# Nietzsche on Women and the Eternal-Feminine

Also available from Bloomsbury

*Joy and Laughter in Nietzsche's Philosophy,* edited by Paul E. Kirkland
and Michael J. McNeal
*Nietzsche and Friendship,* by Willow Verkerk
*Nietzsche's Renewal of Ancient Ethics*, by Neil Durrant
*"Twilight of the Idols" and Nietzsche's Late Philosophy,* by Thomas H. Brobjer
*The Parallel Philosophies of Sartre and Nietzsche*, by Nik Farrell Fox

# Nietzsche on Women and the Eternal-Feminine

*A Critique of Truth and Values*

Edited by Michael J. McNeal

BLOOMSBURY ACADEMIC
LONDON • NEW YORK • OXFORD • NEW DELHI • SYDNEY

BLOOMSBURY ACADEMIC
Bloomsbury Publishing Plc
50 Bedford Square, London, WC1B 3DP, UK
1385 Broadway, New York, NY 10018, USA
29 Earlsfort Terrace, Dublin 2, Ireland

BLOOMSBURY, BLOOMSBURY ACADEMIC and the Diana logo
are trademarks of Bloomsbury Publishing Plc

First published in Great Britain 2023
This paperback edition published 2025

Copyright © Michael J. McNeal and Contributors, 2023

Michael J. McNeal has asserted his right under the Copyright,
Designs and Patents Act, 1988, to be identified as Editor of this work.

For legal purposes the Acknowledgments on p. xii constitute
an extension of this copyright page.

Cover image: Seated Couple, 1915 (mixed media), Egon Schiele (1890–1918)
(© Peter Horree / Alamy Stock Photo)

All rights reserved. No part of this publication may be reproduced or transmitted
in any form or by any means, electronic or mechanical, including photocopying,
recording, or any information storage or retrieval system, without prior
permission in writing from the publishers.

Bloomsbury Publishing Plc does not have any control over, or responsibility for,
any third-party websites referred to or in this book. All internet addresses given in this
book were correct at the time of going to press. The author and publisher regret any
inconvenience caused if addresses have changed or sites have ceased to exist,
but can accept no responsibility for any such changes.

A catalogue record for this book is available from the British Library.

A catalog record for this book is available from the Library of Congress.

| ISBN: | HB: | 978-1-3503-4528-7 |
|---|---|---|
| | PB: | 978-1-3503-4532-4 |
| | ePDF: | 978-1-3503-4529-4 |
| | eBook: | 978-1-3503-4530-0 |

Typeset by Integra Software Services Pvt. Ltd.

To find out more about our authors and books visit www.bloomsbury.com
and sign up for our newsletters.

*This book is affectionately dedicated to Dr. Carol Diethe, who advanced Nietzsche studies throughout her career. A Reader at Middlesex University for twenty-four years, Carol was an original member of the* Friedrich Nietzsche Society *and served as its first secretary. Her scholarship provided valuable insights into Nietzsche's views on women and the role of women in his life. Her notable works include* Nietzsche's Women: Beyond the Whip *(1996),* Nietzsche's Sister and the Will to Power *(2003), the* Historical Dictionary of Nietzscheanism *(2007), and a matchless translation of* On the Genealogy of Morality *(2003).*

# Contents

Notes on Contributors ix
Acknowledgments xii
Abbreviations and References for Nietzsche's Texts xiii

Introduction  *Michael J. McNeal* 1

Part 1  Influential Early Analyses
1  Nietzsche on Woman (With a New Postscript)  *Lawrence J. Hatab* 17
2  Woman as Truth in Nietzsche's Thought  *Kelly A. Oliver* 31

Part 2  The Eternal-Feminine and Future of Philosophy
3  Nietzsche: Psychologist of the "Eternal-Feminine"  *Allison Merrick* 45
4  The "Eternal-Feminine" in Nietzsche's Philosophy: On Nietzsche's Inversion of Goethe's Verse *Ihr "Ewig-Weibliches" zieht uns— hinab!*  *Vinicius Souza de Paulo* 57
5  What If Truth Were a Woman? Metaphors of the Feminine and the Transvaluation of Values in Nietzsche's Philosophy  *Isadora Petry* 73

Part 3  Myth and Self-Creation
6  Nietzsche's Misogyny and a Feminine Philosophy of the Future  *Mat Messerschmidt* 87
7  Nietzsche and Shaktism  *Shruti Jain* 103
8  Nietzsche on Naxos: Ariadne and an Aesthetics of Justification  *Nicholas E. Low* 119
9  The Veiled Mother: Life, Nature, and True Culture in Nietzsche's Early Thought  *Pedro Nagem de Souza* 135

Part 4  Care and the Other
10  Nietzsche's Perfectionism and the Ethics of Care: A Brief Treatment  *Justin Remhof* 153
11  Stendhal, Nietzsche, and Beauvoir on Romantic Love  *Lorenzo Serini* 161
12  Nietzsche on Marriage and the Cultivation of Humanity  *Marina García-Granero* 175

Part 5  Feminist Strategies

13  The Same Instinct Named Twice: The Drive to Possession and the Fettered Spirit in Nietzsche's Middle Period  *Marisa E. Maccaro*   191

14  An Affirming Feminism: Queering Nietzsche with Judith Butler  *Marta Vero*   201

15  Hedwig Dohm's Feminist Revaluations of Nietzschean Nihilism  *Katie Brennan*   215

Bibliography   230
Name Index   243
Subject Index   246

# Notes on Contributors

**Katie Brennan** is Assistant Professor of Philosophy at Temple University and winner of the 2017 Hollingdale Prize for best essay from the *Friedrich Nietzsche Society*. Dr. Brennan's articles have appeared in *The Journal of Nietzsche Studies*, *Memoria di Shakespeare*, and *The Routledge Companion to Shakespeare and Philosophy*. Her current research seeks to rediscover forgotten works of philosophy by women and other marginalized groups, particularly those of Hedwig Dohm.

**Marina García-Granero** earned her PhD in philosophy at the Universitat de València and is currently a postdoctoral researcher with both the Facultad de Filosofía y Ciencias de la Educación at the Universitat de València and the Husserl-Archives: Centre for Phenomenology and Continental Philosophy within the Institute of Philosophy at KU Leuven. In addition to Nietzsche, Dr. García-Granero has published on feminist theory, Habermas, and Kant.

**Lawrence J. Hatab** is Louis I. Jaffe Professor of Philosophy Emeritus at Old Dominion University. A prolific, internationally recognized scholar, Professor Hatab has authored many books and articles, primarily on Nietzsche, Heidegger, and ancient thought. His books include *A Nietzschean Defense of Democracy: An Experiment in Postmodern Politics* (1995), *Ethics and Finitude: Heideggerian Contributions to Moral Philosophy* (2000), *Nietzsche's Life Sentence: Coming to Terms with Eternal Recurrence* (2005), and *Nietzsche's On the Genealogy of Morality, An Introduction* (2008).

**Shruti Jain** is Associate Professor of German Language and Cultural Studies and Assistant Director of the Global Languages Centre at O. P. Jindal Global University. Dr. Jain's current research stems from her doctoral thesis, "Nietzsche and India: The Possibilities of an Arcades Project," which examines the role Indian thought played in Nietzsche's worldview and Nietzsche's reception by prominent Indian thinkers, both pre- and post-independence.

**Nicholas Low** is a PhD candidate in the Committee for the Study of Religion at Harvard University, completing a dissertation on the theme of deification in Nietzsche. Beyond Nietzsche his interests include continental philosophy, the study of religion, and new forms of religion and spirituality in the twentieth century. His research traces the ways that "divinity" is, or might be, reimagined following the "death of God."

**Marisa E. Maccaro** currently teaches philosophy at Reedley College in California. They received their MA in philosophy from Georgia State University in 2020 with a thesis on sex work and empowerment. They have since been conducting research into gender ontology and nineteenth-century German philosophy, specifically Schopenhauer and Nietzsche.

**Michael J. McNeal** is an interdisciplinary scholar and Adjunct Professor at the University of Denver and serves as Secretary of the *Friedrich Nietzsche Society*. Dr. McNeal is co-editor of *Joy and Laughter in Nietzsche's Philosophy: Alternative Liberatory Politics* (2022), *European/Supra-European: Cultural Encounters in Nietzsche's Philosophy* (2020), and *US Approaches to the Arab Spring: International Relations and Democracy Promotion* (2018). In addition, he has contributed chapters to scholarly anthologies and published articles in peer-reviewed journals.

**Allison Merrick** is Associate Professor of Philosophy at California State University, San Marcos. With a keen interest in how moral values shape self-understanding, Dr. Merrick has published articles on the philosophical methods and moral philosophy of Nietzsche in the *European Journal of Philosophy*, *The Journal of Nietzsche Studies*, and *History of Philosophy Quarterly*, among other journals. She has also published a number of chapters in scholarly volumes. Trained as a psychoanalyst, she has a private practice in Southern California.

**Mat Messerschmidt** is a Teaching Fellow at the University of Chicago where he received his PhD from the university's interdisciplinary Committee on Social Thought. His Nietzsche scholarship has focused on Nietzsche's conception of history and importance to Continental philosophy, especially Heidegger. Beyond Nietzsche, Dr. Messerschmidt studies conceptualizations of secularization across disciplines in modernity.

**Kelly Oliver** is W. Alton Jones Professor of Philosophy (with appointments in African-American Diaspora Studies, Film Studies, and Women's and Gender Studies) at Vanderbilt University. Professor Oliver's prodigious scholarship includes fifteen books, including *Earth and World: Philosophy after the Apollo Missions* (2015), *Witnessing: Beyond Recognition* (2001), and *Womanizing Nietzsche: Philosophy's Relation to the "Feminine"* (1995). In addition to having edited numerous volumes and published many journal articles she is also author of the Jessica James Cowgirl Philosopher mystery series of novels.

**Vinicius Souza de Paulo** is a PhD candidate in philosophy at the Federal University of São Paulo, Brazil, in the areas of subjectivity, art, and culture, where he is also co-editor of the virtual magazine "Guaru." His current research investigates Nietzsche's notion of the eternal-feminine and the position of women in Nietzsche's diagnosis of culture.

**Isadora Petry** is a PhD candidate at the University of Campinas, Brazil, writing her thesis on Nietzsche's concepts of *décadence* and revaluation of values in light of nineteenth-century French literature. Her MA, which included research at the University of Montréal, also focused on Nietzsche's philosophy. Her publications on Nietzsche have examined décadence, art and modernity, and gender and feminism.

**Justin Remhof** is Associate Professor of Philosophy at Old Dominion University, specializing in nineteenth- and twentieth-century European philosophy and metaphysics. The author of *Nietzsche as Metaphysician* (2022) and *Nietzsche's Constructivism: A Metaphysics of Material Objects* (2018), Dr. Remhof has also published articles in numerous journals, including *Inquiry, Contemporary Pragmatism, The Journal of Nietzsche Studies, Nietzsche-Studien, European Journal of Philosophy*, and *History of Philosophy Quarterly*.

**Lorenzo Serini** earned his PhD in philosophy at the University of Warwick where he is a Senior Teaching Assistant in the philosophy department. He also serves as a Teaching Fellow at the Institute for Advanced Teaching and Learning, and as an Associate Fellow at the Institute for Advanced Studies. Dr. Serini's current research focuses on post-Kantian European Philosophy, especially Nietzsche, the history of skepticism, and the history of the philosophy of the emotions.

**Pedro Nagem de Souza** is a PhD candidate at the University of Campinas, Brazil, and holds a FAPESP scholarship with the project *Untimely Mimesis—Philosophical Expression in the young Nietzsche*. He also serves on the editorial board of the journal *Discurso* at the University of São Paulo's philosophy department, where he has taught courses on Nietzsche's thought.

**Marta Vero** is a postdoctoral fellow at the Italian Institute of German Studies (IISG) in Rome. She completed her PhD at the University of Pisa-Florence with a dissertation on Hölderlin's philosophy of tragedy. Dr. Vero's research focuses on aesthetics, specifically the twentieth-century reception of the German authors of the *Goethezeit*, and the nineteenth-century German debate over the framing of the image of the South, particularly with regard to Herder and Nietzsche.

# Acknowledgments

I have benefited from the assistance of many people in creating this volume. First, I thank each of the contributors for their work, conscientious engagement, and flexibility. I also appreciate the support of the team at Bloomsbury Academic, particularly Suzie Nash and Jade Grogan, which was crucial to bringing it forth. I am also indebted to the proposal and manuscript reviewers for their feedback.

I am especially grateful to Melanie Shepherd for her thoughtful commentary on my introduction, and to Rebecca Bamford and Martine Prange for their constructive suggestions and support. Throughout the creation of this volume I have benefited from the intellectual engagement of many people. I thank Glen Baier, Marguerite La Caze, Niklas Corral, Christine Daigle, Katherine Graham, Paul Kirkland, Bevis McNeil, Philip Mills, James Mollison, Jamie Parr, Corinna Schubert, Gary Shapiro, Paul Stephan, and Gabriel Zamosc for this engagement, and for their collegiality. Finally, my deepest gratitude goes to Kurt Holzberlein, without whose support and humor I would not have accomplished this project.

Professor Hatab's chapter originally appeared in the *Southern Journal of Philosophy* 19/3 (Fall 1981), 333–45; https://doi.org/10.1111/j.2041-6962.1981.tb01439.x. Professor Oliver's chapter was first published in *Social Theory and Practice*, 10(2) (1984), 185–99; https://doi.org/10.5840/soctheorpract19841028. A version of Dr. Brennan's chapter appeared in *The Journal of Nietzsche Studies*, vol. 52 (2021), 209–33; https://doi.org/10.5325/jnietstud.52.2.0209. For permission to reprint these essays I thank the authors, Wiley, the Copyright Clearance Center, the Philosophy Documentation Center, and Penn State University Press. Early drafts of chapters three through fifteen were presented at the 26th annual conference of the *Friedrich Nietzsche Society*, September 16–18, 2021.

# Abbreviations and References for Nietzsche's Texts

## German Editions Utilized

eKGWB Nietzsche, Friedrich (2009). *Digitale Kritische Gesamtausgabe, Werke und Briefe*, Nietzsche Source, ed. Paolo D'Iorio on the basis of the Colli-Montinari text. www.nietzschesource.org/#eKGWB
KGB Nietzsche, Friedrich (1975–), *Briefwechsel. Kritische Studienausgabe*, ed. Giorgio Colli and Mazzino Montinari, Berlin: De Gruyter.
KGW Nietzsche, Friedrich (1967–), *Werke Kritische Gesamtausgabe*, ed. Giorgio Colli and Mazzino Montinari, Berlin: De Gruyter.
KSA Nietzsche, Friedrich (1980), *Kritische Studienausgabe in 15 Banden*, ed. Giorgio Colli and Mazzino Montinari, Berlin: De Gruyter.

## Abbreviations

Standardized abbreviations of Nietzsche's works in English translation are utilized throughout this volume. Where necessary, numerically distinct books, parts or sections, and abbreviated section titles are employed.

| | |
|---|---|
| A | *The Antichrist* |
| AOM | *Assorted Opinions and Maxims* |
| BGE | *Beyond Good and Evil* |
| BT | *The Birth of Tragedy* |
| CW | *The Case of Wagner* |
| D | *Dawn* |
| EH | *Ecce Homo* |
| GM | *On the Genealogy of Morality* |
| GS | *The Gay Science* |
| HC | *Homer's Contest* |
| HH | *Human, All Too Human* |
| HL | *On the Use and Disadvantage of History for Life* |
| M | *Morgenroete* |

| | |
|---|---|
| NL | *Nachlass Notes* |
| OGS | *On the Greek State* |
| PPP | *The Pre-Platonic Philosophers* |
| PTG | *Philosophy in the Tragic Age of the Greeks* |
| RWB | *Richard Wagner in Bayreuth* |
| SE | *Schopenhauer as Educator* |
| SL | *Selected Letters* |
| TI | *Twilight of the Idols* |
| TL | *On Truth and Lies in an Extra-Moral Sense* |
| TSK | *On Teleology since Kant* |
| UM | *Untimely Meditations* |
| WS | *The Wanderer and His Shadow* |
| Z | *Thus Spoke Zarathustra* |

# English Translations of Nietzsche's Texts

Along with their own translations, authors have utilized numerous translations of Nietzsche's writings, including:

Nietzsche, Friedrich (1968), *The Antichrist*, trans. Walter Kaufmann, in *The Portable Nietzsche*, ed. Walter Kaufmann, New York: Viking Press.

Nietzsche, Friedrich (2005), *The Anti-Christ: A Curse on Christianity*, in *The Anti-Christ, Ecce Homo, Twilight of the Idols and Other Writings*, ed. Aaron Ridley and Judith Norman, trans. Judith Norman, Cambridge: Cambridge University Press.

Nietzsche, Friedrich (1966), *Beyond Good and Evil, Prelude to a Philosophy of the Future*, trans. Walter Kaufmann, New York: Random House, 1966.

Nietzsche, Friedrich (2002), *Beyond Good and Evil, Prelude to a Philosophy of the Future*, ed. Rolf-Peter Horstmann and Judith Norman, trans. Judith Norman, Cambridge: Cambridge University Press.

Nietzsche, Friedrich (2014), *Beyond Good and Evil, Prelude to a Philosophy of the Future*, in *Beyond Good and Evil/On the Genealogy of Morality*, trans. Adrian Del Caro, Stanford, CA: Stanford University Press.

Nietzsche, Friedrich (1967), *The Birth of Tragedy*, in *The Birth of Tragedy and The Case of Wagner*, trans. Walter Kaufmann, New York: Random House.

Nietzsche, Friedrich (1999), *The Birth of Tragedy and Other Writings*, ed. Raymond Geuss and Ronald Speirs, trans. Ronald Speirs, Cambridge: Cambridge University Press.

Nietzsche, Friedrich (1967), *The Case of Wagner: A Musicians' Problem*, trans. Walter Kaufmann, New York: Random House.

Nietzsche, Friedrich (2021), *The Case of Wagner, Twilight of the Idols, the Anti-Christ, Ecce Homo, Dionysian Dithyrambs, Nietzsche contra Wagner*, trans. Adrian del Caro, et. al., Stanford, CA: Stanford University Press.

Nietzsche, Friedrich (2011), *Dawn: Thoughts on the Presumptions of Morality*, trans. Brittain Smith, Stanford, CA: Stanford University Press.
Nietzsche, Friedrich (1982), *Daybreak: Thoughts on the Prejudices of Morality*, trans. R. J. Hollingdale, Cambridge: Cambridge University Press.
Nietzsche, Friedrich (1967), *Ecce Homo: How One Becomes What One Is*, trans. Walter Kaufmann, New York: Random House.
Nietzsche, Friedrich (2005), *Ecce Homo: How to Become What You Are*, in *The Anti-Christ, Ecce Homo, Twilight of the Idols and Other Writings*, ed. Aaron Ridley and Judith Norman, trans. Judith Norman, Cambridge: Cambridge University Press.
Nietzsche, Friedrich (1974), *The Gay Science, with a Prelude of Rhymes and an Appendix of Songs*, trans. Walter Kaufmann, New York: Random House.
Nietzsche, Friedrich (2001), *The Gay Science, with a Prelude of Rhymes and an Appendix of Songs*, ed. Bernard Williams, trans. Josefine Nauckhoff, with poems translated by Adrian Del Caro, Cambridge: Cambridge University Press.
Nietzsche, Friedrich (1986), *Human, All Too Human: A Book for Free Spirits*, trans. R. J. Hollingdale, Cambridge: Cambridge University Press.
Nietzsche, Friedrich (1995), *Human, All Too Human: A Book for Free Spirits*, vol. 1, trans. Gary Handwerk, Stanford, CA: Stanford University Press.
Nietzsche, Friedrich (2013), *Human, All Too Human: A Book for Free Spirits*, vol. II, *and Unpublished Fragments from the Period of Human, All Too Human II*, trans. Gary Handwerk, Stanford, CA: Stanford University Press.
Nietzsche, Friedrich (2005), *Nietzsche contra Wagner: From the Files of a Psychologist*, in *The Anti-Christ, Ecce Homo, Twilight of the Idols and Other Writings*, ed. Aaron Ridley and Judith Norman, trans. Judith Norman, Cambridge: Cambridge University Press.
Nietzsche, Friedrich (1967), *On the Genealogy of Morality: A Polemic*, trans. Walter Kaufmann and R. J. Hollingdale, New York: Random House.
Nietzsche, Friedrich (1994), *On the Genealogy of Morality, a Polemic*, ed. Keith Ansell-Pearson, trans. Carol Diethe, Cambridge: Cambridge University Press.
Nietzsche, Friedrich (2014), *On the Genealogy of Morality, a Polemic*, in *Beyond Good and Evil/On the Genealogy of Morality*, trans. Adrian Del Caro, Stanford, CA: Stanford University Press.
Nietzsche, Friedrich (1998), *On the Genealogy of Morality*, trans. Maudemarie Clark and Alan J. Swensen, Indianapolis: Hackett.
Nietzsche, Friedrich (1999), *Philosophy and Truth, Selections from Nietzsche's Notebooks of the Early 1870's*, ed. and trans. Daniel Breazeale, Amherst, NY: Humanity Books.
Nietzsche, Friedrich (2001), *The Pre-Platonic Philosophers*, ed. and trans. Greg Whitlock, Urbana: University of Illinois Press.
Nietzsche, Friedrich (2005), *Prefaces to Unwritten Works*, ed. and trans. Michael W. Grenke, with additional prefaces by Matthew K. Davis and Lise van Boxel, South Bend, IN: St. Augustine's Press.
Nietzsche, Friedrich (1996), *Selected Letters of Friedrich Nietzsche*, ed. and trans. Christopher Middleton, Indianapolis: Hackett Publishing.
Nietzsche, Friedrich (1968), *Thus Spoke Zarathustra: A Book for All and None*, trans. Walter Kaufmann, in *The Portable Nietzsche*, New York: Viking Press.
Nietzsche, Friedrich (2005), *Thus Spoke Zarathustra: A Book for All and None*, trans. Graham Parkes, Oxford: Oxford University Press.
Nietzsche, Friedrich (2006), *Thus Spoke Zarathustra: A Book for All and None*, ed. Adrian Del Caro and Robert Pippen, trans. Adrian Del Caro, Cambridge: Cambridge University Press.

Nietzsche, Friedrich (1998), *Twilight of the Idols, or How One Philosophizes with a Hammer*, trans. Duncan Large, Oxford: Oxford University Press.
Nietzsche, Friedrich (2005), *Twilight of the Idols, or How to Philosophize with a Hammer*, in *The Anti-Christ, Ecce Homo, Twilight of the Idols and Other Writings*, ed. Aaron Ridley and Judith Norman, trans. Judith Norman, Cambridge: Cambridge University Press.
Nietzsche, Friedrich (2019), *Unpublished Fragments (Summer 1882–Winter 1883/84)*. Stanford University Press, trans. with an afterword, by Paul S. Loeb and David F. Tinsley.
Nietzsche, Friedrich (2020), *Unpublished Fragments (Spring 1885–Spring 1886)*. Stanford University Press, trans. Adrian Del Caro.
Nietzsche, Friedrich (1997), *Untimely Meditations*, ed. Daniel Breazeale, trans. R. J. Hollingdale, Cambridge: Cambridge University Press.
Nietzsche, Friedrich (2009), *Writings from the Early Notebooks*, ed. Raymond Geuss and Alexander Nehamas, trans. Ladislaus Löb, Cambridge: Cambridge University Press.
Nietzsche, Friedrich (2003), *Writings from the Late Notebooks*, ed. Rüdiger Bittner, trans. Kate Sturge, Cambridge: Cambridge University Press.

# Introduction

Michael J. McNeal

Among Nietzsche's numerous reflections on women, the feminine, and feminism, his use of the terms "woman" and "female" as tropes, and his mentions of the "eternal-feminine," some of his comments are notoriously polemical, particularly in sections 231–239 of *Our Virtues* in *Beyond Good and Evil* (BGE). The controversial statements he makes there (as with others) are understood by many scholars as rhetorical goads that are integral to his radical interrogation of truth and values. On this interpretation Nietzsche was challenging his then mostly male readers' paternalistic, masculinist biases in order to prompt them to recognize their similarly absurd faith in received truths. Might Nietzsche have also intended, through his hyperbole, to illustrate how nineteenth-century Europe's male chauvinism symptomatized Europe's worsening decadence? While this could, *prima facie*, be seen to be at odds with the earnest acclamations of masculine virtue that appear throughout his late works, it may be argued that he did so, however intentionally. What is certain is that he thought modernity's decadence, including the aims of realizing radical equality and abolishing all suffering—among other enticements to nihilism—was transforming gender subjectivities in harmful ways and fueling the feminist movement. Less charitably, these comments are frequently taken by unsympathetic critics as demonstrative of sexism—if not outright misogyny—by their author.[1] On this view, they are self-impugning indictments of Nietzsche's judgment that ought to reduce our confidence in his insights and place an asterisk next to his contribution to philosophy. I reject this unsympathetic position, which ignores the complexity of his views, and rebut it in what follows through differing interpretive stances on his writing on women.

The complexity of Nietzsche's critique of modernity coupled with his vituperative rejection of feminism generates difficulties that are as likely to frustrate readers as to guarantee enduring debate about his meaning. His condemnation of feminism was intended to simultaneously illustrate and enact his free-spirited opposition to the decadence he saw debilitating humanity. Therefore what strikes us as indisputable today is that persistent disagreement about the significance of his views on women and their relevance to broader issues in his thought—including his philosophical project—make them worthy of closer scrutiny. Yet one eminent Nietzsche scholar—Walter Kaufmann—explicitly rejected this view. In working to rehabilitate Nietzsche in the postwar United States and Anglophonic world, Kaufmann encouraged his reader to disregard the philosopher's inflammatory remarks about women, stating, "Nietzsche's writings contain many all-too-human judgments—especially about women—but these are philosophically irrelevant; and *ad hominem* arguments against any philosopher on the basis of such statements seem trivial and hardly pertinent."[2] While Kaufmann's latter point is undeniable, the contributors to this volume would disagree that Nietzsche's judgments about women are philosophically irrelevant; quite the contrary. In fact, scholars increasingly appreciate the relevance of Nietzsche's views on women to his critiques of truth and values, and to his philosophical project, namely his aim of initiating a fundamental revaluation of all values toward the transfiguration of humankind. In considering these matters, many of this volume's contributors pay particular attention to Nietzsche's use of "woman" as a trope or metaphor for truth (BGE P1, 220; GS P 4; GM III 1)—which he utilized even in his critique of modern science (HH 257)—and his metaphorical gendering of truth (as feminine) and strength (as masculine). This occurs in various places throughout his late works: "Suppose that truth is a woman— and why not?" (BGE P1), and later, "Carefree, mocking, violent—this is how wisdom wants us: she is a woman, all she ever loves is a warrior" (GM III 1, from Z 1 Writing).[3] Nietzsche appealed to gender stereotypes – women as capricious, elusive, and artificial – to metaphorically convey the thrust of his skeptical epistemological stance.

None of this is to deny that Nietzsche's sexist observations and rehearsal of gender stereotypes implicate him in late-modernity's nihilism, even as they offer us deeper (if unintended) insights into its sociocultural dynamics. This is evinced by the drive psychology he takes to explain what motivated feminists to emancipate themselves from patriarchy and achieve equality with men, which provides valuable psychological and philosophical insights. While some of Nietzsche's expressed views on women are arguably at odds, *prima facie*, with his best insights, they serve to demonstrate his observation that "we cannot look around our corner" (GS 374). Furthermore, it is worth recalling that he reminds his reader that these statements reflect *his* truths (BGE 231), meaning that, consistent with his rejection of dogmatism, they are not for everyone, and his reader need not agree with them (BGE 221, 228). However, while his views should not be judged through the lenses of contemporary liberal values without qualification, we must consider why Nietzsche would take the chance of standing himself in the way of some of his own best insights in such a manner, and risk alienating much (potentially half) of his prospective readership thereby.

Informing his opposition to the decadence he saw afflicting Europe and his perspectivist view of truth as originating in artistic interpretation, Nietzsche's strong opposition to metaphysical and ontological essentialisms prompts us to doubt that he can be entirely in earnest when he endorses traditional sex roles and gender stereotypes, as at BGE 232. We read on hoping for the sardonic humor that otherwise roils the book and would indicate a self-conscious mockery of such chauvinist views. However, in the course of his reflections on women in the aphorisms comprising *Our Virtues*, his possible facetiousness may strike many as insufficient to discredit male-chauvinist views. While some find humorous hyperbole in statements such as "Look out when the 'eternal tedium of woman' (which they all have in abundance!) first dares to emerge"! (BGE 232), to many readers his humor falls flat and does not mitigate the obnoxiousness of his statements anyway. Moreover, the suggestion that such humor ought to temper the offensiveness of the views Nietzsche advanced is likely, at best, to strain credulity as an effort to deny that they are as offensive as they seem, or at worst to constitute an apologia for his sexism.

Nietzsche's controversial assertions were meant to challenge his reader's acceptance of what he saw as modernity's decadent values, particularly its ideals of freedom and its corresponding notion of "emancipation." He took feminism to be a product of post-Enlightenment liberal thought, part of a trend instigated by Rousseau (see D 163, BGE 245, TI Skirmishes 3), which symptomized and advanced antinatural notions of equality that mischaracterize hierarchy as unjust and authority as inherently oppressive. In Nietzsche's view this would invariably poison relations between men and women, erode the privileges that inhered to the traditional, socially formative roles of masculine and feminine, and exacerbate the sickness weakening Europe.[4] The result, Nietzsche feared, would be increasingly effeminate—and spiritually emasculated—men, as well as more miserable, "masculinized" women (see BGE 144, 209, 239).[5]

These decadent trends were exacerbated by the death of God and modernity's post-Christian, yet still life-denying secularized ideals—the inclinations from which feminism stems. Bound to increase *ressentiment*, Nietzsche thought feminists would foment greater discord between the sexes and compromise the traditional privileges of women *vis-à-vis* men (BGE 239). It should go without saying that in his view these ideals also undermined men. For example, at GS 362 ("Our faith in the masculinization of Europe"), he reflected upon Napoleon's legacy and praised him, asserting that "'woman' [... has] been spoiled by Christianity and the enthusiastic spirit of the eighteenth century, and even more by 'modern ideas.'" This was not meant rhetorically. Nietzsche thought such a "masculinization" of European man (by which he meant inuring, desensitizing) was necessary, particularly given the aforementioned effects feminism was having—what he derisively dubbed "the masculinization of women."[6]

A contemporary reader might understandably be perplexed by the fact that a thinker as innovative as Nietzsche would be so threatened by the prospective legal and social equality of women that he would equate it with a diminishment of womanliness and the commensurate emasculation of men. This is especially true given his penetrating critique of values and knowledge of the fact that some of his contemporaries were interrogating and rejecting traditional gender roles as regressive. Is it not counter-intuitive that Nietzsche did not take the gender norms then corseting European society as symptoms of its decadence, as opposed to the loosening of those restrictive customs? Some interpreters of Nietzsche's thought take his condemnations of feminism to exhibit his own interpellation by the decadence of his age, which in other contexts he seemed to acknowledge (e.g.: EH Wise 2; CW P). His opposition to women's liberation in favor of traditional gender subjectivities may well appear to serve unduly restrictive, if not anti-human ends.

According to Nietzsche's critique of decadence values and their diminution of culture, a dogmatic insistence upon any truths—in this case the presumed veracity of conventional gender identities correlated with biological sex—could only amplify the physio-psychological decline afflicting modern life. Conversely, it would also spur agonistic contests between the defenders of such a patriarchal order and its opponents, along with those rare exceptions who possess the strength to experiment with themselves (including, hypothetically, their gender and sexuality). Whereas the strength to experiment with and overcome themselves comprises a key part of the free spirit's type of artistic agency (or capacity for self-creation), the great majority understand themselves as "the oppressed, the downtrodden [… and] believe in an unbiased 'subject' with freedom of choice, because […] that sublime self-deception" enables them to understand "their particular mode of existence as an accomplishment" (GM I 13). How emancipated women and sexual and gender minorities fit into this understanding, *vis-à-vis* its ramifications for identity in our decadent age, is a matter taken up in various ways by a number of this volume's contributors. While Nietzsche apparently did not intend for his critique of values to lend support to the emancipatory social movements with which we are familiar, he would have expected the feminists' challenges to traditional gender identities to increase Europe's decadence and hasten its downgoing.[7] Perhaps counter intuitively (and *contra* Nietzsche), support for feminism would, from this perspective, consist with these tasks he sets for his free spirits—"the new faction in favor of life" (EH BT 4).[8]

Why then did the feminists' agonistic striving to overturn Europe's gender norms not resonate with Nietzsche, given his recognition that Europe's reigning institutions and centuries-old ruling aristocracies were moribund (GS 358; A 43; TI Skirmishes 39)? Significant pieces of the feminist's program would seem to dovetail with Nietzsche's critical perspective on the sources of Europe's malady. Nevertheless, he rejects feminism as originating in the herd instincts driving the democratization that typified his age. Claiming to advance a greater, transcendent good—one intertwined with notions of individual liberty and social justice—these movements signified the shared impulses of sick individuals who had come to oppose all obligation, duty, and rank order of difference as intolerable forms of subjugation; individuals for whom the "desire for *freedom*, […] necessarily belong[s] to slave morals and morality" (BGE 260). Nietzsche therefore took feminism to indicate a "corruption of the instincts" (BGE 233) that would lead people to deny "the necessity of an eternally hostile tension" between the sexes that he thought productive (BGE 238). Characterizing feminists as unwitting victims and propagators "of the most vicious 'idealism,'" Nietzsche asserts that such "emancipated women are basically *anarchists* in the world of the 'eternal-feminine', people in bad shape [i.e.: poor health], whose bottom-most instinct is revenge" (EH Books 5). That instinct was a manifestation of the broader decadence of their age, like the diminution of patriarchal authority in nineteenth-century Europe. These "typical signs of decline and conflicting instincts […]," resulted from the diminished vitality of an age in which "humanity […] has been taught decadence values, and only decadence values, as the highest values" (EH Destiny 7).

While Nietzsche's critique may jar the sensibilities of many contemporary readers, a deeper reading helps us understand his objectives. His rejection of feminism consisted with his critique of liberalism, modernity, and democratization, which, as aforementioned, he took to be poisoning healthy desires and fomenting the rejection of hierarchy and political authority, as well as with his denunciation of the "industrial spirit" typifying these trends (BGE 239). The objections he raises against feminism also consist with his rejection of "the moral judgment and condemnation [that is] the favorite revenge of the spiritually limited on those who are less so" (BGE 219). These comments may be dismissed as reactionary but that would miss radical possibilities in Nietzsche's broader critique of cultural decadence and the profound, if unconventional, opportunities for becoming or post-modern liberatory politics they suggest.

Among the late nineteenth-century contests of meaning that Nietzsche engaged was the place of women in society and rationales for their subordinate status therein. He thought feminists had embraced a reactionary and counter-productive (ant) agonism by insisting upon essentializing themselves anew—qua "women"—"woman *an sich*" (BGE 232). That is, they sought to re-essentialize themselves *against* the patriarchal essentializations that constrained them to become the equals of their oppressors.[9] Nietzsche thought this would further impede women—and by extension, men—from fundamentally reconceiving themselves and undertaking the experiments needed to ensure their becoming and flourishing. Nietzsche takes the increasing desire of women in his era for political and legal equality as a yearning analogous to becoming "scientific"—and he uses this conceptualization as a means of critiquing the broader social change then occurring, as "one of the worst developments in Europe's general trend towards *increasing ugliness*" (BGE 232). This sentence is crucial for understanding the complex meaning of the notorious aphorisms about women that follow, for Nietzsche states that he is taking up just *one* of the life-threatening developments afflicting Europe in the late nineteenth-century. There were other imperiling developments underway, but the a/effects modernity was having on women were especially grave.

It seemed to Nietzsche that by the late nineteenth century the *received* roles of men and women had not fundamentally changed in many millennia, the archetypes (and assumed equivalency between sex and gender) being evident in the earliest records of human history.[10] This is, in part at least, why he modified Goethe's notion of "the eternal-feminine" and described himself as possibly being its "first psychologist" (EH Books 5): women dissatisfied with their received role struck him as exemplifying the declining instincts of his age.[11] Nietzsche obviously could not appreciate the sense many women had of being disadvantaged by traditional gender roles and repressed and exploited by men (see D 227). He did however recognize that this grievance was exacerbated by liberal values, which drove the emancipatory programs of the feminists' and suffragette movements and fostered fanaticism—"the only 'strength of the will' that even the weak and insecure can be brought to attain" (GS 347). This extremism, which compounded the misguided "tendency to think that all human misery and wrongdoing is caused by traditional social structures: which lands truth happily on its head!" (BGE 44), was likely to increase anarchy and weaken Europeans, per his understanding of decadence and fixation on masculine "virtues," including independence, courage, and especially strength. In this regard Nietzsche's comments consist with his broader assessment of the psychological origins of our egalitarian, democratic ethos; namely, the slavish moral imperatives for such change. Yet despite the psychological and sociocultural bases of his critique, his anxiety over the ways in which feminism was likely to transform relations between the sexes was hardly uncommon. The rationale for such fears is captured in the text of a suffragette pamphlet from 1918 that offered marriage advice to women. Appearing less than two decades after Nietzsche's death, and just three decades after his final productive year, it warns "young ladies" not to marry, and cautions that if they must marry they should seek a "tame man." The text further counsels that "most men [...] need taming" before concluding that, *vis-à-vis* marriage, "it is wiser not to chance it, it isn't worth the risk."[12]

Still, there is another perspective from which, as I suggested above, such demands for social change arguably consist with Nietzsche's philosophical psychology and futural thought. That is, by appearing to lend their *support* to movements that aim to fundamentally reorder sociocultural and political institutions, his free spirits would create a space for themselves within which they could engage in experiments, strive to overcome decadence values, and perfect themselves in the process. They would thereby contribute to the subversion of the reigning values of their day and affect the course and success of those liberatory movements, thereby creating further possibilities for revaluing values. Such movements—and the antinatural ideals motivating them— can be deflected, hijacked, and exploited. By doing so free spirits could increase the decadence of their age to hasten the down-going of humankind toward its overcoming and distant transfiguration by philosophers of the future. There is nothing in Nietzsche's critique of values that advances the innate inferiority of women, per se, or could justify their subordination to men and the internalized self-subordination it fosters. That subordination only makes sense within an ascetic values framework like that provided by Christianity, which, discredited by its own emphasis on truth, resulted in the death of God.[13] Efforts to preserve that discredited values framework, as zealous religious fundamentalists do from an incomparable spirit of revenge, are just as harmful as the putatively emancipatory movements Christianity's collapse spawned.

Despite these disparate sociocultural reactions in the wake of the death of God, the last half-century has demonstrated that as the range of permissible gender expressions and sexual identities expands, opportunities for life-affirming becomings increase for everyone. Therefore, maintaining the hegemony of traditional gender roles or even rhetorically defending them becomes more difficult, and those who do so are gradually perceived to be reactionary moral reprobates. Indeed, such outdated beliefs are increasingly seen as antediluvian, and the individuals who espouse them as laughable. Yet while Nietzsche saw the emancipatory movements of his day as indicative of worsening decadence, he also would have interpreted one dimension of those movements positively, that being the way in which it accelerated processes necessary for the future overcoming of humanity. Toward that aim, free spirits would inevitably reconceive secular modernity's heterosexist mores and taboos (a legacy of antinatural Judeo-Christian ideals) to challenge such value norms. In fact, despite not anticipating it, the revaluation of *all* values Nietzsche advocated compelled the reconceptualization of the traditional gender roles integral to them (A 13; A Law against Christianity 4). There is no reason that such a radical challenge could not be understood as a development toward *Übermenschlich* individuals, consonant with Nietzsche's own critical analysis (GM P 3, II 24; TI Skirmishes 37). Indeed, by subversively playing with hegemonic identic categories and defying the prejudices they enforce, Nietzsche's free spirits could affirm life while giving style to their characters (GS 290). The transformation of gender norms would then serve as a basis for further experiments and a means by which free spirits could become who they are. It might also provide a conceptual framework—and a corresponding "Nietzschean" ethic— conducive to new forms of desire and corresponding practices to discredit patriarchy and combat toxic masculinity (such as Nietzsche imparted through his rhetorical, and not only rhetorical, provocations). In addition to empowering women, such practices could mitigate heterosexism, and trans- and homophobia, and succeed, ultimately, in eliminating them. New forms of life and opportunities for becoming can be expected to develop from such a *post-feminist*, or post-gender Nietzschean ethics to emancipate every individual from the anti-human constraints of essentializing gender roles. It would thus seek to move humankind beyond restrictive gender binaries and oppressive norms to realize the crucial role of female human beings to the tasks of comprehensively transfiguring humankind (HH 259, 425; TI Morality 1, Skirmishes 39). Given the changing views of sexual identity and the transformation of gender norms in the post-industrial, advanced economies of the world, where such experimentation is occurring with increasing regularity and acceptance, it is fair to say that this is already taking place.

Despite his masculinist rhetoric there is no reason to think that women would not be integral to Nietzsche's free spirit project. His own flattering comments about the women in his life (Lou Andreas-Salomé, Malwida von Meysenbug, Cosima Wagner, etc.) suggest as much. So it is somewhat unfortunate that he did not simply observe that the feminist movement is a symptom of the affective nihilism plaguing contemporary Europe that will exacerbate the decadence of our age. It may be credibly argued that certain passages about women and/or feminism in Nietzsche's "mature" or "late- period" works generate problematic ambiguities. Yet it would be too simple a reading to conclude that Nietzsche did not care about or was unaware of this, particularly as he was not afraid to make his reader work. Given how concerned Nietzsche was with what he saw as nineteenth-century Europe's cultural and sociopolitical decline it is not, as suggested above, unreasonable to think that Nietzsche's offensive comments about women may have been made as part of a conscious effort to provoke his (then mainly) male readership in a number of productive ways. Simultaneously, and consistent with his reflection in BGE 230, perhaps there is something of his own "will to be deceived" and "joyful self-delight at the arbitrary narrowness and secrecy of a corner," as well as a "not quite harmless willingness to deceive other spirits and to act a part in front of them," expressed in the scornful comments he makes about women in the passages that followed. These suggest that the unwillingness of feminists to act the subservient part traditionally expected of women annoyed him. However, that only accounts for the surface meaning of his assertions, which were also—at the same time—japes. In addition to containing multiple levels of meaning, these comments playfully function as "as if" propositions to spur his readers into reconsidering their acceptance of received truths and the implicit biases enforced by gender stereotypes. They also consist with—and simultaneously enact—his philosophical views on the subversive utility of pranks, jokes, and laughter that express his free spirits' life- affirming ethos.[14]

In considering the probable sources of his truculence in writing about women, "woman," the feminine, and feminists, we should take account of some of Nietzsche's formative experiences. It must be appreciated that he was born into a politically conservative religious family in the patriarchal society of mid-nineteenth-century Germany and came of age in a strict educational environment. At an early age he became the only male in a household of women within which he felt the need to performatively enact the behavioral expectations associated with German men.[15] In his adult life acquaintances described him as having a relatively high-pitched voice, and he was perceived by some to be effeminate (Safranski 2002: 248). Perhaps Nietzsche felt (or recognized?) that he was unattractive to women, but of this one may ask, so what? Students of his work will nevertheless wonder if his disposition toward women arose in part from an injured sense of self-esteem for having been unable to attract them.

A great deal of attention has already been paid to questions about Nietzsche's well-known difficulties with women. It is not well known, however, that Nietzsche's unsuccessful proposal of marriage to Lou Andreas-Salomé was not his first such rejection. He had "made a highly aggressive impromptu proposal to Mathlide Trampedach" in April of 1876, "after they had met on only three occasions."[16] His difficulties finding a spouse and evident inability to enter into intimate relationships with women furthered questions about Nietzsche's sexuality. These were occasionally unkind, given their implications, as when his personal physician communicated with Wagner about his health following the latter's scurrilous suggestion that Nietzsche was a chronic masturbator—an egregious violation of medical ethics today.[17] Likewise, with regard to rumors that he contracted syphilis from a prostitute, little can be known about his unintended visit to a Cologne brothel except that it occurred. Tangentially, no compelling evidence to support speculation that he ever visited an all-male Genovese brothel exists, nor are there any accounts to persuade us that he was homosexual, Kohler's elaborate 2002 conjecture notwithstanding. After he became incapacitated, Nietzsche's *Pforta* schoolmate Paul Deussen—with whom Nietzsche had communicated a first-hand account of the Cologne brothel visit—supposed "that Nietzsche remained a virgin throughout his life."[18] Despite Nietzsche's occasional criticisms of celibates, this strikes me as quite likely.

By his early forties Nietzsche was suffering increasingly severe symptoms of the benign brain tumor—certainly *not* syphilis—that would incapacitate him in January of 1889.[19] Beginning with the debilitating headaches and bouts of nausea that afflicted him from his early teens, that tumor likely also produced the periods of euphoria and frenetic productivity he experienced in the second half of 1888. Disinhibited in his final productive months, many of his statements about women contrast with those of the middle period works, something arguably true of all the works from his final productive years. As one biographer observed "the aphorisms on women in *The Gay Science* are notably positive and sympathetic,"[20] while the bellicose statements in *Beyond Good and Evil* reflect a change in his rhetorical tactics that found their strongest expression in *Ecce Homo*. Whatever the relationship between his deteriorating health and his attitudes toward women, it is ridiculous that Nietzsche's detractors endeavored to smear him with the brothel tale, the syphilis conjecture, and rumors of homosexuality.

There has not been a scholarly anthology in Anglophonic Nietzsche studies to focus on these subjects in roughly three decades. The 1990s saw at least three volumes on its themes: Paul Patton's *Nietzsche, Feminism and Political Theory* (1993), Peter J. Burgard's *Nietzsche and the Feminine* (1994), and Kelly Oliver and Marilyn Pearsall's *Feminist Interpretations of Friedrich Nietzsche* (1998), which reprinted fifteen articles from the preceding decade-and-a-half. In the intervening decades there have been a number of notable articles (including those by Call [1995], Abbey [1996], Appel [1997], Thorgeirsdottir [2004], and Draz [2018], among others), and a few monographs on the subject (including by Krell [1986], Picart [1999], Oppel [2005], and Oliver [2016]), but nearly thirty years stand between those anthologies and this collection, which presents thirteen original articles alongside two groundbreaking essays from the 1980s.

In creating this volume, my principal aim has been to publish exciting new work on Nietzsche's thinking on these subjects. By placing thirteen original essays alongside two articles that have influenced the field over the last four decades, it also provides insight into how scholarship on these topics has evolved over that period—one in which the bulk of Anglophonic Nietzsche studies has occurred. Furthermore, the volume realizes my aim of bringing together scholars from around the globe who represent every academic career phase. This diversity, it is hoped, will contribute to greater intellectual cross-pollination between disparate national-linguistic communities of Nietzsche scholars. By rethinking past and current debates on this volume's themes, its contributors build on existing work in the field and develop novel insights. While this is not a volume about queer-theoretical approaches to Nietzsche's thinking, or its ramifications for transgender studies, as such, a number of chapters (i.e., Brennan, Jain, Petry, and Vero) examine the relevance of his ideas to queer and trans issues, and our contemporary debate about gender and identity. By extension, the perspectives this volume advances may affect thinking on a range of other matters, too, including aspects of the axiological, ethical, epistemological, and ontological importance of Nietzsche's thought.

Divided thematically into five parts, the anthology is oriented around the subject of how Nietzsche's use of "woman" functions as a trope for truth, broadly construed. From this overarching theme the contributors diverge to consider a range of related matters, including his critique of women and gender relations in late-modernity, care, marriage, the instincts, and the feminine, as well as his engagement with and by other thinkers. They variously consider how these connect with his critique of truth and values, the dangers he perceived in feminism's putative intensification of decadence, strategies of emancipation and their viability.

Part one consists of two now seminal essays presented in chronological order of their original appearance. Chapter one presents Lawrence J. Hatab's essay, *Nietzsche on Woman*—originally published in 1981—to which Professor Hatab has also contributed a new postscript. Hatab begins by considering whether and to what extent Nietzsche was a sexist and what that means for his philosophy. He further considers how Nietzsche's thinking on women fits within his philosophy, observing that Nietzsche rejects the mistaken feminist aim of emancipating women by attaining "equality" with men. Rather, this would constitute a loss of women's privileges and power; the repudiation of feminine traits in favor of masculine ones being an exchange of strength for weakness.

All calls for equality rehearse the central theme of Western metaphysics: the attempt to transcend a world constituted by differences and their subsequent conflicts, to abolish suffering and, ultimately, becoming itself. Hatab concludes by posing questions Nietzsche would likely have put to contemporary feminists and suggests the possible characteristics of a Nietzschean "feminism."

This is followed by Professor Kelly Oliver's 1984 essay *Woman as Truth in Nietzsche's Thought*. In it, Oliver examines Nietzsche's use of woman as a metaphor for truth, a subject she examines with an eye toward the power arising from its ambiguity. She notes that truth and woman are both elusive for Nietzsche and the task of formulating his relationship to woman is not simplified by the points of connectedness between them. As we investigate Nietzsche's theory of truth we simultaneously illuminate his thinking on woman, without eliminating all uncertainty. Oliver's analysis takes this ambiguity as productive. She differentiates between the Dionysian, the castrating, and the dogmatist/feminist types of women, their respective expressions of will to power, and their uses of illusion and masks. With this dialectical triad she argues that the constant flux of truth/woman—its ineliminable ambiguity—cannot be endured without being masked. Four decades on, the chapters that follow bring the evolution of the field and some of the most salient questions animating it into perspective.

Part two, entitled *The Eternal Feminine and Philosophy*, addresses Nietzsche's uses of the phrase "the eternal feminine" and its significance to his understanding of "woman," nineteenth-century ideals of the masculine and feminine, his critique of decadence, and what he meant by claiming to its foremost psychologist. In chapter three Allison Merrick questions the significance of Nietzsche's most sustained discussion of woman (*das Weib*) and women (*die Frauen*) in BGE. She considers three influential interpretations of it to argue that each is potentially misleading for downplaying Nietzsche's interpretive stance as a psychologist of the eternal feminine. Closely reading BGE 232, Merrick contends that if the eternal feminine is best taken as a category that no woman could exemplify, then it functions as a shame-inducing ideal. By centering the "psychologist of the eternal feminine" we get a clearer understanding of how shame functions, in addition to how we might overcome our commitment to pernicious ideals. Merrick concludes by reflecting on Nietzsche's description of himself as "the first psychologist of the eternal feminine".

In chapter four Vinicius Souza de Paulo investigates the relation between Nietzsche's inversion of Goethe's verse "Ihr 'Ewig-Weibliches' zieht uns—hinab!," and the position of Goethe in Nietzsche's critique of feminism as a symptom of cultural degeneration. De Paulo argues that Nietzsche uses the expression "eternal feminine" in his critique of culture to denounce the idealized image of the feminine manifested in decadent romantic art and culture. Goethe's value to Nietzsche's thought lies in the contrasting image he presents of a life-affirming Renaissance spirit. De Paulo maintains that Nietzsche's inversion of Goethe's phrase serves him as a means of criticizing modernity. He concludes that Nietzsche's destabilizing use of the eternal feminine serves his aim of revealing the decadence afflicting modern women and the emancipatory movements they support, including feminism, egalitarianism, and idealism.

In chapter five Isadora Petry considers Nietzsche's problematization of the notion of truth by means of the relation "woman/truth," ideal notions which cannot be made comprehensible on the basis of some essential quality or putatively universal foundation. Taking up Nietzsche's question "what if truth were a woman?," she examines metaphors of the feminine and their relevance to a future transvaluation of values. Petry analyzes how the Greek figure of Baubo illustrates the importance of laughter as a strategy for displacing perspectives and producing new realities, *vis-à-vis* discussions of gender. She then problematizes aspects of Nietzsche's philosophy to show how the theme of truth should be understood as intimately related to his questioning of the feminine, and finally, to sexual difference. Petry concludes that by such means we gain tools for examining issues relevant to current debates about gender and transvaluing decadent values.

Part three concerns *Myth and Self-Creation*, interrelated subjects that informed Nietzsche's views of women, the feminine, and future transfiguration of humankind. In chapter six Mat Messerschmidt utilizes the *Dionysian-Dithyrambs*, along with Nietzsche's scattered references to Ariadne to argue that the project of embracing Dionysian flux in the thought of the eternal return ultimately requires a surrender to the greater power of Dionysian becoming, something Zarathustra cannot achieve. However, as Ariadne can do so, the project is gendered as a female endeavor; the highest human task—that of creating a higher human being—is thus the task of female flesh. Messerschmidt maintains that for Nietzsche, Ariadne must ultimately replace Zarathustra and demonstrates that in his late works the paradigmatic higher human becomes female. Messerschmidt concludes by turning to Ariadne's lover Dionysus in order to explicate the limits of Nietzsche's radicality with regard to gender and the feminine philosophy of the future he advances.

Shruti Jain examines the parallels between Nietzsche's thought and Shaktism, or Goddess spirituality, in chapter seven. She notes that while Nietzsche's mature works do not reference the archaic womb, or *Ur-mutter* mentioned in BT, they reference motherhood and pregnancy, which inform his notions of the "artist philosopher," "male mother," and Zarathustra's anticipation of birth. Through them he proffers de-essentialized possibilities for becoming *vis-à-vis* gender and destabilizes traditional gender roles and patriarchy. Contrasting the goddess archetypes of Ariadne with Radha, Baubo with Lajja Gauri, and Hecate with Dhumavati, Jain shows how Nietzsche may be understood to have imbued the Goddess archetype with new meaning. Finally, she explicates relevant parallels between Nietzsche's thought and Shaktism and how they have conditioned his reception in India.

In chapter eight Nicholas Low observes that when Nietzsche characterizes the philosopher of the future as an experimenter and seducer he seems to suggest a radical departure from conventional understandings of truth, and a method for pursuing it. Yet rather than understand Nietzsche's view of truth as comparable to a woman, and the (masculine) philosopher as endeavoring to woo her, Low suggests that for Nietzsche the genuine philosopher is seduced by the truth exemplified in the god Dionysus. Understanding the pursuit of truth as a process of deification complicates gendered accounts of philosophy-as-seduction, showing the Nietzschean philosopher to be a seducer who is also vulnerable to seduction. Low maintains that Nietzsche's Dionysianism undermines any account of self-generating subjectivity. The creative process of "becoming what one is" is better explained by receptivity to a seductive encounter with divinity.

Concluding part three, Pedro Nagem de Souza considers style in relation to the metaphor of nature as a mother in Nietzsche's early work. Assessing the notes to Nietzsche's doctoral dissertation (*On Teleology since Kant*, 1867/8), he observes that the mother-nature metaphor is already evident. Echoed in SE where Nietzsche defines culture as "imitating nature in her motherly mood" and "veiling expressions of nature's stepmotherly mood." This dual act of imitation and concealment is style, which de Souza argues is the means by which we give unity to nature's senseless multiplicity. He further asserts that differences of style engender corresponding differences in the relation between nature and culture, and that the problematic arising from nature's illumination by culture may serve as a hermeneutic for interpreting the evolution of Nietzsche's thought.

Part four, on *Care and the Other*, consists of works examining compassion and dependency, romantic love, and the relation between marriage and breeding in Nietzsche's thought. In chapter ten Justin Remhof contributes a novel argument about Nietzsche and the ethics of care tradition. Examining his apparent disdain for human dependency, Remhof analyzes key statements in Zarathustra and other texts that dismiss the importance of compassion. He argues that any meaningful ethical theory must account for relations between individuals, particularly if it emphasizes an individual's relation to herself over others. Remhof maintains that given its grounding in self-care, Nietzsche's perfectionism can withstand challenges presented by the care tradition and is therefore more responsive to the care tradition than his more inflammatory statements would, *prima facie*, suggest.

In chapter eleven Lorenzo Serini explores the topic of love and relations between men and women in Nietzsche's thought through a comparison with Stendhal and Beauvoir, which he argues provides an enhanced understanding of Nietzsche's discourse(s) on romantic love. He notes the many positive remarks about romantic love in Nietzsche's middle writings. Yet, as a passion susceptible to excesses, Nietzsche is critical of the ideas that love should be non-egoistic or that it requires self-relinquishment. Yet Serini contends that in Nietzsche's view we should not rid ourselves of love's passion because while love can be life-denying, it can also be life-enhancing. Serini clarifies Nietzsche's largely overlooked life-enhancing conception of love to reveal his support for a mode of loving that cherishes duality, diversity, and oppositions. He concludes by showing how Beauvoir re-elaborates Nietzsche's idea that men and women love differently.

In chapter twelve Marina García-Granero examines Nietzsche's views on marriage and its intersection with his aim of transforming humanity, and the implications of this for his thinking about heredity. She argues that Nietzsche's views on marriage can be understood in terms of his desire to promote cultivate—or breed—a future human, an aim that obtains a programmatic character in the mature works. García-Granero analyzes "On Children and Marriage" (Z I 20), which she argues is an implicit discussion of Schopenhauer's thesis regarding the ultimate meaning of the sexual union between a man and a woman. She maintains that Nietzsche deemed the Schopenhauerian conception of love and marriage to be a reactive and ascetic one, and that Nietzsche's notion of marriage is a prolongation of the will to power and a recreation in difference that catalyzes a yearning for the *Übermensch*.

Part five, on *Feminist Strategies*, addresses how Nietzsche's critique of evolving relations between the sexes and excoriation of feminism might serve, however counterintuitively, as a spur to agonistic struggles that enable novel forms of identity, generate higher modes of love and friendship through the passions, and reveal new strategies for self-overcoming. In chapter thirteen Marisa Maccaro scrutinizes the psychological analysis of love in Nietzsche's middle works, in which he suggests that love and greed may be the same instinct named twice (GS 14) and that romantic/sexual love is an egoistic expression of the drives to possess and, elsewhere, to be possessed. Maccaro argues that the expression of these drives, via the gender roles Nietzsche calls "will and willingness," is detrimental to both men and women. Reflecting on Nietzsche's characterization of these drives in conjunction with his praise of friendship as love's highest form, Maccaro concludes that the Nietzschean virtue of curiosity ought to be cultivated between men and women to serve as both a higher ideal and the key to their flourishing.

In chapter fourteen Marta Vero reflects on Judith Butler's reading of Nietzsche to explicate the possibilities that Nietzsche's philosophy presents for contemporary feminism. Specifically, she argues that postmodern feminists should queer Nietzsche by adopting a genealogical methodology to investigate the relationship between power, sex, and gender. Vero maintains that by adopting a Nietzschean genealogy and skeptical perspective on language, feminist theorists can better question gender binarism as a patriarchal construct and overcome it. Vero further claims that by re-articulating anti- (or all-too-)human patriarchal norms through the ironism and drag performances commended by such a queered genealogical inquiry of linguistic-performative acts, future feminist philosophers may invalidate and overcome them.

In the fifteenth and final chapter, Katie Brennan analyzes the work of radical German feminist Hedwig Dohm (1831–1919), to draw out the implications of a Dohmian critique of Nietzschean nihilism. Brennan argues that while existing accounts of Nietzschean nihilism have focused largely on either its cognitive elements or its affective components, Dohm's critique of it provides a framework for developing a more robust account of nihilism's sociocultural effects. Via Dohm, she contends that despite failing to see how social norms and the roles ascribed to women force them into nihilistic predicaments, Nietzsche nonetheless provides conceptual resources for developing an account of nihilism in oppressed peoples.

## Notes

1   Hatab refuted allegations that Nietzsche was a misogynist, noting that "The 'place' of the feminine, for Nietzsche, reflects a Dionysian superiority. So ironically [...] it would not be difficult to interpret Nietzsche's philosophy *literally* as a 'feminism'!" (1981: 339). See D 346, in which Nietzsche criticizes the self-loathing drive that motivates misogyny.
2   Kaufmann (1974: 84).
3   Pippin maintains that read conventionally, "the lesson [...] is that just as women love only 'real men' or warriors, philosophical truth or wisdom is a manly thing, a matter of active, powerful legislation, not supplication or 'feminine' passivity" (2010: 15).

4   In an unpublished note he referred to this threat as the "*marasmus femininus*" or "withering feminine" (KSA 11:37[11]).
5   Diethe observed that "the Wilhelmines' perception of the independent woman as 'manly' was the sanctification of the bourgeois married woman's mothering role," an attitude Nietzsche echoes in places (1996a: 41); cf. Moore (2002: 131–3).
6   Illustrating his contempt for challenges to sexual mores, Nietzsche singled out George Sand for criticism twice in *Twilight of the Idols*. Perhaps the 19th-century's most famous cross-dressing woman, Sand was often described (though not by Nietzsche) as a "cigar-toting sexual outlaw". At TI Skirmishes 1 Nietzsche called the French feminist writer a "milk cow", and derisively associated her with Rousseau at TI Skirmishes 6. Despite his avowed "immoralism" Nietzsche often adopted the conservative rhetorical posture of a moral prig on matters of sex and sexuality, as if to implicitly suggest that his revaluation of *all* values would not extend to such matters. See KSA 13:15[80], on the "erotic precociousness […] of French youths", for example.
7   One may argue that Nietzsche did not fully recognize the revolutionary potentials afforded by his critique of truth and values, but such an oversight would not constitute a betrayal of that critique.
8   Commenting on HH 426, Wolfenstein notes Nietzsche's view that "free spirits […] view women as snares and marriage as captivity" (2000: 172).
9   As Oliver observed, Nietzsche thought that "the 'feminist,' like the metaphysician, worships the 'in-itself,' or the 'as-it-is.' She attempts to pierce the veil forced on the male dominated society in order to reveal woman as she is" (1984: 187–8).
10  This required willfully ignoring myriad exceptions to those roles, which are equally evident throughout recorded history.
11  Nietzsche's references to "the eternal-feminine" are largely disparaging. Apart from EH Books 5, see BGE 232 and 236, TI Skirmishes 4, and CW 3 and 6.
12  The pamphlet was displayed at the Pontypridd Museum in Wales in early 2018. See (under "Representation of the People Act 1918, January–March 2018"): https://www.pontypriddmuseum.wales/exhibitions#Exhibitions&gid=1157491203&pid=3, last visited on February 20, 2022.
13  Reflecting on the ambiguity of the ascetic ideal in the context of self-subordination, Guay notes that for women "this subordination allows for new possibilities of self-expression" (2022: 143).
14  See McNeal (2022).
15  See Bishop (2022: 16–17).
16  Safranski (2002: 250).
17  Prideaux (2018: 169).
18  See Hayman (1984: 64), cf. 11; cf. Pletsch (1991: 66–7).
19  See Hemelsoet et. al. (2008), who conclude that "Cerebral autosomal dominant arteriopathy with subcortical infarcts and leukoencephalopathy (CADASIL) accounts for all the signs and symptoms of Nietzsche's illness."
20  Prideaux (2018: 202).

Part One

# Influential Early Analyses

# 1

# Nietzsche on Woman

## With a New Postscript

Lawrence J. Hatab

Was Nietzsche a sexist, a male chauvinist, a misogynist? In the eyes of many, Nietzsche is one philosopher for whom the question should not even be asked, as if there were any question. Is not Nietzsche surely one of the more striking examples of a philosopher perpetuating a male-dominated culture by arguing for the inferiority of women? I don't think so. With some trepidation, I would like to engage this delicate matter, and take issue with the claim that Nietzsche's views on women reflect "all-too-human prejudices" which are therefore "philosophically irrelevant" (Kaufmann 1974: 84)—and even attempt the impossible, argue for Nietzsche's "feminism."

Was Nietzsche a sexist? If sexism means a belief in necessary and essential differences between the sexes, the answer is a qualified yes. If it means a belief in masculine superiority, the answer is no—in fact, a good case can be made for feminine superiority. If Western culture reflects masculine domination, we will see that Nietzsche presents a decidedly "non-Western" view of the masculine-feminine relation and the priorities disclosed in the nature of that relation.

Like all facets of Nietzsche's philosophy, his thoughts on woman demand a careful reading, with an eye out for links to other aspects of his thinking. We will begin with the longest single treatment of the issue in Nietzsche's writings, found in *Beyond Good and Evil* 231-9.[1] Two important points in section 231 must be noted at the outset: (1) He speaks of "woman as such" (*Weib an sich*), not "women."[2] I take this to be an indication that Nietzsche is pursuing something deeper than sexual differences. Hereafter, the term "woman" is meant to be synonymous with "the feminine" (*Weiblichkeit*), a principle which is neither biological nor sociological but "archetypal" (Neumann 1969: xxii). (2) Nietzsche identifies the thoughts to come as "my truths." Some might take this to be a philosophical disclaimer, or relief for the serious reader, since what follows is a rather idiosyncratic indulgence with no importance beyond a subjective profile of

---

This chapter is a reprint (with some editorial modifications) of my article, "Nietzsche on Woman," *Southern Journal of Philosophy*, 19/3 (Fall 1981), 333–45; https://doi.org/10.1111/j.2041-6962.1981.tb01439.x.

the author. Yet, although Nietzsche was a playful writer, he was never without serious intention. In my view, before we can judge Nietzsche's thoughts on woman, we must first attempt to see how they fit within his overall thought. Let me begin by quoting a good portion of the sections in question.

> Woman wants to become self-reliant—and for that reason she is beginning to enlighten men about "woman as such": *this* is one of the worst developments of the general *uglification* of Europe. For what must these clumsy attempts of women at scientific self-exposure bring to light! ... Woe when "the eternally boring in woman"—she is rich in that!—is permitted to venture forth! When she begins to unlearn thoroughly and on principle her prudence and art—of grace, of play, of chasing away worries, or lightning burdens and taking things lightly .... Is it not in the worst taste when woman sets out becoming scientific that way? So far enlightenment of this sort was fortunately man's affair, man's lot .... But she does not *want* to truth: what is truth to woman? From the beginning, nothing has been more alien, repugnant, and hostile to woman than truth—her great art is the lie, her highest concern is mere appearance and beauty. Let us men confess it: we honor and love precisely *this* art and *this* instinct in woman—we who have a hard time and for our relief like to associate with beings under whose hands, eyes, and tender follies our seriousness, our gravity and profundity almost appear to us like folly .... We men wish that woman should not go on compromising herself through enlightenment .... I think it is a real friend of women that counsels them today: *mulier taceat de mulier!* (Woman should be silent about woman).
>
> (232)

> To go wrong on the fundamental problem of "man and woman," to deny the most abysmal antagonism between them and the necessity of an eternally hostile tension, to dream perhaps of equal rights, equal education, equal claims and obligations—that is a *typical* sign of shallowness.
>
> (238)

> Wherever the industrial spirit has triumphed over the military and aristocratic spirit, woman now aspires to the economic and legal self-reliance of a clerk: "woman as clerk" is inscribed on the gate to the modern society that is taking shape now. As she thus takes possession of new rights, aspires to become "master" and writes the "progress" of woman upon her standards and banners, the opposite development is taking place with terrible clarity: woman is retrogressing. Since the French Revolution, woman's influence in Europe has *decreased* proportionately as her rights and claims have increased; and the "emancipation of woman," insofar as that is demanded and promoted by women themselves (and not merely by shallow males) is thus seen to be an odd symptom of the increasing weakening and dulling of the most feminine instincts. There is *stupidity* in this movement, an almost masculine stupidity .... What is the meaning of all this if not a crumbling of feminine instincts, a defeminization? To be sure, there are enough imbecilic friends and corrupters of woman among the scholarly asses of the male sex who

advise woman to defeminize herself in this way and to imitate all the stupidities with which "man" in Europe, European "manliness," is sick: they would like to reduce woman to the level of "general education," probably even of reading the newspapers and talking about politics .... Altogether one wants to make her more "cultivated" and, as is said, make the weaker sex *strong* through culture—as if history did not teach us as impressively as possible that making men "cultivated" and making them weak—weakening, splintering, and sicklying over *the force of the will*—have always kept pace, and that the most powerful and influential women in the world (most recently Napoleon's mother) owed their power and ascendancy over men to the force of their will—and not to schoolmasters!

(239)

A careful reading of these passages, in the light of certain basic assumptions in Nietzsche's thought, should lead to the conclusion that this is anything but male chauvinism, that is, the belief in the superiority of masculine traits. If the emancipation of women entails equality, namely affirming and recommending the participation of women in "man's world," it is clearly Nietzsche's view that this represents not a step up but in fact a regressive decline and loss of power. If feminine traits could be characterized as playfulness, adornment, instinctiveness, unpredictability, sensuality, nurturing (as in child rearing); and masculine traits as seriousness, rationality, orderliness, de-sensualization, productivity (as in a "career")—then Nietzsche seems to be saying that the repudiation of feminine traits in favor of masculine traits is an exchange of strength for weakness. In other words, not only is the feminine not inferior to the masculine, it may be superior, because according to Nietzsche man is "sick."

If such an interpretation is to make sense, we must draw connections with certain central Nietzschean themes: (1) *the primacy of instinct*. Although Nietzsche never denies the value of reason, he rejects the rationalistic devaluation of passion and instinct—not out of some shallow romanticism, but because he sees reason and instinct as inextricably linked. Reason is in the service of life instincts, the priority of which must therefore always be recognized. (2) *the primacy of will*. Nietzsche never abandoned the Schopenhauerian view that knowledge is subordinate to will, that explanation, measure, and order are epiphenomenal echoes of an inexplicable force of sheer assertion: will. As in the first theme, knowledge is not without value; it simply does not represent the core of human being. (3) *anti-egalitarianism*. Nietzsche opposes all forms of equality, not on social or political but philosophical grounds. All calls for equality, in Nietzsche's eyes, represent variations of the central theme of Western metaphysics: the attempt to transcend the world constituted by differences and their subsequent conflict. In all facets of his thinking, Nietzsche tried to preserve the tension of differences, because in his view the essence of reality (a process of becoming) is fueled by this tension. (4) *the decadence of Western culture*. Nietzsche criticized the spirit of Western civilization because it represents an inversion of the priorities described above. The Platonic-Christian foundation of the Western mind determined the course of culture and history to be a continuing suppression of "nature" in favor of "spirit." Now, in view of the masculine and feminine traits sketched earlier, if one were to admit a common assumption of male chauvinism—that our culture is a masculine product—then then it seems to me that accusing Nietzsche of misogyny or male chauvinism entirely misses the point. There never has been a more severe critic of Western culture than Nietzsche; consequently, he can be seen to be one of the most severe critics of the masculine principle.

We can pursue this matter from another angle by recalling the central theme of *The Birth of Tragedy*: the Dionysian-Apollonian distinction, and with it the issue of truth and appearance, which are most pertinent to our topic. Assuming the reader is somewhat familiar with BT, I will only sketch a bare outline of the fundamental issue in that work. There Nietzsche identifies what he considers to be the two archetypal forces controlling Greek culture, which are embodied in the deities Dionysus and Apollo. Dionysus personifies ecstatic self-transcendence and Apollo personifies the principle of individuation. What is portrayed here is a cosmic relation consisting of a unified formless flux (becoming) and individuated moments within that flux (being), which together constitute the world-process. For Nietzsche, the early Greeks knew both forces well: the cultivation of form and meaning in the plastic and poetic arts, and form-shattering annihilation in the ecstatic practices of mystery cults.

Nietzsche's view of the world gives priority to becoming over being. Consequently, he maintained that Greek tragedy, which was connected with Dionysian religion, represented the culmination of Greek genius, their deepest penetration into the nature of reality. The tragedies could affirm individuation and form (the poetic reflection of the hero) and yet recognize the priority of the annihilating power of flux (the hero's doom). In other words, the tragic worldview saw form (the Apollonian) as "appearance" (a temporary ordering of a primordial chaos) which must consequently yield to a formless power (the Dionysian), symbolized by the priority of destructive fate in the drama. In the tragic age, the Greeks were able to create a world of beauty and meaning and yet affirm the inevitable negativity of life, thereby affirming life as a whole.

With the advent of the scientific spirit (personified by Socrates), the tragic attunement of Apollo and Dionysus was ruptured. The forces of form and formlessness became separated into an antagonistic conflict, where the principle of form was given priority. The Socratic search for truth, understood as an abiding form beyond appearance and change, represented the rejection of the artistic spirit, namely the view that form is a *creation* out of an indeterminate chaos, not "truth." In this way the Apollonian principle is severed from the Dionysian, resulting in the opposition between reason (form alone) and chaos (mystery and destruction), in an attempt to eliminate or at least devalue the latter.

According to Nietzsche, with this Platonic inversion of tragic priorities, where new form takes precedence over formlessness and unchanging form becomes the criterion for truth, the Western mind begins to be alienated from a world constituted by becoming. The ideals of Western (post-tragic) culture represent the predominance of Apollonian-rational tendencies and the subordination of Dionysian instincts, either in the other-worldly form of Christianity or the this-worldly form of scientific rationalism. In any case, Nietzsche sees as a consequence the weakening of life-affirming instincts and the eclipse of attunement to a world of becoming.

Since, for Nietzsche, form is a *process* of creation out of formlessness, not a "substance," then the Platonic inversion represents not only a philosophical mistake, but also an existential barrier impeding the appropriate emergence of form in the aesthetic mode of creativity. Herein lies the background of Nietzsche's critique of truth and promotion of appearance. The continuing references to appearance in Nietzsche's writings point back to this central theme of BT: form *as such* is appearance; there is no "truth," other than the annihilation of form. Form-as-appearance, namely form which admits its "deceptive" character, which yields to the formless, is a more appropriate model of reality. Form is not "objective truth," but rather a creation; and this is why Nietzsche calls the world an "aesthetic phenomenon" (BT 5)—which, as a primal condition, cannot be rendered as "mere" appearance measured against some purported "real" condition.

If we recall Nietzsche's characterization of woman in the passages quoted earlier, we can begin to see the references to "appearance," "lie," and the repudiation of truth in a new light. And if we could match the Apollonian-Dionysian distinction with the masculine-feminine distinction, then Nietzsche's objections to "emancipation" could be translated as follows: woman's equality means (in Nietzsche's view) the adoption of masculine traits; defeminization announces the final victory of the Apollonian/rational over the Dionysian and completes the degeneration and weakening of human beings. Could it be that the woman question represents, for Nietzsche, a specific battle in which he fights for the preservation of the Dionysian?

If we could conclusively equate the feminine with the Dionysian, then in the context of Nietzsche's critique of Western culture we could argue for the "primordiality" of the feminine. To that end, let us hear more from BGE:

> What inspires respect for woman, and often enough even fear, is her *nature*, which is more "natural" than man's, the genuine, cunning suppleness of a beast of prey, the tiger's claw under the glove, the naïveté of her egoism, her uneducability and inner wildness, the incomprehensibility, scope, and movement of her desires and virtues—what, in spite of all fear, elicits pity for this dangerous and beautiful cat "woman" is that she appears to suffer more, to be more vulnerable, more in need of love, and more condemned to disappointment than any other animal. Fear and pity: with these feelings man has so far confronted woman, always with one foot in tragedy which tears to pieces as it enchants.
>
> (239)

We are clearly reminded of the "nature versus culture" tragic tension in BT. In section 231 of BGE, Nietzsche says: "Woman is *essentially* unpeaceful, like a cat." In one of his later writings, Nietzsche says that woman "tears to pieces" when she loves, and he calls women "maenads" (EH Books, 5)—which is clearly a Dionysian reference. In that same passage, he tells us that he "knows women" because of his "Dionysian dowry," and he calls himself in that context the "first psychologist of the eternally feminine." All this suggests that Nietzsche considered the feminine and the Dionysian to be closely linked if not synonymous. We can further elucidate this association by briefly addressing the context of the Dionysian in ancient Greece (see Kerenyi 1976).

The cult of Dionysus was the most successful "Chthonic" counterweight to "Olympian" worship in the sense that it represented elements of nature mysticism and ecstatic self-transcendence to balance the more composed beauty of the Olympian gods. The respective notions of immortality speak to this point: Olympian immortality meant freedom from death; Dionysian immortality meant continual death and rebirth. In this way, Dionysian mythology expressed the cyclic regeneration of nature, the destruction and reconstruction of life forms. Consequently, Dionysian worship embraced the "dark" destructive side of life in order to receive the blessings that stem from harmonizing the self with a necessary natural force. The essence of Dionysian religion consisted in the realization that although nature destroys the individual, the whole is indestructible; therefore, mystical self-transcendence grants religious transformation.

The Dionysian cult was originally a cult of women; only later were men included. Furthermore, Dionysus was frequently characterized as androgynous, that is to say, a male with a feminine manner (as portrayed in *The Bacchae*). Much of the imagery of Dionysian religion suggests that it was derived from an archaic worship of the feminine principle, as in the "Great Mother" theme common to many cultures.[3] The women who worshiped Dionysus were called "maenads," namely those possessed by divine madness. The terrible practices of the cult, such as dismembering live animals and devouring them raw, though "mad" by ordinary standards, nevertheless were religiously significant. They were examples of ritual participation in the destructive force of the god.[4] Although the wild exploits of the Dionysian women offered a stark contrast to other more moderate forces in Greek life, nevertheless Dionysian worship was thought to bring peace and a blissful communion with the god. In fact, since the annihilating force was necessary and inevitable (hence its deification), then failure to revere it would only invite more terrible destruction (as in the brutal consequences of Pentheus's resistance in *The Bacchae*).

Dionysian religion presents the Greek version of a common reverence given to the dark destructive side of nature in many other cultures; and almost invariably, such a power takes a feminine form: in India, *mâyâ* and feminine associations with the god Siva; in China, the *yin* principle. In general, one could summarize the cross-cultural features of the masculine-feminine duality as follows: the masculine as light, knowledge, construction, consciousness, form; the feminine as darkness, mystery, destruction, unconsciousness, formlessness. So, in this respect the Dionysian cult represented a worship of the feminine. One could characterize Western forms of spirituality and intellectual development as the gradual ascendance of the masculine over the feminine principle (beginning with the Olympian victory over the Titans).[5] Accordingly, Nietzsche's critique of the West can be translated into the terms of our discussion: the Apollonian-Dionysian dyad presents a masculine-feminine duality; and Nietzsche's objections to the predominance of Apollonian rationality become an objection to the predominance of the masculine principle; and his respect for the tragic spirit is inspired by its recognition and acceptance of a primordial feminine principle. In this way Nietzsche promotes a decidedly "non-Western" take on the masculine-feminine relation, in that he seeks to elevate the feminine force to equal status with the masculine force.[6] The "destructive" aspect of the feminine, therefore, is not something to be regretted. In fact, it undoes on Apollonian fixation and thereby induces a more holistic vision.

Western culture values knowledge over mystery, reason over instinct, technology over nature. Nietzsche's thoughts on woman present a defense of, and in some ways a preference for, certain sub-cultural forces, the denial of which leads to alienation, weakness, and sickness (or perhaps the fate of Pentheus). Nietzsche thinks that a woman's fight for equal rights is symptomatic of disease. Women should resist "rights," because the state of nature, the "eternal war between the sexes, gives her by far the first rank" (EH Books 5). If Nietzsche were a male chauvinist, we would have to demonstrate his preference for "man's world," and his subordination of women to their place of subservience because of their inferiority. But as we have seen, the superiority of the masculine (intellect, order, the "business of the world") is a reflection of an Apollonian-rational ideology. The "place" of the feminine, for Nietzsche, reflects a Dionysian superiority. So ironically, in the context of our analysis it would not be a stretch to interpret Nietzsche's philosophy literally as a kind of feminism—a unique kind, of course, which would not suit the goals of contemporary feminism; nevertheless, it is clear that Nietzsche would join the fight against "female inferiority." Moreover, in EH, Nietzsche gives a fascinating explanation for the so-called failings of women, fascinating because it sounds so much like a current feminist critique:

> Someone took a youth to a Sage and said: "Look he is being corrupted by women." The sage shook his head and smiled, "It is man," said he, "that corrupt women; and all the failings of women should be atoned by and improved in man. For it is man who creates for himself the image of woman, and woman forms herself according to this image." ... Someone else shouted out of the crowd: "women need to be educated better!"—"Men need to be educated better," said the sage.
> (GS 68)[7]

To better fathom my proposal of Nietzsche's "feminism," we should consider further the relation between the masculine-feminine distinction and the truth-appearance distinction. We can do this by recalling those passages on woman from BGE, this time in terms of their context. The passages conclude the section entitled Our Virtues, which explores two main themes: (1) the creator and the rejection of equality, and (2) the value of "cruelty." These themes are related in the following way: Nietzsche proposes an aesthetic process-model of the world, in which he espouses creative form (form brought forth from formlessness through the creative process) in contrast to "substantial" form, which reifies meaning into fixed, objective "truth"—and which, in order to overcome variability in experience posits some common essence to "equalize" differences, thereby resolving what the conceptualizing intellect takes to be a problematic conflict. It is in this context that we can understand Nietzsche's recommendation for cruelty. He tells us that high culture is the "spiritualization of cruelty" (229) and that there is cruelty in all profound thinking (230). In other words, since any affirmation is at the same time a denial (an overcoming), the nature of thought as a *whole* is process, not fixed substances. The limits of form inherent in process *constitute* the emergence of form. Therefore, no formation can claim to be fixed or objective "truth," but is more accurately "appearance"—that is to say, creative form-ing in a process that cannot be fixed in any form. In this way, Nietzsche inverts Platonic-Western priorities by denying truth and affirming appearance.[8] The traditional notion of truth must be discarded (herein lies the essential meaning of the "death of God" theme in GS); that is to say, the notions of unchanging form, universal concepts, and scientific explanation must yield to something more primordial (as Apollo yielded to Dionysus in tragedy). The result is the aesthetic, creative role of negativity in the constitution of form. It is in *this* context that the passages on woman are placed, indeed they conclude this section. Despite Nietzsche's aphoristic style, he was a careful writer. The "woman question" is not a digression or a sideshow. In fact, the Preface to BGE begins with the sentence: "Supposing truth is a woman—what then?" Put another way: What if truth were appearance?

We should now have a deepened appreciation for Nietzsche's references to certain feminine characteristics such as playfulness, ornamentation, instinctiveness, and unpredictability. If we contrast these with certain masculine values such as seriousness, unmasking through explanation, order, and stability, it is evident that the feminine seems to be more appropriate to the primal aesthetic character of the world process.[9] In this context we note that in GS 361, Nietzsche writes: "Woman is so artistic." And the first set of passages from BGE express Nietzsche's belief that man must continually learn from woman. Feminine naturalness, frivolity, and love of surfaces teaches man the "folly" of his pursuits, makes light of serious things, and in so doing discloses the meaning of appearance.[10] Here we have a contemporary remnant of the Dionysian suspension of "culture" and the salvific effect of loosening the bonds of knowledge. We can now better understand Nietzsche's alarm over the prospect of abandoning the feminine. One could say he feared the loss of an aesthetic "Dionysian connection."[11]

We have seen that in the context of Nietzsche's overall philosophy, the woman question is much deeper than a social, sexual, or biological matter. I hope I have demonstrated the shortsightedness of the judgment that Nietzsche's thoughts on woman are philosophically irrelevant. At this point I would like to link these deeper aspects of the masculine-feminine distinction with the male-female question and consequently speak to certain issues in contemporary feminism. I have to admit my limitations in these matters but in considering Nietzsche's position, I am convinced there is much his thought can contribute to current debates.

Let us begin by considering what in Nietzsche's eyes is the most important distinction in human nature: not that between male and female or even masculine and feminine, but the creator and the herd, that is to say, the distinction between those who enact the creative process and those who simply receive their world as given. How can we characterize the creator? In the light of Nietzsche's archetypes, I would say the creator presents an equal mix of Apollonian and Dionysian features; since creators as such bring forth form from formlessness and clear away old forms to make way for the new, they are attuned to both the constructive and destructive aspects of the *whole* form-as-process represented by the Apollonian-Dionysian dyad. In this way, creators inhabit an equal mix of masculine and feminine qualities. If the masculine-feminine distinction can be summarized as the duality of conscious and unconscious forces (Neumann 1969: 42), we can more clearly see the creative process as a masculine-feminine correlation. Although at times in his writings Nietzsche seems to emphasize unconscious drives, nevertheless the creative process as a whole must involve the gathering in consciousness of unconscious forces (the tragic synthesis). Creators are therefore to be distinguished from either ordinary types who dwell in conscious awareness alone, or purely destructive types for whom de-formation is an end in itself.

In characterizing creators as an equal mix of masculine and feminine qualities, we offer no conclusion about the gender of creators. At this point I will try to organize what I think *could* be a Nietzschean position in this matter. The masculine-feminine distinction is not equivalent to the male-female distinction. The former dyad is much deeper than gender. I think it is clear that creators are *archetypically* "androgynous."[12] The *ordinary* male could be said to represent a predominance of the masculine-Apollonian and the *ordinary* female a predominance of the feminine-Dionysian. Nietzsche's remarks on woman in BGE might have been limited to ordinary types. But even if this were so, we would have to attend to the linkage with the creator, which after all was the *context* for the sections on woman.

For Nietzsche, the creator is a special case of human being. But if we consider the "pyramid" analogy in The Antichrist 57, we should remember that the creator is not an *isolated* case. The peaks of culture are supported by a broad base. Ordinary people "support" the creator, and therefore can even be said to be a "foundation" for the creator. How so? If the creator is a mix of masculine and feminine traits, it might have been Nietzsche's view that the *tension* between the masculine and the feminine, the "eternal war of the sexes," must be maintained as the condition which *generates* the creator—as a *mixture*. If the masculine-feminine tension were blurred or suspended, perhaps there would emerge no creator *out of* this tension. In other words, if the creator embodies a dialectic of opposites, then the opposition must be maintained *as such* in the larger order of things. We can see, therefore, that Nietzsche's objections to equality have their roots in his aim to preserve conditions of creativity. On the one hand, he objects to reducing the creator to conventional values of the ordinary type; and on the other hand, he seems to object to a "unisexual" democratization of the base conditions for the emergence of the creator type—that is to say, the articulated masculine-feminine tension between ordinary males and females.[13]

If the masculine-feminine tension generates the creator, then it is clear why Nietzsche challenges "woman's equality" in the context of his critique of the West. To diminish the feminine principle in an already masculine-dominated culture would only complete the alienated closure of the human spirit and obviate its creative potential. Nietzsche might ask: How much of modern feminism is merely a *continuation* of masculine dominance with its challenge to the feminine (non-Apollonian) roles of ordinary females? In other words, how much of modern feminism is an unwitting "masculinism"? I do not think that Nietzsche's views imply confining all females to certain conventional roles. He consistently opposes any form of "All S is P" universals. I think Nietzsche would simply object to the Democratic view that *all* females are, or could become the same, either in terms of feminine *or* masculine roles. He would object to the idea that women who follow a feminine stereotype are "oppressed," or that women who might *choose* a feminine role are "duped" or coerced by cultural conditioning. He would oppose such ideas because of the implicit theory that all human beings, whether male or female, are capable of or meant for a common form of life, whether that be traditional masculine and feminine roles, or even the masculine-feminine mix of creativity.

I am convinced that Nietzsche would not constrict "masculine" to the male and "feminine" to the female. The fact that Nietzsche fears woman could *lose* the feminine implies that it is not confined to gender. A female can certainly pursue a predominantly masculine role. Moreover, a female can embody the masculine-feminine mix of the creator type—given that the only person Nietzsche deemed worthy of continuing his work was a female, Lou Andreas-Salomé. What *would* Nietzsche oppose in contemporary feminism? Not a woman "liberating" herself, pursuing either a masculine role or a masculine-feminine mix, but seeing liberation not as an *individual* matter but as a "women's movement"—what Nietzsche seemed to resist most in BGE was an "enlightened" woman's pronouncements on "woman as such." Any such "movement" would imply another form of democratization, which for Nietzsche is always an expression of metaphysical fixture (for instance, that human nature possesses a common essence upon which distinctions are added accidentally). Nietzsche's doctrine of rank will not allow the idea of a common human nature. But this does not imply that a hierarchy is forever a fixed thing. Women can become creators; females and males can switch roles; some homosexual relationships illustrate a frequent "relocation" of masculine and feminine qualities, which would suggest that the distinction itself is natural but its location varies. Whatever variation is accomplished, Nietzsche would plead against *universalizing* it. Any idea can succumb to dogmatism; even the proposition "Everyone is a creator" is a dogmatic statement that Nietzsche would reject.[14]

I think Nietzsche would warn modern feminists that within the legitimate pursuits of certain individuals, there is the veiled possibility of a completed form of masculine-Apollonian dominance over the feminine-Dionysian. Nietzsche would want to ensure that the masculine-feminine distinction (and *tension*) is preserved in some form. I think he would ask: How much of contemporary feminism is an implicit preference for masculine traits? Do women simply want an equal share of masculine alienation? Is there not the danger of a powerful and necessary instinctive element becoming extinct? Has everyone come to fear the feminine? Nietzsche could support, and may have himself even proposed a "feminism" with the following characteristics: (1) A recognition of the archetypal masculine-feminine distinction, where each has equal importance (perhaps the feminine could even have priority), where the feminine is protected from extinction or domination by the masculine. (2) The proposal of a new model of human nature, in the form of an androgynous mix of masculine and feminine traits, namely the creator type. (3) The qualification that androgyny is not for everyone. Nietzsche would want to retain the proportionate polarities in ordinary males and females, whose "war" prepares the generation of the exception.

I think we should heed Nietzsche's warnings about "politicizing" individual destinies (even if entrenched cultural barriers to individual freedom incite a politically focused attack as a first step), or universalizing the exception. Any "movement," as such, can only perpetuate in another form the very condition that aroused its opposition in the first place—the suppression of differences. Even a liberation movement can be oppressive. Will we come full circle someday, where a woman will feel guilty if she prefers "homemaking" to a "career"?

In closing, although I have tried to show the legitimate importance of Nietzsche's thoughts on woman, it has not been my intention to argue for the validity of his view of human nature. I am not at all sure about such matters; this essay has been largely exegetical. I *am* sure that most contemporary feminists would object to Nietzsche's elitist exclusion of many persons from the ideal of androgyny. But in my view, at present there is no conclusive evidence that androgyny is the natural state of all persons, or that what Nietzsche calls the creator type lies dormant in every individual. I must say that the burden of proof does not lie with Nietzsche.

## 2022 Postscript

I am grateful to have my 1981 essay included in this collection of essays, which is meant as a gesture to early efforts in Anglophone research engaging Nietzsche on the question of women and the feminine. It's been over forty years, and since my essay was written on a typewriter, there is no original file, and so a new typescript had to be created. This gave me the opportunity to make some minor editorial changes and to include this postscript as a look back after all these years.

I have to admit that I am a little embarrassed by parts of the essay. I stand by most of its exegetical efforts, but some of my remarks about (then current) feminism now seem clunky and misplaced. I was young and cocky and I wanted to be provocative. In my work on Nietzsche over the years, I have "experimented" with challenging supposed contraries like Nietzsche and democracy, Nietzsche and divinity, and in this case Nietzsche and feminism (along with exploring purportedly marginal or incongruous topics like jazz, laughter, and sports). In any case, I was in over my head with respect to feminism and too apologetic about traditional roles. And when I presented this paper at an APA session prior to its publication, my commentator was right in saying that women would be wary of a man speaking on their behalf, even if suggesting a "superior" status for women, which can come across as an underhanded defense of the status quo with exalted veneration of socially restricted attributes. Moreover, as a further sign of my limitations, I was not readily aware of developments in "difference" feminism, which has challenged "equity" feminism. And lastly, my account of masculine and feminine "archetypes" sounds very dated now, given the remarkably fluid senses of "identity" in contemporary LGBT+ movements—although my attempt to decouple the masculine-feminine distinction from traditional gender associations might be relevant. Altogether it might have been better to be silent on sociocultural matters and simply stick to my exegetical task—which I still stand by today—namely, the complexity and ambiguity of Nietzsche's position on the "woman question," the problematic attribution of "male chauvinism," and the philosophical relevance of his approach to matters of sex and gender.

## Notes

1. The translation is from Kaufmann, *Basic Writings of Nietzsche* (Modern Library, 1968).
2. The same distinction is drawn in Z I, On Women.
3. For example, the Dionysian practice of boiling goat pieces in milk expresses this idea of returning to the Mother. See Kerenyi (1976: 256).
4. Herein lies the religious element of Greek tragedy; the recognition of the priority of a destructive force (fate) is derived from the worship of Dionysus.
5. See Campbell (1964, chapter 1).
6. Those who analyze the feminine archetype often overlook the fact that in many cultures the feminine principle not only "nurtures" and creates; it destroys as well. But only a culture like ours, which emphasizes the constructive masculine principle would disdain the feminine. The female personification of terrible natural forces in other cultures is not an expression of a misogynist spirit, but rather a gesture of honor and worship (as deification). Such a cultural view affirms construction and destruction as coequal aspects of an overall world process. In this archetypal light, American woman who protested the exclusive use of feminine names for hurricanes was a concealed furtherance of the Western preference for the masculine. We view the association of women with hurricanes as an insult. In India, such a feminine reference pays homage to a great power. In this respect, the call for "bisexual" hurricanes seems silly.
7. Kaufmann translation (Vintage Books, 1974).
8. It is important to clarify the often-ambiguous references to truth and appearance in Nietzsche's writings. At times he speaks *for* truth, at times *against* truth. I think the solution to this ambiguity is the following distinction: for Nietzsche, becoming is truth; being is appearance. Since the tradition had always seen being as truth and becoming as appearance, Nietzsche must criticize the traditional notion of truth (constancy) so that a more primordial truth (flux) can take its place. In this way, traditional truth is now appearance, which *as* appearance is appropriate to the truth of primordial becoming.
9. At this point we could clearly understand Nietzsche's objections to a frequent assumption of today's thinking about human nature and sexual roles that masculine and feminine traits are precisely that, roles as culturally fashioned "masks" that hide a person's true nature, which is sexually neutral. For Nietzsche, there is *nothing* under the mask. All forms of "nature" are "masks" of a formless flux. Therefore, the adoption of a mask does not hide but rather *constitutes* "human nature."
10. In BGE 232, the reference to gravity (*Schwere*) should recall the "spirit of gravity" (*die Geist der Schwere*) that Zarathustra had to overcome in Part III of *Thus Spoke Zarathustra*.
11. If Dionysian "cruelty" is interpreted as the "dismemberment" of the Apollonian principle, then the connection between playfulness and danger which often comes up in Nietzsche's treatment of woman might make more sense. The playfulness of the feminine is a danger for masculine seriousness. Instinctiveness and naturalness are a danger for masculine order. Many references to this effect occur in Z I, On Women. Moreover, attention to the qualities of danger, play, and man's "fear" of woman described in this passage could possibly redeem the statement which concludes the section, which is often quoted and thought to typify Nietzsche's misogyny: "You

are going to women? Do not forget the whip!" Two remarks are in order: (1) the statement is given not by Zarathustra, but by a woman; (2) in context, it is not clear for whom the whip is intended. The reference is to "the" whip, not "your" whip. And the whip may serve as an image expressing Dionysian (feminine) cruelty in the sense described earlier. It should be noted that this text was written in winter 1883; less than a year earlier, in May 1882, Nietzsche posed for a photograph with Paul Rée and Lou Andreas-Salomé. The pose had Nietzsche and Rée pulling a cart with Lou sitting on top, whip in hand. Apparently, Nietzsche greatly enjoyed this episode (see Binion 1968: 55).

12  For more clues about the complementarity of the masculine and feminine principles, see BGE 248, where Nietzsche describes two types of genius, one that wants to beget, fertilize, and dominate (the Romans), another that wants pregnancy and the task of forming, maturing, and perfecting (the Greeks).

13  The image of woman giving birth to the *Übermensch* (Z I Women) could be interpreted on this level.

14  Nietzsche never argues for the elimination of convention and ordinariness. In fact, the "herd" is needed to maintain the *tension* of the creative process (the fight *against* convention). See Z II Rabble, GS 76, and A 57.

2

# Woman as Truth in Nietzsche's Thought

Kelly A. Oliver

Nietzsche is as notorious for his struggle with woman as he is for his battle with truth: his writings are a mixture of awe and disdain for both. The infamy of Nietzsche's discussions of both woman and truth is not their only relationship, for in several passages, Nietzsche himself connects truth and woman. "Suppose truth is a woman … What is certain is that she has not allowed herself to be won—today every kind of dogmatist is left standing dispirited and discouraged. Both truth and woman are elusive—distance is their power."[1] The connection between truth and woman does not simplify the task of formulating Nietzsche's relationship to woman. Truth is as ambiguous in Nietzsche's writings as woman. This joint ambiguity is no coincidence: for while developing a theory of truth we are unpacking the symbol of woman. Inversely, while developing a theory of Nietzsche's philosophy of woman, we are unpacking a metaphor for truth. Our investigation will take this ambiguity as its axis: at one pole the ambiguity of truth, at the other the parallel ambiguity of woman. This ambiguity need not be read as an amorphous bewilderment; rather, a dialectic triad can serve us well in order to demonstrate one way this philosophical ambiguity can be coherently articulated. A triad borrowed from Derrida's *Spurs*, which describes Nietzsche's relationship to woman, will set up a grid for interpreting Nietzsche:

> He was, He dreaded this castrated woman.
> He was, He dreaded this castrating woman.
> He was, He loved this affirming woman.[2]

Nietzsche both identifies with and reacts against the three positions of woman suggested by Derrida: the castrated woman, the castrating woman, the affirming woman. This tri-positioning woman corresponds neatly to the tri-positioning of truth can extract from Nietzsche's works—truth as a manifestation of the will to truth, the will to illusion, and the will to power. Nietzsche has the same love-hate relationship to woman which he has to truth. The castrated woman embodies truth which results

---

Professor Oliver's chapter first appeared in 1984 as "Woman as Truth in Nietzsche's Writing," in *Social Theory and Practice*, 10(2), 185–99; https://doi.org/10.5840/soctheorpract19841028.

from the will to truth, the castrating woman corresponds to truth as a manifestation of the will to illusion, and the affirming woman is truth as the will to power. Each of these positions is a deception employed by the "avidious will" in order to "detain its creatures in life and compel them to live on."[3] Any deception, according to Nietzsche, can serve either ascending or descending life.

That which serves descending life impoverishes life, and gives a one-sided prominence to some things at the expense of others. The coward who serves declining life sacrifices creative multiplicity for a false security. Those weak wills, claims Nietzsche, who need to discover value rather than create it, are degenerate. Instead of creating their own value out of the flux of their experience, they try to go "beyond" the changing manifold of sensuous experience into a secure world "as-it-is-in-itself." They postulate a preexisting reality, opposed to the variety of our sensuous experience, which needs only to be discovered.

Degenerate life worships this postulated reality which overrides the senses: this transcendent reality demands that we suppress our instincts in favor of its stability. "To be obliged to fight the instincts—this formula of degeneration: as long as life is in the ascending line, happiness is the same as instinct."[4] That which is in the ascending line serves our instincts and thereby enhances life; it accommodates a great and multifarious variety with playful ease. Ascending life "reflects its plentitude upon things—it transfigures, it embellishes, it rationalises the world"; declining life "impoverishes, bleaches, mars the value of things; it suppresses the world."[5]

Each of the three positions of truth and woman can serve either ascending or declining life. Nietzsche identifies with each deception, each position of woman and truth, insofar as it serves ascending life, while he rejects any deception when it serves descending life. "I know both sides," says Nietzsche, "for I am both sides."[6]

The woman who serves ascending life revels in the superabundance of life; while she who serves declining life suppresses it. The castrated woman is the feminist who uses the will to truth either to enhance survival or dominate life. The castrating woman is the artist who uses the will to illusion either to playfully affirm the multiplicity of life or cunningly deceive us in order to gain advantage. The affirming woman is the will to power which either creates or destroys life.

## The Castrated Woman

The castrated woman imitates the will to truth. Just as the will to truth in the services of descending life can be the most tyrannical manifestation of the will to power, so the castrated woman can be the most tyrannical woman. For both betray themselves by identifying with their opposite: truth as the manifestation of the will to truth believes that it is apodictic and necessary when according to Nietzsche it is the opposite, that is, perspectival and contingent. The castrated or de-sexed woman assumes a position as a second type of man. She is the feminist who negates woman in order to affirm herself as man. "There is stupidity in this movement (the feminist movement)," writes Nietzsche, "an almost masculine stupidity." He continues, "Certainly there are enough of idiotic friends and corrupters of woman amongst the learned asses of the masculine sex, who advise woman to defeminize herself in this manner, and to imitate all the stupidities from which 'man' in European 'manliness', suffers."[7]

The "feminist," in Nietzsche's (unjustified)[8] opinion, denies her sexuality, castrates herself, in order to imitate man. In the castrated position woman suffers from the will to truth; that is, she lays claim to objective truth. She wants to create a science of woman. In this way she resembles the dogmatic philosopher; here the castrated woman stands in the same tyrannical relation to truth as the metaphysician. The tyranny of the metaphysician's will to truth manifests itself throughout the history of philosophy from Plato's theory of the Forms to Kant's unknowable *ding an sich*. Knowledge of reality/truth, according to Plato, demands a denial of the changing images presented to the senses in favor of pure reflection which penetrates the multiplicity of sense perception in order to confront reality "as it is" rather than "as it appears." We create a tyrannical truth and then put it beyond our grasp; this is the thing-in-itself. "The true world which is unattainable for the moment, is promised to the sage, to the pious man and to the man of virtue ... Progress of the idea: it becomes more subtle, more insidious, more evasive—it becomes a woman."[9]

The "feminist," like the metaphysician, worships the "in-itself," or the "as-it-is." She attempts to pierce the veil forced on the male-dominated society in order to reveal woman: "Woman wishes to be independent, and therefore she enlightens men about 'woman as she is'—this is one of the developments in the general uglifying of Europe."[10]

Both the feminist and the metaphysician are hypnotized by will to truth. Both seek the in-itself, an objective reality. The position of truth or woman, says Nietzsche, is hostile. Objective truth is hostile to the flux and passions of the sensuous which surrounds us; it is hostile to the multiplicity of interpretations whose flux is the will to power, the very source of life.[11]

> Castration and extirpation, are instinctively chosen for war against a passion, by those who are too weak of degenerate, to impose some sort of moderation upon it—natures who need *la Trappe*, or some kind of ultimatum gulf set between themselves and a passion.[12]

The castrated woman is hostile to the passions of woman sensuous being. She not only de-sexes herself in order to imitate but she also attempts to develop a science of woman, destroying the power of woman which originates, as we from her multiple meanings, her ambiguity. The will postulates a reality, a woman, which needs only discovery and interpretation. We hide truth behind a bush, claims Nietzsche, and praise ourselves when we find it.[13] Just as Nietzsche position of truth "the will to truth as the impotence to create,"[14] he calls emancipated women "abortions who lack the wherewithal to have children."[15]

The castrated position of truth/woman is impotent because it is cut off from the source of its power: illusion. This castrated truth/woman mistakes the means to life for the end of life:

> Man has repeated the same mistake over and over again: he has made a means to life into a standard of life; instead of discovering the standard in the highest

enhancement of life itself, in the problem of growth and exhaustion, he has employed the means to a quite distinct kind of life to exclude all other forms of life, in short to criticize and select life. I.e., man finally loves the means for their own sake and forgets that they are means: so that they enter his consciousness as aims, as standards for aims—i.e., a certain species of man treats the conditions of its existence as conditions which ought to be imposed as a law, as "Truth," "good," "perfection": it tyrannizes.[16]

In the case of the castrated woman, the "feminist," what she began as a movement—a means—to improve the socioeconomic position of women, has become, among some feminists, an end in itself. Feminism has become a type of moral obligation, a truth, rather than a means to improve life. If what began as an instinct to preserve life or a means to life turns against life and begins to tyrannize life by holding itself up as a standard for life, then it serves declining life. According to Nietzsche, a standard is impotent if it does not improve life. In the case of feminism, when it becomes an end in itself, it becomes impotent to further social change. While the will to truth as it manifests itself in feminism is useful to survival, when it presents its fruits as more than the means to survival—as apodictic truths—then it no longer serves life; it no longer helps our survival. Rather, it turns against life and denies life. The will to truth in its dogmatic certitude serves descending life. It sets up a fixed standard, a science of feminism, which life in its changing physicality cannot measure up to; it is therefore eternally frustrated and unhealthy.

When we apply Nietzsche's theory to contemporary feminism, we see that feminists, like metaphysicians, divided the world into true and apparent in order to enhance life. The apparent world is the world women are living in, a world dominated by men, in which even wages reflect the inferior value of women. Since women occupy inferior socioeconomic positions in this world of submission, it appears that they are inferior beings. The feminist's truth about woman "as she is" rather than "as she appears" was intended to change woman's socioeconomic position: what was intended to change appearance in order to create the world (where women occupy equal socioeconomic positions as men) became the criterion of reality, a science of woman.

At the parallel pole, the metaphysician's intention of dividing the world into true and apparent, as Nietzsche tells us the parable,

> was to deceive oneself in a useful way; the means, the invention of formulas and signs by means of which one could reduce the confusing multiplicity to a purposive and manageable schema.
>
> But alas! now a moral category was brought into play: no creature wants to deceive itself, ... consequently there a will to truth ... This is the greatest error that has ever been committed, the essential fatality of error on earth, one believed one possessed a criterion of reality in the forms of reason—in fact one possessed them in order to become master of order to misunderstand reality in a shrewd manner.[17]

Both truth and woman, as a manifestation of the will, began in the service of ascending life. Both were castrated became impotent to serve life when they turned the means to the end of life. The will to truth, whether played out through feminist's science or the metaphysician's truth, only serves ascending life when it recognizes itself as a means to life, a fiction enhances life. When it takes itself for *the* privileged perspective serves degenerate life. Fiction is life-enhancing but only playfully serves the multifarious openness of life. It is, then, only when the will to truth becomes the will to illusion, and itself as illusion, that it is in the service of ascending life. Truth is more primary than illusion; however, in this impotent castrated position we forget that "truth does not count supreme value ... The will to appearance, to illusion, to deception, to becoming and change (to objectified deception) here more profound, primeval, metaphysics than the will to truth, reality, to mere appearance; the last is itself merely a form of the will to illusion."[18]

At times Nietzsche seems to forget that illusion is more than truth. When he attempts to enlighten us about "woman is" he falls back into the impotent, castrated truth. Before his discussion of woman in Beyond Good and Evil, permission to "utter some truths about 'woman as she is,' that it is known at the outset how literally they are merely," says, "—my truths."[19]

Nietzsche identifies with woman in order to describe the nature of woman. Here Nietzsche seems to invoke some reality, the nature of woman "as she is," which is independent of interpretation. This, of course, is also Nietzsche's paradox when he tries, in a sense, to assert that the truth is "there is no truth." In order to enlighten about the real nature of the world about which the will deceives us, Nietzsche himself falls prey to the will to truth. In these passages he seems to rely on some form of the correspondence theory of truth which he rejects: true descriptions correspond to the world. Metaphysicians' descriptions do not correspond to the world "as it is," therefore they are deceptions, while Nietzsche's descriptions are more accurate. When Nietzsche identifies with woman, he must identify with the castrated woman as well as the affirming woman. Recall Derrida's statement: "He *was*, He dreaded this castrated woman." Nietzsche is in the castrated position when he talks of woman "as she is"; he attempts to formulate a science of feminism.

## The Castrating Woman

Although she remains within the discourse of truth, the castrating woman uses illusion craftily in order to cut the power of the metaphysic of truth. She is the actor or the artist who plays with truth; undermining the metaphysician's authority, she will persuade us of one truth only to abandon that one for another:

> If we consider the whole history of women, are they not obliged first of all, and above all to be actresses? If we listen to doctors who have hypnotised women, or finally if we love them—and let ourselves be "hypnotised" by them—what is divulged thereby? That they "give themselves airs," even when they—"give themselves" ... Woman is so artistic.[20]

As the actor the castrating woman assumes a role which she knows is only an illusion yet she convinces the metaphysician and his truth-centered culture that she is for real. She is the woman who uses all of the ideas about woman "as she is," those of the feminists as well as the phallocentric society, never believing them, in order to get what she wants. She is the woman who can play the role of the submissive secretary in order to get a job (she uses the beliefs of the phallocentric society to her own advantage); and then she can play the role of the social-activist in order to demand equal pay (she uses the beliefs of the feminist to her own advantage). Through her illusions and role playing she manipulates the dogmatist's castrated truth. She castrates the metaphysic of truth, cuts its power, by playing it against itself. Like a chameleon, she changes to protect herself from threats in the environment, which undermines the fixity of the metaphysician's reality.

Derrida suggests that "in the *guise* of the christian, philosophical being she either identifies with truth, or else she continues to with it at a distance as if it were a fetish, manipulating it, even as refuses to believe in it, to her own advantage."[21] If the castrating woman is a Christian, she is a heretic. She may pose as a Christian philosopher, but only in order to undermine their authority through her illusion. She poses playfully to her own advantage. In a sense, Derrida argues, the Christian/philosopher/feminist castrates for the sake of a castrated truth; the act of castration, however, self-conscious—the dogmatist does not realize that her power from multiplicity, that variety which she cuts off by identifying the castrated truth. In contrast, the castrating woman intentionally castrates the dogmatist's truth by identifying illusion; she cuts off the authority of the dogmatic truth by asserting equally believable illusions—she poses as the truth, but never herself seriously.

As the artist the castrating woman cuts the power of metaphysic of truth by replacing it with equally convincing guises. She substitutes her illusions for the science of the metaphysician. For, according to Nietzsche, the illusion of the artist, Apollonian will to illusion, is more profound, complete, effective than the will to truth. The castrating woman chooses appearance over reality, the "as-it-appears" over the "as-it-is." She learns that illusion is more effective than reality:

> But after the inventive genius of the young female artists has riot for some time in such indiscreet revelations of youth ... they at last discover, time and again, that they have not been judges of their own interest; that if they wish to have power men the game of hide-and-seek with the beautiful body is likely to win than naked or half-naked honesty.[22]

Honesty is not as powerful as illusion; after all, honest science reaches its limit, while illusion can continue forever. As Nietzsche proclaims, "When the inquirer, having pushed to the circumference, realizes how logic in that place curls about itself and bites its tail, he is struck with a new kind of perception; a tragic perception, which requires, to make it tolerable, the remedy of art."[23]

The castrating woman/artist rejects the limitations of logic and science. She harbors a secret scorn for science:

> For what is rarer than a woman who really knows what science is? Indeed the best of them cherish in their breasts a secret scorn for science, as if they were somehow superior to it.[24]

... clever people frequently have an aversion to science, as have, for instance, almost all artists.[25]

Science worships the Truth and scoffs at the artist's illusions. Artists and actors create illusions which appear real; they tempt science. The castrating woman is the seducer, tempting the metaphysic of truth away from its foundation.

The castrating woman, the artist/actor, can, however, be seduced by her own illusion. She may begin to believe that the illusion she created is the source of her power; she forgets that she created the illusion. She clings fanatically to her illusion. This is the will to illusion as it serves descending life. Here the castrating woman holds fast to one perspective at the cost of all others—life is the price which must be paid. She is the actor as the hysterical little woman.[26] She mistakes the means, her illusion, for an end. The castrating woman becomes another version of the castrated woman.

When, however, the will to illusion is in the service of ascending life, that is, when it playfully affirms multiplicity, then the castrating woman is more powerful than the castrated woman. Her illusions undermine the stifling dogmatism of the will to truth yet they do not destroy truth altogether. Her illusions are Apollonian individuations which save us from the raw Dionysian force—the chaotic source of her power. Without her artistic creations we would be doomed to the limits of science. Nietzsche goes so far as to say that if we had not invented this cult of the untrue, art, the general untruth of science would lead to nausea and suicide.[27]

Art is a woman without which it is impossible to live. "In this supreme jeopardy of the will, art, the sorceress expert in healing, approaches us, only she can turn our fits of nausea into imaginations with which it is possible to live."[28] Art subjugates terror through the sublime and releases us from the tedium of absurdity through the comic. Art enables us to act—she overcomes becoming and thereby gives a reason to act; her illusions give life a foundation (although illusory) more stable than endless becoming, which enables us to act. No longer do we find value behind a bush, we create it. Artistic creation is the manifestation of the will to power as the will to illusion, as an Apollonian mask. "Those Apollonian masks—are necessary products of a deep look into the horror of nature; luminous spots, as it were, designed to cure an eye hurt by the ghastly night."[29]

Without masks nothing can be justified—only as an aesthetic phenomenon can the world be justified. It cannot be justified by logic or science; for there is no justification independent of our interpretations. The will to illusion, then, is a survival mechanism, an instinct which protects us from a deep look into the horror of nature (which, as we shall see, is the affirming woman—the will to power). The castrating woman is the survivor, the artist, the actor. She castrates the metaphysic of truth by creatively interpreting the world. She is the eternal dialectic of masks which perpetuates life. Nietzsche too is a dialectic of masks; he castrates the metaphysic of truth through his creative illusions and metaphors. The fact that he creates different faces leads to his ambiguity about truth and woman; he creates many different illusions about both. He was, he dreaded this castrating woman.

## The Affirming Woman

Whereas objective truth de-sexed the castrated woman, castrating woman, through illusion, de-authorized objective, the affirming woman is outside the discourse of truth. The affirming woman, says Nietzsche, has no need for truth.

> Among woman.—Truth: Oh, you do not know truth! outrage on all our pudeurs?[30]

> Disgust with Truth—Women are so constituted that all truth (in relation to men, love, children, society, aim of life) disgusts them.[31]

The affirming woman has no need for truth; she affirms herself without man and his logocentrism. She is the inarticulate "truth" which is more original than the metaphysic of truth or the illusion of art. Unlike the metaphysician who discovers a foundation for action and the artist who creates a foundation, the affirming woman is the self-perpetuating Dionysian force who has no need for a foundation. "A voice that rings authentic," says Nietzsche, through Dionysian art and its tragic symbolism cries out, "Be like me, the Original Mother, who, constantly creating, finds satisfaction in the turbulent flux of appearances."[32] The affirming woman is the original mother, the unexhausted procreative will of life which is the will to power.[33] She is Dionysus, the desire for change, becoming: a desire which can manifest itself as destruction or creation, which can serve either declining or ascending life. This Dionysian force is an overfull power pregnant with the future.

Nietzsche repeatedly uses such biological metaphors—womb of being, mother eternally pregnant, procreative life—to describe the Dionysian force. The affirming woman is the eternally pregnant mother; she affirms herself continually by reproducing. This position of truth and woman, according to Nietzsche, is the most original, affirmative position which serves ascending life. The perfect woman, then, in Nietzsche's writings, is one who is always pregnant. Her pregnancy is presented as a type of immaculate conception, independent of man—clean, without the mess of the body.[34]

Nietzsche's use of the metaphor of procreation seems problematic. First, it seems inappropriate to speak of the affirming woman *reproducing*: she *produces*; she is original and creative. Reproduction connotes a re-creating, re-making something which is already made. The philosopher, for instance, tries to re-create reality. The affirming woman, however, is supposed to create reality anew, not out of already existing materials. She artistically produces, not reproduces, truth because she is independent of the metaphysic of truth.

Second, in passages where Nietzsche discusses the biological procreation of man, he refers to this instinct as a reactive force rather than an affirming force:

> Procreation ...—only derived; originally, in those cases in which one will was unable to organise the collective mass it had appropriated, an *opposing will* came into power, which undertook to effect the separation and establish a new center of organization, after a struggle with the original will.[35]

Since the procreative force in human beings is not an original force, the use of the metaphor of procreation in order to describe an original force, the Dionysian force, seems inappropriate.

The Dionysian force—the will to power—is not a reactive force; rather, it is the origin of all force. Yet it is a myth, an origin does not exist.[36] The will to power is layer after layer of masks and no face behind the costumes. The will to power is the affirming woman. She is layer upon layer of masks, a papier-mâché balloon.

> MASKS—There are women who, wherever one examines them, have no inside, but are mere masks.[37]

> Man thinks woman profound—why? Because he can never fathom her depths. Woman is not even shallow.[38]

She is hollow like a womb. She is the space, the womb, from which everything originates. This space is distance: the affirming woman is not an object in the distance; she is distance. Her power is distance; as distance she is space, pure womb. Just as there is no woman, there is no truth:

> That the value of the world lies in our interpretations [...]; previous interpretations have been perspective valuations by of which we can survive in life, i.e., in the will to power, growth of power; that every elevation of man brings with overcoming of narrower interpretations; that every strengthening and increase of power opens up new perspectives and believing in new horizons—this idea permeates my writings. world with which we are concerned is false; it is "in flux" something in a state of becoming, as a falsehood always changing but never getting nearer the truth; for there is no "truth."[39]

Truth, like woman, is an interpretation, not an objective reality. According to Nietzsche the power of truth and woman comes their distance and ambiguity. "The enchantment and the powerful effect of woman is, to use language of philosophers, effect at a distance, an *actio in distans*; there belongs thereto, however, primarily and above all,—distance!"[40]

If this distance can never be closed, as Nietzsche suggests, the goal Nietzsche assigns to us is ultimately unreachable. Christian God and the Platonic Forms are replaced by another supersensible force: the will to power. Nietzsche, then, is always castrated woman as well as the affirming woman. He is as sick metaphysicians who prescribe a frustratingly distant "truth."

Nietzsche, however, does not leave us at the precipice of understanding looking longingly down at the distant ground. Although the distance between truth/woman and our understanding cannot be closed, it can be bridged by the artist/castrating woman. The protective instincts of the artist/castrating woman must disguise the power of the original Dionysian womb of being. The eternal torrent of the will to power/affirming woman is too horrible a sight unless masked: it is the hollow womb which needs a wall of tissue layers in order to procreate. "Man is a coward in the face of all that is eternally feminine," says Nietzsche.[41] Therefore this eternally feminine face, which is horrifying because it is hollow, must be masked.

If truth/woman existed as an object for scientific study, as a fact, as the philosopher/castrated woman would have us believe, it would be shallow and harmless; there would be no need for masks. Truth/woman would be stable, easy to fix before our eyes. It is the constant flux we cannot bear, the ambiguity. Truth/woman is not shallow; the aimless spiral of truth/woman is endless.

One possible way we theoretians (or artists) can interpret, create truth/woman is the triad we have developed out of Nietzsche's writings: The Dionysian woman affirms herself outside of the metaphysic of truth. She is the will to power, the original mother, eternally pregnant. Yet this raw force of the womb of being is horrifying; we, therefore, require the masks created through the artist's will to illusion. The castrating woman disguises the Dionysian flux of the will to power through the masks of the artist and actor in order to provide some justification for our existence, no matter how illusory. She also destroys the authority of the meta-physics of truth by substituting a multitude of interpretations for the dogmatist's one, objective, reality. The dogmatic feminist takes an illusion which began as a principle to preserve life, presents it as an apodictic principle, thereby subverting life. Following Derrida's suggestion, we have created a dialectic triad in order to read, interpret Nietzsche's philosophical ambiguity on the question of woman and truth; by unraveling one, we also unwind the other.

## Notes

1   See BGE P; HH, p. 140; TI, p. 3.
2   Derrida (1979: 101).
3   BT 18.
4   TI Socrates 11.
5   CW Epilogue.
6   EH Wise 1.
7   BGE 239; HH I, p. 301.
8   I think Nietzsche's opinion is unjustified because clearly not all feminists imitate men. Some radical feminists want a completely separate feminine society.
9   TI Fable 2.
10  BGE 232.
11  WP 608.
12  TI Morality 2.
13  OTL, in The Complete Works, p. 183.
14  WP 585.
15  EH Books 5.
16  WP 354.
17  WP 385.
18  WP 853.
19  BGE 232.
20  GS 361.
21  Derrida (1979: 97); my emphasis. Some people might argue that castrating woman represents Christian morality and the philosopher, not the will to illusion. Although

this thesis could be defended some passages from Spurs, these and other passages can be interpreted as arguments against this thesis (pp. 89, 97). Moreover, regardless Derrida's interpretation of Nietzsche, Nietzsche's texts can be more neatly deciphered if the castrating woman is identified with the artist—the texts Derrida refers to do not suggest otherwise.

22  WS 215.
23  BT 15.
24  Nietzsche, The Early Greeks.
25  TI, p. 3.
26  GS 208.
27  GS 107.
28  BT 15.
29  BT 15, p. 60.
30  TI Arrows 16.
31  AOM 286, cf., p. 305.
32  BT, p. 102.
33  Z, p. 226.
34  Given Nietzsche's concern with the body and senses, it seems inappropriate for him to present an image of a woman who creates independent of her world.
35  WP 657.
36  BT 18, Nietzsche calls the Dionysian vision a myth. However, in sections of the *Birth*, e.g., §16, Nietzsche suggests that music mirrors the thing-in-itself. He suggests that there is an original Nature which we can uncover.
37  HH I 405.
38  TI Arrows 27.
39  WP 616.
40  GS 60; cf., Z, p. 76.
41  CW, p. 7.

Part Two

# The Eternal-Feminine and Future of Philosophy

3

# Nietzsche: Psychologist of the "Eternal-Feminine"

Allison Merrick

We know, because Nietzsche tells us, that his "perfect reader" is a "monster of courage and curiosity" (EH Books 3). Such a person explores the "abysses into which no foot has ever strayed" (EH Books 3) as they climb "into the caverns" having dared first "to suspect that they are caverns" (EH Destiny 6). "All 'feminism,'" Nietzsche insists by contrast, "closes the door: it will never permit entrance into this labyrinth of audacious thought" (EH Books 3). Nietzsche's inquisitive reader goes where "all 'feminism'"—in scare-quotes, of course—does not: to *their* depths (cf. BGE 238).

In shifting focus from the audience to the practitioner, from spectator to creator, Nietzsche offers a similar provocation. As "psychologist of the eternal-feminine" [*Psycholog des Ewig-Weiblichen*], Nietzsche maintains that he "*know[s]* women" (EH Books 5). By contrast, "dogmatic" philosophers are "inexpert about women" (BGE P). With "gruesome seriousness" and "clumsy obtrusiveness," such philosophers employ "awkward and very improper methods" (BGE P).

From either vantage point, however, we can observe a taxonomy of investigative practices. Intellectual activity is classified: cowardly, superficial, antinatural, dogmatic or courageous, profound, natural, curious. Further, these alternative ways of doing philosophy can either cover over or uncover forms of life: one is, Nietzsche tells us, either a dogmatist or a psychologist.

I am interested in Nietzsche's use of the "eternal-feminine" in this regard. That is, in contrast to other interpretations, I argue that "eternal-feminine" marks out a philosophical approach and a system of value (section 1). At issue, I contend, is an organizational structure (what Nietzsche often calls a "system of purposes") that determines what is deemed good or evil and thereby what is colored, as it were, with a positive or negative hue (GM II 12). For that reason, this philosophical view that is to be found under the label of the "eternal-feminine" nourishes certain forms of existence at the same time as it depletes others. In adopting the role of a psychologist of the eternal-feminine, I suggest that Nietzsche is concerned to specify the psychological origins and impacts of such systems and ways of life (section 2). I conclude (section 3) by addressing the vexed question of whether it is possible to philosophize or psychologize without that particular philosophical ideal—that of the "eternal-feminine."

## On the "Eternal-Feminine"

Rather than centering my analysis on Nietzsche's most sustained discussions of women and of femininity (e.g., GS 60–75; BGE 231–39), my focus is on the "eternal-feminine" [*Ewig-Weiblichen*] (BGE 239; EH Books 5) or "woman as such" [*das Weib an sich*] (BGE 231, 232, 239). As noted above, the concept is especially generative as it serves two functions: (1) to make plainer a philosophical viewpoint, and (2) to further highlight a schematic of inquiry. Let me substantiate and further make my case by holding my re-construction against the backdrop of other interpretations.

For some commentators, the "eternal-feminine" signals Nietzsche's critique of metaphysical dualism (Thorgeirsdottir 2004, Tirrell 1995). At issue is the devaluation of "the whole sphere of becoming and transitoriness" (GM III 11) and the valorization of masculine modes of being. Maudemarie Clark, going further down this line, insists: "Given [*Beyond Good and Evil's*] central claim that *das Ding an sich* (BGE 16) is a contradiction in terms, Nietzsche's use of the phrase '*das Weib an sich*' cannot be accidental. He is probably suggesting that our idea of the 'eternal feminine' also involves a contradiction in terms, and therefore no woman could readily exemplify it" (Clark 1998: 192–3). So understood, the "eternal-feminine" indicates a dualistic metaphysical view that is self-contradictory. While these scholars aptly identify the object of Nietzsche's disdain, as I will too, none takes up the issue, as I do, of why a psychologist is needed on these matters.

Other commentators have drawn upon the "eternal-feminine" for its fundamental psycho-biographical import. On this view, far from telling us something instructive about Nietzsche's metaphysics or the category of "woman-as-such," the notion intimates Nietzsche's experiences with particular women (Young 2013: 62).[1] Nietzsche, of course, lends himself to such an interpretive strategy, when he insists, for instance, that "Everyone bears within him a picture of women derived from his mother: it is this which determines whether, in his dealings with women, he respects them or despises them or is in general indifferent to them" (HH I 380). And, as is well known, Nietzsche candidly claims that "great philosophy" is "a kind of involuntary and unconscious memoir" (BGE 6). Nevertheless, I will take a different interpretive path. Instead of ambling down that far-reaching road that tries to locate "women," within Nietzsche's work, and instead of psychoanalyzing the philosopher, I will direct my attention toward the task that Nietzsche sets *himself*: the psychologist of the "eternal-feminine" (EH Books 5). This will afford a richer understanding of the object of Nietzsche's critique—which I will specify next—and give us a taste of Nietzsche *as* psychologist—which I will address in section 2.

### Idealism

By "eternal-feminine," Nietzsche means to direct our attention to a particular form of idealism (cf. Deutscher 1993). With a nod to the last line of Part II of Goethe's *Faust*—"the eternal-feminine/leads us on high"[2]—Nietzsche equates them: "European *feminism* (or idealism, if you prefer that word) which is forever 'drawing us upward' and precisely thereby forever 'bringing us down'" (D P 4; CW 3; cf. GM III 19; TI

Expeditions 4). Elsewhere he draws the equivalence in this way: "malignant 'idealism'" in the "world of the eternal feminine" is an expression of the "underprivileged whose most fundamental instinct is revenge" (EH Books 5).

The significance of this equation is threefold: First, as I remarked earlier, Nietzsche's objection to the view is on account of its wrong-headedness. It is, in short, a philosophical "error" (BGE P). Speaking more generally: idealism denies "*perspective*" (BGE P), purports to have a monopoly on the unconditional value of "the good as such" (BGE P) and of the truth (GS 344), and takes a number of forms, most notably, on Nietzsche's view, Platonism and Christianity (BGE P). Such a philosophical stance falsifies, Nietzsche contends, on each of these key fronts: knowledge claims are perspectival (GS 374; GM III 12) and our values are conditioned by social, political, historical, and psychological forces (GM, *passim*).

Second, "idealism" denotes a system of value. The schematic devalues the world of instincts and nature, as it elevates "pure spirit and the good as such" (BGE P 5). In its most menacing form, our passions, desires, and instincts are not just suppressed but held in contempt (EH Books 5). Indeed, in championing chastity, in denying the material, in suppressing desires, such a view carries a "deadly hostility to life" (A 38; TI Morality). Further, as I will show, this turning-away from life is also exemplified in the intellectual activity of many scholars, particularly philosophers (EH Clever 8).

Third, though idealism denies this fact, it is a philosophical view, as Nietzsche shows, that finds its origins in a particular psychological need for safety. On Nietzsche's view, and to discern this psychological need, we need to ask a guiding question, namely: what has been *forbidden*? (EH P 3). That is, what feels so dangerously annihilating that it must be defended against? In the case of idealism, Nietzsche's answer is plain: engulfing sensibility engenders disintegration. A fear of being seduced, immersed, and overwhelmed and thereby subjugated by desire, served, at least in Plato's case, as fodder for a philosophy that restricts and keeps desire in check (GS 372). In this way, idealism is a philosophical position with its origins in psychological protection. To put it another way, idealism protects against the crushing "fear of *over-powerful* senses" (GS 372). As the protective measure safeguards a sense of self, it also forbids the vitality that is expressed through the material or the sensual. Hence, and even as I would like to understand the impetus toward idealism as squarely self-protective, we can understand why Nietzsche equates idealism with cowardice (EH P 3; EH Books BT 2; EH Wagner 2). Nietzsche's reason for such an equivalence is that idealism is born from a particular set of fears, notably being overwhelmed, overcome, or even annihilated by sensuality. Hence the question how did "the pure and sunlike gaze of the sage [emerge] from lust?" (BGE 2) can be answered. "Lust" can be overpowering and frightening. "A pure and sunlike gaze" directs one's attention elsewhere and thereby can keep such fear at bay (BGE 2). In this way, asceticism, with "its pure sunlike gaze," functions to ward off or otherwise mitigate the shame, humiliation, and guilt that attend the sage's lustful feelings (BGE 2). Further still such a gaze can be viewed as a means of self-protection: the sage can deny, and thereby keep out of conscious awareness, their lustful longings under the cover of self-discipline and otherworldly contemplation.

So far, and in taking Plato's metaphysics as an example, I have sought to demonstrate that fear of overwhelming sensuality is at the core of the philosophical form of idealism that Nietzsche equates with the "eternal-feminine" (EH Books 5). There is, however, a potentially serious objection to my view which principally concerns how well my account sits with Nietzsche's arguments in *Beyond Good and Evil*. The objection calls our attention to section 232 and to Nietzsche's claim that an altogether different fear appears to animate the turn to the eternal-feminine: "fear of man" (Tirrell 1995: 175).[3] The disputed passage develops as follows:

> Women want to become independent, so they are beginning to enlighten men about the "woman *an sich*"—*this* is one of the worst developments in Europe's general trend towards *increasing ugliness*. Just imagine what these clumsy attempts at female scientificity and self-disclosure will bring to light! Women have so much cause for shame; they contain so much that is pedantic, superficial, and schoolmarmish as well as narrow mindedly arrogant, presumptuous, and lacking in restraint (just think about their interactions with children!), all of which has been most successfully restrained and kept under control by their *fear* of men. Look out when the "eternal tedium of woman" (which they all have in abundance!) first dares to emerge! When, on principle, they start completely forgetting their discretion and their art—of grace, play, chasing-all-cares-away, of making things easier and taking them lightly, as well as their subtle skill at pleasant desires! ... If this is not really all about some woman trying to find a new piece of *finery* for herself (and isn't dressing up a part of the Eternal Feminine?), well then, she wants to inspire fear of herself:—perhaps in order to dominate.
>
> (BGE 232)

As indicated a moment ago, some have taken the significance of these remarks to reside in what they tell us about the psychological origins of this philosophical view. Notably, on such a reconstruction, "woman *an sich*" is underpinned by a "fear of man" (Tirrell 1995: 175). In addition to arguing that fear is the psychological and motivational force that fortifies this philosophical viewpoint—that of the *Ewig-Weiblichen*—some have also suggested that such a fear also explains Nietzsche's skepticism of certain emancipatory political movements. Nietzsche's worry, so the argument goes, is that "modern social movements like women's suffrage and the 'democratic tendencies' of Europe ... have caused woman to 'forget her fear of man: but the woman who "forgets fear" abandons her most feminine "instincts"' (BGE 239) (Brennan 2021: 221). The thought here is that "fear of man" has great explanatory force: it at once accounts for the emotional or psychological impetus that undergirds a philosophical view as it also explains Nietzsche's critique of that view. That is, in Nietzsche's estimation, so this argument contends, fear is healthy and the eternal-feminine is problematic because it suggests one "abandon" such fear.

Because I am in broad agreement that Nietzsche seeks to show that fear is a central motivational force of idealism, and thereby of the eternal-feminine, my aim in what follows is to demonstrate that the arguments that place the "fear of man" (Tirrell

1995: 175) at the center actually displace Nietzsche's broader philosophical objectives as the "psychologist of the eternal-feminine" (EH Books 5). To make this case, let me direct our attention back to the contested passage, *Beyond Good and Evil* 232, where it is important to take notice of Nietzsche's own explanation of the psychic forces that underpin the emancipatory movements of his time. There Nietzsche contends that the cloak of "scientific self-exposure" covers a deeper motivation which is a longing to "inspire fear of herself—perhaps because she seeks mastery" (BGE 232). What we see here, I think, is something of a remarkable convergence: idealism and the current scientism of the "eternal-feminine" both disavow the motivational function of fear. Idealism, on Nietzsche's reading, is born of a devastating "fear of *over-powerful* senses" (GS 372). The "clumsy attempts of woman at scientific self-exposure" are also, or so we learn, philosophical judgments made out of fear and an acute and painful longing for mastery. In both cases Nietzsche shows that those psychological and motivational factors are disavowed (BGE 232). I will return to this issue in the next section, but for now let me hold out the possibility that, here anyway, Nietzsche seems to be suggesting that rather than replacing a life-denying ideal, the emancipatory movements of the day are merely "adorning" themselves with it (BGE 232).

In sum, "idealism," and if I am right its equation with the "eternal-feminine," marks out a set of life-denying philosophical practices and vantage points. The reason is that such a philosophical view sets up a metric of valuation that mirrors its own denial and disavowal of the passions, desires, and instincts. It is worth bearing in mind that Nietzsche was himself seduced, at least at times, by idealism (EH Clever 2). He characterizes this period as "the real catastrophe of [his] life" (EH Clever 2). He goes further to recount that "[he] can explain all [his] mistakes as a result of this 'idealism': it is responsible for all the time [he] really strayed away from [his] instincts" (EH Clever 2). However, in keeping my word I will not psychoanalyze Nietzsche, but simply underscore the deeply personal nature of his encounter with this philosophical view.

## Psychologist of the Eternal-Feminine

Supposing that what I have said so far is plausible and we do indeed have some good reason to equate idealism with the eternal-feminine, nevertheless an open and pressing question remains: why does Nietzsche assume the role of psychologist of the eternal-feminine? This question can be addressed and the response, as I will demonstrate in this section, runs along three trajectories: first, in section 2.1, I argue that Nietzsche takes issue with the eternal-feminine on the grounds that it assumes and purports a false view of human personhood. Next, I show in section 2.2 that this false view of subjectivity and of sociality nevertheless functions as a system of evaluation. Hence, Nietzsche shows how the "eternal-feminine" works to advantage certain forms of life as it disadvantages other ways of making sense of ourselves. The framework (the view of human personhood) and the forms of life it valorizes (those systems of evaluation) are thereby reciprocally co-constructive. Such a framework and a system of evaluation exert a grip on us, a dominance over us, because we often and unreflectively grant such a philosophical view an unquestioned authority. Hence, as I demonstrate in section 2.3, a psychologist is needed to help us disentangle ourselves, wrest our longings and our understanding of ourselves from those that the system dictates. We can, with the help of Nietzsche as psychologist, begin to free ourselves from this view of human personhood and its system of evaluation without reinforcing its supremacy. I will return to this question in due course, but for now must turn to a much more preliminary one: what is the view of human personhood that the eternal-feminine purports and on what grounds does Nietzsche contest such a view?

## A Naïve Mistake: Nietzsche on the "Ego"

Nietzsche first challenges his readers to see one of the core tenets of the "eternal-feminine" doctrine as an error. The mistake, Nietzsche contends, is the metaphysical belief in the "ego" and the reified conception of human personhood it entails. More precisely, "the naïve mistake" on Nietzsche's view is that such an interpretation takes the "the 'unegoistic' and 'egoistic'" as "opposites," when, as Nietzsche holds, "the ego is itself just a 'higher lie,' an 'ideal'" (EH Books 5). In its most condensed form, the reason that this is a mistake is that the "ego," "egoistic," and "unegoistic" are not ahistorical psychological categories, but conceptual responses to a particularly punishing set of social and political conditions, which predate and explain their emergence (GM I 13). A clear-eyed reading of history shows that, as Paul Patton neatly has it: "Just as all perception is perspectival, so is all *conception*" (1993: 213). The "ego" is born of socio-political struggle. Hence, on Nietzsche's view, to consider the "ego" as a philosophical conception that is anything other than the result of psychological privation is to tell some version of that "higher lie" (EH Books 5).

Furthermore, and as a way of lending some further shape and nuance to these ideas, let me highlight another of Nietzsche's claims. Both egoistic and unegoistic acts, Nietzsche holds, "are psychological absurdities" (EH Books 5). Yet, what makes those beliefs psychologically absurd? To answer such a question, let me return us to the First Essay of *On the Genealogy of Morality* and to the section in which Nietzsche suggests that the "subject" is not given but is itself the result of a complex social and political process (GM I 13). According to Nietzsche's argument, the "ego," the "unbiased 'subject,'" finds its origins in a subordinated mode of subjectivity (GM I 13). A belief in the "ego" or an "unbiased subject" preserves and allows those so subordinated to affirm their particular mode of life (GM I 13). As such, the construction of an "ego" allows this psychological type to engage in "that sublime self-deception whereby [they] … could construe weakness itself as freedom, and their particular mode of existence as an accomplishment" (GM I 13). Accordingly, to maintain that there is an "ego," a "subject," a "doer" (GM I 13) that exists independently of such a process is to tell some version of that "higher lie" (EH Books 5). The reason, once more, is that the formulation of this "subject" is a response to a punishing set of social and political conditions, which by necessity predate the emergence of the subject as a concept (GM I 13).

## On Learning How Not to Look for Your Own Advantage

I have argued that by positioning psychology within the scene of sociopolitical and historical struggles, Nietzsche's account shows that psychological structures work to privilege certain forms of life as they disadvantage other ways of being. Conceived in response to sociopolitical subordination, we can ask: what did such system of evaluation allow to come to be? The answer, on Nietzsche's view: the unegoistic, the selfless, self-denial, self-sacrifice. Also of note is the question: what was prohibited from growing? The answer, on Nietzsche's view: the egoistic, the selfish, self-interest, self-advantage. Indeed, the prohibition on self-advantage, to take but one example, leads to atrophy. As is the case with atrophy, plainly enough, Nietzsche suggests that within this system of evaluation, the ability to identify our desires degenerates and deteriorates. This renders us further obscure to ourselves because we struggle to determine what it is we desire. Here is how Nietzsche puts the point: "'Not to look for your own advantage'—that is just the moral fig leaf for an entirely different, namely physiological, state of affairs: 'I do not know how to *find* my own advantage anymore'" (TI Skirmishes 35). Not being able to find our advantage leads to uncertainty, anxiety, and helplessness. It also reproduces and reinforces the safety to be found in such a structure: one need not worry about finding one's own advantage because, so the system suggests, it is the other's advantage that is of superior conceptual and moral worth. Hence, the eternal-feminine viewpoint has a clear psychological function: to ward off debilitating uncertainty and immobilizing anxiety (TI Errors 5). The psychological relief from such painful disquietude, however, is purchased a tremendous cost: ever further obscurity from one's own desires and interests. Hence, the eternal-feminine view makes it ever increasingly difficult to "find [one's] own advantage" and, as a result, ever further locks one into its system of evaluation (TI Errors 5).

We might already have gone some way toward seeing how the system conserves itself (cf. GS 347), but what of its origins? This requires us to make that "backward inference" Nietzsche heralds: "from the work to the maker, from the deed to the doer, from the ideal to those who *need it,* from every way of thinking and valuing to the commanding need behind it" (GS 370). The "eternal-feminine" was born of need: to keep the overpowering senses at bay; to keep in check the passions, longings, yearnings, and instincts; to quell anxiety.

Noticing this, let me return to the issue I set aside at the end of the last section. Nietzsche accuses feminists of his day of perpetuating "the eternal-feminine": bringing us down to the other, failing to draw us up, by impeding a re-evaluation of idealism. This critique requires that we attend to another metric: what is the creative force behind the feminist movement of his time, overfullness or impoverishment? (GS 370). Nietzsche suggests the latter, impoverishment. This is the stuff of idealism: reaction, "instinctive hatred," and "revenge" (EH Books 5). Re-evaluation, born of overfullness, of those pregnant with the future, is possible but cannot be achieved, Nietzsche maintains, by those who remain enchanted by idealism, with the "eternal-feminine," with those who elevate "*themselves* as 'woman *an sich,*' as the 'higher women' as the 'idealists' of women" (EH Books 5). This conceptual move, according to Nietzsche, "*lowers* the rank of women in general" by returning to and restoring the evaluative framework of idealism, of the "eternal-feminine" (EH Books 5). In sum, on Nietzsche's view, the feminist movement of his time, rather than revaluating or re-making, merely re-inscribes a life-denying metaphysical ideal, namely, that of "the eternal-feminine."

Here, however, a detractor might worry that there is more than one way to understand a worldview born of impoverishment or lack. In addition to explaining the anti-sensualism of idealism, as I have done, as primarily, if not exhaustively, a fear response, one might suggest that the philosophical view of the eternal-feminine is born of physiological impoverishment: a sickliness of the body (GM III 17). Such a detractor might further point to *On the Genealogy of Morality* where Nietzsche argues that: "every table of values, every, 'thou shalt' known to history or ethnology, requires first a *physiological* investigation and interpretation rather than a psychological one" (GM I 17). Indeed, one might conclude that this gives us strong evidence that the physiological reading of sickness as impoverishment is the correct one (cf. Morrison 2021).

There are a couple of ways of responding to such a challenge. One option is to suggest that even as Nietzsche distinguishes a "physiological investigation and interpretation" of morality from a "psychological one" (GM I 17), in his late philosophy, the two function as but "two sides of the same coin" (Stellino 2015: 113). At any time, then, rather than assuming we have either a physiological or a psychological explanation, we have both. So, on this view, a proper account of the eternal-feminine would account for impoverishment in all of its forms. Another and perhaps far more promising response is to point to the role that Nietzsche assigns himself in this regard: he does not claim to be a physiologist of the eternal-feminine, but a "psychologist of the eternal-feminine" (EH Books 5).

## Toward New Psychological Horizons

Why might such a role be necessary? Indeed, how might a psychologist of the eternal-feminine help us to expand our views, to see, as Nietzsche describes the idea in the Preface to *On the Genealogy of Morality*, "as though through new eyes?" (GM P 7). It is worth bearing in mind that we might need to see through such "new eyes" because we are caught in an ensnaring perspective: that of the "eternal-feminine." Such a perspective, as we have seen, denies its own perspectival nature, operates largely outside of our awareness, and is the framework that forms and shapes our experiences.[4] One form that our bondage can take is that of the assumptions we make about our place in the world. These presuppositions are so fundamental, so elemental, that they can often escape our conscious awareness. Freud marked this out as our "internal foreign territory" (2001: 57)—the strange land within. Others capture this as our "prereflective unconscious" (Stolorow, Brandchaft, and Atwood 1987), or as "unformulated experience" (Stern 2009) even the "unthought known" (Bollas 2018). Hence, a psychologist is needed to help us discern that which so often remains unformulated by us or ever elusive to us. They help us to discern that we often find ourselves "trapped in an unreflected perspective, one that [we do] not recognize as a perspective but accept ... as not-to-be-questioned reality" (Brandchaft 2010: 143).

On Nietzsche's view, Neo-Platonic Christianity is one such system of evaluation (BGE P). Unegoistic acts born of selflessness, self-denial, and self-sacrifice are commended and considered good. Egoistic acts born of selfishness, self-interest, and self-advantage are disparaged and considered evil. Indeed, as we have seen, such a prohibition on self-advantage leads to atrophy: in not knowing how to locate one's advantage, one comes to believe that one *should not* look for one's own advantage. This is an example of a vantage point that often operates pre-reflectively. To give another example of a "not-to-be questioned reality" (Brandchaft 2010: 143), let us consider what Nietzsche says about the nature of the feeling of obligation. "Duty," Nietzsche writes, "is a compulsive feeling [that] impels us to some action and which we call good and regard as undiscussable (we refuse to speak of its origin, limitation and justification or to hear them spoken of)" (WS 43). Here Nietzsche demonstrates that our feeling of obligation compels us to act because its validity is assumed and unquestioned. Indeed, they are undiscussable. In this way, even as such duties organize our experiences—they tell us what we must, what we must not, what we ought, what we ought not, what we should, or what we should not do—the key historical and psychological questions—"Whence does it come? What is its purpose?"—remain stubbornly out of view (WS 43).

Nietzsche takes on the role of a psychologist, then, because that role permits and opens up, rather than forecloses, a wide range of questions: what are the origins of these moral obligations? What needs do they serve? Why does any given duty feel necessary, obligatory, beyond discussion? Nietzsche's psychological studies of the "eternal-feminine" demonstrate that our values indeed have their origins in needs. Having answers to the questions "Whence does it come? What is its purpose?" (WS 43), we can ask whether those inherited ways of viewing ourselves serve our current needs and purposes. Indeed, through such an investigative practice, we might learn to see that which we could not before: our values developed as responses to acute needs. As such, our strange land within may indeed become more familiar. The perspectival freedom provided by such psychological accounts creates the space for us "to run through," as Nietzsche explains it, "the range of human values and value feelings and *be able* to gaze with many eyes and consciences from the heights into every distance, from the depths up to every height, from the corner onto every expanse" (BGE 211). Such an expansive view allows us to see that whatever feels necessary, in this case the eternal-feminine worldview, is but one way of ordering things.

## Conclusion: Can We Philosophize and Psychologize without the "Eternal-Feminine"?

By way of conclusion, let me consider one outstanding issue: is it possible to philosophize without the metaphysical ideal of the eternal-feminine? Indeed, it might be objected that Nietzsche himself re-establishes this life-denying ideal. Is it not the case that Nietzsche himself, or so the argument might go, smuggles "in, Trojan horse style, inherited values that must themselves be resisted or transvaluated[?]" (Zurn 2021: 70). Is it not the case that Nietzsche himself, after all, is simply evoking the ideal he denounces?

The most persuasive version of this charge runs as follows: is it not the case that the creative overfullness Nietzsche imagines, his "ethics of affirmative self-creation require[s] the same image of the eternally feminine to guarantee its value"? Indeed, the argument continues, the "enigmatic image of the eternally feminine" functions as "the mirror that gives [Nietzsche] back his own reflection" (Diprose 1989: 32; cf. Deutscher 1993: 165). Hence, according to this line of thought, Nietzsche needs the authority of "the eternal-feminine" to underwrite his philosophy. Thus, one might conclude, Nietzsche too reproduces rather than re-evaluates "the eternal-feminine."

In response, it seems to me that the suggestion that one requires idealism to philosophize is but an expression of the strength and domination of that picture, of "the eternal-feminine." In making such a suggestion, one forgets the multiplicity of perspectives. One fails to see that there are other ways of viewing oneself than through the mirror that "the eternal-feminine" holds up and requires. One forgets the origins of "the eternal-feminine" in specific needs. One fails to recall how, as Nietzsche puts it, "highly conditioned its right to exist really is" (TI Skirmishes 5). One neglects that which came before "the eternal-feminine," namely a reverent, rather than reactive, way of making sense of oneself (BGE 287).

This is to caution us, as Nietzsche might, against remaining enchanted with morality, with idealism, with "the eternal-feminine" here especially where it matters most. Instead, let us take up the psychologist's questions: Why is the ideal needed? What does it conceal? What does it reveal? What does it forbid? What does it allow to come to be? How does the ideal organize experiences? These are questions of acute need and of dire motivation. Once we understand these fears and prohibitions, these motives and desires, then the question of how we might view ourselves differently becomes available to us, by which I mean conceptually possible. That is, it is here, by seeing "the eternal-feminine" as one conceptual possibility, that we might begin to free ourselves from its dictates, from its mandates, from its unique form of life.

In closing, let me say that I do not propose that my analysis goes any way toward absolving Nietzsche of charges of misogyny, nor do I suppose that this settles the issue of "women" or "femininity" in his writings. Rather, I hope to have shown why we should read Nietzsche, on this score at least, as he asks to be read and thereby go some way toward seeing Nietzsche, just as he asks to be seen, as "perhaps the first psychologist of the eternal-feminine" (EH Books 5).

## Notes

1   These categories need not be discrete. For instance, Maudemarie Clark, an advocate of the first interpretive option, also argues for the second: "[Nietzsche's] nasty comments about women have always seemed to me a reflection not of his basic ideas, but of his understandable, if human, all-too-human need for revenge against Lou Andreas-Salomé. And Nietzsche himself gives us theoretical resources to understand them in this way" (Clark 2015: 142).

2   Here I make use of Judith Norman's translation.
3   I am grateful to Iain Morrison for bringing this issue to my attention.
4   Here I would like to extend the ensnaring perspective from the "eternal-feminine" to idealism to Christianity. Such equivalences are useful as a way of explaining how we are often trapped by philosophical perspectives and are warranted, I think, by Nietzsche's own such equation: "Christianity" is, Nietzsche writes, "Platonism for 'the people'" (BGE P).

# 4

# The "Eternal-Feminine" in Nietzsche's Philosophy: On Nietzsche's Inversion of Goethe's Verse *Ihr "Ewig-Weibliches" zieht uns—hinab!*

Vinicius Souza de Paulo

Although Nietzsche uses the term eternal-feminine in a unique sense the term itself is not new. Variations of it have been used to express a range of characteristics that describe a feminine essence, a series of values that are inherent to women that have long been taken as intrinsic signs of a feminine expression.[1] Although the term appears just a few times in both Nietzsche's works and unpublished notes, each instance of it shares a similar background, as I reveal in this chapter.

At first glance Nietzsche seems to use the term in a way that perpetuates the same eternal image of the woman, an immanent femininity distinct from the goals and will of man. He may therefore appear to support a nostalgic desire to rescue a value that remains preserved in the condition of women. This in evident in notes in which the philosopher affirms typical female characteristics, biological aspects of women emphasizing procreation and the pregnancy of the woman, as a symbol of fertilization and life, to the detriment of the "women of emancipation." This was expressed, for example, at EH Books 5, where Nietzsche writes "Do I dare to suggest that I *know* women? This is part of my Dionysian dowry. Who knows? perhaps I am the first psychologist of the eternal-feminine." These statements are followed by severe criticisms of nineteenth-century feminists: "Emancipated women are basically anarchists in the world of the 'eternal-feminine', people in bad shape whose bottommost instinct is revenge" (EH Books 5).

Contrary to this statement, which seems to attribute intrinsic biological characteristics to women, Nietzsche's writings also exhibit a concern not only to avoid such essentialisms, but also to denounce this idealization of the feminine. By denouncing the dogmatism pertaining to any pretension to a fixed essence of woman, he rejects the metaphysical character of the eternalization of a subject, an idealization of woman "in itself."

These contradictory features of the eternal-feminine underscore one of the greatest points of conflict in Nietzsche's philosophy regarding women, that is the essentialization of women via his affirmation of stereotypical feminine characteristics, with emphases on the biological aspects of women, including issues of procreation, pregnancy, and as a symbol of fertilization, life, and eternal becoming.² One of the questions that emerges from this problem, and which I investigate in this chapter, is how Nietzsche's use of the term eternal-feminine corresponds with his critique of modern women. Moreover, I examine his choice of this particular term. Why does Nietzsche employ a term that apparently raises such contradictions if what is being questioned is the conventional notion of a metaphysical essence of women? By extension, I consider the relation between the eternal-feminine and the Dionysian, as it comprises a part of his "Dionysian dowry."

In attempting to answer these questions I also examine the role that Goethe played in relation to Nietzsche's philosophy throughout this chapter, starting with Nietzsche's inversion of Goethe's verse—*ihr "Ewig-Weibliches" zieht uns—hinab!*: "the 'eternal-feminine' draws us—downwards!" This sentence appears where Nietzsche employs the term eternal-feminine, in direct relation to the problem of art and culture, especially in his critique of romantic art. Therefore I approach the question of the eternal-feminine in Nietzsche's philosophy as an aesthetic problem that sees in art the possibility of subverting the dogmatic metaphysical logic that limits modern perspectives, as Nietzsche understood it. This entails examining how Nietzsche affirms women and the feminine, according to values that are necessary for a new perspective on art as a force transformative of culture—a perspective that embraces, above all, the same values Nietzsche attributes to the Dionysian.

By illuminating the relation between Nietzsche's and Goethe's respective uses of this term, it can be better understood, as it expands the critique of modern woman from the point of view of the Nietzschean critique of modern art. This approach to the problems of the modern woman and modern art goes some way toward clarifying the relationship between women and the Dionysian. It illuminates Nietzsche's suggestion in EH that—speaking as the "first psychologist of the 'eternal-feminine'"—he "know[s] women" (EH Books 5).

## The Eternal-Feminine in Goethe's *Faust*

There is a direct relation between Nietzsche's account of the eternal-feminine and Goethe's notion of it. In the 1886 preface to the second volume of *Human, All Too Human*, Nietzsche inverted the final verse of *Faust*, perhaps one of Goethe's most important works, at a point where Nietzsche's critique is directed at modern culture, more specifically to romantic, Wagnerian music. The passage reads:

> I began by forbidding myself, totally and on principle, all romantic music, that ambiguous, inflated, oppressive art that deprives the spirit of its severity and cheerfulness and lets rampant every kind of vague longing and greedy, spongy desire. "*Cave musicam*" [Beware music] is to this day my advice to all who are man enough to insist on cleanliness in things of the spirit; such music unnerves, softens, feminizes [*verweiblicht*], its "eternal feminine" draws us—downwards!³ ... [*ihr "Ewig-Weibliches" zieht uns—hinab!*].
> 
> (HH II P 3)

The use of the term eternal-feminine in quotation marks accentuates both the problematic character of the term and Nietzsche's ironic tone. The eternal-feminine is equated here with romanticism, this "ambiguous art." As romanticism is a form of idealism, the ironic effect of the sentence suggests an inversion of Goethe's idea of the eternal-feminine, as initially indicated by Nietzsche's placement of "downwards," *hinab*, instead of "upwards," *hinan*, as the German poet wrote.

This difference underscores a key element of Goethe's meaning, which Nietzsche preserved in his use of the term: it is the eternal-feminine of romanticism that drags us down. This is echoed in the aforementioned passage from EH, where Nietzsche states that the emancipated are the anarchists in the world of the eternal-feminine. By "raising themselves higher, as 'woman in herself,' as the 'higher woman,' as a female 'idealist,' they want to lower the level of the general rank of woman" (EH Books 5). In this context, it is this emancipationist "anarchism" and its eternal-feminine that "draws us downwards." Regarding the term "anarchism" here, Goethe's approach is also significant, as it indicates the lack of a hierarchy that Nietzsche values in the figure of Goethe, who represents a strong culture and "aristocracy" of spirit. That is, contrary to what Nietzsche criticizes in modern culture, it is less about the political connotations of the word anarchism and more about his critique of culture, specifically the lack of an order of strong values. This issue will be addressed more fulsomely below.

The Goethe verse that Nietzsche refers to "*ihr 'Ewig-Weibliches' zieht uns—hinab!*" is found at the end of the second volume of *Faust*, in a line pronounced by the *Chorus Mysticus*, which exalts the following verse:

> What is destructible
> Is but a parable;
> What fails ineluctably,
> The undeclarable,
> Here it was seen,
> Here it was action;
> The Eternal-Feminine [*Das Ewig-Weibliche*]
> Lures to perfection [*Zieht uns hinan*]⁴

(Goethe 1962: 503)

Trying to understand the meaning of Goethe's verse in a work that already presents interpretive difficulties exceeds the scope of this chapter. However, in light of the question raised here about the relation between Nietzsche's and Goethe's respective use of the term eternal-feminine, it is necessary to highlight some central features surrounding Goethe's notion of the feminine to better illustrate how Nietzsche's reference corresponds with the meaning Goethe expressed in his work.⁵

In Goethe's passage the eternal-feminine functions as a symbol. In a pioneering essay Harold Jantz addressed this, writing: "The passage itself plainly states that it is couched in symbolic language. The 'womanly', therefore, is an earthly, humanly accessible symbol for a divine eternal mystery which can only be thus indirectly suggested" (Jantz 1953: 791). According to Jantz, the interpretation that has the greatest consensus among interpreters is that this eternal-feminine means "the feminine principle of love, of mercy and grace, which leads the spirit upward to the highest perfection" (Jantz 1953: 792). Nonetheless, Jantz also emphasizes the background through which Goethe was inspired in relation to the divine aspect of this feminine symbol, a concern that draws upon the spirit of the Renaissance. According to Jantz, "Goethe was using Renaissance symbolic language here within an established traditional frame of reference" (Jantz 1953: 792). For Jantz the union of feminine images, Margarete, the Mater dolorosa, the Mothers, etc., is a direct reference to the Renaissance spirit, where one can find a "fusion of pagan and Christian imagery, from a time when a devout poet could without offense address God as mighty Jove, or the Virgin Mary in terms of the goddess Aphrodite" (Jantz 1953: 793).[6]

From a similar perspective, Ernst Osterkamp expands on the issue, emphasizing this movement in Goethe's work when he states:

> The female forms in the final *Faust* scene are not redemptive Christian forms, but aesthetic figurations of that productive force of love, which Goethe in the end names "the Eternal-Feminine", and which he could also, in this scene outlined on the margin of mystical silence, having given the name of God or Nature, since he is always aware that for the absolute there is no language.
> (Osterkamp 2012: 46–47)[7]

However, this notion of "nature" has a precise meaning according to Osterkamp: "First of all, there are no historical-philosophical models in Goethe of an original unity of self and Nature, from which auxiliary theoretical articulations would derive—something like the Schillerian paradigm: naivety, sentimentality, ideality" (Osterkamp 2012: 45).[8]

In this context, a passage from Jantz's work best defines this eternal-feminine in Goethe's work, where he asserts:

> The "Eternal-Womanly", therefore, was unmistakably intended by Goethe to comprise in symbolic form the great creative continuity of life, birth and rebirth in constantly renewed forms, the ultimate resolution of death, destruction, and tragedy in new cycles of life, constructive activity, and fulfillment. [...] The "Eternal-Womanly", pregnant with the future, draws the heroic soul upward to a higher sphere of existence. The heaven into which Faust enters is clearly and expressly one of change and development, not a terminus of rest but a way-station to a higher life.
> (Jantz 1953: 804)

Goethe's interpretation of the eternal-feminine is echoed at several significant points in Nietzsche's own philosophy, especially in values he expresses about the feminine.[9]

These are, above all, some of the main values emphasized by Nietzsche in relation to Goethe—the Renaissance spirit above all Christian morality and romantic mendacity—these are all aspects of the great values communicated by Goethe's poetry, which distances him from Romantic, and above all Germanic art. At WS 125 Nietzsche questions whether it is possible "to speak of a 'German Classic'" to underline what a surprising event Goethe was for the Germans. When he goes on to note that Goethe "belongs in a higher order of literatures than 'national literatures'" (WS 125), he is criticizing the nationalist tone of Germanism that seeks a properly Germanic identity.

Such a nationalist identity would advance an impoverished vision of culture mediated by reactionary ideals and a jingoistic political spirit that, for Nietzsche, serves decadent values. "Goethe, not only a good and great human being but a *culture*, Goethe is in the history of the Germans an episode without consequences: who could, for example, produce a piece of Goethe from the world of German politics over the past seventy years!" (WS 125). If Nietzsche ironically inverts the meaning of Goethe's sentence about the eternal-feminine in *Faust* by changing its end, the German poet remains exalted throughout his work. This appreciation of Goethe is crucial for the proposed problem surrounding Nietzsche's eternal-feminine.

## The Value of Goethe to Nietzsche's Philosophy in Relation to the Eternal-feminine

In *HH* Nietzsche presents Goethe as a model of "noble" art, especially in sections 162 and 221. In this sense, the inversion of Goethe's verse indicates a similar concern, that is, something that holds, that preserves a value Nietzsche perceives in the figure of Goethe, and the poet's "gaze". But it also denounces the romantic, metaphysical idealization that Nietzsche condemns, by referring to the eternal-feminine of modern culture as an element that demeans, that drags downward.

In other places Nietzsche's criticism and subsequent use of the term eternal-feminine can be better understood. In the 1886 preface to *Daybreak*, Nietzsche makes the same allusion to Goethe's verse, expanding his critique of romanticism, as mediated by feminism as idealism:

> hostile to the half-and-halfness of all romanticism and fatherland worship; hostile, too, towards the pleasure-seeking and lack of conscience of the artists which would like to persuade us to worship where we no longer believe—for we are artists; hostile, in short, to the whole of European *feminism* [*Femininismus*] (or idealism, if you prefer that word), which is eternally "drawing us upward" and precisely thereby eternally "bringing us down."[10]

(D P 4)

At this point, Nietzsche's critique turns to various forms of idealism that have Romanticism at the heart of the problem, as a kind of art that "persuade" us to "old ideals" that we "no longer believe." Nietzsche thereby synthesizes the moral problem of European culture, uniting Romanticism, idealism, and patriotism, with a decadent notion of "feminine," or "feminism," to indicate that they all have the same background, are derived from, or are symptoms of the same problem. The form of "feminism" referenced here entails an idealism that draws us toward metaphysical concepts, truths, and values beyond life itself. His criticism of idealism is implicit in the famous preface to *Beyond Good and Evil* where Nietzsche opposes dogmatic truth via the rhetorical question "suppose that truth is a woman?"

In this context, Oswaldo Giacoia (2002) interprets the issue of the feminine and Nietzsche's provocative critique of feminism, as presented in BGE, relating it to Nietzsche's philosophical enterprise of overcoming Platonism and transvaluing decadent moral values. In the aforementioned preface, he begins by directly confronting dogmatism and, above all, "Plato's invention of the pure spirit and the good as such [...] the worst, most durable, and most dangerous of all errors" (BGE P). In effect, Plato turned the truth upside down, thus denying "perspective, the basic condition of all life" when "one spoke of spirit and the good as Plato did" (BGE P). In Giacoia's words:

> Driven by the belief in the Platonic invention of pure spirit and the Good itself, philosophical gravity, with its ingrained and atavistic condemnation of sensibility, has always devalued what is subjective—perspectivistic, as if it represented the zero degree of truth, that is, the error, deceit and illusion.[11]
>
> (Giacoia 2002: 12)

Therefore, what in BGE (and relatedly in the aforementioned prefaces for the second volumes of HH, and D) constitutes a critique of dogmatic truth also entails a critique of art and romantic music. Nietzsche's critique of the eternal-feminine resides in his subtle play of meanings and ironies, which becomes clearer in other places where the term appears.

These include some unpublished fragments from the period of TI in which Nietzsche conveys a mature conception of the eternal-feminine. In fragment 15[118] from the spring of 1888, which addresses themes found in the chapter *Maxims and Arrows* of TI Nietzsche writes, "The woman, the eternal-feminine: a merely imaginary value, in which only the man believes"; then, in the same block of posthumous fragments Nietzsche would use in *TI*: "Man created woman—but out of what? Out of a rib from his God,—from his 'ideal'" (TI Maxims 13). From these sentences what is at stake for Nietzsche becomes clear: the necessity of a critique of the "feminine" in romanticism, its idealism of the "soul" at the expense of the body, and of sensuality. In this critique of the idealist, Nietzsche rejects that romantic conception of modern man, of the man who "created" this idealized metaphysical image of woman, who built this feminine ideal, this romanticized eternal-feminine, which is the fruit of a decadent value, of a narcotic, resentful, moralistic culture, that lowers the general condition of women, as Nietzsche himself expressed in EH.

It is in TI that Nietzsche perhaps best expresses what he understands by this type of romantic idealism, where he describes Rousseau as the exemplar that best defines such idealism:

> I still hate Rousseau *in* the Revolution; it is the world-historical expression of this duality of idealist and rabble. I do not really care about the bloody farce played out in this Revolution, its "immorality": what I hate is its Rousseauean *mortality*— the so-called "truths" that give the Revolution its lasting effectiveness, attracting everything flat and mediocre. The doctrine of equality!
>
> (TI Skirmishes 48)

Rousseau is a synthesis, like this romantic "feminine," of all modern values, equality, revolution, idealism, equal rights; Nietzsche uses all these elements as synonyms of a decadent, nihilist culture, as symptoms of the "disease" of this romanticism that dominates modern culture. In fact, regarding this diagnosis of the "revolution," this "'modern idea' *par excellence*," Goethe is preserved, as Nietzsche writes right after the excerpt above: "I see only one person who perceived it correctly: with disgust - Goethe" (TI Skirmishes 48). Thus, Goethe is an antipode of Rousseau, "not a German event but a European one: a magnificent attempt to overcome the eighteenth century by returning to nature, by coming towards the naturalness of the Renaissance, a type of self-overcoming on the part of that century" (TI Skirmishes 48). Goethe opposed the eighteenth century's romanticism. As Nietzsche wrote, Goethe is "a magnificent attempt to overcome the eighteenth century by returning to nature, by coming towards the naturalness of the Renaissance, a type of self-overcoming on the part of that century" (TI Skirmishes 49). For Nietzsche, Rousseau represented the spirit of an anti-Germanic, anti-Wagnerian culture via a "feminine" idealism of mendacity and "unbridled self-contempt" best expressed by the sign of romanticism, by the image of Rousseau.

It is, however, through this correlation of meanings that Penelope Deutscher approaches the similarity between what Nietzsche characterizes as "feminism" and Rousseau's problem, as explained above. In her words:

> It could even be said that when Nietzsche denounces what he terms "feminism", there is little difference between the sense that Nietzsche has given to the term "feminism" and the sense that Nietzsche has given to the term "Rousseau". Antithetical when represented in terms of their precise content, they nevertheless take on almost the same meaning in Nietzsche's texts: reactivity, idealism and egalitarianism.
>
> (Deutscher 1993: 164)

In this sense, the condition of the modern women is, from Nietzsche's perspective, also related to Rousseau's influence and the impact of his decadent values on modernity. However, as Deutscher points out, the problem of "feminism" in Nietzsche "is comprehensible only if read as a foreshortening of the terms 'idealism' and 'feminism' to the point of their being interchangeable" (Deutscher 1993: 165).

Nietzsche had already problematized these issues in his early writings and related them to this image of the eternal-feminine. In HL Nietzsche critiques the notion of science in modernity and how history is being shaped by it. He also uses the term eternal-feminine for the first time in his published work, in a passage regarding the modern historian:

> But, as I have said, this is a race of eunuchs, and to a eunuch one woman is like another, simply a woman, woman in herself, the eternally unapproachable - and it is thus a matter of indifference what they do so long as history itself is kept nice and "objective", bearing in mind that those who want to keep it so are forever incapable of making history themselves. And since the eternal-feminine[12] will never draw you upward, you draw it down to you and, being neuters, take history too for a neuter. But so that it shall not be thought that I am seriously comparing history with the eternal-feminine, I should like to make it clear that, on the contrary, I regard it rather as the eternally manly: though, to be sure, for those

who are "historically educated" through and through it must be a matter of some indifference whether it is the one or the other: for they themselves are neither man nor woman, nor even hermaphrodite, but always and only neuters or, to speak more cultivatedly, the eternally objective.

(HL 5)

Through the metaphor of the eunuch Nietzsche relates the objectifying aspect of the modern historian. Among those belonging to this, "race of eunuchs [...] individuality has withdrawn within: from without it has become invisible; a fact which leads one to ask whether indeed there could be causes without effects" (HL 5). This movement of withdrawing from oneself, from one's interiority, this "withdrawn within," this "becomes invisible" is the most pertinent point in relation to the critique of the eternal-feminine in this passage. In its false "neutrality" this purely objectivizing character of events, which lacks the instinct of life, neglects the perspectival dimension and instinctive sphere of knowledge. As Nietzsche asserts, "If one watches him from outside, one sees how the expulsion of the instincts by history has transformed man almost into mere *abstractis* and shadows: no one dares to appear as he is, but masks himself as a cultivated man, as a scholar, as a poet, as a politician" (HL 5). He clearly impugns the metaphysical element in this process. This makes it possible to better understand the meaning of the eternal-feminine for Nietzsche and his differentiation of it from what he dubs the eternal-masculine.

However, the same allusion to the passage from Goethe's *Faust* here does not contain the inversion that the texts from 1886 onward exhibit. The Goethean sense is preserved here, without any ironic tone that is noticeable in the other references. Here it is possible to understand the meaning that Nietzsche gives to the passage from *Faust*. The feminine that "elevates" here in Goethe's sense, as Nietzsche argues, is not "simply a woman," "woman in herself," "the eternally unapproachable," that is, something "neutral," without instinct, without body, something dissociated from life. Nor, however, is it metaphysical. On the contrary, Nietzsche's argument claims that it is the eternal-masculine that, without the necessary strength to "draw up" history, like Goethe and his eternal-feminine, ends up "draw[ing] it down," for it "neuters, and take[s] history too for a neuter" (HL 5).

In fact, the opening of the essay presents a significant quotation from Goethe on which Nietzsche begins his argument, "In any case, I hate everything that merely instructs me without augmenting or directly invigorating my activity" (HL Foreword). He explains:

why instruction without invigoration, why knowledge not attended by action, why history as a costly superfluity and luxury, must, to use Goethe's word, be seriously hated by us—hated because we still lack even the things we need and the superfluous is the enemy of the necessary.

(HL, Foreword)

In this context, the metaphor of the eunuch is also significant, for it underscores the absence of the sexual element, that is, sexuality referring to women and the body. This affirms "woman" not as an ideal, as a metaphysical "thing in itself," but as a singular subject that includes drives, desires, passions, and sensuality. Part of his critique of essentialist idealism in relation to women pertains to the absence of this erotic element (*eros*), of sexuality as a symbol of what is earthly, corporeal, and contrary to life-denying ascetic ideals.

Therefore, to my argument that the values preserved in the eternal-feminine are similar to what Nietzsche sees as necessary for a strong culture, the instincts, rooted habits, that aspect of "nature," or a "return to nature," are antithetical to Rousseau's vision. Indeed, it is here that the allusion to Goethe becomes significant because he is the antipode of Rousseau, and what is at stake is an artistic element, which is not a "neutral" objectification or a "nature" in Rousseau's sense. Rather, it represents a value in which Goethe's own image is the counterpoint, as a representation of another cultural disposition, that is, the argument takes place within the cultural aesthetic field, because this "modulating force" of life that should guide culture is, above all, mediated by the Dionysian dimensions of art.

It is in this sense that Nietzsche exalts Renaissance culture as an opposing ideal to Romanticism. In the words of Giuliano Campioni: "The Renaissance, as a return to the values of Hellenism, is a glorification of the reality of the body against the sick ghosts and the contradictions of the spirit of the Middle Ages" (Campioni 2016: 197).[13] Indeed, it is Renaissance values that Goethe symbolizes via the noble sensibility he conveyed in his works and which Nietzsche valued in the poetry of vital cultures. As Campioni observes, "Goethe as a Dionysian nature and 'man of the Renaissance', has, in Nietzsche's eyes, high symbolic value against the Germans […] and against Wagner" (Campioni 2016: 240).[14] Campioni also maintains that for Nietzsche

> Goethe represents superior health and a classic balance in relation to the disease of 'modern man', which is the 'exaggeration of sensitivity', of the 'disproportion' between their desires and their potency, of *dismembering* and the incurable contrast between their faculties.[15]
>
> (Campioni 2016: 240)

Therefore, the critique contained in Nietzsche's inversion of Goethe's eternal-feminine also reinforces the distinction between a conception that affirms, that values the whole perspective of artistic life against a conception that builds values "beyond" life, which romantically idealizes the concept of "soul" and privileges it over the body. As Nietzsche writes: "you first need to persuade the body" (TI Skirmishes 47), and this relates to the larger problem of German culture:

> It is crucial for the fate of individuals as well as peoples that culture begin in the *right* place—*not* in the "soul" (which was the disastrous superstition of priests and half-priests): the right place is the body, gestures, diet, physiology, *everything else* follows from this.
>
> (TI Skirmishes 47)

This distinction, ultimately, is what fundamentally characterizes the critical difference between the ideal "feminine" of Romanticism and the image of women as life, as affirmation, as pudency and truth throughout Nietzsche's work. In Romanticism there is an idealization of the woman that denies everything that is body, instinct, and "Dionysian"; it eternalizes a Christianized ideal of "woman" in which there is no seduction, body, or fruition.

This whole movement appears in a particularly significant way in the debate that Nietzsche has with himself in BT A 7 in which the subject is the critique of romanticism,

> But, Sir, if your book is not Romanticism, what on earth is? Can the deep hatred of "the present", "reality" and "modern ideas" be carried further than in your artiste's metaphysics, which would prefer to believe in nothingness or in the devil rather than in "the present"?
>
> (BT A 7)

Nietzsche self-reflectively questions what is at stake about Romanticism and modern art, which includes music. This includes the work of Wagner as a symptom of the same problem, no longer a hope for the transformation of German culture as Nietzsche suggested in 1872. As Nietzsche wrote in a passage from CW, "Modernity speaks its most *intimate* language in Wagner" and "Wagner sums up modernity" (CW P). This is the context of his "Attempt at Self-Criticism," more particularly section 7 in which Nietzsche reiterated his position on Wagner and romantic art. In the following passage this issue becomes more evident:

> are you telling us that this is not the genuine, true Romantic's confession of 1830 beneath the mask of the pessimism of 1850, behind which one can hear the opening bars of the usual Romantic finale—fracture, collapse, return, and prostration before an old belief, before *the* old god? Is not your pessimist's book itself a piece of anti-Hellenism and Romanticism, something which itself "both intoxicates and befogs the mind", at any rate a narcotic, a piece of music even, of *German* music?[16]
>
> (BT A 7)

Here Nietzsche questions his approach to Wagner with German music, questioning the difference between his position on art and that of Romanticism, and that of Richard Wagner. Following the same passage, continuing the questioning of his own work, Nietzsche evokes Goethe, quoting a significant passage from *Faust*:

> would not the tragic man of this culture, given that he has trained himself for what is grave and terrifying, be bound to desire a new form of art, the art of metaphysical solace, in fact to desire tragedy as his very own Helen, and to call out along with Faust:
> And shall I not, with all my longing's vigor
> Draw into life that peerless, lovely figure?
>
> (BT A 7)

In relation to the passage from *Faust*, this "art of metaphysical solace" this Helen due to him is particularly important. This excerpt takes place in a scene entitled "On the banks of the Lower Peneu," in which Faust, aided by the centaur Chiron, sets out to search for Helena in the realm of the dead. In Goethe's *Faust*, the full passage reads:

> And shall not I, sustained by poignant longing,
> endow this perfect form with life–
> this timeless being, the true peer of gods,
> tender but grand, august yet gracious too?
> You saw her long ago, but I this very day–
> the dream of beauty, charm, and loveliness.
> *My* whole existence now is held in bondage,
> and I shall die unless I make her mine.
>
> (Goethe 2014: 190)

This frenzy of desire, which describes the romantic eagerness in the search for that "art of comfort," is precisely what Nietzsche evokes in his argument when quoting this passage from *Faust*. It is also significant from the point of view of the problem surrounding the eternal-feminine. Such a consolation, Nietzsche states immediately afterwards, would not be necessary: "No, three times no, you young Romantics; it should *not* be necessary!" (BT A 7). Soon after, Nietzsche reiterates his comparison of romanticism with Christianity: "But it is very probable that it will *end* like this, that *you* will end like this, namely 'comforted', as it is written, despite all your training of yourselves for what is grave and terrifying, 'metaphysically comforted', ending, in short, as Romantics end, namely as *Christians*" (BT A 7). On the contrary, the "art" required, says Nietzsche, is the art of laughter:

> No, you should first learn the art of comfort *in this world*, you should learn to *laugh*, my young friends, if you are really determined to remain pessimists. Perhaps then, as men who laugh, you will someday send all attempts at metaphysical solace to Hell—with metaphysics the first to go!
>
> (BT A 7)

The "art of comfort *in this world*" is a Dionysian laugh, is the laugh of Zarathustra the dancer, soothsayer, sooth-laugher. Nietzsche ends the preface by quoting a passage from part four of Z, indicating a path for a new value in art, not the romantic frenzy of desire expressed in the ideal of the eternal-feminine, but an eternal-feminine that like Baubo (GS P), expresses a Dionysian life-affirming disposition guided by art.[17] This is also the value of Goethe for Nietzsche. Where it is possible to understand Goethe's position in relation to the Dionysian, Nietzsche wrote,

> A spirit like this who has *become free* stands in the middle of the world with a cheerful and trusting fatalism in the *belief* that only the individual is reprehensible, that everything is redeemed and affirmed in the whole—*he does not negate any more* … But a belief like this is the highest of all possible beliefs: I have christened it with the name *Dionysus*.
>
> (TI Skirmishes 49)

## The Eternal-Feminine and the Dionysian

The critique of Christian Platonic asceticism that Nietzsche provides in his critique of Romantic art—in which he rejects the denigration the physical body and the notion of a soul—is a major part of Nietzsche's diagnosis of decadence as a cultural psychologist, or the "first psychologist of the eternal-feminine" (EH Books 5). In this context the association between the feminine and the Dionysian becomes understandable.

In TI, for example, Nietzsche makes the following statement to clarify what he understands by "Dionysian":

> Saying yes to life, even in its strangest and harshest problems; the will to life rejoicing in its own inexhaustibility through the *sacrifice* of its highest types—*that* is what I called Dionysian, *that* is the bridge I found to the psychology of the *tragic poet*. [...] And with this I come back to the place that once served as my point of departure—the "*Birth of Tragedy*" was my first revaluation of all values: and now I am back on that soil where my wants, my *abilities* grow—I, the last disciple of the philosopher Dionysus,—I, the teacher of eternal return.
>
> (TI Ancients 5)

This important passage puts the Dionysian at the heart of the problem addressed in the final phase of his philosophy. This "saying yes to life," this "will to life" that constitutes what Nietzsche calls Dionysian is the "bridge" to the "psychology of the tragic poet." With this passage it is possible to better understand the passage from BT, mentioned before, namely that one must "first learn the art of comfort in *this* world [...] then learn to *laugh*" (BT A 7). What is at stake is the valorization of a psychology of the tragic poet against the psychology of romantic and modern art and its nihilistic tendency.[18] This is also what is at stake in relation to the question of women and the eternal-feminine. The Dionysian psychology of the tragic poet exalts a perspective affirmative of the body, instincts, and life's suffering. This becomes clearer where Nietzsche references pregnancy in relation to the Dionysian, to the psychology of the tragic poet of the ancient Greeks:

> The *fundamental fact* of the Hellenic instinct—its "will to life"—expresses itself only in the Dionysian mysteries, in the psychology of the Dionysian state. What did the Hellenes guarantee for themselves with these mysteries? *Eternal* life, [...] the *true* life as the overall continuation of life through procreation, through the mysteries of sexuality. That is why the *sexual* symbol was inherently venerable for the Greeks, the truly profound element in the whole of ancient piety. All the details about the acts of procreation, pregnancy, and birth inspired the highest and most solemn feelings. [...] There has to be an eternal "agony of the woman in labour" so that there can be an eternal joy of creation, so that the will to life can eternally affirm itself. The word "Dionysus" means all of this: I do not know any higher symbolism than this *Greek* symbolism of the Dionysian.
>
> (TI Ancients 4)

Here Nietzsche not only reaffirms the value that he attributes to the feminine from BT onward, but also expands his conceptions of pregnancy and the fecundity of women in their relation to the Dionysian. Nietzsche directly assimilates the value of pregnancy and the "woes of a woman in labour," which "sanctify pain in general" as a living expression of the eternal return, the deepest instinct of life and "the pathway to life." For Nietzsche the meaning of procreation lies in its affirmation of becoming.[19]

At this point, it is not a question of a simple appropriation of gestation. As Thorgeirsdottir points out, the

> concept of birth in Nietzsche's philosophy is here primarily interpreted from this perspective of giving birth as a metaphor for a creative, transforming, mutually empowering experience. Less emphasis is put on other aspects of birth, such as parturition, the succession of generations, and genealogies.
> (Thorgeirsdottir 2010a: 163)

The pain of childbirth is, above all, an appreciation of life that cannot be dissociated from the religious impulse of the Hellenic mysteries, which for Nietzsche constituted the heart of the tragic feeling of the Greeks. It corresponded with the Dionysian impulse that was fully manifested in the tragic period of ancient Greece. This aesthetic and physiological value permeated the image of the Greek woman that Nietzsche thinks has been lost in modern culture, a loss he attributes to Christianity, which made sexuality impure and removed erotic pleasure and pregnancy from its ideals of women.[20] The sphere of values that for the Greek constituted the will to life, the most fundamental Hellenic instincts is, according to Nietzsche, the element that configures the necessary condition for a transvaluation of all values and renewal of culture in our late-modern age. The Dionysian, with its "psychology of the orgiastic," is this force of affirmation of the will to life, as opposed to the Christian-Platonic will to truth that generates a will to nothingness and nihilism.

This interpretation provides a broader understanding of the feminine that Nietzsche seeks to "redeem" from an essentialist conception of woman and gender advanced by a metaphysical semantics. Nor does it concern a determined social individual, as a fixed and predetermined subject, or "I," because this whole conception is the result of a metaphysical idealism, as well as the idea of man, of a humanity idealized through a fixed and universal concept. As Thorgeirsdottir writes:

> The fear of the natural and bodily nature of women is in effect terror of the finiteness of human life. This fear results in an ambivalent view of women, who are seen either as earthly and akin to animals, or as pure, ethereal, unearthly beings, often in the guise of angels or fairies. Images of women as sublime beings disconnected from nature serves as a denial of the natural and bodily aspects of human life. Nature is thus denied a place in accounts of what makes human life noble.
> (Thorgeirsdottir 2010a, 170)

Nietzsche's Dionysian conception of subjectivity, of the self, emphasizes the animal aspect of the human and the genealogical constitution of values, which is developed through constant struggle, the conflict of active forces as conceived in the Nietzschean concept of will to power, as an expanding will to life. At BGE 23 Nietzsche remarked that "psychology is again the path to the fundamental problems," which helps explain the meaning of his assertion that he is "a psychologist of the eternal-feminine." He continues,

> all psychology so far has got stuck in moral prejudices and fears; it has not dared to descend into the depths. to understand it as morphology and the doctrine of the development of the will to power, as I do—has nobody yet come close to doing this even in thought—insofar as it is permissible to recognize in what has been written so far a symptom of what has so far been kept silent.
>
> (BGE 23)[21]

On this matter Scarlett Marton states that "the body consists of impulses which, acting and resisting one another, give rise to different configurations and assume various forms of coordination and conflict, organization and disintegration. In a word, it is a complex of impulses in permanent struggle" (Marton 2009: 56).[22] More emphatically, the Dionysian is "the interconnected totality of dynamic *quanta* or, if you like, of unstable force fields in permanent tension, it is process" (Marton 2009: 73). Therefore, it represents a conception of the body as a process, as opposed to a fixed, "eternal" metaphysical idea of subject, of woman, of the "*homo natura*" (BGE 230). It is this meaning that Nietzsche seeks to restore and affirm through the Dionysian.

## Conclusion

Ultimately, the relation between Nietzsche and Goethe is typified by an essential difference between the eternal-feminine of Goethe and the Dionysian feminine of Nietzsche. If Nietzsche sees Goethe's art and poetry as expressing a set of important values and a renewed cultural disposition in opposition to the German nationalist/idealist spirit, he does not fail to emphasize a fundamental lack in Goethe's tragic idea, that being the Dionysian. Following Nietzsche's own words: "We get a very different impression when we examine the idea of 'Greece' developed by Winckelmann and Goethe and find that it is incompatible with the element at the root of Dionysian art—the orgiastic rite" (TI Ancients 4). It is the absence of the "orgiastic rite" characteristic of Dionysian art that diminished Goethe's image of the Greeks. Nietzsche reiterates his point by asserting that, "As a matter of fact, I have no doubt that Goethe would have excluded anything of this kind from the possibilities of the Greek soul. *That is why Goethe did not understand the Greeks*" (TI Ancients 4). Years earlier Nietzsche had suggested that Goethe was not truly tragic, when he wrote, "Goethe once said that his nature was too conciliatory for real tragedy" (WS 124). Consequently, it is possible to say that the Goethian eternal-feminine is too conciliatory for real tragedy because it omits the central element, the "orgiastic rite" that typifies the Dionysian. That aphorism is significant for understanding the difference between the eternal-feminine as Goethe expressed it in his work, and the eternal-feminine from which Nietzsche was inspired when referring to the term in *Faust*. In it Nietzsche argues that the "idea of Faust" is not truly tragic to demonstrate what consists of Goethe's conciliatory nature. Initially, what Nietzsche is calling into question in WS 124 is the German "tragic idea." Without the assistance of the devil in person the great scholar could not have seduced and dishonored Margarete. As Nietzsche wrote, "after the little seamstress, 'the good soul who erred but once', had suffered an involuntary death, his [Goethe's] gentle heart could not refrain from transporting her into the proximity of the Saints" (WS 124). This is the meaning of Goethe's conciliatory nature, "indeed, in due course he even sent to Heaven the great scholar, the 'good man' with the 'impulse obscure', through a trick played on the Devil at the decisive moment:—up in Heaven the lovers find one another again" (WS 124).

There is no tragic element here, for Goethe cannot resist the urge to seek for reasons and compensations. There is no room for something irreconcilable, there is no room for the irrational, for disorder, for chaos, for "the demand for ugliness, the older Hellenes' good, severe will to pessimism, to the tragic myth, to affirm the image of all that is fearsome, wicked, mysterious, annihilating and fateful at the very foundations of existence" (BT A 4). As the Dionysian is described in BT, there is no room for the tragic Dionysian, which for Nietzsche comprises the central element of Greek tragedy.

From the point of view of the eternal-feminine, Goethe's conciliatory nature is also central. His conception of an eternal-feminine that leads the spirit to the highest perfection and draws the heroic soul upward to a higher sphere of existence lacks the Dionysian, tragic element. It is in this sense that Nietzsche's conception and use of the phrase "the eternal-feminine" differs from Goethe's conception in *Faust*. What Nietzsche seeks is the tragic element of the Dionysian, the permanent tension it creates and the process of becoming it embraces. This is the value of life for Nietzsche, as he writes in an aphorism entitled *"vita femina"*: "perhaps this is the most powerful magic of life: it is covered by a veil interwoven with gold, a veil of beautiful possibilities, sparkling with promise, resistance, bashfulness, mockery, pity, and seduction. Yes, life is a woman" (GS 339).

## Notes

1   In her thesis on the eternal-feminine in Goethe's *Faust*, O'Brien argues that the notion dates back to Plato and is most evident in medieval Catholic idealizations of feminine types, especially in images of the Virgin Mary (see O'Brien 2012). Perhaps the most significant feminist employment of it is found in Simone de Beauvoir's work *The Second Sex*, in which she took the myth of the eternal-feminine as a starting point of her inquiry into the question of women, particularly in its diverse cultural manifestations.

2   This problem has been addressed by several feminist philosophers and historians. From the standpoint of a feminist approach, there is a movement to interpret Nietzsche's more aggressive statements according to his critique of modernity, thereby preserving a positive core in Nietzsche's text about women. There are some who disregard Nietzsche's so-called positive assertions and still others who denounce them. Regarding the defense of a more positive perspective on the issue, see Derrida

(1979), Kofman (1995), Picart (1996), Bergoffen (1996), and Thorgeirsdottir (2004). About Nietzsche's denunciations of women, see Irigaray (1991) and Oliver (1995); for a reading of his denunciations with some reservations, see Higgins (1996) and Ansell-Pearson (1993).
3   Translation modified slightly.
4   The last word pronounced by *Chorus Mysticus* is the adverb *hinan* ("above" or "up"). In literal translation: "The Eternal-Feminine / Pulls us up."
5   For a more profound analysis of Goethe's work see van der Laan (2007).
6   Also, according to Jantz: "Such syncretism is to be found in Renaissance art also, and young Goethe was certainly acquainted with its elaborately intertwining connotations from the art books in his father's library and elsewhere, from the great and small art collections he knew, not to mention his broad acquaintance with Renaissance literature" (Jantz 1953: 793).
7   My translation.
8   My translation.
9   For example, in GS 339 Nietzsche affirms that life is a woman, *Vita Femina*, as well as the famous passage from the preface also to *The Gay Science* in which he approaches the question of truth in relation with the female image of Baubo.
10  Translation modified slightly.
11  My translation.
12  Translation modified slightly.
13  My translation.
14  My translation.
15  My translation.
16  Translation slightly modified.
17  For an in-depth analysis of Baubo's female image in relation to laughter and the Dionysian, see Thorgeirsdottir (2012).
18  "Every art, every philosophy can be considered a cure and aid in the service of growing or declining life: it always presupposes suffering and sufferers. But there are two types of sufferers: first, those who suffer from a *superabundance* of life—they want a Dionysian art as well as a tragic outlook and insight into life—then, those who suffer from an *impoverishment* of life and demand quiet, stillness, calm seas *or else* intoxication, paroxysm, stupor from art and philosophy" (NCW, We Antipodes).
19  For a detailed study on Nietzsche rescue of the Greek female image in its relationship with the "mysteries," with the Eulesian rites concerning the female Greek religions of worship of the goddess Demeter, which has a particular relation with the female figure of Baubo, that Nietzsche rescues here indirectly, see Behler (2010) and Thorgeirsdottir (2010a, 2012).
20  See D 74 and A 56.
21  For an in-depth analysis of will to power, see Müller-Lauter (1999).
22  My translation.

# 5

# What If Truth Were a Woman? Metaphors of the Feminine and the Transvaluation of Values in Nietzsche's Philosophy

Isadora Petry

## Introduction[1]

Nearly a century and a half has passed, and Nietzsche is still the target of criticism and accusations of misogyny due to certain affirmations in his works. "You are going to women? Do not forget the whip!," muttered the old woman in *Thus Spoke Zarathustra*. While speaking "about woman" Zarathustra asserted that "woman must obey and find a depth for her surface [...]. Surface is the disposition of woman: a mobile, stormy film over shallow water" (Z I "Old and Young Women"). In *Beyond Good and Evil*, Nietzsche wrote that "[w]oman has much reason for shame; so much pedantry, superficiality, schoolmarmishness, petty presumption, petty licentiousness and immodesty lies concealed in woman" (BGE 232). These are a few examples of some of his most appalling statements. Despite all this, even today, Nietzsche's works spark debate among philosophers and feminists who continue to read them. As Tamsin Lorraine point has observed, although we cannot ignore the trace of misogyny in Nietzsche's philosophy, we should not fixate on it, as this would prevent us from taking a careful and creative look at the possibilities that certain metaphors on the feminine in his works offer us even today (Lorraine 1998: 120). If we do read Nietzsche as feminists, it is not because we "ignore the way in which Nietzsche's texts exclude or belittle women" but rather "because Nietzsche himself gives [us] some suggestions as to how to transform the often ugly and nauseating 'truths' that are [our] cultural resource into something [we] can affirm in the present" (Lorraine 1998: 120).

However, determining if Nietzsche is misogynous is not the object of this chapter, nor do I intend to defend him as a feminist philosopher. Instead of assuming either view, I am interested in finding ways to extract elements from Nietzsche's work that help further feminist thought. To do so, I base my inquiry on the literature of women philosophers who have dedicated themselves to studying Nietzsche from a pluralist and feminist perspective.

Lorraine also affirms that if "the feminist virtue is the hope for a non-oppressive society," then we must go beyond certain boundaries and categories to "honour this hope" (ibid., 128). In my view, it is possible to read and interpret some cardinal elements in Nietzsche's philosophy, such as the revaluation of values, from a feminist perspective. When we read Nietzsche from this perspective, it contributes to philosophical research in at least two ways. The first is to the specific area of research carried out by *Nietzsche-Forschung*. It was common for Nietzsche's early interpreters to skip the paragraphs with words such as "woman" or "feminine" and to avoid hermeneutical interpretations of these terms. As a result, they ended up with an interpretation that did not take account for the plurivocity of meanings derivable from these terms or from the texts that contained them. It was as though the questions that could emerge from the terms "woman"/"feminine" were not worthy of philosophical investigation.

This strategy was adopted by Kaufmann, then followed by the majority of students of Nietzsche who "[dismissed] his comments on women as unfortunate products of his time and irrelevant to his philosophy."[2] Heidegger had the same attitude. When he interpreted the fable "*The Story of an Error*," in Twilight of the Idols (TI), he analyzed all the elements of the text *except* the "becomes female" of the idea [*sie wird Weib*]:[3] "The true world, unattainable for now, but promised to the man who is wise, pious, virtuous ('to the sinner who repents'). (Progress of the idea: it gets trickier, more subtle, less comprehensible,—*it becomes female* ...)" (TI Fable 2).

Both when Nietzsche used the term "woman" and when he evoked images and metaphors of the "feminine," it was commonly seen as secondary to his philosophy and lacking hermeneutic importance. This started changing in 1972 with Derrida's lecture "The Question of Style," in which he opened the way for exploration of the theme of the woman in Nietzsche's philosophy from a variety of perspectives.[4] Interpreting certain concepts in Nietzsche's philosophy from a feminist perspective provides a key for a hermeneutic reading of Nietzsche that had long been overlooked. A feminist hermeneutic approach to Nietzsche would also be fruitful for recent gender studies. Although it is not my goal to go into the details of these studies here, with regard to the overall framework for research on the philosophy of gender, I believe it is fundamental to highlight the importance of Nietzsche and certain women philosophers' interpretations of his works—as is the case of Butler, which I will focus on here—to reflections on the issues of gender, the feminine, and sexual difference.

## Switching Perspectives

As early as *Human, all too Human*, Nietzsche reflected on the need to overcome certain categories from the metaphysical tradition such as the matter of the origin of things: "how can something originate in its opposite, for example, rationality in irrationality, the sentient in the dead, logic in unlogic, disinterested contemplation in covetous desire, living for others in egoism, truth in error?" (HH I 1). According to the philosopher, the problem of the origin is a constant in metaphysical thought and if we examine it closely, we see that it raises the issue of differences. How can good and evil have the same origin when they are opposites? The same holds true for man and woman, or the masculine and the feminine. According to the German philosopher, by conceiving all these things as opposites, the tradition of metaphysical philosophy appears to answer this question by "denying that the one originates in the other, and by assuming for the more highly valued things some miraculous origin," directly from its own essence, whether "it" be the "true world," "God," or the "thing as such."

While in HH Nietzsche focused on questioning metaphysical categories, in *On the Genealogy of Morality*, he provided the tools for a new way of thinking that aims to go beyond these categories. By no longer questioning the origin or the belief in the origin of these values, but the *value* of the values themselves, he unveiled a new approach and more importantly, the possibility of revaluing values and switching perspectives.[5] In his later works, Nietzsche recognized the "revaluation of values" as his biggest philosophy project—so much so that the subtitle he was going to use in the book *Will to Power* he was planning to write was "An Attempted Revaluation of All Values." In 1887, Nietzsche abandoned his attempt to write the book, but not his work on revaluation. Together with the issue of nihilism and *décadence*, the revaluation of values is evident in Nietzsche's works, especially those written in late 1888.[6] For Nietzsche, revaluation is not merely about questioning the truthfulness of the "truth" but also and mainly about switching perspectives. This change, which requires tremendous effort to avoid succumbing to static positions, was Nietzsche's main concern from the time he diagnosed Greek *décadence* as being at the root of Socratic-Platonic-Christian thought.[7]

The transvaluation of values and Nietzsche's criticism of metaphysics offered certain contemporary feminists an important basis and fertile ground for discussions on gender. In her book, "*Gender Trouble*," Judith Butler acknowledges the importance of Nietzsche's critique of metaphysical thought on "substance" and its concept of genealogy in the construction of her own critique of the concept of gender identity. It is precisely the idea of a "metaphysics of substance"—which Butler takes from Nietzsche's critique of dogmatic philosophy—that characterizes the way in which the binary logic of sex has become embedded in our imaginary. Therefore, in reflecting on sexuality, Butler not only draws on fundamental elements from Nietzsche's thought but also embraces his philosophy to undertake the challenge of rethinking gender categories outside the metaphysics of substance. In her book, she explains:

> [G]ender is not a noun, but neither is it a set of free-floating attributes, for we have seen that the substantive effect of gender is performatively produced and compelled by the regulatory practices of gender coherence. Hence, within the inherited discourse of the metaphysics of substance, gender proves to be performative—that is, constituting the identity it is purported to be. In this sense, gender is always a doing, though not a doing by a subject who might be said to pre-exist the deed. The challenge for rethinking gender categories outside of the metaphysics of substance will have to consider the relevance of Nietzsche's claim in *On the Genealogy of Morals*.
>
> (Butler 1999: 33)

Butler is referring to GM I 13, in which the philosopher affirms that the subject is merely a category invented by reason. In the words of Nietzsche,

> For just as the popular mind separates the lightning from its flash and takes the latter for an *action*, for the operation of a subject called lightning, so popular morality also separates strength from expressions of strength, as if there were a neutral substratum behind the strong man, which was *free* to express strength or not to do so. But there is no such substratum; there is no "being" doings, effecting, becoming; "the doer" is merely a fiction added to the deed—the deed is everything.
> (GM I 13)

Butler adopted Nietzsche's genealogy, using his idea that there is no subject behind the action to propose her own corollary: "there is no gender identity behind the expressions of gender." She goes on to assert that "identity is performatively constituted by the very 'expressions' that are said to be its results" (Butler 1999: 33).

With the deconstruction of the concept of the subject as her starting point, which is the foundation of Nietzsche's genealogy, Butler does not view gender as a "thing as such." Instead, she reflects on *how* we came up with certain constructions of gender identity and what these constructions reveal about ways of life. For her, laughing in the face of serious categories—such as "subject" or "gender"—is "indispensable for feminism." That is not to say, however, that feminism does not require its own forms of seriousness. Butler defends genealogy as the best method for discussing gender issues because when we use it as a lens for our analysis, the "female no longer appears to be a stable notion, its meaning is as troubled and unfixed as 'woman'" (Butler 1999: xxix). For Butler, laughing at serious categories is fundamental for feminism, whereas for Nietzsche, laughter itself, as we will see shortly, is one of the primordial characteristics of the woman—or better, the feminine, which is not necessarily related to women.

Therefore, readers looking for some "truth" in the German philosopher's statements on what he really thinks about women or the feminine will come up empty-handed. As Oliver noted, ambiguity is the hallmark of Nietzsche's texts on women—and on truth. He establishes a similar relationship with both of them: a mixture of "awe and disdain" (Oliver 1984: 185–200). In his works, therefore, Nietzsche does not appear concerned with constructing a coherent image of the woman or the feminine. For one, in Nietzsche's view, all constructed images are merely fiction invented by reason in alliance with language. Secondly, all images interest him insofar as they have the potential to reveal something about life itself or the living—that is, a symptom of life. Thus, reading Nietzsche as a feminist is not about extracting feminist concepts *about* women from his philosophy but rather taking note of the nuances in his thought that help us overcome boundaries and categories to honor that feminist virtue.

**Truth Is a Woman?**

Since we cannot avoid the fact that ambiguity is a hallmark of Nietzsche's writings on women and truth, my goal here is to explore a bit further the relationship that Nietzsche establishes between woman and truth in his revaluation of values project (ibid., 185). I will show how this line of interpretation opens up new perspectives for the current debate on gender. In the preface of BGE, Nietzsche addresses the issue of the feminine and the truth by associating them directly to the fundamental challenges of deconstructing metaphysics and revaluing values. "Supposing truth is a woman—what then?," says Nietzsche,

> Are there not grounds for the suspicion that all philosophers, insofar as they were dogmatists, have been very inexpert about women? That the gruesome seriousness, the clumsy obtrusiveness with which they have usually approached truth so far have been awkward and very improper methods for winning a woman's heart? What is certain is that she has not allowed herself to be won—and today every kind of dogmatism is left standing dispirited and discouraged. *If* it is left standing at all!
>
> (BGE P)

In Nietzsche's view the fact that dogmatic philosophers since Plato have tried at all costs to uncover and conquer the truth or the ultimate foundation of things reveals a lack of bashfulness on their part. Here, bashfulness is a characteristic of the woman who, unlike the dogmatists, is aware of the transitory and perspectivistic nature of the truth. Nietzsche therefore argues that the philosophers' fanaticism in relation to the truth demonstrates their incapacity to understand the fleeting and ephemeral nature of existence. The complete lack of mastery with which they purported to know the truth/woman led them to try to dominate her through the use of force, keeping her under lock and key and promising her only "to the wise man, the pious man, the virtuous man ('to the sinner who repents')" (TI Fable 2). As a result, the truth/woman becomes all the "more cunning, more insidious, more incomprehensible," as Nietzsche explains in "How the 'true world' finally became a fable." But the attempt to render the truth/woman inaccessible, though promised, exposes an even greater problem: it indicates that nihilism—the inhospitable guest—is finally knocking on the door. The "progress" of the idea of the truth/woman thus corresponds to our descent into nihilism.

In the fall of 1887 (NF 9[35]), Nietzsche wrote, "[W]hat does nihilism mean? That the highest values devaluate themselves."[8] If nihilism represents the loss of belief in the values that justified life and if *décadence*, the source of nihilism's logic, runs so deep that it is no longer possible to create new values, then the only escape from impotent dogmatic rationality would be to turn the truth/woman into a promised and inaccessible, yet desired, thing—a fetish.

**Truth/Woman as a Fetish**

Even though "fetish" is not a common term in Nietzsche's philosophy, as Kofman (1998: 21–22) shows, it does appear a few times, such as at TI Reason 5 to describe the rudimentary belief in language, reason and metaphysics that Nietzsche discusses in HH, as we saw earlier. But in TI, Nietzsche explains that it is the "crude fetishism" of reason that impels us to identify and discriminate between agents and acts and to believe in the will and in the "I" as a Being, as substance. It leads us to *project* "the belief in the I-substance onto all things" and, consequently, see it as the "cause" of the concept of the "thing." Thus, the belief in language reveals a fetishistic attitude toward reason because, as Freud has shown us, the object of a fetish is always a substitute for something hidden in our subconscious, thus revealing a difficulty of accepting what is *lacking*.[9] Obviously, Nietzsche did not know about Freud at that time, nor had the psychoanalyst written his works on fetishism by then. Even so, the image of the fetish in Freud's work illustrates well what Nietzsche diagnosed as the root for Socratic fanaticism for rationality that Western metaphysical philosophy and Christianity continue to pursue:[10] the desire for the truth, which expresses human *horror vacui* [fear of the vacuum].[11]

In GS 60 Nietzsche brings women as distance to the scene: "the magic and the most powerful effect of women is, in philosophical language, action at a distance, *action in distans;* but this requires first of all and above all—*distance*" (GS 60). The play on words Nietzsche makes with "distance"/"*distans*" confirms one element that Oliver highlighted: woman—as the affirmative woman, as we shall see—"is not an object in the distance; rather she is distance" (Oliver, op. cit., 196). Just as distance and space do not exist "on their own," "the" woman also does not exist. "As distance, as space— pure womb—she does not exist. Just as there is no woman, there is no truth" (ibid.). Contrary to the dogmatic philosophers, who needed to dig down to the foundation [*Grund*] to extract the meaning of existence, the woman, understood as distance and surface, moves "*over* existence!" [*über das Dasein hinlaufen*] (GS 60).

Incapable of admitting that the desire for truth was what motivated them and served as the foundation for their "crude fetishism" about the metaphysical categories that they themselves had created, the dogmatic philosophers needed to believe in the existence of an eternal and immutable feminine. They remained trapped in an eternal quest for "the" truth/woman as they were unable to think outside of a binary logic. Incapable of understanding the truth/woman, dogmatic reason needed to fetishize her to be able to find satisfaction in its own fetish so as to fill the void from its lack of purpose.

## Baubo: The Deepest Is the Surface

In contrast to the fixity of the truth that the dogmatists sought to establish, which Nietzsche discusses in *Beyond Good and Evil*, and the second preface of *The Gay Science* (1886), he evokes the image of another truth. Using the metaphor of the truth/ woman, Nietzsche presents the image of Baubo—or Iambé, as she is referred to in the *Homeric Hymn to Demeter*—where he writes:

> One should have more respect for the bashfulness with which nature has hidden behind riddles and iridescent uncertainties. Perhaps truth is a woman who has reasons for not letting us see her reasons? Perhaps her name is—to speak Greek— *Baubo*? Oh, those Greeks! They knew how to live. What is required for that is to stop courageously at the surface, the fold, the skin, to adore appearance.
>
> (GS P 3)

According to Nietzsche, like this affirming truth/woman mentioned by Oliver, the Greek were "superficial—*out of profundity!*" (GS P 3). But who is Baubo, the woman and goddess with a vulva for a face? As Lubell explains in *The Metamorphosis of Baubo*, there are records of cave drawings dating to the Palaeolithic period that depict a robust woman with the image of a vagina where her face would normally be. In these images, the woman is often dancing and laughing, and her face, which is the vulva itself, is always uncovered. In *Homeric Hymns*, which Nietzsche was familiar with, Baubo or Iambé makes a subtle appearance only twice. Even so, she is of fundamental importance because thanks to her joking and gesticulating, Demeter manages to smile again and recover from the mourning of the loss of her daughter Persephone. The image of Demeter before and after her mourning is rich in nuances. When the goddess hears her daughter's screams, which echoed on the stones right after she had been abducted by Hades, she immediately put a dark cloak over her shoulders, hiding her blond hair that used to bring light to the world. Shrouded in melancholy, Demeter takes on the appearance of an old lady and decides that nothing will grow on the earth again. She then begins to wander aimlessly until she comes to Celeu's palace where the servant Baubo jokingly approaches her. Baubo's playful teasing causes a moment of rupture. Demeter's aged face gives way to laughter, and she puts an end to her refusal to drink by accepting a glass of water mixed with a touch of pennyroyal. The laughter that Baubo causes with her merrymaking was enough to change the goddess's mood, enabling her to muster up enough courage to devise a plan and persuade Zeus to bring Persephone back.

What interests Nietzsche in the figure of Baubo appears to be precisely the fact that her laugh comes from the belly and is expressed on her face and that this is the only laughter capable of switching perspectives. This shows that there is no opposition between depth and the surface. Moreover, the deepest laughter appears on the surface—in the folds of the vulva. Could this be the laughter that Butler argues is so indispensable to feminist practices and theories? Nietzsche warns us that laughter cures: "Objections, digressions, gay mistrust, the delight in mockery are signs of health: everything unconditional belongs in pathology" (BGE 154).

In his book *Baubo: la vulve mythique*, Georges Devereux affirms that in the passage of the myth that narrates Baubo's antics, it is clear that the jokes she tells are not verbal but visual ones. Dismissing the rationality of words, Baubo heals Demeter's suffering by showing that she is not the only castrated one there and especially by reminding her that she can get pregnant and give birth again. As such, despite its comical nature, Baubo's jest carries the promise that Demeter's daughter will return. Another interesting aspect of Baubo's jesting according to Devereux is the way that sex is exhibited: playful and irreverent but only among women. This could imply that dogmatic men do not understand anything about the feminine, and therefore, they cannot laugh like women laugh of themselves, nor can they revalue perspectives.

Montinari indicates that Nietzsche acquired his knowledge of the myth of Demeter not only from *Homeric Hymns* but also by reading *Protreptikos* (Exhortation to the Greeks) by Clement of Alexandria. In the version of the myth narrated by Clement, who was a Christian apologist, the transformative nature of Baubo's actions is even more evident:

> This said, she drew aside her robes, and showed
> A sight of shame; child Iacchus was there,
> And laughing, plunged his hand below her breasts,

> Then smiled the goddess, in her heart she smiled,
> And drank the draught from out the glancing cup.
>
> (Clement of Alexandria 1960: 43)

In this version, there is yet another important aspect that Thorgeirsdottir (2012: 69) comments on where she notes that one can see the head of Iacchus, also known as Dionysus, inside of Baubo's vagina. Some interpret this as meaning that Baubo was giving birth to Dionysus, and it was precisely when Demeter was watching the spectacle of the birth that she experiences the only laughter capable of displacing perspectives.

## Giving Birth to New Perspectives

The metaphor of birth thus contains the experience of otherness and the encounter with difference—a condition required for the gestation of philosophical thought that is capable of going beyond metaphysical opposites.[12] For Nietzsche, what was of interest in the experience of birth was not the ability to give birth *per se*. According to Thorgeirsdottir, what interests him is the metaphor of birth as the only experience that produces both pain and pleasure at the same time: "Birth is for him a paradigmatic example of a phenomenon in which great pain and lust come together, in which something ends and something new begins" (2010a, 158). From this perspective, then, the experience of birth holds the possibility of revaluing perspectives precisely because it brings together in the same act opposing experiences and sensations: life and death, pain, and joy. Furthermore, death is a precondition for life, which indicates that life is not necessarily opposed to death; instead, there is an eternal continuum between the two: "The dead and the living are both aspects of the same organic and inorganic process of what we call 'life'" (NF 1874, 168[109]).[13]

The metaphor of birth has both an aesthetic and an epistemological meaning because it renders explicit and affirms both the interdependence of joy and suffering and the inseparability of life and death, thus asserting the possibility of creating *new* values.[14] Therefore, the laughter in the story of Baubo and Demeter may come from its subversive nature, as she brings to the surface what is deepest in a woman's body—the vulva—and by doing so, claims to have overcome opposition. The laughter may also be a sign of relief and the promise of the future, as it is the result of the experience of birth which unites suffering and joy, thus showing that both sentiments are not necessarily opposed to one another.

This brings to mind something that Nietzsche wrote in *Ecce Homo*: to see sickness from the perspective of health and health from the perspective of sickness is a sign of one's ability to revalue and overcome oneself.

> Looking from the perspective of the sick toward *healthier* concepts and values and, conversely, looking again from the fullness and self-assurance of a *rich* life down into the secret work of the instinct of decadence—in this I have had the longest

training, my truest experience; if in anything, I became master in *this*. Now I know how, have the know-how, to *reverse perspectives*: the first reason why a "revaluation of values" is perhaps possible for me.

(EH Wise 1)

When discussing the philosophy of birth in Nietzsche from a feminist perspective, Thorgeirsdottir emphasizes the importance of the figure of Baubo for reflecting not only on how to go beyond metaphysical philosophy but also the possibility of using it to question masculine/feminine dichotomies—that is, the binary logic of sex (2010a: 159). Even though we can say that Baubo is a woman and Dionysus, a man, they are both full of transgender characteristics that are masculine and feminine at the same time. And it is precisely this multiplicity of erotic possibilities, performed in the transgender body, that brings into question and destabilizes the oppositions between natural and artificial, depth and surface, internal and external, through which metaphysical and, to an extent, totalitarian discourses always operate. By associating Dionysus with pregnancy and birth, Nietzsche deconstructs all essentialist ideas on the sexes, as Dionysus represents "a possibility of a plurality of sexual identities" in one body (ibid.). He is the spokesperson of great style, the one capable of synthesizing oppositions.

For Thorgeirsdottir, the metaphor of birth is the prime example of the encounter with otherness, which is the prerequisite for seeing oneself and the other in a new and different light. As birth creates a moment of awe—the astonishment that comes from being confronted with the encounter of the other—it places the subject in the dimension of the unknown and difference. In Zarathustra's view, creation "is the great redemption from suffering, and life's growing light. But that the creator may be, suffering is needed and much change [...]. To be the child who is newly born, the creator must also want to be the mother who gives birth and the pangs of the birth-giver" (Z II Blessed Isles). It is a way of thinking that both challenge and affirm the difference between the I and the Other, which is a necessary condition for the gestation of philosophical thought.

## Woman as Such, Thing as Such?

Yet, if Nietzsche aims to overcome the dichotomies and question the veracity of the truth, then how can he claim to speak of "the woman as such" as he does, for example, in BGE 231? In his analysis of the aphorism in question, Andreas Urs-Sommer (2016: 652) explains that when Nietzsche speaks of "the woman as such," he is ironically referring to the Kantian "thing as such" [*Das Ding an sich*]. While Kant believes that it is impossible to know the "thing as such," Nietzsche seems to suggest that it is impossible to know the "woman as such." Because he sees both as categories invented by reason, Nietzsche would only be able to speak of the woman if he performatively inserts her in this dogmatic discourse, and he is well aware of this. However, when Nietzsche launched his critique of the "woman as such," he did so because he saw in the feminism of his time a return to the belief in the metaphysics of the dogmatists. Therefore, he does not talk about "the woman" per se but only the idea that one has of the woman or, in other words, "the woman as such." As we learn from the words of Zarathustra himself, speaking "about" (*überreden*) is always a device that the dogmatists use.[15] This is precisely why he could only speak "about" women to men and to the old woman who, just like dogmatic philosophy over time, became increasingly skeptical as they collected "small truths."

One cannot talk about the woman precisely because "the" woman, like "the" truth, does not exist. To say that she does not exist means that she is "outside the discourse of truth," the dogmatic and metaphysical truth (Oliver 1984: 194). The truth and life should be treated the same way as "judgments, value judgments on life, whether for or against, can ultimately never be true: they have value only as symptoms, they can be considered only as symptoms—in themselves such judgments are foolish" (TI Socrates 2). Nietzsche knows, then, that all truths about the truth/life/woman are only *his* truths; they are perspectives and reveal only the values and symptoms of the one who is judging.

## Conclusion: A Love/Truth/Woman

Nietzsche suggests that dogmatic philosophers relate to the truth the same way they do to women: with "clumsy obtrusiveness" and "very improper methods," they try to undress them. He argues that these men treat women "like birds who had strayed to them from some height: as something more refined and vulnerable, wilder, stranger, sweeter, and some soulful—but as something one has to lock up lest it fly away" (BGE 237[a]). They do not understand the tragic irony that permeates the truth/woman and love. This tragic irony compels us to heed yet another woman in Nietzsche's philosophy: Carmen, from Bizet's opera based on Mérimée's novella. She alone comprehends what Nietzsche sees as the only conception of love worthy of a philosopher: "love as a fate, as a fatality, cynical, innocent, cruel,—and precisely in this way *Nature*! The love whose means is war, whose essence is the *mortal hatred* between the sexes!" (CW 2). In the opera *Carmen*, which Nietzsche watched for the first time in 1881, we find the gypsy's famous line: "love is a wild bird that nothing can tame" (The Metropolitan Opera 2014: 42). The love/truth/woman is elusive and shrewd like a bird that does not allow itself to be captured. Incapable of accepting the ephemeral nature of the love Carmen offers him, which is the only kind of love worthy of a philosopher, Dom José murders her. Unlike Carmen, he is incapable of remaining bravely in the fold, on the surface.

Now, is this not the same way philosophers treat the truth/woman, as Nietzsche shows in the preface of BGE? Unable to access the truth/woman, like Dom José, they massacre her. Dom José is incapable of living with the difference between his and Carmen's love and he believes he is doing justice by murdering her. He does not understand that the irony of love lies precisely in the fact that such justice is unattainable because "man and woman have different conceptions of love—and it is one of the conditions of love in each sex that neither sex presupposes the same feeling, the same concept of 'love' in the other" (GS 363). Therefore, justice could only be done if differences are maintained and allowed to grow.

Even though it is understandable why Nietzsche is often accused of misogyny, I believe that his philosophy and way of thinking can effectively dialogue not only with feminist theories but with all ways of thinking that are open to dialogue with the other and with differences. When Nietzsche expresses his opposition to the ideas of "equality" between men and women—going so far as to accuse women seeking their independence of being "one of the worst developments of the general *uglification* of Europe" (BGE 232)—his position is understandable, according to Thorgeirsdottir, because Nietzsche "does not want men and women who would end up having the same attributes and outlooks" (Thorgiersdottir 2012: 69). Instead, he wants both to be maintained with their differences. Moreover, while it is true that he does not thoroughly examine these issues in his works, it is clear that by challenging the limits of reason and language—or, in other words, the "crude fetishism" of reason in language—he wants us to understand that what we call sex, gender, and desire are mere fictions. According to Butler, the first step we need to take to be able to think of gender not as something given and natural, but something that becomes, is transformed and, above all, performed, is to eliminate the belief in the existence of a subject. For Nietzsche, if the subject is nothing more than a fiction of seductive language, then "we are not getting rid of God because we still believe in grammar" (TI Reason 5).

# Notes

1 This chapter was supported by grant number 2016/23514-8, São Paulo Research Foundation (FAPESP).
2 Oliver and Pearsall (1998: 1).
3 Derrida (1998: 59). Here Derrida referred to the second half of the section entitled "The story of an error" under "How the 'True World' Finally Became a Fable" in TI, which is about the consolidation of Christianity.
4 Cf. Derrida, op. cit., 51: "The title kept for this conference shall have been *the question of style*. But—it will be woman who shall be my subject. It would remain to ask whether that amounts to the same—or to something other."
5 Nietzsche explores the idea of "*switching perspectives*" [*Perspektiven umzustellen*] as the basis of the task of revaluating values [*Umwerthung der Werthe*] further, primarily in EH Wise 1.
6 Montinari comments that when Nietzsche abandoned the idea of using his project of revaluation of all values (*Umwerthung aller Werthe*) as a subtitle for the work *Der Wille zur Macht* (which he never wrote), the philosopher ended up focusing on this project in the works he wrote in the final productive year of his life. See Montinari (1982: 118).
7 TI Socrates.
8 Translation from eKGWB—*NietzscheSource.org*.
9 Freud discusses this idea of a "lack" by associating it to "castration." The fetish of the man generally reveals his incapacity to accept the woman's castration—her lack of a penis (Freud 1961).

10  According to Nietzsche, "Christianity Is Platonism for 'the people'" (BGE P).
11  GM III 1.
12  This idea is developed by Thorgeirsdottir (2010).
13  Transl. from eKGWB—*NietzscheSource.org*.
14  By "*new* values," I refer to Richardson's hypothesis on Nietzsche's *new* values as strategies for what he considered one of his "meta-values": life and truth (Richardson 2020: 354).
15  "Über das Weib soll man nur zu Männern reden" (KSA 4:I, 84).

Part Three

# Myth and Self-Creation

6

# Nietzsche's Misogyny and a Feminine Philosophy of the Future

Mat Messerschmidt

## Nietzsche Scholarship and Nietzsche's Misogyny

Is Nietzsche a misogynist? Nietzsche's texts abound with statements that the average, non-professionalized reader of Nietzsche surely understands as hostile and derogatory to women. In Nietzsche studies over the past half century, however, it seems that the most conventional way of responding to this question has been to emphasize the ways in which Nietzsche, contrary to appearances, in fact gives us the tools to challenge traditional dichotomies—dichotomies which often have the ability to limit our power to "become who we are" by confining our sense of ourselves to false essences. Two such constricting false essences are "man" and "woman." The prevailing line of thought regarding Nietzsche on gender, then, has come to be that Nietzsche offers us a path to liberation from gender norms that have potentially stunted avenues of human growth. For this reason, to the question "Is Nietzsche a misogynist?," the array of answers coming from Nietzsche scholars has often been quite favorable to Nietzsche. Not everyone goes so far as to decisively answer in the negative, claiming that Nietzsche is *not* a misogynist but, for a large number of charitable readers, the importance of the specific histrionic claims against woman made by Nietzsche pales in comparison to the importance of the methods Nietzsche develops that can be turned against oppressive gender hierarchies. On the whole, within Nietzsche studies, it has become almost the standard position to read Nietzsche as basically a salutary force when it comes to gender relations.

While this general tendency might be surprising to someone who is not a Nietzsche expert, it is certainly not without reason. One might not expect to see Nietzsche's name mentioned favorably in the opening chapter of Judith Butler's *Gender Trouble*, but the point Butler makes there about Nietzsche is quite accurate. She observes that Nietzschean genealogy's general tendency to question the intrinsic, substantialized status of merely *current* formations of subjecthood empowers the project of challenging the essentialized status of today's "man" and "woman," configurations that have been naturalized into eternal types.[1] Even if Nietzsche cannot be said, in any straightforward way, to have himself conducted such a deconstruction of the genders as they are experienced today, we can certainly see how his genealogical approach could help paved a path for such an endeavor. Establishment ideology tends to found itself in sacred origins; Nietzschean genealogy refutes both the illustriousness[2] and the unity[3] of such origins. Michel Foucault, perhaps the most famous self-described inheritor of Nietzsche's historiographical paradigm, says that in Nietzsche's historical investigations, "What is found at the historical beginning of things is not the inviolable identity of their origin; it is the dissension of other things. It is disparity."[4] These tendencies clearly point to an iconoclastic, anti-establishmentarian disposition inherent to Nietzsche's genealogical strategy. The fact that Nietzsche's methodology itself (as distinguished from his substantive claims about this or that object of historical analysis) has this radical bent means that even where Nietzsche's conclusions are conservative, his approach can be used toward revolutionary or hierarchy-challenging ends. In this sense, Nietzsche's appeal for feminist readers is less strange than it might at first seem to be, despite all his attacks on women.

It seems to me, though, that we must distinguish between *appropriations* of Nietzsche, on the one hand, and Nietzsche *scholarship*, on the other, when we ask the question of how to approach the issue of Nietzsche and misogyny. The intellectual projects of Butler and Foucault are not, by and large, projects of Nietzsche scholarship, of course. Their implementations of some aspects of Nietzsche's historical approach can be endorsed without concern as to whether these implementations exhibit rigid fealty to Nietzsche—they do not. When one is claiming to practice Nietzsche scholarship, however, the situation is different. If we go too far in suppressing, ignoring, or defanging Nietzsche's misogyny, we run the risk of failing to read Nietzsche as Nietzsche. Gender is an important category for Nietzsche—the Nietzsche text is, we might say, heavily "gendered," in obvious ways. From the sexualized dynamics of the Apollo-Dionysus relationship to the designation of philosophers as overweening male lovers in pursuit of the woman "truth,"[5] to the emergence, in Nietzsche's last productive years, of the woman Ariadne as a kind of higher human being, "man" and "woman" are clearly important concepts for Nietzsche, even when he is complicating them. We cannot afford to misunderstand their operation in Nietzsche's thought because we have avoided discussion of the most unsavory Nietzsche passages on the topic.

In the rest of this article, I will begin with an analysis of the exact dynamics of Nietzsche's misogyny. I will argue, against some other scholars, that Nietzsche's disclaimers about his views on women cannot be taken to fully undo what he says about man and woman in those passages and that we must, therefore, confront and analyze Nietzsche's misogyny. Woman is condemned for being constituted as a fundamentally reactive configuration of the will to power. I will then show, however, that there is a line of thought internal to Nietzsche's own thinking that challenges this devalued status of the "woman" described in the section on the sexes in BGE 231–9, and that we see this contrary line of thought begin to emerge even in that section itself, toward the end (239). The inversion of reactive woman's denigrated status is carried through more fully in the figure of Ariadne, whose presence in Nietzsche's late works undermines the masculinist ideal of "active force." We should read Ariadne, I argue, as a representative of Nietzsche's own philosophy, such that Nietzsche covertly aligns himself with some of the same "feminine" traits denigrated in the misogynist passages of *Beyond Good and Evil*. We can thus see an underground "feminization" of philosophy taking place in Nietzsche's references to Ariadne.[6] In this way, a head-on engagement with Nietzsche's misogyny leads us to more interesting places, I think, than we might first imagine.

## Nietzsche on Woman

What is the basis of Nietzsche's attack on woman? It would probably be giving Nietzsche far too much credit to look for a coherence uniting *all* of his misogynist comments throughout his corpus, but we can, I think, identify some common threads to Nietzsche's statements in *Beyond Good and Evil*'s final sections to the chapter "Our Virtues," §231–9. This is a convenient place to start in part because it is here that the highly aphoristic writer, whose attention can pivot from one topic to another on a dime, writes about woman at some sustained length. Another reason to begin here is the simple fact that these passages have attracted a fair deal of scholarly attention, so that we can justifiably speak of and respond to general trends in responses to them.

These passages proceed with a sort of present-perfect tensing. Nietzsche is concerned both with who woman has always been and with what he claims she has become. We can thus identify two different levels of argument—one suprahistorical and one historical. The suprahistorical argument speaks of who woman has always been. The "Seven Epigrams on Woman" that make up BGE 237 present themselves as timelessly valid sayings and depict woman as a being who is constituted in reaction to man. Like the "reactive" slave in the soon-to-be-written *Genealogy*, she seeks to control man ("How the longest boredom flees, when a man comes on his knees!"[7]) but must seek this control from a position of apparent weakness ("Up till now, men have treated women like birds that have come to them after having lost their way from somewhere high above: they are finer, more vulnerable, wilder … but as something that must be locked up, so that it does not fly away."[8]). Her ability to achieve power over man in this way is founded in sexual attraction ("Whom do I thank for my success? God!—and my dear tailoress"[9]). Although some scholarship has implied that woman's status as "weaker sex" is, for Nietzsche, a specifically modern result of modern ideology (more on such readings momentarily), Nietzsche's invocation of this phrase clearly speaks of a modern constellation of gender relations being imposed upon a sex that was already "weaker." He says, "In no epoch has the weaker sex been treated with such respect as in our epoch."[10] Throughout these sections, Nietzsche frequently describes female "instincts" as being under serious threat in modern Europe. For example, "the 'emancipation of woman'" is a "symptom of the accelerating weakening and deadening of the most female instincts."[11] What exactly are the "most female instincts"? Nietzsche has a clear answer: woman "is unlearning how to *fear* man: but the woman who 'unlearns fear' abandons her most female instincts."[12] Fear is the basis of (transhistorical) "female instincts." More specifically, woman definitionally fears man. For Nietzsche, woman is always a reaction to man, and this reaction is founded in fear. In this sense, woman—not just today, in this historical moment, but always—is a picture of "reactivity" itself.[13]

The criticism launched more specifically at *modern* woman and, at modern society's treatment of woman, bases itself on Nietzsche's sense that woman has forgotten or suppressed the above "facts" about herself. Modern woman aspires to equality with man, which means, for Nietzsche, that she aspires to *be* man. "Insofar as [woman] claims new rights for herself, strives to become 'master' [*Herr*] and writes the 'progress' of woman on her flags and banners, she accomplishes the opposite with frightening clarity: *woman is regressing*."[14] Here, the word "*Herr*" must be translated as "master" or "lord," but we should also note that it is a necessarily gendered word that can also mean "gentleman." In modernity, woman seeks to become man. The modern stance of woman is thus a kind of inauthenticity about woman's basic "instinctual" configuration in relation to man.

## The Difficulty of Minimizing Nietzsche's Misogyny

At this point we should note that the above reading cuts against the grain of much Nietzsche scholarship by emphasizing what lies on the face of the text: that these passages are not sympathetic to women. Since efforts to downplay or mitigate this aspect of the passages in question are so widespread, I will address the weaknesses of such an approach at some length here. To be clear, no one of whom I am aware actively resists the idea that Nietzsche makes clearly misogynist statements here, but many scholars do suggest that there is a way to dramatically undercut, or even dissolve, the force of the anti-woman element of Nietzsche's commentary on the sexes. This notion has been advanced in two different ways. Some scholars suggest that Nietzsche shows, in these passages, how the "woman" whom the text appears to scorn is in fact the modern product of a historical development that Nietzsche condemns. Citing §239, for instance, in which Nietzsche argues that "[s]ince the French Revolution, the influence of woman has *decreased* in proportion to the increase of her rights and entitlements,"[15] Vanessa Lemm argues that, for Nietzsche, "liberal rights have disempowered women by decreasing their influence."[16] Nietzsche wants to "[remind] modern women of the Dionysian, 'Asian' link between naturalness, sexuality, and political power."[17] Lemm thus links premodern woman to a constellation of terms that suggest a healthier kind of power that is endorsed by Nietzsche. Similarly, Sarah Kofman writes that, for Nietzsche "'[w]oman' as 'weaker sex' is not an essential determination of woman, but a historical event that threatens to become definitive and to constitute henceforth the feminine 'type' par excellence."[18] Certainly, there is something to this line of thought: Nietzsche describes recent history as a "defeminization" or "de-womaning" [*Entweiblichung*] of woman.[19] Woman, he seems to say, has lost herself in modern times. This line of reasoning, however, cannot paper over the fact that, as we noted above, Nietzsche, without apparent irony and with clear transhistorical meaning, calls woman "the weaker sex"—a fact which directly and unambiguously refutes Kofman's claim. Similarly, the assertion that woman is founded in a fear of man does not appear to be historically contingent in any way. In summary, against these readings (against them to a degree, at least), the reactivity of woman appears to be suprahistorical.

A more pervasive tack taken by scholars seeking to downplay Nietzsche's sexism is to rely on the notion that Nietzsche's text is, to use Bernard Williams's phrase, "booby-trapped"[20]—that the text undermines its own statement. Jacques Derrida may have been the first to employ this idea when talking specifically about Nietzsche's thoughts on women. For Nietzsche, "[t]here is no such thing as a woman, as a truth in itself of woman in itself," Derrida says, in his well-known *Spurs*.[21] He appears to be referring to BGE 231, where Nietzsche places the phrase "woman in herself" [*Weib an sich*][22] in quotation marks that seem to suggest that the phrase itself is dubious.[23] Derrida apparently believes that this implies that the following anti-woman passages that follow, which speak of woman, orient themselves around a concept whose coherence has been questioned beforehand. Maudemarie Clark focuses on a different phrase in the same section in order to make a similar claim. She points out that Nietzsche introduces his thoughts on women by stipulating that they are "only *my* truths."[24] Clark believes that, with this phrase, "Nietzsche is letting us know that he is not claiming that his comments on woman are true."[25] The general idea uniting readings like this, then, is that before Nietzsche goes on his sexist screed, he preemptively disqualifies everything he is about to say, detoxifying his text for today's reader in advance. As the examples of Derrida and Clark show, different sorts of Nietzsche readers have taken this approach to these passages.[26]

One problem with this approach is that it implies a standard of skepticism regarding the Nietzsche text that may be extremely difficult to employ comprehensively across Nietzsche's corpus. He claims that every philosopher's *entire philosophy* is a "personal confession."[27] If we were to read this assertion the way Derrida and Clark read the phrase "my truths," we would be compelled to read *all* the "truths" put forth by *any* philosopher as *only* "their truths"—or, if we do not grant Nietzsche the right to speak for all philosophers, then certainly we would have to read Nietzsche's own "truths" this way, at the least. In other words, if emphasis on the notion that these or those "truths" come from me is equivalent to saying that (to paraphrase Clark's wording) "I am not claiming that these assertions are true," then any and all assertions in Nietzsche's corpus must be preemptively asterisked as "not claiming to be true." This would seem to disintegrate more or less all of Nietzsche's claims, philosophical or otherwise.[28] As the price of saving Nietzsche from misogyny, we would commit ourselves to losing Nietzsche entirely as a writer making philosophical claims if we were to remain consistent.

There is a more directly textual reason, though, to question whether a phrase like "my truths" is really enough to disqualify everything that follows in the sections on woman as somehow not seriously meant. The context in which the words "my truths" appear—in the last words of §231—strongly suggests that this phrase does not mean anything as totalizing and unnuanced as, say, "statements that are not actually true." The entire passage up to that point discusses the connection between belief and "physiology," arguing that the two must be seen as deeply intertwined. Having named this theme, Nietzsche quickly turns to the example of relations between the sexes. He argues that "[f]or every cardinal problem there speaks an unchangeable 'this is what I am,': when it comes to man and woman, for example, a thinker cannot unlearn, but can only complete his learning [*auslernen*]."[29] Having indicated that he is speaking as "the physiologist,"[30] this "unchangeable 'this is what I am'" can only be taken, I think, in physiological terms. For Nietzsche, this means the terms of drive configuration. In the phrase "my truths," then, Nietzsche is indicating that he is speaking from his own sexed perspective, from the perspective of his own drive configuration. But nothing about the passage indicates that this is tantamount to a total disavowal of the notion that he is actually making claims about the broader social world. To the contrary, the social world is about to be understood, in the passages that follow in "Our Virtues," as an interplay of male and female physiologically founded perspectives. Certainly, Nietzsche admits his bias, but the same acknowledgment of bias simultaneously positions Nietzsche as a seasoned participant in—and, thus, perhaps, knower of—the world he is about to comment upon.

My broader point about Nietzsche's misogyny is this: there is no textually defensible way to explain it away or mitigate it. Rather than to try to defuse his statements, as often occurs in Nietzsche studies, I follow the thread of Nietzsche's thinking on women in these passages to see where it leads. What Nietzsche has said is the following: woman is constituted in reaction to man. Woman, he says, lives in fear, and her response to man is colored by fear. Woman, like man, is equipped for conflict between the sexes, for their "abyssal antagonism,"[31] but her weapons in this combat are different than those of man: lacking the active power for open combat, she holds back, submits, and manipulates in and through submission. She is, for Nietzsche, the weaker sex.

Throughout BGE 231–239, this picture of woman is delivered in a mostly derisive tone, but, toward the end of 239, Nietzsche pivots—not substantively, but tonally. He writes with apparent admiration that woman "suffers more deeply, is more easily injured, more capable of love … than any other animal."[32, 33] This makes her "nature … more 'natural' than man's."[34] In the *Genealogy*, the strong "activity" of the noble is clearly more "natural" than the at times submissive, at times passive-aggressive "reactivity" of the slave. Here, that appraisal is reversed.[35]

I will argue in the rest of this essay that this revalorization of the feminine represents a major internal correction in Nietzsche's late work and that this reversal is radicalized in the figure of Ariadne.

## Ariadne: The Feminization of Philosophy

I have been trying to show that, while we must acknowledge Nietzsche's misogyny, this does not mean that this is all there is to say about Nietzsche and the sexes. To the contrary, in his last few productive years, Nietzsche makes a female figure, Ariadne, into an emblem for a higher form of humanity. On one level, the choice of Ariadne can be explained in simple terms: Nietzsche declares himself to be the "last disciple and initiate of the god Dionysus,"[36] the god of Becoming. Nietzsche orients his philosophical project around an engagement with Dionysian Becoming:[37]

> Philosophy, in the only way that I will still allow it to hold any validity, as the most general form of history [*Historie*], as the attempt to somehow describe Heraclitian Becoming, and to abbreviate it in signs (to *translate* it, so to speak, into a kind of semblance of Being, to mummify it).[38]

Ariadne, as the human lover of Dionysus in Greek mythology, is accordingly heralded by Nietzsche as the human being who achieves the desired engagement with Dionysian Becoming. It will become clear that, in Nietzsche's thought, the fact that Ariadne is female is critical to our understanding of her success in engaging Dionysus. What is interesting here is that, as we will see, Ariadne's femaleness is defined in the same terms as the femaleness that had been denigrated by Nietzsche in *Beyond Good and Evil*—but this same collection of traits now points to a higher kind of humanity.

How could the constellation of traits understood as femininity by the overbearingly masculinist Nietzsche come to be understood as the pathway to a higher human being? To answer this question, we must observe first that Nietzsche's valorization of masculinity is not nearly as straightforward as a casual reading (or Nietzsche's reputation!) might lead one to believe. When one perceives what a foundational role male sexual possessiveness plays in Nietzsche's story of how Western thought goes wrong, we can begin to see why the emblem for a move against this history of error would be female. *Beyond Good and Evil* famously opens with the question, "Assuming that truth is a woman—what? Is there no justification for the suspicion that all philosophers, insofar as they are dogmatists, understand women poorly?"[39] Philosophers make "eternal demands"[40] on truth and want to possess her permanently, whereas truth does not permit such static, permanent possession.[41] Nietzsche identifies this impulse as beginning with Plato, who, as Heidegger memorably illustrates in his four-year lecture course on Nietzsche, places "Being" over "Becoming" in his hierarchy of reality.[42] The association of the male possessiveness shown by philosophers hitherto with the suppression of Becoming becomes clearer in *Twilight of the Idols*, where Nietzsche says that a "hatred of even the representation of Becoming"[43] is a basic stance of the philosopher. The philosopher seeks a sense of control over reality by congealing Becoming into Being. The "true world," for the philosopher, is a static world of Being, accessible to reason. Becoming is thus controlled, disempowered, *owned*, as it is submitted entirely to a picture of Being that is accessible to the philosopher's "reason"[44] in the form of the "true world." Since Nietzsche goes on to give what seems to be a brief history of the "true world" as the basis of Western thought as a whole in the chapter "How the 'True World' Finally Became a Fable," it may not be too much to say that overweening male possessiveness is itself the basic sickness that grounds Western thinking.

Before Nietzsche focuses increasingly on the figure of Ariadne in 1886, 1887, and, especially, 1888, he had been preoccupied with a different fictional character who had been pitted against the paradigm of the "true world": Zarathustra, whose title work appears in four parts between 1883 and 1885. Zarathustra dramatically declares his intention—in opposition to the philosophers, we might say—to "remain true to the earth."[45] Western philosophy, following Aristotle, had strategically defined the human being as the rational animal. This allowed the philosopher, as the *most* rational animal, to pose as the paragon of the human essence and to assert various versions of the decidedly supra-earthly "true world" as the highest reality, the realm of Being. Nietzsche's philosophy, he tells us repeatedly, will not understand the human being first and foremost as a reasoning entity but as a "physiological" entity. In defiance of the tradition, Nietzschean philosophy-as-physiology will follow the "guiding thread of the body" [*Leitfaden des Leibes*].[46] Zarathustra vociferously endorses the fundamental Nietzschean position that says that the human being is always in the first instance a *Leib*, that the human being *is* only insofar as it is an *embodied* human being. He castigates the "Despisers of the Body," presumably the philosophers,[47] and himself clearly gives the body pride of place over the soul or reason. "[Y]our little reason is an instrument of your body,"[48] he says, implicitly rejecting the Aristotelian view of the human being as ζῷον λόγον ἔχον, *the animal constituted in reason*.

However, if we take a closer look at Nietzsche's understanding of the *Leib* as articulated in his own voice (as opposed to that of Zarathustra), we are forced to come to the conclusion that Zarathustra does not really fully grasp Nietzsche's lesson about what the transition from the soul to the body as the core of the human really means: he does not understand it as a lesson in human finitude. Nietzsche consistently shows the body, as embodied will to power, to be a hierarchy of drives whose power to advance its interests in the world is always finite.[49] It is hard to summarize Nietzsche's conclusions in this regard in a succinct way, but we can try to do so with the help of some other scholars. Nietzsche sees the *Leib* as constituted in *Einverleibung*, incorporation. In order to create a world of which it can make sense, through the process of incorporation, the body necessarily ossifies the becoming world that it finds itself facing into a *being* world, a world with a degree of solidity and perdurance.[50] Its power to do so, however, is always strictly delimited.[51] As Barbara Stiegler puts it, "No human flesh can coincide with the excess of all possibilities"[52]—no human body can truly engage Becoming in its pure flux. Eric Blondel speaks of the "tragic gap" implied in the *zur* of "*Wille zur Macht*":[53] the body's striving after "power" [*Macht*] always involves the project of "stamping Becoming with the character of Being,"[54] but the body's ability to perform this "stamping" is limited. This means that the task of self-empowerment is always an ongoing, incomplete one, as implied by the directionality of the word "*zu*" (in *zur*), the "to" of "will to power." The body is finite; it can never truly "incorporate" Becoming in an immediate, direct, or complete way.[55]

Zarathustra cannot be said to have learned this lesson of human finitude that is embedded in Nietzschean physiology. For Zarathustra, it is not reason, as it was by "the philosophers," but "the will" that aspires to assert itself over the entirety of cosmic Becoming, in the form of the golden ring of the eternal return. Zarathustra's "thus I willed it,"[56] directed toward the entirety of the past and thus the future— toward, therefore, the entirety of cosmic happening—repeats the male hubris of the philosophers in a different guise, indulging in the fantasy of human dominance over all reality. As with "the philosophers," Nietzsche actively and explicitly emphasizes Zarathustra's maleness, especially in his interactions with the women Wisdom, Life, and Eternity.[57] Many scholars have recognized that Zarathustra is not presented by Nietzsche as a perfect character; my intention here is to point out that his imperfection is gendered as male.

We should therefore not be surprised when, after the completion of *Thus Spoke Zarathustra*, Nietzsche turns to a female character as his new figurehead in the quest for a higher engagement with Becoming: Ariadne. Now, to be clear, my intention is not to argue that the mature Nietzsche utterly rejects Zarathustra, whom he is still referring to favorably in *Ecce Homo*, his last full-length work.[58] We can, nevertheless, follow a strain of thought in the Nietzsche corpus whereby, for the reasons described above, the male hubris we might associate not only with Zarathustra but with Nietzschean ideals such as active force or the dominant noble must give way to a stance of comparative humility. This stance of humility acknowledges that the human being is radically and fundamentally finite in the face of Becoming, that Becoming, as the "ultimate truth,"[59] must always remain incomprehensible to us outside the domain in which either human reason or human will hold sway. In the imagery of Becoming that is related to Ariadne, the eternal, Dionysian flux of Becoming is no longer represented as a beautiful, visible golden ring but, instead, as a dark, incomprehensible labyrinth.[60] Dionysus, as a figure who represents Becoming, is now spoken of as an alterity that a human being—even his lover—cannot hope to comprehend: he is the "Concealed One," "Unnamable One" [*Unnennbarer*], and "Unknown One" [*Unbekannter*].[61]

In Ariadne, the human stance toward Becoming endorsed by Nietzsche becomes considerably more fearful and less assertive—on Nietzsche's terms, more feminine. This shift is made nearly explicit in the repurposing, in 1888, of two passages from *Thus Spoke Zarathustra*, such that both passages are now associated in some way with Ariadne. The two passages I am thinking of are "The Night Song," originally appearing in Book II of *Zarathustra* and reappearing in 1888 in *Ecce Homo*'s chapter on *Zarathustra*, and the lament of the sorcerer in Book IV, which comes back as "Ariadne's Complaint." In both pairs of passages, a fictional character is speaking for the duration of the passage. My argument here is that, in the shifting framing of the two passages from the *Zarathustra* years (1883–1885) to 1888, we can see a reappraisal of Zarathustra's attempt to will his way into a positive relationship with cosmic flux. In both cases, this reappraisal is executed subtly and employs the insertion of the figure of Ariadne. "The Night Song" is sung by Zarathustra himself in Book II of *Thus Spoke Zarathustra*. He tells us that he gives abundantly, out of an excess of wealth. There is no question in the mind of any reader of *Zarathustra*, I think, that the title character is an imperfect, and decidedly human, individual. Yet, having reprinted this song in 1888, Nietzsche comments upon the painful excess of wealth spoken of in the song by saying, "this is the way *a god*, a Dionysus, suffers" (emphasis mine).[62] He names Ariadne as the one who would be the "answer" to such suffering.[63] It is easy to miss the fact that an important change has taken place: the fundamentally active position of needing to "give" out of a kind of radical excess has been taken from the merely human Zarathustra and given to a god, Dionysus. Furthermore, the comparatively passive position of receiving the overabundant gift has been given to a new specific, valorized individual: Ariadne. This merely forecasts a dynamic that becomes much more explicit in the other *Zarathustra* passage that gets a cast change in 1888, the sorcerer's speech, which becomes "Ariadne's Complaint" in the *Dionysus-Dithyrambs*. With more emphasis this time, the identity of the speaker changes from *Zarathustra* to the *Dithyrambs*, as the sorcerer is originally the speaker, but then disappears entirely from the equation in 1888, when the speech becomes an apostrophic address to Dionysus delivered by Ariadne. In this speech, the speaker assumes a relatively passive position in relation to an unseen deity, who only becomes explicitly identified as Dionysus in the 1888 reprinting. In the original version in *Thus Spoke Zarathustra*, Zarathustra immediately greets this position, so at odds with his aspirations of an unharnessed will, with scorn.[64] In the 1888 version, however, where Ariadne is the speaker and assumes the exact same stance as did the sorcerer, her speech triggers a five-line response from Dionysus,[65] confirming her status as his lover (this is the only difference between the *Zarathustra* version of this song and the 1888 version, besides the title, which is what makes clear that Ariadne is the one speaking in 1888). Using a flurry of images of penetration, she asks the god to "plunge deeper / Plunge one more time"[66] with the "cruel barb" of his love,[67] to "puncture, shatter my heart!"[68] She invites Dionysus to "torment" her and describes his assault upon her with "icy frost-arrows"[69] or, in a different moment, with "blunt arrows."[70] The reader is given the vague sense that Ariadne may be bound to a spot, given the fact that she makes no attempt to go to Dionysus herself, even when she reports that he is close enough to hear her breathe.[71] Finally, when Ariadne begs Dionysus one last time to come to her, calling him "my *pain*! / my last happiness!"[72] he arrives and delivers a short response, which ends with "*I am your labyrinth* …" [*Ich bin dein Labyrinth* …].[73]

In contrast to philosophy's attempt to dominate Becoming with reason, and in contrast to Zarathustra's attempt to dominate Becoming with the power of his will, here we have a picture of a human orientation toward Becoming that assumes that it will always, ultimately, be at the mercy of Becoming. Ariadne's stance is not one of *total* passivity—her tone, as we can see above in the imperative voice she uses with Dionysus, can be combative. But it is a stance that does not intend to attempt to overpower that which cannot be overpowered. Fundamentally, it is a stance of receptivity. If, for Nietzsche, Becoming is fate, and *amor fati* is the love of fate,[74] then loving fate-as-Becoming, as only Ariadne succeeds in doing, means accepting it as our "labyrinth," as the inescapable and incomprehensible. This means a renunciation of the masculine dream of control that animated both philosophy before Nietzsche and Nietzsche's own fictional character, Zarathustra.

At this point, the importance of confronting and really *reading* Nietzsche's misogynist reading of "woman" becomes clear. Ariadne, who, near the end of *Beyond Good and Evil*, is explicitly designated as the sort of human being whom Dionysus could love,[75] is a move beyond Zarathustra precisely in her embodiment of the feminine traits scorned by Nietzsche in the earlier chapter "Our Virtues," which we discussed above. Ariadne is resigned to the superior power of Dionysus yet orients her existence toward him. Inheriting "woman's" tendency toward injury, she is constantly injured by Dionysus and asks to be injured again. In "Ariadne's Complaint," it might not be too much to say that Ariadne's orientation toward Dionysus is one of *fear*—from the beginning to the end of that poem, she exhibits a paranoia regarding the proximity of the unseen, powerful god. Fear, remember, is the defining characteristic of woman in the "Our Virtues" passages on the sexes. Ariadne is woman but radically revalorized.

It must be emphasized that Ariadne is not merely a recurrent literary figure sporadically used to personify a certain ideal. Her first substantive appearance in Nietzsche's published works occurs at BGE 295, most famous as the passage in which Dionysus returns after a long absence after *The Birth of Tragedy*.[76] It is here that Nietzsche memorably declares himself to be "the last disciple and initiate of the god Dionysus."[77] In ancient Greece, Dionysian religiosity was often associated with women,[78] as Nietzsche the philologist must have known, so this phrase might be taken as an oblique association of Nietzsche's philosophical self with the feminine. This oblique association becomes far more direct in the closing part of the section. Dionysus, represented here as speaking directly to Nietzsche, acknowledges Ariadne as the kind of human being whom he could love. Then he names the ability to find one's way around any labyrinth as the quality specific to this lovable sort of human being.[79] This statement appears, of course, to refer back to Ariadne, whose ball of thread helps Theseus find his way out of the labyrinth. Surprisingly, though, Nietzsche then reports having seen a smile on the god's face, "as if he had just given *me* a charming compliment."[80] Clearly, this compliment would most naturally belong to Ariadne, yet Nietzsche says it is given to him. Here again, Ariadne's importance is not exactly trumpeted by the Nietzsche text, but it is indisputable once we see what is going on here: Nietzsche is associating himself with Ariadne. In this passage, they appear to collapse in on each other.

This one, limited moment in the text in which Nietzsche associates himself with Ariadne can become a key with which to understand much of Nietzsche's later thought if we are willing to consider an 1885 note in which Ariadne makes an appearance.[81] In that note, Nietzsche associates the *Leitfaden*, the guiding thread, from his motto "Follow the guiding thread of the body," with Ariadne's *Faden*, the thread with which Ariadne endures the labyrinth.[82,83]

The fact that Nietzsche tells us to associate Ariadne with the "guiding thread of the body" elucidates her stance of relative submission to Becoming, as opposed to Zarathustra's "masculine" attempt to dominate Becoming. As I pointed out earlier when discussing Zarathustra's shortcomings, Nietzschean physiology illuminates the necessarily finite body's limited power to face Becoming, to engage Dionysus, who represents a power who will always outstrip human power. Human finitude is revealed by the philosophy that follows the guiding thread of the body. This philosophy examines and exposes human physiology's inability to incorporate or engage the radical Dionysian flux, which always must remain beyond the limits of human comprehension. Ariadne's acknowledgment of Dionysus as the dominant partner in their love affair is indicative of a certain covert humility in Nietzsche's philosophy of the guiding thread: the guiding thread does not claim for itself the possibility of comprehending all reality. We can thus see, in Nietzsche's thought, a tendency toward a break with the male hubris that has dominated Western thought, the hubris of metaphysics, which wants, Nietzsche tells us, to grasp all reality via a static, rational picture of Being. In this way, I think it is right to speak of a "feminization of philosophy" in Nietzsche to slightly alter the phrasing of Sigridur Thorgeirsdottir, who has written about a "feminization of metaphysics" in Nietzsche. As Thorgeirsdottir says, this "feminization" is executed by orienting philosophy toward "the body and the earth."[84] The philosophy of the future, as a higher form of thought belonging to a higher human being, will be, on Nietzsche's own terms, a more feminine form of thought.

It may be, though, that it is not only a *higher* humanity but also humanity generally that gets "feminized" in Nietzsche's philosophy-as-physiology. The terms in which we have traced Nietzsche's engagement with "the feminine" and "the masculine" up to this point are certainly, in a certain sense, conservative. What I mean by this is that the classic Aristotelian association of the feminine with the passional and the fleshly, and of the masculine with the rational and ideal, does not undergo a sustained challenge in Nietzsche's thinking. Yet Nietzsche unambiguously insists that it is the passional and the fleshly—the will to power as studied by physiology—that constitutes the human being. In other words, the allegedly feminine side of the human is treated as basic or paradigmatic.

## Conclusion: Nietzsche and Misogyny

Nietzsche's misogyny cannot be explained away—nor should it. It is only by attending to Nietzsche's understanding of woman as reactive, weak, and fragile, as articulated in his notoriously misogynist passages, that we understand the dynamics of the femininity that surprisingly become associated with Nietzsche's own philosophy in the figure of Ariadne. In the guise of Ariadne, this same femininity is celebrated. At this point, however, a disclaimer is in order. It bears repeating that Nietzsche never finally and unambiguously rejects Zarathustra and that it is extremely doubtful that Nietzsche himself would ever describe his project as a "feminization of philosophy." I have been following a line of thought in Nietzsche's thinking that is not consistently maintained, a line of thought that puts some strain on other tendencies that never fade away in Nietzsche's thinking. I do not think that the Nietzsche of the swashbuckling active will—the *male* active will, we might say—ever goes away. I do believe, however, that Nietzsche's "feminized" philosophy stands in easier relationship to his picture of the human being as necessarily finite, embodied will to power, than do his more masculinist visions that celebrate "noble" action, aggression, and uncompromised self-assertion.

In twentieth-century Continental philosophy Nietzsche is frequently invoked in connection with that century's preoccupation with the project of "overcoming" or "surpassing" metaphysics. The exact path by which Nietzsche seeks to "overcome" metaphysics is understood differently by different twentieth-century philosophers. For Heidegger, the Nietzschean body wants to "incorporate" the entirety of the cosmos, in a grandiose gesture of self-empowerment, taking the helm of the sensual world in the act of willing representation.[85] For French deconstructionists, Nietzsche rejects the hegemonic unity of metaphysical visions of Being and instead celebrates the play of active forces that affirm and celebrate the uniqueness, the "difference," of their own perspective. What these readings of Nietzsche have in common is their disregard for the fact that Nietzsche speaks clearly and enduring about the *limitations* not only of the human being but of the organic, of life, in general—something that is taken into account by neither of these visions of unfettered empowerment. The surpassing of metaphysics will not, then, be any kind of power play but, to the contrary, will be a recognition of the absolutely delimited horizons of our thought. Ariadne, as the last emblem of Nietzsche's philosophy, reflects this sobriety. Dionysian Becoming, as the highest reality, is an alterity that we can love, but not one we can comprehend, not one that we can subdue with reason. To believe otherwise would be to participate in the "history of error"[86] that is the course of male Western metaphysics—a history which Nietzsche wishes to overcome.

## Notes

1. Butler (1990: 28).
2. Nietzsche exclaims in the *On the Genealogy of Morals*, "How much blood and horror is at the bottom of all 'good things'!" GM II 3; KSA 5:297.
3. Raymond Geuss has done a good job of explaining how it tends to be the case, in Nietzschean genealogy, that showing a practice or belief to have multiple origins, instead of just one, tends to go hand in hand with the devalorization of that practice or belief. See Geuss (2002, 1994).
4. Foucault (1977: 142).
5. See BGE P; KSA 5:11–13.
6. I am borrowing the phrasing here of Sigridur Thorgeirsdottir, who speaks compellingly of a "feminization of metaphysics" in Nietzsche. See Thorgeirsdottir (2004: 51–68).
7. KSA 5:173.
8. KSA 5:174.
9. KSA 5:174.
10. KSA 5:175.
11. KSA 5:176.
12. KSA 5:176.
13. Gilles Deleuze, who popularizes the strong emphasis on Nietzsche's terms "active" and "reactive," clearly positions the notion of "active force," which always celebrates its own difference with its other, as an idea with an implicit bias against hegemonic power that would suppress, vanquish, or consume its other. In response to this political reading of Nietzsche it should be noted, however, that it is precisely politically disempowered parties, such as women and slaves, who are repeatedly associated *not* with active force but with reactivity. See Deleuze (1983), and GM II 11–12 (KSA 5:309–16) for Nietzsche's introduction of the concepts of active and reactive force.
14. KSA 5:176.
15. KSA 5:176.
16. Lemm (2020, 149).
17. Lemm (2020, 159).
18. Kofman (1995: 180).
19. KSA 5:177.
20. Williams (1993: 4).
21. Derrida (1979: 101).
22. KSA 5:170.
23. In German, it is clearer than it is in English that "*Weib an sich*" is a play on "*Ding an sich*," Kant's thing in itself.
24. KSA 5:170.
25. Clark (1998: 191).
26. We can add to the list Sarah Kofman, discussed above, who, like Clark, emphasizes the phrase "*Weib an sich*," using it to come to the emphatic conclusion that Nietzsche is not a misogynist: "to consider Nietzsche a misogynist is to forget what he always emphasizes: [...] there is no woman 'as such'" (Kofman, "The Psychologist of the Eternal Feminine," 189). Acampora and Ansell-Pearson provide another example, mostly focusing on the phrase "my truths," as does Derrida. They say that this phrase

reveals the misogynist statements that follow to be "assumptions, presuppositions, prejudices" (Acampora and Ansell-Pearson 2011: 168).
27 KSA 5:19 (*Beyond Good and Evil*).
28 Or, alternatively, it would reduce the entirety of Nietzsche's thought to a single, endlessly repeating meditation on the dissolution of propositional meaning. This is something like the conclusion of Paul de Man, who claims that in "the general structure of [Nietzsche's] work" we find an "endlessly repeated gesture" whereby "philosophical rigor" is reduced to the act of an "artist 'who does not learn from experience and always again falls in the same trap'" (de Man 1979: 118).
29 KSA 5:170.
30 KSA 5:170.
31 KSA 5:175.
32 KSA 5:178.
33 The word "animal," it should be noted, carries largely positive connotations for Nietzsche. Lemm's book *Nietzsche's Animal Philosophy* discusses how "animality engenders culture … how animal life becomes the source of creativity" (Lemm 2009: 154). Reading this *Beyond Good and Evil* passage in *Homo Natura*, she speaks, rightly, of "woman as nature or naturalness threatened by male civilization" (Lemm 2020: 145).
34 KSA 5:178.
35 I am aware that the *Genealogy* is written after *Beyond Good and Evil*, meaning that the "naturalness" of reactivity, if we can call it that, as it manifests itself in the passages on woman, is not a position that consistently endures in Nietzsche's thought. As I will acknowledge below, my stance is not that the shift I am tracing in Nietzsche's thought on women leads us to Nietzsche's "final position," but that it reflects a tendency that repeatedly threatens to complicate Nietzsche's masculinist outlook as it manifests itself elsewhere.
36 KSA 5:238.
37 For an excellent articulation of Nietzsche's relationship to Becoming, see Dries (2008a, 2008b).
38 KSA 11:562 1885 36[27].
39 KSA 5:11.
40 KSA 5:12.
41 Robert Pippin's 2001 essay on philosophers as "clumsy lovers" in Nietzsche illustrates the extent to which this possessiveness with regard to truth is erotic in nature. Pippin points out that the idea that philosophy begins in erotic desire is a notion that Nietzsche is taking from Plato, most notably the *Symposium*. He observes that the theme of exaggerated possessiveness is a recurring one in *Beyond Good and Evil* (Pippin 2001: 90–1) that is not limited to the preface. I find Pippin's observations there quite right, but I would add that the gendering of this possessive desire is important—the "clumsiness" and greediness of philosophers are that of a specifically male heterosexual desire.
42 Heidegger's 1936–1940 lectures on Nietzsche can be found in the *Gesamtausgabe* 6.1 and 6.2 (Collected Works).
43 KSA 6:74.
44 In this context I am following Nietzsche in placing "reason" in quotation marks: clearly Nietzsche questions whether this basic approach to understanding reality deserves the title of "reason."
45 KSA 4:15.

46  For exemplary uses of this phrase, see *Nachlass* 1885, 37[4], KSA 11:577–8 and *Nachlass* 1884, 27[27], KSA 11:282.
47  KSA 4:39–41.
48  KSA 4:39.
49  On the finitude of the body in Nietzsche, see my forthcoming article in *Nietzsche-Studien*, "The Body and the Completion of Metaphysics: A Critical Analysis of Heidegger's Nietzsche."
50  Although, like most scholars today, I have great reservations about many aspects of Heidegger's reading of Nietzsche, this particular aspect of the dynamics of *Einverleibung* is addressed well, I think, in Heidegger's lecture course *The Will to Power as Knowledge*: see especially lecture sessions 11–13 (Martin Heidegger, *Der Wille zur Macht als Erkenntnis*. In *Gesamtausgabe* 6.1, 496–519). William McNeill's excellent analysis of these sections is germane here for its lucid positioning of the Nietzschean body (on the Heideggerian reading) in terms of Becoming and Being. He writes of the body as a process of "individuation arising out of the very midst of chaos," where I take "chaos" to be equivalent to "Becoming" (McNeill 2006: 159).
51  For indications of the body's necessarily limited power of incorporation, see *Nachlass* 1881, 11[134], KSA 9:490; *Nachlass* 1886–1887, 7[25], KSA 12:304; *Nachlass* 1885 40[7], KSA 11:631.
52  Stiegler (2005: 163).
53  Blondel (1991: 47).
54  *Nachlass* 1886/1887 7[54], KSA 12:312 (*Will to Power* §617).
55  This point is driven home in numerous places. Nietzsche says in the *Nachlass*, for instance, that "the ultimate truth [*die letzte Wahrheit*] of the flow of things does not tolerate *incorporation*; our *organs* (in order to live) are configured for error" (*Nachlass* 1881, 11[162], KSA 9:504). More well-known is the passage of the *Gay Science* in which Nietzsche asks, "To what extent does truth tolerate incorporation [*Einverleibung*]?—that is the question" (GS 110, KSA 3:471).
56  KSA 4:181.
57  The idea that Zarathustra exemplifies a stereotypically male hubris for which the text implicitly takes him to task is by no means my original observation, and it is a point that has been made in greater textual detail than we can go into here. T. K. Seung, for instance, observes of Zarathustra's interaction with the woman Life: "Zarathustra confronts life with power, first as a hunter and then with a whip. But he gets nowhere. He wants to control and dominate her" (Seung 2005: 210). Henry Staten similarly observes of this scene that it "clearly undercuts the blustering ideology of male dominance that the whip symbolizes" (Staten 1993: 172).
58  Jean-Luc Marion and Barbara Stiegler have already made the claim that Ariadne serves as a kind of replacement for Zarathustra. Their reasons for doing so do not follow the thread of gender the way that I do in this essay. I also wish to stake out a degree of distance between my reading and their readings by acknowledging that, for me, this transition from Zarathustra to Ariadne is never firm, decided, and final. See Marion 2001, and Stiegler 2005.
59  *Nachlass* 1881, 11[162], KSA 9:504.
60  From the poem "Ariadne's Complaint," KSA 6:401, l. 25.
61  KSA 6:398, 399.
62  KSA 6:348.
63  EH, KSA 6:348.
64  KSA 4:319.

65  KSA 6:401, ll. 21–5.
66  KSA 6:398, ll. 20–1.
67  KSA 6:400, ll. 2–5.
68  KSA 6:398, l. 22.
69  KSA 6:398, l. 8.
70  KSA 6:399, l. 1.
71  KSA 6:399, ll. 14–16.
72  KSA 6:401, ll. 17–18.
73  KSA 6:401, l. 25. The ellipsis is in the original and ends the poem as a whole.
74  GS; KSA 3:521.
75  KSA 5:239.
76  Strictly speaking, it is not the first time she appears in the published works, as her name completes a turn of phrase in UM I, wherein Nietzsche exclaims that he cannot find the "thread of Ariadne" in Strauss's insufferably labyrinthine prose (KSA 1:234).
77  KSA 5:238.
78  Silk and Stern (1983: 181).
79  KSA 5:239.
80  KSA 5:239. Emphasis mine.
81  *Nachlass*, 1885 37[4], KSA 11:576–9.
82  Stiegler (2005) comments at length upon the association of Ariadne and the body.
83  Nietzsche's imagery regarding Ariadne and the "Dionysian" labyrinth is often elliptical with regard to the actual Greek myth, as it usually excludes Theseus. In the conventional telling of the story involving the thread, Ariadne helps Theseus out of the labyrinth.
84  Thorgeirsdottir (2004: 61).
85  See, for instance, Heidegger, *Gesamtausgabe* 6.1, 295.
86  From the subtitle of the history of Western thought called "How the 'True World' Finally Became a Fable," referenced above: "History of an Error" (KSA 6:81).

# 7

# Nietzsche and Shaktism

Shruti Jain

## Introduction

Goddess spirituality, "the reverential experiencing and expressing of divine female energies within the universe," has been known to mankind since the Paleolithic age (Keller 2014: 729f.). *Shaktism*, a form of Goddess spirituality that developed in India, in its great as well as the little traditions, speaks of the worship of the Mother Goddess principally as a procreative power and nurturer. From the exalted *Durga* or *Kali* to the ubiquitous *gram devi* (village deity), she is present to this day all over the country in her myriads of forms. Although the tradition of the Mother Goddess in India can be traced back to the Indus Valley civilization, it was during the latter half of the nineteenth century and the beginning of the twentieth century, especially during the Indian Independence struggle, that the Mother Goddess was invoked with great fervor by modern Indian poets and thinkers. During the nationalist struggle, the metaphor of the Mother was often used for the Nation in order to arouse nationalistic sentiments among the "sons of the nation" to free the Mother from the British colonizers. *Shakti* as a political ideal of *swadeshi* was fed by the literary experiments of Bankim Chandra Chattopadhyay and the Kali cult of Sri Ramakrishna and popularized by Swami Vivekananda and Sister Nivedita (see Bagchi 2017: 51–79).

Interestingly, it was during this time that Nietzsche's teachings were being interpreted as being essentially the worship of Shakti. In his book titled *India and Its Faiths* published in 1915, James Bissett Pratt, in his unique style of using anecdotal information from his travel experiences, writes: "When Mazoomdar returned from a visit in Europe he told Ramakrishna—the devout worshiper [sic] of Kali—that the philosophers of Europe were not atheists, since they believed in an 'Eternal Energy— an unknown Power behind the Universe'—[...] And a recent writer in the 'Prabuddha Bharata' interprets the teaching of Nietzsche as being essentially the worship of Shakti" (Pratt 2005: 62).[1] In the 1915 January issue of the magazine *Prabuddha Bharata*,[2] there is indeed an article on "The Philosophy of Nietzsche," which clearly states: "The quintessence of Nietzscheism is the worship of Shakti."[3] The writer however adds that Nietzsche was "a poor worshipper at the altar of Power" (ibid.).

Can Nietzsche's philosophy possibly be understood in terms of the Shakti philosophy? Shaktism as a way of life predates Nietzsche by centuries and nowhere in his entire *oeuvre* does he mention the term "Shakti." But there do exist many parallels between Nietzsche's philosophy and Shaktism. I examine these similarities to help explain the response to his thought in India and to explicate some important connections between deities in the ancient Hindu and Greek pantheons, the latter of which strongly influenced him. The latter illuminates some of the underappreciated ways in which Nietzsche's appeals to and creative employment of mythic themes in his thinking contain echoes of ancient Indian ones. Finally, I consider the relevance of all this to the place of women and the feminine in his philosophy.

## Sacredness versus Demythologization

Mythological narratives about goddesses play a crucial role in Shaktism. They are an inherent part of the sacred traditions and have hidden meanings of yogic significance. Packed with sacred symbolism, various intriguing plots—depicting the Goddess and her battles with *asuras* to help alleviate crisis and her more human-like qualities of wife, mother, and daughter—are presented in texts like the *Devi Mahatmaya* or the *Srimad Devi Bhagvatam*, among many others. These invite readers to participate in a dialogue with the texts, see beyond the veils of the plot, and "learn" from the life of the Goddess. Parallel to the stringent rules of worship to the Goddess, the practice of Shaktism (especially the Bhakti-Shakta-tradition introduced by Sri Ramakrishna) also constitutes of a tradition of "Devi-in-everydayness" (Mukhopadhyay 2019: 49). Within this tradition, Devi becomes the friend and guide of the *sadhaka*, inspires and listens to the devotional songs composed by the spiritual aspirant, makes her devotee a poet/singer, in effect synchronizing the song with the flow of everydayness, thus "turning mundane life into life divine" (Mukhopadhyay 2019: 52).

Nietzsche made both explicit and implicit use of mythology in his philosophical explications. His endeavor to introduce classical Greek mythology[4] into his philosophy should be seen as an effort to counter the over-valorization of science and of historiography in modern Europe. According to him, "the enormous historical need of dissatisfied modern culture" emanated from "the loss of myth, the loss of a mythical home, a mythical, maternal womb" (BT 23). He states: "Without myth […] all cultures lose their healthy, creative, natural energy; only a horizon surrounded by myths encloses and unifies a cultural movement" (ibid.). Authentic cultural rejuvenation, according to Nietzsche, occurs only through a critical appreciation of the myth based on an interpretative participation in its symbolism that leads to the activation of the subject. The activation of the subject and its assertion of power can be achieved through what Paul Ricoeur describes as a process of *demythologization* (Ricoeur 1967: 162). The process of demythologization involves not only destruction but also reinterpretation (Malan 2016: 5). The reinterpretation of a myth or myth making is an exercise in epistemology. It consists of displacing the existing language-meaning-constellations and retelling of the myth which not only involves applying the myth to the immediate socio-historical context of the subject but also may incorporate its traditional meanings that were misunderstood or forgotten with the passage of time. Nietzsche makes surplus use of women figures from Greek classical mythology as a substrate for his own philosophizing. Through his intertextual experimentation with the Eleusinian mysteries and other works of classical antiquity, he pulls the Greek goddesses from their sacred pedestals into the realm of the secular.

## Gender Essentialism versus Anti-essentialism

In the Rig Veda (1700–1100 BC), there are references to female deities such as Prithvi (the goddess of Earth) or Usha (the goddess of dawn) among many others who are personifications of nature, but the Mother Goddess is essentially ungendered. Her name is Aditi. She is the sky, the mid-air; She is all gods. She is the Mother, the Father, and Son; Aditi is whatever shall be born (Book 1, Hymn 89, Verse 10).[5] However, by the Puranic times (350–750 CE), Shaktism came to exclusively attribute the female gender to the Goddess. Paramount importance was given to the body of the primordial Mother Goddess. There are in fact fifty-one *Shaktipithas* in India, which according to popular belief came into existence when Sati's dead body was cut by Vishnu into fifty-one parts that fell on Earth (see Singh 2020). Each *Shaktipitha* is a center of power which is believed to alleviate the suffering of devotees and to bring about a spiritual transformation in them. By virtue of their common feminine nature, women are in some contexts regarded as special manifestations of the Goddess, sharing in her powers. Thus, the Goddess is viewed as a mythic model for Hindu women. "There is evidence to suggest that Shakta traditions tend to be more inclusive of women as practitioners and more accepting of women as leaders or gurus than do Vaishnava or Shaiva traditions" (Erndl 2000: 93). A prominent example of a woman saint is Anandamayi Ma. "In Tantric circles, women gurus are also commonplace. A famous example is the Tantric holy woman called the *Bhairavi* who was for a time Ramakrishna's guru. The fact that holy women or women gurus can exist at all in male-dominated Hindu society is due to the divine model of femaleness which the Goddess provides" (Erndl 2000: 94). Nevertheless, some feminists and scholars of religion have argued that the existence of the Hindu Goddess has not appeared outwardly to have benefitted women's position in Indian society (Erndl 2000: 11), with good reason. Indian women continue to face gender-based violence even today. Female infanticide, resistance to educate the girl child, gender discrimination at the workplace, domestic violence, and sexual abuse—all of these are real-life issues that women in India combat till date and which a mere veneration of the Goddess can hardly address. What is needed is an *actio in distans*, which Nietzsche proposes through his anti-essentialism.

Nietzsche sees through the problem of essentializing woman and strikes at the root of the problem. Firstly, he separates Nature from its perceived femininity and substitutes it with the Dionysian chaos (BT 16). This complies with Nietzsche's critique of the myth of *das Ewig Weibliche*. In *Ecce Homo*, Nietzsche calls himself "the first psychologist of the eternal feminine" (EH Books, 5). The eternal feminine is according to Nietzsche a male construct that creates woman in man's image to suit his patriarchal aspirations. "Woman, the eternally feminine: a merely imaginary value in which only man believes."[6] One is reminded of Nietzsche's poem "To Goethe" from *The Gay Science*.[7] Goethe, at the end of Faust II, promises redemption for the erring Faust in the eternal feminine that draws him upward on the moral and spiritual path (Goethe 1984: 305). Nietzsche reacts critically toward this proposition. Through his poem, he draws attention to the underside of mystifying feminine attributes. The imperishable, the absolute, the permanent, he writes, is not true but only a "simile." God is the awkward trickery of a poet. By doing so, Nietzsche rejects any promise of salvation. In order to disenchant, Nietzsche replaces the words "eternal feminine" with "eternal fool" and debunks the theory of the ascent of the soul replacing it with frightening imagery of an eternal fool in two forms—one that is a rolling world wheel, mixing being and appearance, and the other that is a cauldron mixing all of us in it, not out of any moral obligation but simply as random play.

In his later writings too, Nietzsche continues to debunk the idea of the eternal feminine as something profound and mystical and brings it down to the realm of society and real feminist issues. As a self-proclaimed psychologist of the eternal feminine, Nietzsche equates the eternal feminine, not with a mythical Goddess as was the case in Faust II but with "idealism" or, as he puts it, with "anti-nature" (EH Books 5), which is a result of wanting to "copy all the stupidities that the 'man' in Europe, that European 'manliness' suffers from" (BGE 239). In this way, emancipated women, "whose bottom-most instinct is revenge" (EH Books 5), had fallen prey to slave morality by devaluing what men, the so-called masters, valued. Nietzsche also relates the idea of the eternal feminine with the "[w]oman as such" (ibid.)—which is, according to him, just another fabricated ideal generated by the reactive "eternal *war* between the sexes" (ibid.).

Nietzsche's idea of revaluation of the notions of "[w]oman as such" and the eternal feminine hence leads to their double semantic displacement. The first displacement occurs when Nietzsche critiques the traditional understanding of the Eternal Feminine—thereby opening a way for women who are entrapped in the sexed discourses of dilution, manipulation, and control of women's identities by patriarchy. Similarly, while he deconstructs the eternal feminine, he also equates woman with life and life's teachings. "Yes, life is a woman!" (GS 339), thus freeing women from the confinement of gender essentialism and compelling his readers to find newer ways of penetrating the veils of the myth of the eternal feminine that has been passed down to them.

## Metaphysical Pluralism versus Anti-metaphysical Perspectivism

The philosophy of Shaktism has a non-dualist metaphysical foundation; however, there is an underlying pluralism that is characteristic of Shaktism. Shakti, the formless source of everything, is understood to take forms—as goddesses, personifications of the different energies that make up the multiple dimensions of existence and of our own consciousness (Kempton 2013: 7).

Nietzsche's thought is non-dualistic too, but he rejects the existence of an absolute consciousness. Unlike Shaktism, there is no place for a formless, transcendent, metaphysical objective truth in the Nietzschean scheme of thought. He set out to find the answer to how to maintain, in Sloterdijk's words, "the vertical tension" if the higher region has been removed (Sloterdijk 2013: 39). After announcing the death of the Christian God, and with that the denial of hope and other worldly salvation, he devotes most of his thought to the world of appearances or to life. But while doing so, he heavily relies on gods and goddesses from Greek mythology and treats them not as divine entities but as forces that drive human life. Like Shaktism, Nietzsche too endorses an "aesthetics of everydayness" (see Mukhopadhyay 2019)—the difference being, that Nietzsche only strives toward a meaningful life and certainly not a "life divine." According to Nietzsche, "the main thing in life is to take the minor things seriously" (Sloterdijk 2013: 39).

In addition to its metaphysical foundation, Shaktism is characterized by a distinct epistemological pluralism. In Shaktism, every goddess is a source of knowledge. It "is not the intention of the Tantra to limit the capacity of the individual to a particular realisation however perfect it may be [...] the seeker can aspire for an integral knowledge, and he may, depending on his capacity, come nearer the Total Divine, by having as many realisations as he can" (see Shankaranarayanan 2002: 7f). This epistemological pluralism of Shaktism partially resonates with Nietzsche's perspectivism.

To undermine the traditional perception of absolute knowledge and to overcome the epistemological nihilism caused by it, Nietzsche introduces the concept of perspectival knowledge. For Nietzsche, any knowledge is embedded in "the affects and values of the audience—it positions them to notice, find salient, and be disposed to act in relation to certain (aspects of) things while ignoring, finding less salient, and being disposed to neglect (aspects of) other things" (Alfano 2019b: 127). Hence the greater the number of perspectives, the closer toward completeness would be our knowledge. "There is *only* a perspectival seeing, *only* a perspectival 'knowing'; and *the more* affects we allow to speak about a matter, *the more* eyes, different eyes, we know how to bring to bear on one and the same matter, that much more complete will our 'concept' of this matter, our 'objectivity', be" (GM III 12). One is reminded at this point of the iconography of the *Goddess Shatakshi*—the goddess with innumerable eyes—eyes that incessantly shed tears for nine days creating rivers that renourished the world undergoing a calamity caused by the usurping of the knowledge of the Vedas by the demon *Durgamasur* (Srimad Devi-Bhagavatam, Book 7, Chapter 28).[8] Could the rejuvenation of the earth by the tears from the innumerable eyes of Shatakshi Devi possibly be interpreted as a Nietzschean perspectivist response to epistemological nihilism (knowledge becoming *durgam* (inaccessible, abstruse)?

## *Mayashakti* and Nietzsche's Dionysiac Power of Art

According to the Vedanta, the supreme consciousness manifests itself into many and creates an illusion of Maya. The world of appearances or of Maya is compared to the dream world. Just as the dream world disappears when one awakens, so is the world of appearances also unreal or false (Shastri 1911: 87ff.). Instead of treating *Maya* or the phenomenal world of becoming as illusion, Shaktism treats *Maya* as *Mayashakti*, as an immanent creative operational force of the Absolute consciousness. Hence, a Shakta acknowledges Maya as true, sees it as an inseparable part of the Supreme consciousness, and steers the *sadhana* through its many layers (see Woodroffe 2009: 276). Interestingly, in Nietzsche's view too, "the Dionysiac shows itself, […] to be the eternal and original power of art which summons the entire world of appearances into existence" (BT 25). The Dionysiac power of art resonates greatly with the notion of *Mayashakti*. Nietzsche does not treat the world of appearances as an unreal separate entity; rather he summons the Dionysiac power of art to critique the wrongs in this world of appearances.

An important technique in Shaktism is the technique of *Jivanyasa* (infusion). In this technique, "the sadhaka infuses his body with the life of the Devi, the Mother of All" (Woodroffe 2009: 517). The *mantras* that are chanted during the sadhana are physical descriptions of the Goddesses. Through the repetition of the sounds and the focus on the Yantra, the infusion is achieved. Whether looking inward in meditation or gazing outward upon the world, the fully realized *sadhaka* sees the same thing: the blissful projection of the Self—as—Goddess. This radical bifocal vision, born of sadhana, confirms that the Sakta universe is the holographic projection of the Goddess's I-consciousness (Lidke 2017: 30).

In his seminal commentary on Heidegger's Reading of Nietzsche, *Spurs*, Derrida writes, "He [Nietzsche] is the thinker of pregnancy which, for him, is no less praiseworthy in a man than it is in a woman" (Derrida 1979: 65). In a similar vein, David Farell Krell argues in *Postponements* that to write without dogmatism, Nietzsche found himself "writing with the other hand," the hand of woman, who is just veils and style (Krell 1986: 10). Nietzsche himself writes: "As my father, I am dead, as my mother, I am still alive and growing old" (EH Wise 1). One might be tempted to draw a direct parallel between Nietzsche's style of writing and the Shakti path of infusion. As a "contemplative type" Nietzsche does need to work toward becoming a "male mother"; still, the "spiritual pregnancy" that his contemplative disposition indicates is an important motif in his writings (GS 72). It is vital to understand that there is a basic difference regarding the imbibing of the Goddess. Whereas in Shaktism there is a set pattern of rituals that are prescribed for the *sadhaka*, Nietzsche strives to give a psychological meaning to the female deities who he possibly emulates. In doing so, he unveils various archetypes, creates interesting topoi from the Eleusinian Mysteries, and deals with them artistically. The archetype of the old woman for instance seems to have inspired him on several occasions.

There are traces of Hecate in the old woman who suggests to Zarathustra: "You go to women? Do not forget the whip!" (Z 1 On Little Women). In making her utter these words, Nietzsche intends to provoke. The whip evokes fear; it threatens. But looking at the iconography of Hecate (see Weber 2021: 29f.) one learns that the whip/rope of Hecate traditionally "symbolizes the umbilical cord or represents her role of bringing souls into the underworld and helping them to be reborn" (Reichard 2011: 170). Could Nietzsche have been misunderstood as being a misogynist? Closely related to Hecate is the figure of Baubo (GS P 4) who is also an old woman and takes a comical crouched position, showed the despairing Demeter her genitalia to make her laugh. "Besides mythic connections, Baubo's crouching position clearly referred to delivery and underlined the generative power of the feminine" (Autiero 2014: 93). A similar posture is seen in the statues of the ancient Goddess Lajja Gauri, who is equated with Aditi, the Mother of the Universe. Here the Goddess is seen in *uttanapad*—a "birth position" where "the broadly spread-out legs are drawn up laterally and bent at the knees. The soles of the feet are turned upward. Their modelling and the contraction of the toes show the tension and struggle which attend the process of giving birth" (Kramrisch 1956: 1). This is a yogic position and a bodily experience of birthing and experiencing labor pain which are indeed experienced by *sadhakas* (male or female) on the path of self-realization.

At this juncture one is reminded of Osho who described his experience of enlightenment as being "painful. It was like when a woman goes into labor when a child is to be born, and the woman suffers tremendous pain—the birth pangs" (Osho 1976: 201). At another place, he writes: "when that energy awakens, a second birth happens. In this birth you are both—you are the mother and you are the child. [...] You are taking birth, and you are also giving birth; your birth is happening through you. So the pains can be very severe and intense" (Osho 1997: 16). Similarly, a look at Nietzsche's biography tells us how he endured debilitating pain from headaches from the age of thirteen (Prideaux 2018: 34). Is it possible that he too might have been experiencing something like a yogic transformation but resisted interpreting his suffering as such? It is impossible to say, but his praise of suffering as necessary for creation and self-overcoming is evident later, as when his Zarathustra asserts that "[i]n order for the creator himself to be the child who is newly born, he must also want to be the birth-giver and the pain of giving birth" (Z II Blessed Isles). Zarathustra is a would-be mother who seeks to give birth to himself.

Undoubtedly, Nietzsche's work is characterized by derisive comments on woman. "'Woman' appears as 'pretty sweet little girls', as 'a lustful sexual being, a bitch', as 'slaves, tyrants, cats, birds, and cows', as 'a little old woman, endless mothers', as 'piece of merchandise on the marriage market', as 'manly woman', as 'breasts', as 'dancing mothers' or as 'wicked girls dancing naked'" (Oppel 2005: 140f.). However, these references are masculine stereotypes and do not refer to actual women, but parodize cultural assumptions about the women of Nietzsche's time. Through such comparisons, Nietzsche points at a "man's world" where men speak to each other about women in conventional, stereotyped and belittling or sexual terms. Nietzsche's picture is beyond caricature; it is satire (Oppel 2005: 142). While satirizing this masculine position and appropriating the myth of woman as being elusive, Nietzsche carries on a "feminine operation" (Derrida 1979: 57) of masquerade, "that gives itself for what it is not." Woman, as "veil," as "simulation," is "but one name for that untruth of truth" (Derrida 1979: 51). Commenting upon Nietzsche's style of writing, Oppel highlights his use of irony. "Nietzsche disguises his honesty with 'devilishness' (BGE 227) and seems something other than what he actually is by wearing masks, playing parts, and standing above his creations like the ironist he often is" (Oppel 2005: 90). This device of irony ensues from Nietzsche's Dionysiac power of art—that transfigures *Maya* as illusion into *Maya* as *Shakti*, hence attempting to rebalance the world.

By contrast, Janaway (2007) offers a semantic interpretation of perspectivism. On his view, Nietzsche aims to induce affects and evaluations in his audience, thereby shaping their perspectives. In GM, Nietzsche warns against the dangerous old conception of fiction that posited "pure, will-less, painless, timeless subject of knowledge." He is suspicious of concepts such as "pure reason," "absolute spirituality," or "knowledge as such" (GM III 12). Further, he is acutely aware of the self-trickery involved in act of devotion to a deity and explains why human beings needed to split the self into a lower and a higher being in the first place. In his notes, Nietzsche explains this self-created distance within the self—as the "pathos of distance" which is supposed to be the base of every high culture: that craving for ever greater expansion of distance within the soul itself, the development of ever higher, rarer, remoter, wider, more encompassing states, in short (to use a moral formula in a sense beyond morality), the "self-overcoming of man" (WLN, Notebook 2, autumn 1885 – autumn 1886, 2[13]).

## Non-dichotomy between Body and Soul and the Body as a Labyrinth

Shaktism teaches that the world is not unreal. For this reason, *Shaktas* worship for material benefit as well as final liberation, which is attained not through abstinence or abnegation of the body but through the body itself. The aim of Shakti sadhana is to achieve embodied self-realization. For Nietzsche too, there is no distinction between the body and soul. In *Thus Spoke Zarathustra*, he strongly attacks the despisers of the body. This becomes clear when we compare the figures of Radha as it appears in the *Gita-Govinda* by Jayadeva and Ariadne as Nietzsche portrays her in the poem *Ariadne's Lament* from the *Dionysian Dithyrambs*. From the same works we may also profitably compare Jayadeva's poem *Krishna* to Nietzsche's poem *Dionysus*.

Both Ariadne, who was abandoned on the island of Naxos by Theseus, and the sorrowful Radha who is yearning for Krishna symbolize the anguish of separation, a deep sense of despair and loneliness that the soul experiences when separated from the cosmic beloved. In both the texts, the lover returns at the end. In the Greek legend, Dionysus comes and saves Ariadne. In the Gita Govinda, Krishna returns to Radha. Krishna and Radha unite and bond emotionally in a *unio mystica*.[9] Nietzsche, on the other hand, chooses a dry tone that does not contain any euphoria of mystical union. Dionysus merely points out that he is Ariadne's labyrinth and that he and Ariadne are primarily not separated from each other.[10] Although Radha and Krishna are not separate entities in the Bhakti tradition, they are in common parlance perceived as two. Dionysus telling Ariadne that she has *small ears* and is not listening to her inner voice is Nietzsche's way of pointing toward the sufficiency of the self. This thought is echoed in Zarathustra's statement: "the awakened, the knowing one says: body am I through and through, and nothing besides" (Z 1 Despisers of the Body).

Nietzsche understands the body as a labyrinth and the human condition as analogous to living within it. It is his aim to affirm human life "to value living in this labyrinth, rather than to attempt to escape from it. This is the affirmation that completes nihilism, surpassing both the religious nihilist's desperate conviction that there must be a way out, and the radical nihilist's vilification of a labyrinth from which there is no exit" (White 1990: 14). The labyrinth is the way and also the goal. There is nothing beyond.

Interestingly, Nietzsche's concept of the labyrinth comes close to the sacred geometrical *yantra* used in the visualization of the Devi in Sri-Chakra Shaktism (see Rashinkar 2019: 29–36). Sri-Chakra Shaktism sees the human body as a microcosm of the universe and the yantra is a geometric representation of the cosmos/body. The Sadhaka navigates through the body to achieve a state of enlightened action. One focuses on the Bindu (the central point) in the yantra, which stands for the point of creation and to which all shall return after death. To move beyond the powers of will, knowledge, and action and to remain in the Bindu state steadily is the aim of Sri-Vidya.

Nietzsche's method of operation may be interpreted as an anthropomorphizing of this mystical geometry of Shaktism. His way is to equate the labyrinth with life—a life that is lived dangerously. In his labyrinth there is the possibility of going wrong ways, getting lost, and failing. Every path taken can be the wrong one; it can lead further and finally end in complete disorientation. It can also become a deadly prison from which there is no way out.

## Kundalini Shakti and the Seven Solitudes

According to Shaktism, the macrocosmic Goddess becomes embodied in the subtle physiology as the microcosmic kundalini shakti. It is she who assumes the form of the serpentine power coiled up at the base of the spine in the *Muladhara* chakra. And it is she who, when awakened, assumes the form of a blazing fire and ignites an alchemical transformation so profound that the human psychophysiology becomes the vehicle by which the Goddess accomplishes her highest aim: the transformation of the finite into the infinite. This she accomplishes through uniting the female half of her bipolar being with the male half, the Siva principle, situated in the *Sahasrara* cakra at the crown of the head (Lidke 2017: 30).

Zarathustra is seen to carry a *caduceus*, the staff of Hermes, everywhere he goes, and the caduceus is the symbol of the Kundalini shakti. The energy centers, the chakras, have been known since Plato. In his work *Timaeus*, Plato looks at the seven areas in the body that the soul must pierce to achieve self-realization. In his 1994 analysis of Plato's theory of the soul, Opsopaus finds parallels with the Indian Chakra system. He equates *Koruphe* to *Sahasrara*, *Enkephalos* to *Ajna*, *Trachelos* to *Vishuddha*, *Phrenes* to *Manipura*, *Gaster* to *Swadhistana* and *Gonades* to *Muladhara*.

Yet, against the undemonstrable soul hypothesis, Nietzsche is critical of any supposed *Hinterwelt* (Z 1 Hinterworldly). This includes super-sensuality, the notion of salvation in a hereafter, contempt for the body, the deification of ecstasy, and above all the resulting corruption of life that results from the preaching of the *Hinterwelt*. Even the *Shaktas* would admit that the Kundalini experience can make the mind heavy, which may become a major obstacle on the way to a corruption-free, balanced life. But

Nietzsche does not give up all vestiges of thinking he associated with the hinterworldly. Instead, he attempts to psychologize it. To Nietzsche's thinking the seven chakras become the seven solitudes. In *The Beacon*, from his *Dionysian Dithyrambs*, Nietzsche describes what can be interpreted as a mystical experience of a fisherman and refers to the "seven solitudes." It is evident in this poem that the fisherman is unable to know the seventh solitude. Yet another set of notes from the year 1883 throw further light on what Nietzsche exactly meant by the seven solitudes.[11] Nietzsche's first solitude is that of shame and weakness and silence before a great thought. The second solitude is that one that has lost all old grounds for consolation. The third solitude is the solitude with temptations. The fourth solitude is the awareness of sacrificing friends. The fifth solitude is that of supreme responsibility. The sixth solitude is the solitude in eternity, beyond morality: the creative and the good. The seventh solitude is that of the sick, of getting tired, getting still and that which is sanctified by suffering. Nietzsche clearly states that all these concerns are signs of the will to suffer, a deepening of the pain.[12]

At another place in his notebooks, the seventh solitude is, interestingly, equated with the decapitated head of Medusa. "Seventh Solitude:—lastly '*The Head of Medusa*'".[13] The figure of Medusa, as represented by Ovid in the fourth book of *Metamorphoses*,[14] is characterized by a dyadic development: first she appears as an innocent girl in the temple of Athena; later she transforms into a terrifying monster. Medusa's terrifying eyes are unforgivable. Not only do they turn the other person into a stone, but Medusa herself is not spared by her own gaze. Medusa's gaze thus contains both a critical and a self-critical element. Nietzsche associates the medium of Medusa's decapitated head with the seventh solitude. This dyadic state of the outer and inner critique seems to be the final stage of Nietzsche's spirituality: it consists of both an outward critical gaze as well as a self-critical gaze that is willing to overcome the outward gaze.

Medusa's head can gain another dimension when compared with another Indian Shakti, the goddess *Chhinnamasta*, who according to Shankaranarayanan has her seat in the head, in the place between the eyebrows, in the *ajna* center. She is the power of will and vision (see Shankaranarayanan 2002: 72). In contrast to Medusa, whose head was severed by Perseus, *Chhinnamasta* cuts off her own head and nourishes herself and two yoginis with the blood flowing out of it. *Chhinnamasta* symbolizes according to the Shakti tradition a high state of yogic consciousness. The head is considered to be the seat of the human ego, the I. By severing it with her own hands, *Chhinnamasta* shows her willingness to overcome any one-dimensional dogmatism. Nietzsche might have experienced this yogic state as he also vehemently critiqued dogma. Be it the dogma of the sciences or of the sacred—his writings seem to contain criticisms of both. Medusa's head is likewise a double-edged sword, which cuts through such dogma.

It is evident that Nietzsche equates the self with an aggregate of forces or drives that are struggling to gain control over one another. Clearly, for Nietzsche, the seven solitudes are states of mind that need to be overcome—not to attain salvation but to come to terms with the pain and suffering of the self. Nietzsche accurately deciphers and explicates the traditional theory of the soul and makes it more accessible to the modern reader. By replacing the ancient spiritual jargon with solitude, a term that is existentially and emotionally closer to the human experience, Nietzsche achieves a semantic displacement that opens the ground for new meaning making. Traditionally, the *Sahasrara* is the plane where the soul unites with the Divine and attains salvation. Interestingly, for Nietzsche, the seventh and the last solitude makes one still and perhaps therefore sick. This can be understood in terms of Nietzsche's contempt for the escapist view of the promise of salvation in the otherworld. It is not stillness but action in this world that Nietzsche aims at. Hence, he deliberately resists interpreting the last solitude in the traditional sense, almost willing an eternal postponement of his salvation.

## Shakti versus Will to Power

*Shaktas* aim to work their way out through navigating through the body and gaining control over bodily instincts to reach their fullest potentials. The word "*Shak*" implies "to be able to." Shakti is also interpreted as energy or force. The main aim of Shaktism is embodied self-realization. On the way toward self-realization however the practitioner attains powers (*siddhis*) (see Ganapathy 2003: 232–52). These are however seen as temptations on the path of self-realization and the ultimate aim to achieve a state of desirelessness. As Shaktism is based on art and storytelling, psychological interpretation plays an important role in it. There are several stories woven around the Devi. For example, in the *Devi Mahatmyam* (Leelamma 1998), the Devi is often seen fighting several demons such as *Dhumralochana*, *Chanda* and *Munda*, *Mahisasura*, *Shumbh* and *Nishumbh* or *Raktabeej*. These battles and these demons are however not to be taken literally but must be interpreted psychologically as they symbolize not war but human weaknesses and temptations, arrogance and pride, ego or tendency toward violence.

One of the reasons why the author of the article from Prabuddha Bharata considers Nietzsche to be "a poor worshipper at the altar of Power" is that Nietzsche has "a restricted view of power." It says, "Nietzsche made his mistake in accepting biology instead of psychology as the foundation of his system."[15] Clearly, this assumption does not hold true. Nietzsche's doctrine of the will to power has not just the biological premise but also has a prominent psychological premise (BGE 23). Nietzsche strips the will of its metaphysical dimension. His notion of will to power echoes the Aristotlian idea of *entelecheia* (power coming to itself) devoid of the divine involvement (Heidegger 1991: 64). As Hatab observes:

> For Nietzsche, "natural powers" would no longer follow Aristotle's proviso that they are developments toward actualities inscribed in reality by being fixed in divine form [...] With will to power, Nietzsche turns this principle around: all actualization of form emerges within an irreducible force of power-relations. With the death of God, natural forms can no longer be traced to any "supra-dynamic" divine actuality.
>
> (Hatab 2015: 38)

Instead, Nietzsche advances the psychological thesis of a will to power as the ultimate motivation of all human behavior. He writes: "My idea is that each specific body strives to dominate all space and to expand its power (—its will to power:) and to repel everything that resists its expansion."[16] Power, in Nietzsche's view, is a necessary striving to expand itself. Power is only power insofar as it can maintain itself against other powers and strives to predominate over them. After extending a diagnosis of the nature of interpersonal human power dynamics, Nietzsche also prescribes via the will to power a corrective measure. The will to power is also a tool of resistance that manifests itself against a blind will to truth. "The will to truth needs a critique—let us define our own task with this—, the value of truth is tentatively to be *called into question*" (GM III 24). Will to power is hence Nietzsche's counter construct to the will to truth which is an "always-being-on-the-way" (Aydin 2007: 26) and hence "implies willing to have determinate desires *and* resistance to their satisfaction" (Reginster 2006: 135) at the same time.

The eternal postponement of the birth of Zarathustra's children can be seen as an act of will to power. "Every actualization is for Nietzsche the realization of only one possibility" (Aydin 2007: 27), which may lead to the rise of dogma. This is precisely what Nietzsche also resists. Zarathustra calls upon the readers to be aware of the chaos in them, which is a condition for discovering ever more and alternative possibilities of meaning making. Chaos "is the basis for all creation and creativity. Without it nothing *novel* could emerge. The more that chaos breaks into our ordered world, the more our creative power is stimulated" (Aydin 2007: 27). This recalls Zarathustra's statement, "I say to you: one must still have chaos in oneself to be able to give birth to a dancing star. I say to you: you still have chaos in yourself" (Z P 5). Heidegger too understands will to power as manifesting itself in art (see Heidegger 1991: 69–76)—art that implies an activity of creating, exerting, transforming, and changing. Expressed through artistic modes of being that impel the questioning of existence, stultifying notions of "the truth," and conventional notions of power (as power over others), will to power entices those with the requisite health to reinvent themselves in the service of life.

## Three Metamorphoses versus Shakti *under Erasure*[17]

"Three metamorphoses of the spirit I name for you: how the spirit becomes a camel, and the camel a lion, and finally the lion a child" (Z 1 16). With these words, Zarathustra describes what might be interpreted as Nietzsche's view of the process of spiritual transformation. The stages of this conversion coincide with decisive moments in the myth of Psyche and Cupid depicted in the second-century text titled *Metamorphoses* written by Apuleius (see May and Harrison 2020: 5–8). Although there is no mention of a camel in the text, one can find a stone relic at the Louvre in Paris in which Psyche is depicted riding a dromedary,[18] most probably on her way to the Underworld where she has to meet Persephone in order to get from her the golden box containing the secret of beauty that she has to bring back to Aphrodite. In the myth, Psyche also meets Ceres, the equivalent of Demeter or Cybele, the Goddess with a Lion, who advises her to meet Aphrodite after Cupid has left her. After finally uniting with Cupid, Psyche gives birth to a girl, Voluptas (see May and Harrison 2020: 5–8).

As is evident, the motifs of the camel, the lion, and the child are all present in Nietzsche's creative representation of spiritual transformation; however, they are presented without the Goddess. If the Nietzschean stages of transformation were to be searched in the *Shakti* pantheon of Goddesses, a similar absence of the Mother Goddess can be observed. The camel figures as the companion of Dashaa Ma—a local folk goddess from Gujarat who is a popular variant of the Momai Maa (Mahamaya, i.e., Durga). She is worshiped mainly by women during a five-day fast to improve living conditions, known as *dashaa* (Pande 2003: 208). The lion accompanies the Goddess Durga, who symbolizes strength and vitality. She is the mighty one who killed the demon Mahishasura. The child Shiva is seen breastfeeding in the lap of the Goddess Tara who is found in the sacred shrine of Tarapith, in Birbhum, West Bengal. The forms of sadhana performed in Tarapith are more *yogic* and *tantric* than devotional, and they often involve sitting alone at the cremation ground in the "*shava-sadhana* corpse ritual" (McDaniel 2004: 115), surrounded by ash and bone.

We may question whether Nietzsche commits matricide by omitting the Mother (Irigaray 1991: 26–7). Should he to be held responsible for thereby dis(re)membering the Mother (Oliver 1995: 156)? Does his philosophy close "off the possibility of a specifically feminine other" (Oliver 1995: 25)? Is his posing woman as the absolute Other "denying against all experience that she is a subject, a fellow human being" (Beauvoir 1953: 260)? On the contrary, Nietzsche's engagement with the feminine is intensive and passionate—not only does he deeply engage with the traditional perceptions of the feminine, but he is also able to establish the link between the myths surrounding the feminine and their repercussions on flesh-and-blood women. While seemingly dismembering the Mother he does not commit matricide but assists in reviving her meaning and keeping her alive. Nietzsche employs an effective artistic device that reinforces his becoming the M(other) and reinstates the power flesh-and-blood women had lost. Nietzsche displaces the elements from their traditional contexts and subjects the Goddess to what Heidegger called a crosswise striking through technique (Heidegger 1976: 385ff.). The crosswise crossing is not simply to be understood as a mere negative sign. Under its lines, the presence of a transcendental signified disappears and still remains legible. By doing so, Nietzsche diverts one's attention from the blind habitual pious fervor of ritual and prayers and invites one to contemplate what the goddess means. One is forced to abandon the transcendental meaning attached with the iconography of the Mother Goddess and to actualize one's own meaning making capacities. One is further compelled to ponder what her companions—the camel, the lion, and the child—mean, as well. While the camel and the lion seem to suggest an existential turmoil and the overcoming of that turmoil through assertion of power in both the Greek/Roman mythology as well as in the constellation of the Indian goddesses sketched above, it is constellation in which we see the child that grabs one's attention the most. The child according to Zarathustra "is innocence and forgetting, a new beginning, a game, a wheel rolling out of itself, a first movement, a sacred yes-saying" (Z I 17). In the absence of Goddess Tara, the subject is left alone in the overcoming the fear of death, one becomes the self-propelling wheel of total surrender to itself deriving soul nourishment not from any external source but from being in harmony with oneself. This is quite different from the child that is

Voluptas. She stands not merely for hedonistic pleasure but for the pleasure of self-affirmation amidst adversities. As in the myth of Psyche, which marks the future with the birth of a child (and coincidentally a girl child), Zarathustra's children are also children of the future.

## Conclusion

It is certain that Nietzsche was no worshiper of Shakti, for in addition to being unfamiliar with the sect, the worship of any metaphysical being was anathema to him. Yet there are striking parallels between key elements of Shaktism and Nietzsche's philosophy: both are world affirming, in that they both propound a creative engagement with worldliness in the form of an aesthetics of everydayness, and both place emphasis upon the non-dichotomy of body and soul. By explicating key connections between the ancient Greek and Hindu pantheons I have illuminated the important role that related mythological narratives played in the respective conceptions of the feminine and the self in both philosophies. Furthermore, I have demonstrated that *vis-à-vis* Nietzsche's views of women and the feminine, an appreciation of this is necessary for an adequate understanding of the parallels between Shaktism and his philosophy, and the reception—and resonance—of his thought in India.

## Notes

1   In all probability, it is Pratap Chandra Mazoomdar who is being talked about here. Mazoomdar was a well-read scholar who also wrote the first biography of Sri Ramakrishna in English.
2   *Prabuddha Bharata* or *Awakened India* is an English-language monthly journal of the Ramakrishna Order, in publication since July 1896. It carries articles and translations by monks, scholars, and other writers on humanities and social sciences including religious, psychological, historical, and cultural themes.
3   http://library.bjp.org/jspui/bitstream/123456789/874/2/prabuddh%20bharata%20-%2001PB-Jan1915.pdf (Last accessed: July 24, 2022).
4   Nietzsche came to see "Greek" and "Indian" as *modes of being*, which informed his own ideas on normativity, providing an alternative to the Christian slave morality he so despised (Syea 2016: 266). Figl, in his compelling account of Nietzsche's transcultural thought, informs readers inter alia about how Nietzsche was already learning words in Sanskrit while still at high school and undertook a comparison of Germanic and Greek mythological epics with the great Indian epics *Mahābhārata* and *Rāmāyana* (Figl 2007: 104). Another valuable account of Nietzsche's readings on India can be found in the research of Thomas Brobjer (2008a). A close analysis of Nietzsche's intellectual biography however shows that his knowledge of India lacks accuracy. This leaves scope for complementing Nietzsche's thoughts through a more extensive contextualization of Nietzsche in the Indian mythological and philosophical traditions.
5   https://www.sacred-texts.com/hin/rigveda/rv01089.htm (Last accessed: August 6, 2022).

6  eKGWB/NF-1888, 15[118]—Frühjahr 1888.
7  See GS, *Songs of Prince Vogelfrei*.
8  See Swami Vijnananda (1921–1922), *The Srimad Devi Bhagavatam*, at https://www.pdfdrive.com/srimad-devi-bhagavata-purana-english-by-sw-vijnanananda-d39957378.html (Last accessed: August 6, 2022).
9  See Goswami 2017: Act 2, Verse 10, 77 and Act 3, Verse 9, 100.
10  See Nietzsche's *Dionysian Dithyrambs*, "Ariadne's Lament."
11  eKGWB/NF—Herbst 1883, 16[64].
12  Nietzsche seems to anticipate the subject of modern Chakra healing therapy which is, after Carl G. Jung, a part of analytical psychology today. See Judith (2004: 8).
13  eKGWB/NF-1884, 31[9], Winter (1884–1885).
14  http://ovid.lib.virginia.edu/trans/Metamorph4.htm (Last accessed: July 24, 2022).
15  http://library.bjp.org/jspui/bitstream/123456789/874/2/prabuddh%20bharata%20-%2001PB-Jan1915.pdf, p. 8 (Last accessed: August 6, 2022).
16  eKGWB/NF-1888, 14[186]—Nachgelassene Fragmente Frühjahr (1888).
17  I borrow the term "under erasure" from Gayatri Chakravarty Spivak's preface to her translation of Derrida's "Of Grammatology." Inspired by Heidegger, Derrida uses the philosophical device of "sous rature"—which Spivak translates as "under erasure" (Derrida 1997: xiv). *Sous rature* means the word that is visibly crossed out but which should not be considered completely deleted when reading. Because the word is imprecise, it is crossed out. But since it is necessary at the same time, it remains visible.
18  See https://www.livius.org/pictures/turkey/dalyan-alexandria-in-troas/alexandria-troas-psyche-on-a-dromedary/

8

# Nietzsche on Naxos: Ariadne and an Aesthetics of Justification

Nicholas E. Low

## Introduction

From his earliest writings, the goal of Nietzsche's philosophical practice seems to lie beyond traditional or received conceptions of truth. Even in *The Birth of Tragedy* his analysis of tragedy in terms of Dionysian and Apolline forces is meant less as a description of reality per se and more as an answer to the question of how human life might be redeemed in view of suffering and transience. In this first book, truth matters just so far as it pertains to the aesthetic justification of the world, which relies on the seduction of semblance rather than any conception of truth in itself. For the Greeks, the effect of tragedy was an experience that provided an aesthetic justification for existence:

> For what must be clear to us above all, both to our humiliation *and* our elevation, is that the whole comedy of art is certainly not performed for us, neither for our edification nor our education, just as we are far from truly being the creators of that world of art; conversely, however, we may very well assume we are already images and artistic projections for the true creator of art, and that our highest dignity lies in our significance as works of art—for only as an *aesthetic phenomenon* is existence and the world eternally *justified*—although, of course, our awareness of our significance in this respect hardly differs from the awareness which painted soldiers have of the battle depicted on the same canvas.
> 
> (BTF 5)

The contention in this passage that humans exist as miniscule elements of a grand comedy created by and for superhuman forces has a decidedly transformative vector: the perception is meant to "humiliate and elevate" and thus provide existential solace by transforming the individual's experience of suffering. And while interpreters have debated how seriously to take the ostensibly metaphysical dimensions of this picture, whatever conception of truth may lie behind it is not the primary focus of the work but one feature of the broader project of justification. If Nietzsche's thought is famously protean, this goal of justification is nevertheless a perennial concern. Even in his putatively "positivistic" middle works, Nietzsche's philosophy never aims to arrive at a fixed perspective on "the way things really are" but to discover a practice and experience that justifies and redeems life.[1] In this sense, Nietzsche is more concerned with presenting a particular type of theodicy, a justification of suffering in the world, than he is with formulating a theory of truth.

However, Nietzsche is of course no traditional theologian, and so his peculiar approach to theodicy eschews orthodox formulations in favor of a novel philosophical practice aimed at the transfiguration of suffering itself.[2] Across his writings, Nietzsche often describes a justified life as one that has been transfigured: in *The Birth*, this transfiguration is the "humiliation and elevation" that results from the identification of the individual with a primal creative force, the *Ur-Eine*, achieved through tragedy. And while accounts from later works vary, they retain crucial features from this earliest presentation. As in the passage above, these justifying transfigurations don't necessarily aim to alleviate suffering, or cause its cessation, but to enact a shift in the individual's perspective that allows them to revalue suffering: they articulate the redemption *of* suffering, rather than redemption *from* suffering.[3]

Centering this theme of transfiguration illuminates two major problems of interpretation: it clarifies Nietzsche's primary philosophical "method" as a practice of aesthetic self-transfiguration aimed at the justification of life, rather than the discovery of inert truth, and it enables us to better imagine the form of subjectivity that is the "goal" of that practice. Alexander Nehamas and Robert Pippin propose competing resolutions to these interpretive problems, agreeing that Nietzsche's works pursue the transfiguration of the self, but disagreeing about the adequacy of the method to the stated goal. Nehamas argues that for Nietzsche, the self can be transfigured in literature and that his texts are demonstrations of this practice. Pippin points to an apparent weakness in Nehamas's interpretation, questioning whether literature really has such transformative efficacy. I argue that we should read Nehamas's ambiguity on this point as an opportunity for a more expansive interpretation of Nietzsche's "aesthetics," one which permits us to see that in his works, the transfiguration of the self involves experiences of deification,[4] in which the human subject is both "elevated," beautified and celebrated but also "humiliated" in its mortality and transience. Nietzsche's philosophical method is therefore, as Nehamas claims, a form of "aesthetic" self-cultivation but one that thoroughly explodes modern, post-Kantian conceptions of aesthetics. In this chapter, I explore some of the possible ramifications of appreciating this Nietzschean revision of aesthetics. Specifically, I argue that the ideal of aesthetic unity that Nietzsche envisions for the self is purchased at the cost of embracing the risk of subjective disintegration. Additionally, my account shows that Nietzsche constructs his own written works as experiments meant to engender experiences of deification, meaning that they mirror the effect of tragedy as described in *The Birth*. Finally, I reflect on the role of the semi-divine figure of Ariadne and her relationship to Dionysus and argue that Nietzsche imagines the philosopher of the future, and himself, through this deified feminine character. In closing, I consider how these arguments might suggest an alternative way of thinking about the living Nietzsche's tragic fate.

## Nehamas: Life as Literature, or Literature Instead of Life?

In his influential book, *Nietzsche: Life as Literature*, Nehamas articulates and obeys an important imperative: that any student of Nietzsche should treat the question of style with all seriousness. For Nehamas, Nietzsche's literary styles are an integral element of his philosophical method, generating a mosaic of self-presentations that, when taken together, reveal a holistic strategy of aesthetic self-cultivation. The figure "Nietzsche" is on this account a deliberately portrayed character, a literary self that emerges in the published works, espousing multifarious perspectives and performatively demonstrating a philosophical life beyond good and evil. This argument relies on two related yet distinct ideas. First is the claim that Nietzsche conceives the self, or subject, as a particular kind of aesthetic achievement that involves embracing the instability of becoming. Nehamas spells this claim out in terms of Nietzsche's formulation of "becoming what one is":

> To become what one is, we can see, is not to reach a specific new state and to stop becoming—it is not to reach a state at all. It is to identify oneself with all of one's actions, to see that everything one does (what one becomes) is what one is. In the ideal case it is also to fit all this into a coherent whole and to want to be everything that one is: it is to give style to one's character; to be, we might say, becoming.
> (Nehamas 1985: 191)

On this account, the self is not a static condition, but rather an eventual and mutable emergence of a coherent form governed by a sense style.[5] However, this first claim is complicated by the related claim that for Nietzsche, writing is the integral feature of this philosophical self-formation. Nehamas writes that "we might with some appropriateness attribute to him the hyperbolic view, which this book aims to investigate, that writing is also the most important part of living" (Nehamas 1985: 41). Writing and the production of literary works is thus the means by which Nietzsche fashions a self with style and channels the vicissitudes of becoming into an aesthetic whole.

This account coheres with my opening claim that for Nietzsche, philosophy represents first and foremost the pursuit of some form of justification. For Nehamas, Nietzsche's particular claims, so often hyperbolic, vituperative, or even contradictory, are less important than the effect of the kaleidoscopic figure "Nietzsche" that emerges from the texts. Indeed, the primary function of the texts is to constitute this character: "Nietzsche's texts therefore do not describe him but, in exquisitely elaborate detail, *exemplify* the perfect instance of his ideal character. And this character is none other than the character these very texts constitute: Nietzsche himself" (Nehamas 1985: 233). Through literature, Nietzsche-as-author creates himself as Nietzsche-as-character: the various disparate perspectives and attitudes espoused by this character are shaped into an aesthetic unity, justifying each of its minute parts with respect to the whole. For Nehamas, Nietzsche's philosophical method is therefore a literary form of self-stylization, and the resultant form of subjectivity is a shifting and multiple, yet finally unified self that transfigures and justifies life beyond moral categories.

There is however an apparent ambiguity in this account. If writing is indeed the most important part of living for Nietzsche and is a central feature of his philosophical practice aimed at justification, then we might expect the process of producing his works to have had a transformative effect on Nietzsche's own life. However, Nehamas indicates that this is not the case. He writes that "[i]n engaging with [Nietzsche's] works, we are not engaging with the miserable little man who wrote them but with the philosopher who emerges through them" (Nehamas 1985: 234). This seems to expose a major flaw in his interpretive strategy. If Nietzsche the author, the living breathing human, remains a miserable little man, it's hard to see how the character's achievement of aesthetic unity affects any meaningful transfiguration or justification of life itself. In another essay responding in part to various criticisms of *Life as Literature* (including those of Robert Pippin), Nehamas clarifies how he understands the aesthetic as a *model* for life. Nehamas distinguishes between two potential meanings of this claim:

> It may mean that the choice of a particular mode of behavior is like an artistic decision concerning, say, the adoption of a particular style. But it may also mean that the choice of a mode of behavior is itself an artistic decision, focusing only on the aesthetic features of the course of action in question. The first alternative concerns the basis on which choices and decisions are made: It holds that *artistic decisions provide the model for all action*. The latter refers to the very content of the decision itself: It holds that all decisions are straightforwardly artistic. And though the two interpretations are probably inter-connected, my own view is that the former is more likely to be correct.
>
> (Nehamas 1996: 233)

In this passage, Nehamas favors the somewhat weaker form of the claim, supporting the notion that artistic decisions, or perhaps *aesthetic judgments*, could function as "the model for all action," rather than arguing that such judgments and actions are in fact artistic. There's a lot at stake in this distinction, but for the purposes of understanding Nietzsche's philosophy, it seems to imply that Nehamas interprets Nietzsche's writing practice as a model for philosophical living. In other words, the artistic choices that Nietzsche makes in composing his works could serve as an example of the sort of choices that I might make as a living breathing human operating in the world. On such an account, from reading Nietzsche I would learn to emulate his multifarious art of style; adopt its flexibility with respect to perspective, its anti-dogmatic orientation; and so learn to operate as a multivocal yet unified character in my own individual and social pursuits.[6] In such a way, I might give aesthetic unity to my entire self and so justify the full range of my experiences. This interpretation makes sense out of the distinction between the magnificent character and miserable little man, but it radically devalues the power of literature: Nietzsche the living human surely managed to produce a brilliant literary model for pursuing a transfigurative philosophical life but presumably failed to apply the practices necessary for achieving such a transfiguration in his own life. In other words, the power of writing to aesthetically justify life is drawn into significant doubt.

This is precisely the point on which Robert Pippin most wants to push Nehamas. In a response intended to clarify what he takes Nehamas's somewhat obscure position to be, Pippin emphasizes this discontinuity between life and literature:

> Nehamas asks, again with a clear, silent reference to Proust, "What, then, if the work itself, in its totality, results in the construction of a character whose biography it turns out to be?" His answer to this question appears to be: It is this created character who is important; we need to pay attention to another character, the living character who created this character, only for the actual biography of Nietzsche the person, not the one of significance in historical memory. But then we would not have Life as Literature. The subtitle should read: Literature Instead of Life.
>
> (Pippin 2014: 128)

Pippin highlights the extent to which Nehamas's interpretation *replaces* the living figure of Nietzsche with the literary character: for the purposes of philosophy, as well as historical memory, the character supplants the living Nietzsche; the literary self is the one that actually matters. The stakes of Pippin's intervention are substantial for how we think about the purpose of philosophy: if our goal is the radical and justifying transfiguration of the self, as Nietzsche seems to believe, then the practice of writing philosophy can only succeed in the realm of literature, not life. If our goal as philosophers were to leave historical and literary imprints then we might be satisfied with this "literature instead of life," though Pippin leads us to ask the question of whether this is in fact a satisfying goal. At the very least, it does not seem to have been Nietzsche's.

However, in the final chapter of *Life as Literature*, and indeed as the title implies, Nehamas's account of Nietzsche's achievements is more elevated than the creation of a merely literary character. Just prior to his comment about the "miserable little man," Nehamas describes a more intimate connection between literature and life:

> The final consequence of the reading this book has attempted is that it is not only Nietzsche's model that is literary. In a serious sense, his product is literary as well. Nietzsche *created a character out of himself*. "Fortunately," he writes, "for the great majority books are mere literature" (A 44); for him *they are life itself*. As he thought Goethe had done, *he too created himself*.
>
> (Nehamas 1985: 233; italics mine)

Throughout the book, Nehamas argues clearly that literature is a model for thinking about life; here in the final pages, he seems to suggest that literature has some power to transfigure life itself. Nehamas states, in sequence, that Nietzsche "created a character out of himself," that literature is "life itself" for him, and that he "created himself" through writing, like Goethe. These formulations transcend the neat separability between the character and the author: the character Nietzsche emerges out of and transforms the life of the author, and indeed, it is the practice of writing with style that produces this transformation. There is then, as Pippin notes, a tension in Nehamas's account with respect to the effect that literature has on life: does the creation of the self as a literary character have the capacity to transfigure life or merely to model such transfiguration in the form of a fantastical literary self?

## Pippin: Nietzsche's Psychological Antinomies

In forwarding his critique of Nehamas, Pippin develops his claim about this tension between life and literature along two specific lines: first, he argues that Nietzsche seems less concerned with "aesthetics" insofar as the term traditionally denotes a concern with beauty; and second, that Nehamas either presumes a self-creating subject (which does not seem to be evident in Nietzsche's writings) or, as we have seen, leaves an unbridgeable gap between "life" and "literature," and so drains Nehamas's intimations of the transfiguring power of literature of its force. Extending his critique of Nehamas, Pippin provides an alternative interpretation of Nietzsche's philosophy of self-transfiguration that emphasizes the extent to which these problems are features of Nietzsche's own philosophy. Ultimately, Pippin thinks, unlike Nehamas, that Nietzsche fails, both as a human and as an author, to achieve the too-ambitious philosophical task that he set for himself.

As for the first charge, Pippin is correct to suggest that Nietzsche's enduring focus on the problem of justification is hard to explain in terms of a conventional understanding of aesthetics for which beauty is the ideal. He writes, "Even [Nietzsche's] early notion of an 'aesthetic justification of existence' does not trade much on traditional aesthetic properties of Greek tragedies and focuses instead on tragedy as if it were a distinct ethical category, a worldview of compelling power" (Pippin 2014: 122). Indeed, Nietzsche's account of "aesthetic justification" in BT, while it does involve beauty at the level of Apolline figuration, is undeniably grounded in the somatic and disruptive forces of Dionysian intoxication and, as I have shown, functions as a peculiar form of theodicy, rather than a theory of beauty: the subject is aestheticized, but this aestheticization indicates the perspective from which one sees oneself as part of a larger work of art created by and for superhuman forces. Pippin prefers to locate this phenomenon within the domain of "ethics," on the grounds that it does a better job of accommodating the "compelling worldview," which tragedy seems to be for Nietzsche. However, in differentiating between aesthetics and ethics in this way, Pippin overlooks the extent to which Nietzsche's thought challenges such modern, post-Kantian categorical distinctions. Part of the gambit of BT is precisely to reinvest the aesthetic with a fuller range of meanings, including not only threatening experiences of sublimity, still recognizably "aesthetic" for Kant, but indeed with transfiguring encounters with embodied divine presences (BT 8). In BT, Nietzsche describes the tragic effect as a deifying experience in which spectators encounter an aestheticized, Apollinian representation of the violent impersonal force of the Dionysiac: if this transformation is to be described as aesthetic, then that term will have to bear substantially more weight than it does in post-Kantian philosophical parlance. So while Pippin is right that the modern, academic philosophical sense of aesthetics is much too limited a term to capture the justifying power of transfiguration in Nietzsche's works, he reinforces the siloing of ethics and aesthetics in contemporary philosophy, forcing Nietzsche into a conceptual framework that he ultimately wants to resist. For Nietzsche, neither "ethics" nor "aesthetics" conventionally construed are adequate to the scope and power of the tragic effect, which involves the justification of suffering through the intoxicating and transfiguring performance of tragedy.

Pippin's second objection is more substantive than the first. The implied reliance on a conception of a self-creating self in Nehamas's interpretation does not seem to comport with many of Nietzsche's own statements about subjectivity. For Pippin, Nietzsche's biggest issue is precisely that the conscious self doesn't have any purchase on the various unconscious and prevoluntary forces that contribute to its own development:

> The sort of language just cited suggests that being a subject is a matter of being subject to, rather than a subject of, dominant inclinations, passions, and drives, which group, arise, and subside as subject-less events, but if left at this impression, any unity (subordination of counter instincts and drives) would be in effect something that contingently happens, not something I could be said to do or to achieve. And the unity would be hard to understand since the main engine of that unification, "interpretation," is not and cannot be something that happens to me, but something I reflectively do.
>
> (Pippin 2014: 127)

Pippin rightly notes that much of Nietzsche's own language defies the notion that there is any such unified or autonomous self to do the reflective interpretive work of self-organization that Nehamas seems to impute to him. Indeed, the factors involved in producing a "self" are, according to Nietzsche, things as ungovernable as the age and culture that one is born into, one's parentage and genetics, one's various and conflicting instincts, and one's alimentary inclinations and digestive capacities. Furthermore, Nietzsche is deeply suspicious about whether a "self" emerges from these factors in any real sense; he often avers that the self is an illusion of unity born of the temporary dominance of a given impulse or set of impulses.[7]

In his own monograph, Pippin draws this issue out further in psychological language. He asserts that Nietzsche's philosophical method involves experimental strategies for the management of these various unconscious or prevoluntary impulses, focusing primarily on what he describes as erotic attachments. The problem for Pippin is that erotic commitments are not the sort that consciously deliberating subjects volitionally make. This leads Pippin to construe Nietzsche's project of "becoming what one is" as an attempt to think through the problem of freedom in terms of the ideal of self-overcoming (Pippin 2010: 106). Nietzsche's articulation of freedom or agency comes in the form of a "psychological self-relation" that never settles but defines itself in agonistic relation to a set of constantly shifting possibilities. While Pippin hedges by insisting that this achievement might "perhaps exclusively" be the work of forces like history or fate, agency nevertheless involves a state of self-relation or, in other words, an achievement of a particular form of subjectivity (Pippin 2010: 112).[8]

Pippin, acknowledging that Nietzsche fails (or more likely refuses) to define this form precisely, describes it variously as "attitudinal and dispositional," as an "achievement," and additionally as a "state of mind" (Pippin 2010: 112, 114). Whatever this subjectivity might ultimately look like, it is at least clear that it is *not* an artistic creation (Pippin is at pains to forward this interpretation as a "more promising" counter to Nehamas's "literary" proposal), that it is *not* something achieved through mastery or conscious choice, and that it involves a productive tension between affirming one's erotic commitments, yet always remaining open to their dissolution or abandonment (Pippin 2010: 109). Thus, Nietzsche's ideal subject is conditioned by the "psychological realization of the ineliminable need for self-overcoming," even though that realization is "largely prevoluntary" (Pippin 2010: 116).

The difficulties of this view lead Pippin to conclude that Nietzsche doesn't ultimately have a satisfactory explanation for how his own practical philosophy manages or affirms such prevoluntary inclinations. Pippin avers that Nietzsche, in trying to emulate the cheerful ideal of the French moralists, finally fails to live up to that ideal: he cannot make himself into the serene type of a Montaigne, being an individual plagued by a "sickness with man himself" (Pippin 2010: 123). Pippin wonders whether this sickness is the result of a certain historical difference—whether a Montaigne could have retained his *Heiterkeit* in the ostensibly less cheerful late nineteenth-century—but seems to finally answer no, imputing to Nietzsche a damning vestigial longing for a perspective from eternity and transcendence. This longing seems to be what prevents Nietzsche from realizing his own ideal of self-overcoming, representing a stubborn, obsessive neurosis. Pippin insinuates that Montaigne is successful in a way that Nietzsche is not because he tempers his expectations regarding justification: "[Montaigne] has found a way of addressing what we now call the everyday … without the expectations of a religious transcendence … while still being receptive to small-scale moments of grace and even a kind of redemption" (Pippin 2010: 123). For Pippin, Nietzsche's efforts strive toward a life that is radically transfigured and redeemed but ultimately fail, both in the case of his writing, which is pervaded by neurotic anxiety and anger, and in the case of his own life, which as Nehamas reminds us was "miserable." Nietzsche's writings are on this account a record of his own psychological antinomies and reflect certain failures to live a properly humble philosophical life, rather than a life transfigured and redeemed.

Pippin's attribution of a vestigial longing for transcendence to Nietzsche is crucial, though misguided. While Montaigne managed to shrink his conception of redemption to the everyday, a sign of his own healthy cheerfulness, Nietzsche remains yoked to a higher expectation, a longing for something far beyond the human. In Pippin's psychological presentation, precisely such longing betrays the ideal of a self in flexible and mutable relations with its erotic commitments: while Nietzsche at his best recommends such an ideal, at his worst and most enduring, his narcissistic and neurotic desire for godlike self-determination keeps him from this ideal. There is detectable in Pippin's critique of Nehamas a hint that such a vision of self-determination and self-mastery perhaps illuminate Nietzsche's own "miserable" end:

> As Nehamas himself indicates frequently, virtually no one succeeds in being the poet of his own life. However creative we may be, we cannot secure our

interpretations, reassure ourselves about them, ward off suspicions about self-deceit, and properly understand the right way to react to others' responses to them. We never reach any stable point of view in such a process, never simply become who we are. This is reflected in Nietzsche's own fate. There are far more and far more incommensurable "Nietzsches" among his audience than there are "Socrateses."

(Pippin 2014: 130–1)

To offer an ideal of self-creation is to imagine, or fantasize, that we can all be the Plato to our own Socrates, while the truth is both more mundane and more desperate. Our inexpungible opacity to ourselves suggests to Pippin that an ideal of self-creation lacks in practicability, as most of us are subject to all manner of uncontrollable factors, in Nietzsche's case, his persistent and ultimately terminal health issues. If this is the case, then a sober cheerfulness with respect to the everyday a la Montaigne would perhaps be more commendable and help one to affirm, in more modest terms, the hands that they're dealt in the game of becoming.

However, in what remains of this chapter, I want to propose that Nietzsche has something quite different in mind and suggest an alternative interpretation of the fate of the living Nietzsche. As I argued in the introduction, Nietzsche's philosophy, as a practice of justification, is directed toward the *redemption of* suffering, rather than to its minimization. As such, to interpret the living Nietzsche's painful "fate" as a sign of his failure to achieve his ideal is a mistake. Indeed, Nietzsche's philosophical practice involves an openness to the mutability and fragility of the self as much as it involves notions of mastery and organization. As such, to truly follow Nietzsche's thought requires us, and him, to try and affirm his fate, to see what sort of transfiguration might make it appear as something other than an objection to his life. The key to such an effort is to think of Nietzsche's writing practice as central to his notion of transfiguration, which in turn demands a substantially expanded conception of aesthetics. Specifically, we must understand Nietzsche's aesthetics as involved in a practice of deification that radically affirms suffering and seeks to transfigure life with respect to it, indeed rendering suffering and the sufferer "divine." In this sense, Nietzsche does not ultimately abandon his attempts at the revaluation of the titanic and the horrifying that he began in BT: deification means, for Nietzsche, both elevation *and* humiliation, a divine brilliance as well as abjection and torment. As such, his own living "fate" poses a particular challenge: can we see Nietzsche's suffering as justified by his writing practice?

## Writing as Deification

Defining the transfiguring power of literature in Nietzsche's thought requires that we go beyond Nehamas and Pippin and take their disagreement as an opportunity to expand our understanding of Nietzsche's aesthetics. More specifically, it requires that we appreciate that Nietzsche's writing practice aims at the deification of the subject. As a rejoinder to Pippin, this practice certainly does signify a longing for eternity: such a perspective describes part of the desired effect of deification. However, a "longing for eternity" does not necessarily imply impossibility or a narcissistic fantasy of transcending one's boundaries as a subject. Rather, Nietzsche's longing for eternity emphasizes the justification of suffering through the radical affirmation of life in eternal return. In "the Heaviest Weight," one of Nietzsche's earliest articulations of eternal return, he intimates that affirming the eternal return involves deifying what, in "The Wanderer and His Shadow," he calls the "closest things": it is *this* spider, *this* moonlight, *you* speck of dust that must be willed to return (WS 6). The demon in the night asks the reader whether she has ever experienced a moment of such elevation that all of this, all of these closest, which is to say most mundane but also potentially *most painful* things, appear justified and redeemed. And the reader's imagined ideal response is a deifying proclamation: "You are a god, and never have I heard anything more divine" (GS 341). The force of this affirmation reveals the human being at her most elevated, but only through the inclusion and affirmation of the most humiliating, the point at which she is reduced to mere dust. Eternity does not signify an escape from time but rather a transfiguration and deification of everything within it. Setting aside for the moment the question of whether Nietzsche himself ever achieves anything like such a perspective from eternity, we must ask why Pippin forecloses the possibility from the outset. To read Nietzsche's writings as failed attempts to find "small moments of grace" in the "everyday," as Pippin does, is to fundamentally misunderstand the stakes of Nietzsche's project: what Nietzsche desires is rather an experience that unites the heights of elevation with the nadir of mortal humility, in other words, a recognition that suffering and death too are divine.

Even if we accept that such deification is the goal of Nietzsche's philosophy, there remains the problem of what "becoming what one is" means *vis-à-vis* prevoluntary drives, as well as the question of how we address the apparent gap between the "author" Nietzsche and the literary character. In both cases, the answer has to do with Nietzsche's writing practice. For Nietzsche, writing itself has the power to transfigure prevoluntary or unconscious creative impulses and thus to transfigure the author himself. Indeed, this is precisely the function of artistic creativity as Nietzsche often describes it. Certainly in BT, but in later works as well, Nietzsche talks about the capacities of the artist as the channeling of superhuman, pre-conscious and pre-voluntary drives. In *Ecce Homo*, Nietzsche elucidates the process of writing *Zarathustra* in rather astonishing terms, insisting that meditations on the type of Zarathustra, one who possesses a great health, lead to a perspective from which one beholds "a world so over-rich in what is beautiful, strange, questionable, terrible, and divine that our curiosity and our thirst to possess it have veered beyond control, also, so that nothing will sate us any more!" (EH Books Z 2). This nearly ecstatic condition not only echoes the language of the demon in "The Heaviest Weight"—the divine and beautiful are again paired up with the strange and the terrible—it also recalls the superhuman *Ur-eine* from BT, the force of creativity that compels individual artists. Nietzsche describes his inspiration as follows:

... someone being just an incarnation, mouthpiece, or medium of overpowering forces. The idea of revelation in the sense of something suddenly becoming *visible* and audible with unspeakable assurance and subtlety, something that throws you down and leaves you deeply shaken—this simply describes the facts of the case.

(EH Books Z 3)

Nietzsche writes about his own writing in such a way that composition appears as the conscious translation of superhuman forces into human language. Crucially, this conception of writing parallels Nietzsche's depiction of Greek tragedy, in which the tragedian produces the Apollinian figuration of the Dionysiac.

In effect, we can read many of Nietzsche's texts as Apolline representations of Dionysiac impulses. As in tragedy, the creative energy for this task comes from an alliance between conscious and unconscious forms of artistry. Elsewhere in EH, when Nietzsche explains what it means to "become what one is," he makes it clear that this process is, at least in part, necessarily unconscious. The author "Nietzsche" describes himself as a product of forces and impulses both internal and external (climate, diet, nutrition, etc.) as much as a product of conscious creativity. The "artistry" involved in producing a self which is an "incredible multiplicity that is nonetheless the converse of chaos" belongs not to "Nietzsche" but to his *instincts*, which operate at a necessarily unconscious and prevoluntary level. It is only through the process of writing, of becoming who he was as a philosopher, that his instincts find their fated expression or, as he bombastically claims, allow him to become "a destiny" (EH Clever 9). The task of writing is thus to bring conscious creativity into a harmonious relation with unconscious artistic impulses or, in other words, to give the dark and obscure Dionysiac radiant Apolline form. Becoming what one is signifies not only a "being subject to" the prevoluntary impulses that makes one what one is but also a bestowing of subjective form to those impulses.

However, this doesn't yet fully explain how writing deifies the living subject, justifying the life of the author. This claim relies on a dramatic redefinition of aesthetics. We moderns take Pippin as an example and don't typically think of writing or reading as having the power to affect transformations of subjectivity. For Nietzsche though, writing, and creativity in general, is a practice with immense transfigurative potential. In the preface to EH, Nietzsche claims that he'd "rather be a satyr than a saint." To be a satyr, as Nietzsche taught in BT, means to experience the transfiguring presence of Dionysus in the tragic festival and thus to become ecstatic. It is in such states that one becomes capable of lending form to chaos, of channeling prevoluntary and unconscious impulses into an aesthetic whole. However, the effect of tragedy is also a transfiguration of the viewer: it is not only the satyr who is transformed; the audience too experiences the justifying effect and beholds itself as an aesthetic product. The satyr is directly exposed to the deifying, and dangerous, presence of the Dionysiac, while the audience receives this presence in its safer Apolline representation. In EH, Nietzsche places himself in the position of the satyr, dangerously proximate to the unruly Dionysiac, but acting as a lens through which the reader glimpses the Apolline form of a life redeemed. Nietzsche's texts are themselves exercises in Dionysian transfiguration: they seek to invoke the inspiring and dangerous presence of the god to potentially transfigure both author and reader. In this sense, Nietzsche's writing practice is indeed a form of aesthetic self-formation, but only if we allow "aesthetics," as well as "literature," to involve the invocation of divine presences and the justification of life itself through a process of deification. However, expanding aesthetics to include deifying writing practices, while it opens up the possibility of an aesthetically justified life, also necessitates the affirmation and embrace of suffering: to be divine is not to be immune to suffering and transience but to be transfigured in light of it. The satyr is a semi-divine and beautified figure, but this divinity also requires a fatal embrace of the eternal flux of becoming.

## Ariadne's Deification

To further illustrate these claims, I want to turn to the final passages of BGE, in which the god Dionysus makes his dazzling reappearance in Nietzsche's texts after a nearly decade-long hiatus. As the book approaches its theophanic denouement, Nietzsche reminds the reader that he had dedicated BT, his firstborn book, to the god Dionysus, and that he was the last to make such an offering. In other words, Nietzsche certifies his credentials as an initiate and disciple of Dionysus. To be such a disciple means to be a satyr, one of those who are ecstatically transfigured by the presence of the god. Following an anticipatory string of blandishments—Nietzsche's performative invocation of the god—Dionysus himself appears in the flesh and begins to speak. With this appearance, the reader, along with "Nietzsche," is transported to Naxos, and made privy to a dialogue between the god and his newfound human bride, Ariadne. The tableau portrays the encounter between human and divine as an erotic scene, a scene of seduction. Dionysus declares: "I love humans under certain circumstances." This statement is followed by a contextualizing remark indicating that Dionysus's circumstantial love is directed toward his bride Ariadne, "who was present." Dionysus then goes on to say that he desires to make humans "stronger, more evil, more profound than they are." This is precisely how we might expect a seducer-god to speak to a mortal partner following, or perhaps leading up to, a romantic tryst: he offers words of condescending praise but also an invitation to a more divine way of being (and of loving) unbounded by moral concerns. Importantly, it isn't Nietzsche who receives this seductive invitation, but rather the apparently silent figure of Ariadne. At this point an ambiguous voice interrupts the god's discourse. This voice speaks aloud, implying that the speaker too is present on Naxos, but also narrates its speech in the first person, as if remembering a past event: "'Stronger, more evil, more profound?' I asked, startled" (BGE 295). Who is the "I" that speaks these words? Nietzsche, the last disciple and initiate of Dionysus? Or Ariadne, the god's lover? Are we meant to imagine three figures present in this scene? Or only two? And what happens if we read "Nietzsche" into the text, as this "I"? Is Nietzsche recalling an encounter with Dionysus and his soon-to-be-deified bride, Ariadne? Or is Nietzsche perhaps inhabiting the perspective of Ariadne as she is seduced by the god?

The ambiguity of the voices and identities in this passage is a literary representation of the effect of deification, which blurs the boundary between chorus and god, seducer and seduced. The presence of the god is itself seductive, transfiguring, and even impregnating—it "fills one with new wills, and new desires," a new way of pursuing truth and of doing philosophy. In this text, Ariadne is in the position of the satyr, of drawing perilously close to Dionysus's erotic embrace: to be the god's wife or lover is to be deified oneself. It is she who gives Apolline form to the outpouring of Dionysus's passion, translating it into a literary image that reveals the justification and transfiguration of human subjectivity. While "Nietzsche" is the author of this text, his voice here unites with that of Ariadne, and the two become indistinguishable through their mutual proximity to divinity: together they represent the one who is seduced and impregnated by the transfiguring god but also the one who delivers the philosophical child in the form of the text, the offspring of this unadmitted seduction. As readers, we must then ask what the intended effect of this philosophical offspring is: Nietzsche seeks through his work to seduce us; BGE is an "attempt to tempt" us into a new way of doing philosophy, of being open to divine seductions, which in part means to forsake stable accounts of truth and subjectivity in favor of deifying transfigurations. And in this case, it also means to take on the countenance of Ariadne, a woman, the *bride of Dionysus*. To conclude, I will offer a few more reflections on what this openness to divine seduction might entail.

## Conclusion

Nietzsche's aesthetics—that is to say, the intended transfiguring power of his writings—entails a practice of deification that seeks to mirror and reproduce the justifying effect of tragedy. Beyond traditional aesthetics, as well as ethics, we might say that this practice has an explicitly religious dimension. By this, I mean that it introduces the promise, but also the danger, of a transfiguring encounter with, or even seduction by, divinity. And while it is true that the Nietzschean self is defined by the constant destabilizing process of self-overcoming, as both Pippin and Nehamas recognize in their respective ways, acknowledging the possible presence of divinity in this process introduces a further caution: if in pursuing justification one pursues erotic encounters with deities, then the problem isn't the impossibility of stability so much as the threat of being destroyed in the pursuit. As Pierre Klossowski reminds us, the prose of Actaeon—the one who seeks to behold nude deities—becomes unrecognizable and inhuman, even insane, before ultimately falling silent (Klossowski 1990). Nietzsche himself maintained that the deifying power of Dionysus represents the imbrication of sexuality and death, creation as well as destruction (BT 8). As such, to seek to behold the god, to prefer to be a satyr, or to take the place of the god's bride Ariadne means to risk becoming illegible, to no longer be recognizably what one was before. In this erotic encounter, it is not the philosopher who seduces but rather the god who seduces the philosopher, subjecting her to his deifying power, enriching but also shattering in its force. The deified subject is not only elevated and glorified, but humiliated and subjected to suffering, perhaps even ritually dismembered in festival ecstasy.[9]

Of those who encounter Dionysus, Nietzsche writes: "they are made richer in themselves, newer than before, broken open, blown on, and sounded out by a thawing wind, perhaps less certain, more gentle, fragile and broken, but full of hopes that do not have names yet, full of new wills and currents, full of new indignations and countercurrents" (BGE 295). Who are these philosophers of the future, broken but transfigured, less certain but more hopeful, caressed by the divine and pregnant with the future? Nietzsche is strategically coy about the precise features of such a figure, but in the finale of *BGE*, Ariadne, the wife of Dionysus, is the figure through whom Nietzsche imagines divine seduction and impregnation. In other words, in identifying himself with the figure of the philosopher who deifies life and is herself deified, Nietzsche imagines himself as a woman.

These considerations lead me to two final points. First and foremost is the reminder that for Nietzsche, the task of being a philosophical self, of becoming what one is, is to realize one's place within the chaos of becoming and to be simultaneously elevated and humiliated through this realization. As Nehamas indicates, this elevation is achieved through the practice of artistry, specifically writing: through artistic creation, Apollinian expression is given to prevoluntary Dionysian forces. However, to approach Dionysus also means to risk dismemberment: to deify and elevate life, one must also affirm the depth and inevitability of suffering. As such, the living Nietzsche's fate, indeed the misery he experienced before and after his loss of sanity, should absolutely not be interpreted as a reason to separate the value of his life from that of his literature: in his case, becoming what he was meant precisely to suffer unto madness and death; the living, suffering Nietzsche is integral and constitutive to the literary character. In this sense, his suffering was *necessary*; we would not have the literary character without it. We must therefore try to read his writings as an attempted affirmation, and indeed a deification of his own embodied life, no matter how "miserable" it may have been. This is obviously not to say that Nietzsche should be worshiped as a god or even as an especially exemplary individual: he himself would have reviled such ideas. The point is that Nietzsche's writing teaches that suffering can be justified through deification, rather than interpreted as an objection to life. His own fate exemplifies a powerful test case: while we can rarely control our own destinies, what agency we have as subjects and artists lies in how we respond to suffering, whether we lapse into *ressentiment*, or affirm and deify that suffering. To draw near to Dionysus means to experience the joy and elevation of deification through the pain and suffering of dissolution: such is Nietzsche's Dionysian dowry.

## Notes

1   Allowing that Nietzsche is both verbose and voluble about the many problems and errors that characterize various other conceptions of "the way things really are." My contention here is not that Nietzsche is never interested in truth and related epistemological questions, but that his criteria for thinking about such questions are generally governed by whether or not their answers are positive or negative for life, and as such, indexed to the more important problem of justification.

2   While Nietzsche departs radically from Christian orthodoxy especially, his own recommended philosophical practices share many points of continuity with both classical Hellenic and Roman philosophies, as well as those of some less-orthodox Christian thinkers. On the former, see Ure (2008); Faustino (2017); and for the more surprising Christian resonances, see Roberts (1998).

3   The word Nietzsche uses in BT, "*gerechtfertigt*," implicitly alludes to the Christian conception of God's redemptive bestowal of grace to assuage sin. This idea is decidedly transformative according to traditional Christian uses, denoting the conversion of the individual from a state of sin to one of grace. Nietzsche uses *Erlösung* more frequently in his writing, which has a similar connection to Christianity and was also more common in the philosophical parlance of his era. Schopenhauer wrote of the redemption of the Will, and Philipp Mainlander, another disciple of Schopenhauer whom Nietzsche read, published his *Philosophie der Erlösung* in 1876. While differentiating between these two concepts in Nietzsche's works is a worthy project, for the sake of this chapter, I will use them interchangeably, maintaining that they both indicate a similar notion of transfiguration.

4   "*Vergöttlichung*." Nietzsche occasionally uses this term, or other forms of the word, in both his published works and unpublished notes. My contention is that when we encounter a variety of other terms in Nietzsche's writing having to do with transformation, transfiguration (*Verklärung*), for example, we are entitled to imagine how thinking about those transformations as deifications might affect our reading of those passages. As this paper will make clear, Nietzschean deification has to mean something different than other uses, specifically the sense in which it indicates an affirmation of all that exists, rather than transcendence. This proposal has a number of interpretive virtues, but the most relevant one for my purposes is that it illuminates some of Nietzsche's most important invocations of the language of divinity, and deployments of divine figures like Dionysus and Ariadne, and shows how that language relates to the sort of transfiguration that Nietzsche envisions as one of the central goals of his philosophy.

5   One of Pippin's main objections to Nehamas, which is that he necessarily presumes a self-creating self, is relevant at this point. If the self is a constantly shifting sense of wholeness, then who or what imbues the preexisting chaos with the sense of style that gives it that aesthetic shape? Mustn't one on this account already *be* a self to achieve a self?

6   Many commentators, including Pippin, have pushed Nehamas on his admission that adopting such aesthetic criteria for self-formation and behavior leaves one in a difficult position with respect to ethics. Nehamas readily admits that an ideal Nietzschean character may be morally repugnant, as the formal criteria of aesthetic wholeness could encompass many different types; even decidedly evil characters can exemplify aesthetic wholeness.

7   Examples include D 109 or Nietzsche's discussion of the doer and the deed in the first essay of GM.

8   This account has more similarities to Nehamas's than differences, although it emphasizes that the achievement is a "state" of self-relation where Nehamas eschews that language and carefully avoids the language of self-creation. Crucially, both acknowledge in different ways that the ideal of a Nietzschean self, while it necessitates some dimension of unity or organization, also involves an embrace of the instability and mutability of the constitution of the self.

9  This account moves us well beyond Pippin's reading of Nietzsche's philosophy as a strategy of seduction. Extending the comparison to Montaigne, Pippin imagines Nietzsche's ideal as a philosopher who pursues truth through a strategy of deft seduction. What has inhibited previous metaphysical philosophers is their clumsy and ham-handed approach to truth: in dogmatically positing metaphysical accounts of truth, philosophers frighten away their shy quarry. Thinkers like Nietzsche, but even more so Montaigne, realize that truth is always shifting, implying an unsettled relationship with oneself, and so one must bring the skill of a philosophical Don Juan to the game of philosophy. On my reading, Nietzsche pushes us not only to be open to the vacillations of truth, our erotic quarry, but also to open ourselves to *seduction by* superhuman forces. In this sense, the issue isn't only how we can voluntarily affirm unconscious erotic commitments but also how prevoluntary and unconscious forces might seduce us. As such, to "become what one is" means, in part, to cede some quantity of agency to the nonhuman.

9

# The Veiled Mother: Life, Nature, and True Culture in Nietzsche's Early Thought

Pedro Nagem de Souza

In "Schopenhauer as Educator," Nietzsche's third *Untimely Meditation*, he defines culture as, among other things, "imitation and worship of nature where nature is in her motherly and merciful mood," implicating that culture also "draws a veil over the expression of nature's stepmotherly mood and her sad lack of understanding" (UM III §I, 130). In this metaphorical setting, we can see two opposite images of nature: one being a merciful mother and the other an intransigent stepmother. Meanwhile, culture is described as a veil covering expressions of the latter. And in this sense, the image of the veil simultaneously lies between the two, differentiating them, as well as between stepmotherly expressions of nature and a certain hidden viewer, protecting its eyes from such an uncaring vision.

This metaphor summarizes a series of problems faced by Nietzsche in his early thinking about culture, signaling to his complex comprehension of the relation between nature, life, and truth. This relation is not restricted by the idea of illusion as a necessary illusion in order to preserve beings in life, presented in the *Birth of Tragedy* (BT). The veiling, as I will show, is not just a condition for bearing the vision of life, but the quality of such veiling has implications in the authenticity or falsification of culture. The occurrence of the same mother metaphor in the early period texts sheds light on its significance within the broader context of Nietzsche's thought.

In the first part of this chapter, I explore the conceptual, epistemological, and metaphysical determinations laid out by Nietzsche in his early writings circumscribing this mother metaphor, concentrating on the consequences of its use to the notions of nature and life. I focus on the notes to his uncompleted 1867–1868 doctoral dissertation *On Teleology since Kant* (TSK) to conceive a notion of unity that will inform Nietzsche's comprehension of organicity, health, and culture.

In the second part I focus on Nietzsche's notion of a "true culture," showing how it stems from his thoughts on the relation between human conditions of knowledge and the background of life. The criteria of truth applied to culture are determined by those early remarks on nature, and thus the metaphor of the mother is essential for understanding the relation of nature and culture as carrying some kind of truthfulness. Providing a background of interpretation to this metaphor, I argue that the aforementioned formulation of the veiling of nature in SE is best understood as a culmination and a touchstone of the Nietzschean problem of culture. I further maintain that Nietzsche's first woman, and maybe the model for all the later ones, is the veiled mother.

## Nature as Fiction in the Notes on *Teleology since Kant*

Returning to the notes on TSK, the metaphor of nature as a mother is already present, as is the emphasis on her moods: "[she] is an impartial mother, equally hard with inorganic and organic children" (TSK 248). The focus on impartiality and hardness could suggest that this is a more neutral approach, and nature would be objectively such an impartial mother, which would later be anthropomorphized by the cover of culture's veil. In this interpretation, the veil would be equivalent to a protective Apollonian illusion, shielding humanity from the sight of an all-consuming and merciless nature.

But this immediate correlation with the context of BT is not sufficient since even this portrait of nature as an impartial mother is knowable only through human lenses. This is made clear by the way Nietzsche deals with mechanical causality: "Final causes," he says, "as well as mechanisms, are human ways of perceiving" (TSK 246). The mechanical indifference of matter is not treated as a simple statement of fact but as a specific way of human perception, and as such, it is not more objective than the perspective of a "final cause."

The epistemological equivalent (a "human way of perceiving") of the metaphor of the indifferent mother, this mechanical perspective is the reign of cause and effect, where objects and animals alike are swallowed by the causal sequence of becoming and vanishing ("equally hard with inorganic and organic children"); and still, this merciless chain of mechanical causality remains the projection of an all-too-human way of perceiving. From an epistemological point of view this already suggests that Nietzsche's idea of nature is modulated by the conditions of human perception. Developing this idea, he states that "our intellect is too dull to recognize continuous change: what is knowable to it is called form" (TSK 249); these forms are all contingent conditions of human knowledge, shaping the otherwise "completely dark" background of life. In other words, both the mechanical and teleological ways of perceiving are formal conditions of knowledge, projected toward a background which is, in extremis, inapprehensible.

Throughout his notes Nietzsche refers to this indeterminate background toward which we project our perspectives as "life." It is always characterized by analogy, be it as "multiplicity," or as the "eternally becoming," and this analogy is always rooted in human conditions: "We cannot conceive of 'life,' that is, sensate, growing existence, other than as analogous to the human" (TSK 251). In this sentence, the term "life" is put in scare quotes, signaling that even its naming is the result of analogy with the human sphere, not the precise designation of an entity.[1] This "life" is not knowable in itself. "Not even by final causes," he says, can we illuminate it (TSK 249).

The emphasis on human conditions of perception and knowledge is in part due to the theme and nature of the work, a draft for a doctoral dissertation on the post-Kantian discussion on teleology. But Nietzsche's drafted position in the wider discussion about teleology also anticipates some key aspects of his own philosophy, to the extent that some readers see this text as the "matrix of the future theory of perspectivism" (Marques 2003: 55).[2] The main element of this position is the concept of expediency (*Zweckmäßigkeit*), which, as a form of our intellect, is not an objective aspect of reality but only a conditioned appreciation of living beings: "what we call expedient is nothing other than that we find a thing capable of life and as a result of that we find the conditions to be expedient" (TSK 247). With this, even the concept of organism, inseparable from its own expediency, is considered a formal projection of human conditions upon the multiplicity of life.

Without the idea of an end of nature as prior to human projection, objective teleology is discarded since the organization of living beings is not due to an objective organizing principle—a preestablished harmony, for example. But we also cannot suppose a higher rational unity which would maintain this idea of expediency as a necessary condition given by a rational principle: "We can at best decide upon a reason, but have no right to indicate it as higher or lower" (TSK 240). In other words, there's no guarantee of an ultimate totalization of principles in the unity of reason, which would ensure a subjective teleology based on the necessity of rational laws.

In this sense, Nietzsche's approach to expediency radicalizes Kant's *Critique of Judgement* by making expediency a contingent form and, thus, not even a purely rational necessity. With this weakened concept of expediency, Nietzsche "aims to circumscribe the *subjective-utilitarian* status of that which for Kant had yet a *purely cognitive* value, so to speak" (Marques 2003: 54). By attacking the teleological consequences of the Third Critique, Nietzsche removes the last traces of an objective necessity to human forms of knowledge.

Going back to the metaphor of nature as an indifferent mother, it is after we humans project our own conditions of knowledge upon an unknowable multiplicity that we can qualify this multiplicity in any way. Our ability to refer to a motherly or stepmotherly nature follows this veiling—one of our own making—and it is then that we can we refer to any nature at all, since before this projection the designation of "life" to this background is merely an approximation.

In this sense, the background of life and this first projected nature are almost interchangeable, but there is a crucial difference between them: nature is only conceivable after the projection of the veil of the forms, while life is the unconceivable in itself, so to speak. Nature occupies the same "place" as life, but since life is not conditioned by space, it is not in any "place" whatsoever; as if nature only exists "after" human forms are projected toward life, but since life is not conditioned by time, it does not lie "before" anything.

In terms of the broader significance of this to Nietzsche's views on women, to take any of these images of nature as objective is to suppose a will to truth that could grasp a "real nature," positioning the viewer as a castrated woman in front of a castrating nature. Neither the merciful nor the indifferent mother is really affirmative if they are posed as objective, as existing independently of the children's own gaze.[3] "It is (...)

when the will to truth becomes the will to illusion, and recognizes itself as illusion, that it is in the service of ascending life" (Oliver 1984: 190). To pose nature as a projection toward life is to radicalize the complementarity of truth and illusion, preparing an affirmative approach of both the mother and the veil.

Nature is already veiled life, and even hardness and mercilessness are not the naked truth of the original mother. The idea of a naked truth is, in the context of the mother metaphor, a little too Oedipean, and its rejection may serve as a precedent to the later Nietzschean critique of the clumsiness of dogmatists with regard to women. What we see in this early text is a relational concept of nature, conceivable only in opposition or continuity to the human sphere, itself the superficial face of the ever-changing background of life. The conditions for this visibility are the intellectual forms, which project unity toward the multiplicity of life. The complementary images of nature as a mother and as a stepmother are projective resultants of a fundamental act of veiling by humans. There is no nature prior to this veiling, no original Mother Nature before the glimpse, no final layer of skin to which the veil could allude or betray.

Here, as in later texts, the feminine aspect of nature is not an invitation to nudity but to modesty. "With this, one suppresses, as something null, the very concept of a truth *beyond* appearances, above or below the veil" (Blondel 2009: 65). Nature itself is always a second nature, in the sense that it is a result of human projection toward an always distant and intangible origin. Nietzsche will later refer to this operation when showing the limits to a critical approach to history. Objecting to the unrestricted condemnation of the historical past (which is treated as inherited nature[4]), he says:

> The best we can do is to confront our inherited and hereditary nature with our knowledge, [...] and implant in ourselves a [...] second nature, so that our first nature withers away. It is an attempt to give oneself, as it were *a posteriori*, a past in which one would like to originate in opposition to that in which one did originate.
> (UM II 76)

Regardless of the success of the attempt, the fact that humans can try to give themselves another nature stems from the fictional basis of the image of nature projected toward life. The notion of an a posteriori origin goes well with the metaphor of the mother since the aspects and moods of such an image of nature depend on the human perspective. We, the children of nature, search for nature's moods where there is nothing but the multiplicity of life itself, and we actually see these moods, unaware that we only discover in our mother's eyes the light we ourselves project.

## Life and Its Manifold Manifestations

Nietzsche's remarks on teleology provide another indication of his comprehension of nature as a veiled mother. Despite the inherent distance between the core of "life" and what we apprehend as nature through the forms of intellect, this fictionalized approach does not imply a radical solipsism.[5] The restriction of human knowledge to intellectual forms is accompanied by the emergence of the "forms of life" as the knowable aspect of things, which is nevertheless founded in the primordial unknowability of life.

The intellectual forms are "all of 'life' that appears visible at the surface" (TSK 250). Life is made visible through the projections of human beings. The abyss between the multiplicity of life and the unitary forms of human intellect is epistemological, but metaphysically life engulfs the whole range of its forms. From the start, human beings are immersed in the *continuum* of life, which will be later categorized and veiled by their intellect. But this veiling doesn't conceal more than it reveals since the background has no intelligibility prior to the veiling of human forms.

This is made clear in the case of the organism, which will be one of the main focuses of the notes on teleology since it is the typical projection of final causes and the form of expediency toward unintelligible life. "The organism," says Nietzsche, "is a form. If we look away from the form, it is a multiplicity" (TSK 243). There is a continuity between the perspective of life and the perspective of its forms. "Looking away" entails a change in perspective over one and the same form—seen either as a unity in opposition to the multiplicity around it or as one of the many possible manifestations of said multiplicity in a singular form. The possibility of looking away indicates how the points of view on "life" and form are intrinsically united.

The organism will also be characterized as a surface of life, its visible side: "what is an organism other than form, *formed life*?" (TSK 248). As unintelligible as life is, it cannot be separated from the "astonishing number of forms" in which it takes expression (TSK 248). If nothing can be said about life in itself, its manifold manifestations are still linked to it, expressing in the knowable surface the eternally becoming, which is inconceivable in itself though always present in absentia.

Here, the Schopenhauerian influence is clear. As with the distinction between will and representation, the epistemological distancing between the two "domains" is complementary to the metaphysical unity of the world. The world as representation is constituted from the standpoint of the individuation of will, and the world as will still resides as the moving background of all things—just as with "life" and its forms. The complementarity between the two points of view doesn't exclude their intrinsic tension since the permanence of a given form always stands *against* the eternally becoming. The preservation of the form is never pacific, and the agonistic struggle at the basis of any form of life is first and foremost a struggle of an individual form of life against its own dissolution into the unknown at its own core. We can only know the forms of life, not life in itself. However, since the analogical operation happens in the midst of life, there's but a formal distinction between life and its specific forms. An individual form is maintained in existence through the fine tension between its individuation and the multiplicity from which it arises.

When Nietzsche says the judgment of whether something is expedient or not designates the "ability to live," he is circumscribing the form of the organism to this same tension.[6] Not an external teleological unity applied to the multiplicity, nor a simple objective fact, the capacity to live of an individual form of life is the capacity of forming life in this or that individual living being. The circularity of the definition deflates the idealistic implications of the concept of expediency: "A thing lives—thus its parts are expedient: the life of things is the purpose of the parts" (TSK 250).

The excessive "treasuring of teleology in its valuation for the human world of ideas" (TSK 241) and its consequent presupposing of a deep link between our forms of perceiving and the true reality of the world based on the mere fact of expedience are all locked inside this circle of deflated expediency. Life in itself is unknowable, and the life of things is as far as the concept of expediency goes. The internal articulation between the parts of a living unity is maintained in regard to the life of this unity as such. Inversely, the capacity to articulate its parts into a unity is synonymous with the life of *this* individual being.

The notes on TSK delineate a judgment on organisms and their expediency which is immanent to the forms themselves without a reason that would function as an "original core of meaning that would be regulatorily presupposed" (Marques 2003: 61). At the same time, this judgment allows for the ineffable aspect of existence to be the constant ground for apprehensibility itself. Expediency is the ability of living/existing, and all living beings have around them a contour of indiscernibility. Such a judgment does not ask "what is life in itself?," nor "why do things live?," but only "what are the conditions for the maintenance of *this* singular life in *this* singular form?"—knowing in advance that it won't find in this explanation more than was previously projected.

But even though the circular notion of expediency considers the forms of life without substantializing them and the formalist/fictionalized aspect of this perspective rejects the qualification of a "life in itself," the qualification of nature will not be empty of meaning. The continuity between the manifested life and its manifestations in the forms is revealing, not of a previous reality of "life" but of the image of nature resulting of a human projection of forms. Here, the aforementioned distinction between "life" and nature is crucial since the latter expresses life through a human form.

An image of nature is at the same time the precondition of human knowledge and the expression of the particular human life that engenders it. The position of nature in the early Nietzschean texts is certainly singular: a means for apprehending life, it also involves the sphere of human projections, never coinciding with the nakedness of the eternally becoming. Making possible our apprehension of the world, nature is humanity's first lens, but also, it's first veil since it draws the boundaries of human perception, also in a negative sense. This relational conception of nature comes rather easily to the metaphor of the mother. Not simply as a generative force but as a first image of the world which will structure the limits of the child's worldliness—what is to be seen and what is to be forever hidden.

The images of nature Nietzsche describe therefore function as both a barrier and an openness, the original castration that puts in motion both the will to truth and the will to illusion. Nietzsche does not refrain from postulating a "primal mother, eternally creative beneath the surface of incessantly changing appearances, eternally forcing life into existence" (BT 16). Nevertheless, this postulating is possible in the context of an artificial separation of Dionysian and Apollonian impulses—a didactic exposition, so to speak. Life continuously manifests itself in myriad forms yet remains unknowable. Always pregnant, never naked. As the unattainable yet necessary affirming woman, "she is hollow like a womb. She is the space, the womb, from which everything originates. This space is distance: the affirming woman is not an object in the distance; rather she is distance (…) As distance, as space—pure womb—she does not exist" (Oliver 1984: 196).

The constitution of human knowledge as intrinsically limited and conditioned by the unknowable background of life is the basis of any perspective on nature. Humans are never to unveil life in itself, and yet they never cease to hear, as if from behind the threads of nature, the singing of a distant, more original truth of the eternally becoming—*"Frisch weht der Wind der Heimat zu: mein irisch Kind, so weilest du?"*[7]

## Mother Nature and True Culture

There is yet another notable implication of Nietzsche's mother metaphor to his later thought, which is recognizable in his early concept of culture. It concerns the differentiation between true and false cultures, or between culture and its philistine counterpart. Such a qualification sounds strange in the wider context of Nietzsche's thought—its occurrences in the *Untimely Meditations* making it even stranger (see UM I 7, UM II 80 and 123, UM III 142). Nevertheless, the notion of "true culture" plays a role of differentiating Nietzsche's conception of culture from what he sees as the mainstream philistine conception, a mixture of bourgeois, modern, and erudite ideals. Most importantly, this terminology sends us back to the mother metaphor with the question of whether there is a specific relation to nature and life (metaphorically, to the Mother) that could evoke some notion of truthfulness or authenticity.

We must note that the acts of imitating, worshiping, and hiding have the same projective origin, the same throwing of the veil over the unconceivable face of life. This common ground identifies each human activity and its resulting products as cultural activities and products, up to and including the first act of instituting the difference between culture and nature. Considering the mother metaphor in the light of this identity, the duplicity between a "positive" aspect of worshiping a motherly nature and a "negative" aspect of veiling the stepmotherly one becomes a two-fold act of distinction between nature and its unseen core. This veiling and re-veiling of "life" will constitute both a culture's first image of nature (be it a mother or a stepmother) but also this same culture's image of itself.

The development of the problem of culture throughout the early texts deepens the unitary aspect of this fundamental act. Even though the notes on TSK focus on epistemological and metaphysical questions and do not mention the concept of culture, the later descriptions of and prescriptions for culture will have similar horizons.[8]

### (1) Culture as an Organic Unity

First and foremost, the criterion of *expediency* is maintained throughout the period. The joint action of each part directed at the production of the whole and the consequent internal unity of this whole will be the main criterion for Nietzsche, not just in this early phase[9]. It applies to individuals, to cultures, to worldviews,[10] to organisms, and to works of art. Regarding the last two, Lacoue-Labarthe notes that "artwork [*oeuvre*] and organic are the same word, and it remains to be seen which one is the model to the other, either art or life. Or to see which one is dominant in Nietzsche's thinking: an onto-zoology or an onto-mimetology" (Lacoue-Labarthe 1986: 108). The fictional aspect of the formalist comprehension of the notion of expediency tends to equate the many levels of expedient unities and to blur the supposed originality of one or another. In any case, expediency is the element in common between artwork and organicity, and it's an aspect of the organicity and liveliness of the former and of the beauty and harmony of the latter.

This is also true for the unity of culture as a whole. Thus, it is no surprise that restoring the "health of a culture" will be equivalent to "re-integrate the individuals back to the group," in opposition to cultural pathology, where "the tension between [culture] and its individual components was slack" (PTG 27). If forms are characterized by their unity, and if their individual "lives" consist in the unity they can maintain between their parts, then the degree of this unifying capacity is the measure of health.[11]

Again, it is precisely because of that fundamental identity of human acts in face of life that Nietzsche can talk about culture as a unity, to which the many activities and impulses work as parts or functions. The integrity of the veil gives it a form and figure, which sustains the whole as such against the omnivorous flux of life. In this sense, while maintaining the unity of a people in existence, culture conveys its capacity to live.

The cultural act of constituting such unities against the background of multiplicity will be referred by Nietzsche as style. I would argue that even the "legislation of greatness" (PTG 43), the defining activity of the tragic philosopher, is an equivalent of stylization since it's carried out while having the health of culture as its main objective. Both style and the legislation of greatness have the same function of directing and restraining the impulses, of submitting the many instincts to a single desire and thus giving order to a plurality.

The designation of culture as a "unity of artistic style in all the expressions of the life of a people" (UM I 5) is directly linked to this conceptual framing. It is both a touchstone to later texts and a result of Nietzsche's first thoughts on the notion of organism—a second one being the aforementioned metaphor of the mother and the veil presented in *Schopenhauer as Educator*. It allows us to think of culture as a unity expressing life in a determinate form and of style as the internal unification of the multiplicity of its expressions.

Extending the mother metaphor to the notions of health and style, we can see a remarkable coherence in these early Nietzschean remarks on culture. Health can be seen as the active conjoining of impulses toward a culture, while culture is the resultant unity which, at the same time, conveys its unitary aspect to its parts. In short, health is to expediency what culture is to the organism. At the same time, style both distinguishes human life from nature and projects human forms toward life, a phenomenon evident in each level of culture and identical—in healthy conditions—to the founding act of culture. The metaphor of the veil synthesizes the act of stylization, the forming of a culture, and its internal, healthy coherence.

As Sarah Kofman says, "artistical unity of style and unity of the living being are one and the same" (Kofman 1985: 92). The vitality of a culture is comparable to its discernability as a unity, its capacity of affirming itself in the midst of life's eternal becoming. And that applies also to the cultural construct of nature produced by such a culture since nature is not a separate entity but already a stylized image.

## (2) Culture as Continuous with Nature

Since the act of veiling is contiguous with both culture and the produced image of nature, the resulting culture will be deeply linked with the image of nature at its roots. This continuity is essential to human beings:

> When one speaks of humanity, underlying this idea is the belief that it is humanity which separates and distinguishes human beings from nature. But there is, in reality, no such distinction: the "natural" qualities and those properly called "human" grow inseparably.
>
> (HC 277)

The fictional character of nature makes it all the more human, and this continuity implies a certain transmission of character between the two spheres since a healthy culture will produce a healthy image of nature. The cultural idea of nature being the product of an exchanging between culture and life (the re-veiling act of style), it will express more or less vitality depending on the quality of this same foundational act. Sickly peoples will project a sickly image of nature.

But this continuity is not total identification. The image of a caring mother is not necessarily linked with a healthy culture, and the stepmotherly mood is not a direct sign of sickness. This is made clear by the terrible picture of nature and existence as a whole painted by the Greeks, healthy as they were. "What kind of earthly existence," Nietzsche asks, "is reflected in these repulsively terrible theogonic myths," and his answer emphasizes the *worldview* of the Greeks as engendering these same myths of origin: "[their] uninterrupted view of a world of fighting and cruelty [brought them] towards a disgust with existence, toward the interpretation of this existence as punishment and atonement" (HC 279). Considering the role of the Theogony as a founding myth, with Gaia as the typical mother-nature, the tragic Greek style so exalted by Nietzsche starts by postulating a terrible origin and a senseless mother surrounded by the lineage of Nyx and its own titanic offspring.

The Greek health did not reside in a joyful picture of nature, but in the quality of the stylization contained in the first veiling of life and developed, not by negating such a nature but by submitting it to higher hierarchies of culture. "If Nietzsche designates nature as an original text (…) is because she is, as long as alive, stylized. Stylization, by submission to a dominant instinct, is constitutive to nature's text" (Kofman 1985: 94ff.). This constitutive character of style implies that a sickly image of nature could only be diagnosed as such by the analysis of the culture from which it emerges.

This continuity between culture and nature is twofold: on the one hand, the expressive relation between nature and culture resides on the fictional/projective character of nature; on the other, since the unity and liveliness of a culture are its defining aspect and health, the veiling of Mother Nature must not oppose the two spheres as estrange to one another.

This brings Nietzsche to one of his principal concerns in this period, which was to differentiate a *true culture* from a false one. If we consider culture only as a stylistic unity and expressive continuity with its natural ground, there would be no way to assert the authenticity of any cultural expression. Our artificial modern culture could also claim to be a legitimate veiling of nature inasmuch as its fabrication has all the traces of a fictionalized unity.

This point is best expressed in the following passage of the first *Untimely*: "even an inferior and degenerate culture cannot be thought of as failing to exhibit a stylistic unity within which the manifold phenomena which characterize it are harmonized" (UM I 8). The superficial similarities between such a degenerate culture and an authentic one threaten the identity of a supposedly authentic culture. How can we distinguish one veil from another if the human condition as a whole is characterized by this veiling? If we all project our formal conditions of knowledge toward an unknowable life, how can a set of conditions be more legitimate than the other? What is the "truth" in, or genuine about, a "true culture"?

## (3) The Philistine Problem

The choice of the cultural philistine as an antipode illuminates the difficulties of establishing a clear distinction between a true and a false culture. What characterizes such an opponent is "he fancies that he is himself a son of the muses and a man of culture" (UM I 7). In this assumption of inheritance, the role of son is challenged by Nietzsche, a problem of legitimacy and succession that puts us again at the heart of the mother metaphor.

But we cannot ignore the initial insult in a challenge: the jealousy of the muses. This jealousy is aggravated by some superficial resemblances between the contenders: like Nietzsche, the philistine also "invents for his habits, modes of thinking, likes and dislikes, the general formula 'healthiness'" (UM I 12). And in fact, this philistine efficacy in removing disturbances and bringing the nonconformed to conformity is not that unsimilar to the expediency of a healthy culture with a unity of style.

Even though Nietzsche hurries to remove from the philistine practice any cultural meaning, designating it as a senseless "barbarism with style," this rush reveals the conundrum of the philosopher-physician trying to lean away from his opponent as not to be confused with him. The problem is that there is no human community without some sort of internal coherence between its parts (some minimal health), and even the philistine pseudo-culture articulates itself as a "system of un-culture."

If one of the main advantages of the Nietzschean conception of expediency is the dismissal of a teleological valorization of ideal forms, its main risk is to fall into a lack of differentiation between the many manifestations of cultural unity. If the simple maintenance of a certain unity of impulses were enough to maintain the life of a culture, the philistine would also have his share of reason, and it would suffice to administer a certain symmetry of disposition of said impulses. In this conceptual mist where all cultures are gray, the health of a culture is not that distinguishable from its sickness, and the physician/philosopher is dangerously near to his antipode to the point that the philistine believes to be "a judge of classical taste" (UM I 12).

We should neither take the philistine for granted nor dismiss his claim only by Nietzsche's authority. "Discovering everywhere identical reproductions [*gleichförmige Gepräge*][12] of himself, he infers from this identity of all 'cultivated' people the existence of a unity of style and thus the existence of a German culture" (UM I 8), and his inference has some grounding, given that there would be a certain "symmetry of character" in such homogeneity and consequently an appearance of unity. It is a misleading appearance, from the order of the artifice, lacking in style and fluent in "arabesque flourishes," and yet it is an appearance similar to what is apparent. The philistine *seems* to possess a culture and deceives even himself.[13]

Nietzsche's "conception of 'true culture' subscribes also to a whole metaphysical tradition" in which the task of true culture is to negate the artifice: "it would suffice to free man from false culture, free him from conventions, from public opinion, from the common culture" (Kofman 1985: 84). In fact, it is necessary to liberate oneself from this deceiving appearance in which the interior and exterior don't correspond, for it is such an exact opposite of true culture that it appears to mirror it—hence Nietzsche's insistence upon reinforcing the artificial character of modern/philistine culture.

It is not a condemnation of masks per se, which could suggest an excessive will to truth. The problem of artificial culture is its "breaking of man into two parts (…) it hides, by the veil, that there is nothing to hide" (Kofman 1985: 85), just as in the case of an exclusively Apollonian culture in the *Birth of Tragedy*, which takes its strength of the negation of the Dionysian that goes through it.[14]

The philistine, in his stylized barbarism, maintains the unity of his falsified style by negating nature and life in their most proper aspects: "For that uniformity which is so striking in the cultivated people of Germany today is a unity only through the (…) exclusion and negation of every artistically productive form" (UM I 8). The mere collection of cultural products and manners in symmetrical fashion is far from enough to characterize a culture, and the negative aspect of the philistine culture resides in the fact that this pseudo-unity is never affirmed from within the natural realm but always in spite of everything that comes from nature. In the context of the mother metaphor, he is either an orphan or, worse, an ungrateful son.

"Separated from culture," nature is "a force of death, as much as a culture that was separated from nature" (Kofman 1985: 90). While it portrays itself as makeup, artifice, and *trope-l'oeil*, a fake culture splits its source of meaning and its natural grounding. Even more, this split may radicalize to the point of opposition, mortifying both poles. Though it is a permanent human possibility, since the fiction of nature is based on human projection, this philistine separation of nature and culture is far from paramount.

Nietzsche is opposed to the philistine on behalf of "naturality," "honesty," and "naivety" to the same extent that on behalf of culture. The distinction of truth and falseness is valid when the return to nature of a true culture is not a return to the ideal by elimination of the apparent but the search for a continuity of meaning and value between nature and its apparition in culture.

Even in this early phase, the essence/appearance dichotomy is never solved by Nietzsche through a rejection of one of the poles. His critical-philosophical work does not negate the similarities of a philistine pseudo-culture and a healthy culture but opposes them regarding their relation of affirming or negating life. Only a genuine tragic culture can claim to behave in true continuity with nature, assisting her and "taking her at the same time as a model: [culture] must pursue the same ends as nature, but use more effective means" (Kofman 1985: 88). The natural realm is corrected by human hands, but every pruning is also optimization and, therefore, a reaffirmation of the original impulse. The limit is not imposed by the outside since there is no conceivable "outside" of nature but occurs through life's continuous process of development and the limitation of nature over itself.

## (4) A Dynamic Culture for a Dynamic Nature

The pseudo-culture has the dubious merit of expressing its sickness in its deranged manifestations and even exhibits some resemblance of style in this expressiveness. Nevertheless, it loses sight of what deeply characterizes a true style and a true culture:

> But if an author possesses genius, he betrays it in more than simplicity and precision of expression [traces of naturalism and naivety]: his abundant power plays with his material even when it is difficult and dangerous (…) [the genius] runs nimbly along such paths with daring or elegant strides and disdains cautiously to measure his steps.
>
> (UM I 46)

These "runs" and "strides" of the genius bring us to the last aspect of a true culture I want to emphasize. And that's because if we consider this continuity of meaning between nature and culture, there must be an essential character in common between the two spheres, one that the philistine doesn't apprehend.

Nietzsche repeatedly accentuates the productivity of a healthy culture, correcting and continuing the intrinsic movement of life. This movement neither ends in the collection of objects produced by culture nor restricts itself to the sterile reproduction of ideals. Culture, being continuous activity of self-affirmation of nature and liveliness, must absorb in itself the movement inherent in the eternally becoming. If Nietzsche's search is for the "natural ground on which a cultural unity can be established" (Jeong 2021: 240), then this cultural unity retains the activity and movement that define this ground—an always moving, ever-changing ground.

This is directly linked to the fictional basis of nature and the human sphere, fiction being thought, in a positive sense, as poetical creation: "For Nietzsche, to be is to be produced. If being—life—is thought of as potency, as *dynamis*, it is because it is first thought, in a certain echo of the Greek interpretation of being, as production" (Lacoue-Labarthe 1986: 109). As I've shown above, the original product of such a movement is an image of nature, and the relation of affirmation/negation of such natural ground is the basis of a healthy conformation of multiplicity in a cultural unity. But since life implicates movement and becoming, only a productivity that has its foundation in the productivity of nature is up to the cultural task.

Undoubtedly, his task oscillates between the search for a true culture, for the art that would bring this culture to light,[15] for the kind of philosophy that would prepare his task, in short, for all the modulations of figure and function involved by the problem of culture, which are never taken in isolation. But this oscillation reveals the main difference between the physician of culture and the philistine. The philistine assumes the *possession* of the concept of culture at exactly the point where this idea can only determine a *search* without any guarantee—hence the seduction that the philistine's symmetrical heap exerts on conformists, since it gives, in its systematicity, the false appearance of a finished product that would cease all need for productivity, all efforts, all search for a true culture.

In this point, there is no possible reconciliation: "For it seeks, this German spirit! and you hate it because it seeks and refuses to believe you when you say you have already found what it is seeking" (UM I 9). The indistinction between a true culture and a false one occurs in terms of the general unification of a multiplicity or yet of the internal confluence *directed toward* a style. But while the philistine nullifies this direction, this tensioning of seekers, in a conformed satisfaction, a healthy culture draws its unity from the movement itself, from the very act of seeking.

This act of seeking is also a certain modesty toward nature and life, engaging in the game of veiling and re-veiling without ever supposing to tear apart the distance. This total possession of life would lead to her imprisonment and ultimately to the death of the cultural dynamic. Without this preoccupation, the philistine simply wants to possess, and he even stimulates the drive for knowledge in the hopes that it would ultimately lead to a full possession of life as one of the many products on his shelf.

Nietzsche even fancies himself as "lightly clad," again mobilizing the metaphor of the veiling to say: "perhaps the expression 'lightly clad' is only a euphemism for naked" (UM I 46). The absence of any modesty leads inevitably to decline, which is why Nietzsche's rejection of the philistine is so important to his project. The philistine is sickly and probably contagious: "Ours is a cold clime, and it is precisely because he goes around so lightly clad that he runs the risk of catching cold more often and more gravely than others" (UM I 67). To protect culture from sickness, one must reinforce the necessity of movement, as to generate the warmth that will keep it alive.

It is precisely where the indistinction seemed insurmountable that the abyss between the organicity of culture and the system of un-culture is most acute. The philistine's imperative, hidden under the mask of symmetry of character, is to "cast suspicion on seeking as such and to promote a comfortable consciousness of having already found" (UM I 10). Therefore, he is hostage to his own "negative being," and even those systematic customs are not enough to speak of a culture, but only of an enduring continuity of an artificial unity, like a clock or a sandcastle.

The *foundation* of literate barbarism is confused with its *duration* precisely because, by drawing its unity from the constant negation of the movement of becoming (that is, of "life"), un-culture is essentially infertile, incapable of conceiving a vivacity that goes beyond its own self-enduring. Meanwhile, the fertility of a healthy culture far outlasts its own duration, as in the case with Greek culture.

It is worth noting that, referring to the philistine pseudo-culture, Nietzsche tends to use metaphors suggesting the inorganic and stale ("amassing," "juxtaposition," "convention," etc.) in opposition to a true culture. If a culture is not unified, but plastic and fertile, it is also never satisfied, never resolved, in continuity with the background of life, which itself must be conceived as "sensate, growing existence" (TSK 251) to do justice to the obscure multiplicity hinted at through the veil of nature.

To those who refuse contentment—the tacit inertia of the "real," a bourgeois quotidian—culture imposes itself as a task. It entails a dynamic configuration of activities, values, and impulses, which, instead of aiming at a final resolution that would ultimately negate the eternal becoming of life, augments the movement and increases the tensions that comprise the culture and sustain its existence. In this sense, culture is always the problem of culture.

## Conclusion

The concept of nature inhabits a fine line in this first period of Nietzsche's thought, being at the same time the surface of "life" (its skin) and the cultural clothing that makes life visible and bearable. The artistical style gives the limit of any culture's individuation, which is why the unity of style is (at least in this period) the main definition of a "true culture." The tighter the thread, the more it hides Mother Nature's thighs.

Yet at the same time, the dynamic aspect of this veiling is essential to differentiate a true culture from a false one and to avoid the philistine claim of authenticity in cultural terms. Without this dynamic aspect, we would compromise the whole cultural endeavor by blurring the productive aspect of a lively culture. The fabric of culture must bring warmth without losing movement. The claim of being a "true culture" demands both the continuity with Mother Nature and the dynamic aspect of culture derived from this continuity. To deserve the title of nature's son, one must see his mother as a moving being, lively and hollow, as an affirming woman.

Nietzsche's dispute with the philistine is for the legitimate claim of consanguinity to Mother Nature. Nietzsche absorbs nature's "true self" (the unknowable and ever-moving life) by not removing or negating her inherent movement and bringing this dynamic aspect to his own conception of culture. Hence, by dancing with nature, he imitates and worships her, honoring the life which is always insinuated behind the veil.

As what turns a woman into a mother is, by definition, having children, the metaphor contains the reciprocity between the seer and the seen. Nature can only be a true mother to cultured humans, which select some of her features as essential through the veil of cultural fiction. Only a fool would want to look behind his mother's veil, and the Nietzschean criticism of the untamed impulse to knowledge can be traced to this same conceptual and metaphorical framing. Like Oedipus, the modern man insists on knowing his *true* origin, even if it means moral ruin and *blindness*.

Throwing a veil over nature's nudity is the precondition to see it as a mother or a stepmother, as an "*a posteriori* origin."[16] But to a sickly animal as the cultured human, all concealment instigates unveiling. Therefore, this first act of motherly modesty puts in motion the seductive game of sickly hide-and-seek that permeates all cultures and contains the key to both their coherence and disintegration. The key to health is to maintain the truth of life at a distance, to engage in her dance, and to worship the veiling of nature as the movement of life herself. And to her warnings, "If I love you, look out for yourself!," respond not as the foolish Don Jose, who ultimately kills his love trying to possess her fully, but as Escamillo, who pays homage to his love in the midst of the bullfighting and hears from the choir: "And remember, yes, remember as you fight, that two dark eyes are watching you, that love awaits you! Toreador, love awaits you!"[17]

## Notes

1 "Life," in this radical sense, is the name of the ever-growing obscure "X = " behind nature. I will return to the parallel with Schopenhauer but note here that Schopenhauer also refers to the will as an analogical designation of an obscure ground of existence.
2 See Cruz (2015: 67–82), for a detailed description of Nietzsche's dialogue with the Hegelian and Aristotelian views of teleology, with special attention, in the post-Kantian context, to Trendelenburg.
3 The castrating aspect of the "merciful" mother was not strange to Nietzsche: "it matters little to them whether their children are happy or not; what counts is that they can bestow kindness on them and, in this way, exercise power" (Marton 2022: 27).
4 The relation between history and nature is well developed in many commentaries on UM; see for instance Heidegger (2009) and Zuckert (1976: 55–82).
5 I take the term from Temp (2019: 203–22); also see Toscano (2001: 36–61).
6 There is an oscillation in the texts between the phrases "ability to live," "ability to exist," and "capacity of life."
7 From the opening scene of Wagner's *Tristan and Isolde*. Freely translated, "Fresh the wind blows towards home: my Irish child, where are you?"
8 On the descriptive and prescriptive meanings of *Kultur*, see Kopp (1974).
9 See Jeong (2019).
10 For example, Schopenhauer's "greatness lies in having set up before him a picture of life as a whole, in order to interpret it as a whole" (UM III 141).
11 For a broader analysis of the idea of cultural health, see Ahern (1995). The later notion of great health and its relation to ways of living is compellingly examined in Faustino (2016).
12 Considering the role of allegory and similarity in Nietzsche's early theory of language, it is worth noting that both "identical reproductions" and the term "identity," which follows, translate this same expression in German. See Cavalcanti (2005).
13 I generally agree with Jeong's statement that "it is a delusion that there is a culture, in a genuine sense, to which the cultivated philistine [*Bildungsphilister*] belongs" (Jeong 2021: 239). He stresses the unitary aspect of Nietzsche's definition of culture against the notion that *noble ideals* would be the defining feature of a true culture. Also see Huddleston (2019). Nevertheless, we should not dismiss the philistine illusion so fast; I will show how the natural/vital grounding of culture qualifies the unity of a true culture as dynamic.
14 As Machado observes, "[a]iming to replace the world of truth, or the truth of the world, with beautiful forms, Apollonian art leaves something essential aside" (Machado 1984: 30).

15  Among the many commentaries on this theme, see Gemes and Sykes (2015). Also, Jeong, op. cit.
16  Marton generalizes this notion of "second nature," stating: "masculine and feminine are converted in a second nature, which is also in constant mutation" (Marton 2022: 25).
17  Both references are to Bizet's *Carmen*: the first to the *Habanera* aria and the second to the *Toreador* aria.

Part Four

# Care and the Other

10

# Nietzsche's Perfectionism and the Ethics of Care: A Brief Treatment

Justin Remhof

Nietzsche appears antithetical to care ethics. He often mocks human dependency, for instance, sometimes in ways that appear sexist (see, e.g., Z I Women), and he famously challenges the legitimacy of compassion. Nietzsche's positive ethical position is arguably some form of anti-egalitarian *perfectionism* which holds that goodness is constituted by individual human excellence. Perfectionism, however, coupled with a rejection of the ethical significance of dependency and virtues like compassion, can seem dangerous to modern sensibilities—especially to those in the care tradition. We typically believe that a plausible ethical theory should function to ensure positive rather than negative relations between individuals, and it looks like perfectionism is not up for the task.

I think we should put Nietzsche's perfectionism to the test. In this chapter, I briefly explore whether Nietzsche's perfectionism might not only be consistent with but possibly even support several core features of care ethics. I cannot possibly hope to accomplish a sufficiently detailed comparison of Nietzsche and the ethics of care. I merely want to introduce something new worth thinking about: Nietzsche's perfection is arguably closer to the care tradition than might originally be thought, and, as I see things, this makes his perfectionism more plausible that it might otherwise appear.

The Nietzsche that emerges from this chapter is not a full-fledged care theorist. Nietzsche is certainly not interested in systematically assessing and accounting for the ethical significance of various forms of dependency, for example, and it will emerge that his positive view of compassion seems to be much more demanding than what care ethicists often advance. But no matter: I do not plan on arguing that Nietzsche is a care theorist. I want to explore a reading of Nietzsche's perfectionism that might align with care ethics. From this reading a form of care emerges that appears to be specifically Nietzschean.

## Central Features of Care Ethics

Let me lay out six central features of care ethics. For this task, I primarily draw on Held (2006), Kittay (1999 and 2019), Norlock (2019), Noddings (2003), Tronto (1993), and Sevenhuijsen (1998). The care tradition fundamentally focuses on how all people are *dependent* on others from survival to living well. When we are young and old, and oftentimes in between, we depend on others. The fact that we are all dependents implies two further features of care ethics. Care ethicists call attention to the fact that we are all *vulnerable*. Dependent persons are noticeably open to attack, harm, or damage, whether mentally, physically, or emotionally. Dependency also entails that we are all sometimes in *asymmetrical power relationships* to others, especially when needing or giving care. We are not all equal all the time. Dependency, vulnerability, and asymmetry are undisputable realities of human life. In virtue of these realities, care ethicists argue, we all need care. At the least, care is *ethically significant*. Care enables living well given the reality and implications of dependency.

Further features of care ethics emerge when we look at how we might provide considerate care relations. First, considerate care seems to require a sense of *compassion* that involves an attachment and responsiveness to others. Attachment demands that we recognize that others have needs which need care. Responsiveness might best be understood as a sense of reciprocity: one must consider a person as having certain needs that must be met as that person expresses those needs while not presuming that the person is exactly like oneself. Arguably, attachment and responsiveness primarily arise from some form of compassion, that is, an awareness of others' distress together with a desire to alleviate it. Compassion appears to be crucial for establishing positive rather than negative care relations.

Care theory also contends that *emotions* are ethically significant. Emotional responses can help concerned persons understand and respond to others in a helpful manner. This is not to countenance the legitimacy of any raw emotion whatsoever. Emotions most suitable for enabling considerate care relations should be refined over time through evaluative reflection. Emotions are often other-directed, of course, and care ethicists hold that strategically developing emotional sensibilities can help render dependency relations between people more constructive than non-emotional consideration.

Finally, care ethicists hold that relations between *particular* people are ethically significant. Care theorists are skeptical about attempts to establish universal, agent-neutral ethical principles—principles sought after in traditional ethical programs—on the grounds that such principles intentionally disregard ethical features of specific relationships. As Held says, "the ethics of care *respects* rather than *removes* itself from the claims of particular others with whom we share actual relationships" (Held 2006: 11). Care ethicists do not necessarily close off the possibility of establishing or giving priority to impartial principles. But they often focus on how partial, agent-relative ethical claims might supersede impartial, agent-neutral ones.

The core features of care ethics are then (1) dependency, (2) vulnerability, (3) asymmetry, (4) the development of compassion, (5) the development of emotions, and (6) prioritizing partiality over impartiality. The first three are facts of human life and the last three concern ways in which care ethicists address those facts.

## Perfectionism as Self-Transformation

Now that we have a basic understanding of care theory on the board, I want to look at Nietzsche's perfectionism from the perspective of self-transformation (for alternative accounts of his perfectionism, see Cavell 1990, Hurka 2007, Conant 2001, Rutherford 2018). Self-transformation locates the good in cultivating one's highest values. In *Thus Spoke Zarathustra* I: "On the Three Metamorphoses," Nietzsche lays out three stages of self-transformation. He elaborates on the first stage in the first four sections of *Schopenhauer as Educator* and the second stage in the first five sections of the 1886 preface to *Human, All Too Human*. In principle, each stage of self-development is open to all. Indeed, although I cannot argue for it here, I think Nietzsche's anti-egalitarianism is often best understood in terms of those who can and cannot enact self-perfection.

In the first stage ("camel") one begins searching for one's highest values by engaging in a wide array of difficult but inspiring tasks associated with different and possibly conflicting values. In SE 1 Nietzsche suggests that this process begins when one's conscience calls one to become who one is. In SE 2 he adds that one can avoid value conflict in this stage by determining a dominant highest value around which to order or ground peripheral values. Peripheral values might then mutually support each other by co-supporting the dominant value. In SE 2–3, Nietzsche suggests honesty, cheerfulness, and steadfastness as three possibly dominant values to help those in the first stage.

In the second stage ("lion") one embarks on challenging values adopted in the first stage. This includes, generally, traditional moral values which dominate the Western tradition and, more broadly, values one feels comfortable with—and maybe even complacent toward—after the first stage. The aim is to facilitate self-sufficiency, which consists in rendering one's values more one's own by purging traditional, assimilated values and igniting recommitment to a select few of one's first stage values on the condition that they remain inspiring after being provisionally superseded. Unsurprisingly, then, successfully completing this stage of self-transformation requires hard work and intense discipline.

In the last stage ("child") one's highest values become part of one's habitual nature, which frees one to create new values from a child-like "innocence." Ideally, this process leads to the production of values that give rise to higher humanity. Achieving the last stage is the ultimate goal of Nietzsche's perfectionism.

Can the process of self-transformation account for the central features of care ethics? A major worry is that dependency both precedes and enables the development of one's highest values—it comes prior to any "call of conscience." Perfecting oneself cannot be successful without somehow accounting for dependency and somehow safeguarding positive dependency relations. Call this the "care challenge." Does this challenge undermine the viability of Nietzschean self-development?

## Care Ethics and Self-Transformation

What follows is a sketch of how account of self-transformation might respond to the care challenge. I focus on the first stage ("camel") in conjunction with elements of Nietzsche's philosophy that might account for the features of care ethics described above. I proceed by examining how the first stage of Nietzsche's perfectionism might affirm (6) partiality, (5) emotions, and (4) compassion (in that order) to handle (1) dependency and by implication (2) vulnerability and (3) asymmetry.

First consider partiality. The first stage of self-transformation assumes that partiality may take precedent over impartial ethical codes, just as care ethicists argue. This largely follows from Nietzsche's attack on traditional ethical programs, which require impartiality to eclipse partiality by demanding universal applicability. For Nietzsche there are simply no features all individuals share which could justify the universal applicability of any one value, principle, or ethical code. Indeed, for Nietzsche different kinds of values should be applied to help navigate unique, individual experiences.

The fact that one's relation to oneself should have priority over allegiance to agent-neutral ethical principles, then, given that the latter explicitly intends to overlook individual distinction, is secured in the first stage. Nietzsche gives individual preference priority. If we make the reasonable assumption that individuals often find features of particular relationships much more ethically significant than features of relationships without personal connection—and I see no reason to think Nietzsche would deny this—it looks like the ethical significance of values developed and sustained between people in close relationships will likely contribute substantially more to self-transformation than any attempted adherence to universal values, principles, or codes. Again, Nietzsche provides all sorts of arguments against the viability of the traditional focus on universality. This suggests that the particularity of specific relationships can and likely do play a central role in the process of self-transformation.

The ethical significance of particular connections to others in the camel stage is reinforced when we notice that for Nietzsche emotions, which he often regards as passions, have significant ethical importance. For him emotions are not mere feelings but much more meaningful: they convey worldly orientations. To use Robert Solomon's (2003) nice example, infantile rage is meaningless, while resentment is meaningful. Resentment showcases an understanding of history, involves a complex sense of injustice, and projects an imaginary future. An emotional orientation might be seen as providing a helpful *strategy* that can be refined over time. Nietzsche says that one moves from "the weight of stupidity" of being passive with respect to passions to "spiritualizing" them through gradual control and eventual mastery (TI Morality 1).

Cultivating passions is necessary in the first stage of self-transformation because for Nietzsche passions are fundamentally constitutive of one's highest values. Indeed,

Nietzsche thinks that emotional development enables flourishing. He describes high values as "refined passions and enhanced states" (KSA 10:24[31]). These enhanced states inculcate a "way of thinking and behaving that, once it has become habit, drive, and passion, will rule in [the individual]" (GS 21, cf. Z I Passions). Developing emotional responses creates a path to one's highest values. This path is often shared with others. Indeed, experimenting with realizing our highest values likely always requires participation in social contexts that involve dedicated others, such as friends and mentors, that support progressive movement. This suggests that developing deeply meaningful and inspiring emotional connections with others is central for self-development.

The fact that emotional orientations are ethically significant, however, does not yet tell us which kind of emotional strategies one might develop into values that can ensure considerate care relations. Some form of *compassion* seems to fit the bill. One might reasonably hold that Nietzsche should appeal to compassion in the first stage of transformation, perhaps as a dominant value around which to structure other values, to properly answer the care challenge. Yet Nietzsche is a powerful critic of compassion (see, e.g., HH 50, 103; D 132–142; GS 271, 338; Z II Pitying; GM P; BGE 222, 225, 260; TI Morality 1). I now discuss one key passage where Nietzsche details specific worries about compassion. My goal is to suggest that a positive view of compassion can be salvaged and should be integrated into the first stage of self-development.

In *The Gay Science* 338 Nietzsche asks two questions. First, is it good for those who suffer if one is compassionate toward them? Nietzsche anticipates an affirmative reply but provides three reasons for a negative response. I am going to comment on what form of compassion Nietzsche *allows* with each negative reply he gives. Nietzsche does not attack compassion as intrinsically wrongheaded. Rather, his remarks suggest that compassion is instrumentally problematic on the grounds that it can hinder the possibility of self-development. This means that Nietzsche might be amenable to a form of compassion that contributes to self-transformation. This is what I focus on.

Nietzsche first says that since one's suffering is "inaccessible to nearly everyone," whenever we are "*noticed* to be suffering, our suffering is superficially construed," which "strips the suffering of what is truly personal" (GS 338). Notice what this criticism leaves open: Nietzsche allows individuals to feel compassion if they can have a genuine understanding of someone's suffering. This form of compassion aims at helping those who suffer embrace their suffering for self-development. Indeed, Nietzsche then says that those who are compassionate "want to help and have no thought that there is a personal necessity of misfortune" (GS 338). So one who recognizes when another might benefit from suffering will understand when to be responsive and when to abstain from premature help.

Nietzsche finally tells us that ethical systems which "command [one] to help" many times result in one thinking that "they have helped best when they have helped most quickly!" (GS 338). Again, we have space for compassion. Those who take the time to be responsive in the right kinds of ways, eschewing external ethical imperatives and making compassion a personal virtue, may help best. All three difficulties with compassion can be avoided with the right kind of orientation toward being compassionate.

The second question Nietzsche asks in GS 338 is whether it is good for *us* to be compassionate. The first reason he gives against a positive answer is that the demands of reducing suffering may likely disrupt self-transformation. He writes, "[T]here are a hundred decent and praiseworthy ways of losing myself from my path" (GS 338). Attending to our own distinctive needs can be incompatible with attending to the needs of others. Giving aid might be admirable, but we may become overwhelmed. Care theorists have expressed similar worries. For instance, Meyers worries that the demands of care may result in a "plague of commitments" that may blur one's identity (Meyers 1989: 152).

This worry, however, concerns only those whose engagement in aiding others diminishes their own resources for becoming who they are—and this result need not be the case. Nietzsche additionally suggests that aiding others might give one sanctuary from attending to one's own needs—we "take refuge in the conscience of others" (GS 338). Yet it is consistent with these criticisms to claim that one should compassionately provide care if the task is not debilitative and engaged with a proper grasp of one's motives.

Each space I have carved out for compassion names a legitimate form of appropriately attending to and responding to another's suffering. Nietzsche seems to affirm the sense of reciprocity in which one should be attentive to an other's needs while not presuming that the other is exactly like oneself. He requires that we understand when, how, and why compassion can be put to good use. At the end of the day, he even appears to offer a positive view of compassion. He ends GS 338 like this:

> [Y]ou will want to help—but only those whose distress you properly *understand* because they share with you one suffering and one hope—your *friends*—and only in the way you help yourself: I want to make them braver, more persevering, simpler, more full of gaiety. I want to teach them what is today understood by so few, least of all by these preachers of compassion: to share not pain, but *joy*!

Compassion is effective if one can adequately understand another's suffering by recognizing what needs require attention, and for Nietzsche this possibility occurs in close relationships under the goal of working toward mutual perfection. Nietzsche countenances compassion not merely for alleviating distress, then, but to help someone develop the kinds of sensibilities necessary to face inevitable suffering and arouse what Nietzsche calls a fellowship in "*joy*" (GS 338). Indeed, by "learning better to feel joy," Zarathustra tell us, "[W]e learn best not to hurt others or to plan hurts for them" (Z II Pitying). Seeking joy can decrease potential problems with dependency. Zarathustra later adds: "But if you have a suffering friend, be a resting place for his suffering, but a hard bed as it were, a field cot: and thus you will profit him best" (Z II Pitying). Compassion should be implemented carefully for the purposes of helping someone become their highest self. Indeed, "compassion for the friend should conceal itself under a hard shell, and you should break a tooth on it. That way it will have delicacy and sweetness" (Z I Friend). Rather than condemning compassion tout court, Nietzsche embraces a form of compassion characterized by "delicacy and sweetness."

It is reasonable to suppose that this Nietzschean form of compassion should be used to support the self-transformation of those who are dependent, vulnerable, or asymmetrically situated in relation to oneself. Nietzsche's remarks on compassion show that we need not avoid compassion when embarking on self-transformation. We might instead integrate a specific form of compassion into the first stage. Given the reality of dependency, which Nietzsche appears to acknowledge, the likelihood of seeking out and maintaining a beneficial form of compassion can be essential for self-transformation.

## The Process of Self-Transformation

I want to point out one final thing. It looks like the process of self-transformation *itself* might help to ensure considerate care relations. Being alive to what constitutes one's own flourishing shows that one has grasped the value of attentiveness, and learning to discriminate and act upon one's own needs arguably enhances the ability to discriminate and act upon the needs of others. Neglecting responsibilities to oneself may likely hinder one's capacity to adequately respond to others. Being responsive to and taking care of oneself help one be responsive to take care of others, albeit for Nietzsche those committed to perfecting themselves.

## Conclusion

Care ethicists have typically ignored Nietzsche—and, as I suggested above, it looks like they have good reason to. But this dismissal could be considered shortsighted. By affirming partiality, deliberate emotional development, and a certain kind of compassion, Nietzsche's perfectionism, understood as a form of self-transformation, can to some extent acknowledge and address the realities of human life care ethicists find ethically significant. To reiterate, I do not think Nietzsche can *sufficiently* account for realities like dependency. At the least, though, Nietzsche can provide a substantive response to the care challenge, and I think drawing out the ways in which Nietzsche's perfectionism can support core features of care ethics makes his perfectionism more worth taking seriously.

# 11

# Stendhal, Nietzsche, and Beauvoir on Romantic Love

Lorenzo Serini

## Introduction

It is quite common among specialists and nonspecialists alike to regard Nietzsche as someone embittered about love. Many commentators would agree with Simon May that "[s]exual or romantic passion is not the sort of love between two people that most interest Nietzsche" (May 2011: 197). Indeed, the standard interpretation is that Nietzsche is deeply critical of romantic love and much more interested in other forms of love such as friendship, which he deems to be superior. (It might be tempting for some to reconnect Nietzsche's embitterment about romantic relationships to his unrequited love for Lou Andreas-Salomé and other women—and, in turn, even to his misogyny.) Although the standard interpretation is not erroneous, I suggest, it does not do full justice to the complexities and nuances of Nietzsche's thinking about romantic love.

It is true that Nietzsche is often critical of romantic love; however, it would be mistaken to conclude that he has no serious interest at all in these topics. In fact, in many of his writings, and starting at least from *Human, All Too Human*, Nietzsche can be found continually returning to the theme of loving relationships between women and men—albeit, as is typical of him, he never articulates it in a sustained, systematic discussion.[1]

As Robert C. Solomon noted, Nietzsche distinguishes between "life-stultifying" and "life-enhancing" passions (Solomon 2003: 63–88). In this chapter, I want to argue that for Nietzsche romantic love may take both life-stultifying and life-enhancing forms. His conception of romantic love as a life-enhancing emotion, one that engenders an authentic, flourishing relationship, is largely overlooked in the secondary literature.[2] By drawing attention to Nietzsche's conception of life-enhancing romantic love, I contend, we can gain a different, more positive perspective on his views on the relationship between women and men.

In this chapter, I will explore the topic of romantic love in Nietzsche by inviting a comparison with Stendhal (Marie-Henri Beyle) and De Beauvoir.[3] There is a strong philological motivation for comparing these three figures: Nietzsche read Stendhal, and Beauvoir read both Nietzsche and Stendhal. I will specifically focus on Stendhal's

*On Love* (1822), Nietzsche's middle writings (1878–1882), and de Beauvoir's *The Second Sex* (1949). Not only are their views on romantic love interconnected, but, as I will show, they also complement one another philosophically. While the connection with Stendhal can help us to better understand some of the premises of Nietzsche's psychological observations on romantic love, the link with de Beauvoir will help us to identify Nietzsche's conception of a life-enhancing form of the passion and to appreciate some important implications and uses of his considerations of gender roles in romantic relationships—especially, with respect to feminist theory.

**Stendhal on Love: The Concept of "Crystallization"**

Stendhal is most famous for his literary works—for novels such as *The Red and the Black*. In this section, I exclusively focus on his essay "On Love." This essay, as Stendhal himself presents it, is not a novel but "a philosophical work in which the author coldly describes the various phases of the disease of the soul called love" (Stendhal 2004, "First attempt at a Preface")—a disease that like "a fever [...] comes and goes quite independently of the will" (Stendhal 2004: Ch. 5). With such a philosophical description, Stendhal wants "to establish exactly what this passion is" and to offer a cure for the great pains frequently caused by this disease-like passion (Stendhal 2004: Ch. 1 and Ch. 3 n. 1). Although for Stendhal love is "the strongest of the passions"— the most volatile and violent—it is not to be completely eradicated, for in love we can find the greatest enjoyment and delight (Stendhal 2004: Ch. 12). Rather, we need to better understand and appreciate the process of falling in love and the workings of this passion, so as to cool it down, to get more control over it, and to properly prepare ourselves for its great pleasures.

According to Stendhal's philosophical description, love is a kind of madness because it brings us to see reality—especially, our beloved—in a distorted way: "from the moment he falls in love even the wisest man no longer sees anything as it really is" (Stendhal 2004: Ch. 12). Whereas all the other passions "have to adapt themselves to cold reality," Stendhal claims, "in love realities obligingly rearrange themselves to conform with desire" (Stendhal 2004: Ch. 12). In other words, unlike other passions, love has the power to reshape the lover's reality: the lover "loses his sense of the probable; judging by its effect on his happiness, whatever he imagines becomes reality" (Stendhal 2004: Ch. 12). A large part of the essay is devoted to explaining this phenomenon.

Central to Stendhal's philosophical analysis of love is the concept of "crystallization," a term that he coins "to express the impulse of folly that makes us see all beauties and perfections in the woman we are beginning to love" (Stendhal 2004: Ch. 3, n. 1). The word "crystallization," in Stendhal's opinion, "express[es] the principal process of the madness known as love, a madness which nevertheless provides man with the greatest pleasures the species can know on earth" (Stendhal 2004: Ch. 3, n. 1). Stendhal famously explains the concept of "crystallization" through the metaphor of the salt mines of Salzburg. Here, after throwing a branch in the salt mine, "[t]wo or three months later [people] pull it out covered with a shining deposit of crystals," to the point that "[t]he original branch is no longer recognizable" (Stendhal 2004: Ch. 2). Crystallization, as described by Stendhal, is a "mental process" of projective idealization, through which the lover projects crystals, beauties, or perfections onto the beloved, distorting and transfiguring their image of them (Stendhal 2004: Ch. 2). For Stendhal, then, love is akin to an optical illusion, and the moment we fall in love with someone, we no longer see them as they really are. Under the spell of this illusion, the lover bestows value on our beloved and even "overrate [her] wildly," coming to see her in a different, special light (Stendhal 2004: Ch. 2). While for Stendhal the process of crystallization needs to be stimulated on an ongoing basis to keep love healthy and pleasurable, as we will see in Section 3.1, Nietzsche finds the delusion involved in such a process highly undesirable.

## Nietzsche's Reception of Stendhal

As reported by Thomas H. Brobjer, Nietzsche reads Stendhal starting from 1876 (Brobjer 2008a: 256). By querying the *Nietzsche Source*, we find evidence of a recurrent engagement with Stendhal, who is directly mentioned in Nietzsche's writings, both published and unpublished, as well as in his letters, from the posthumous fragments of 1879 to *Ecce Homo*. From these mentions, it is clear that Nietzsche holds Stendhal in great esteem (see, for example, BVN-1885, 583; EH Clever 3, especially as a "deep psychologist" (EH CW 3; cf. TI Skirmishes 45). Campioni specifies that Nietzsche knows Stendhal's *On Love* and is well aware of his famous concept of crystallization (Campioni 2009: 49). Now, I want to argue, Nietzsche draws on Stendhal's concept of crystallization in the context of his psychological observations on romantic love in his middle writings.

## Nietzsche's Criticisms of Love

As Keith Ansell-Pearson and Rebecca Bamford note, "[i]n his middle writings [...] develops a powerful set of criticisms of love in its idealized romantic form [...]. He is suspicious about cases of romantic love that assume an obsessional form simply because it makes fools of us as we become so prone to self-deceit and world-deceit" (Ansell-Pearson and Bamford 2021: 182). I identify three specific criticisms Nietzsche directs to romantic love in the middle writings.

### *Love as a Crime against Knowledge*

In *Mixed Opinion and Maxims*, Nietzsche criticizes people who speak in praise "of 'forgetting oneself in love' and of 'dissolving one's self in the other person'" (MOM 37). Those people, for Nietzsche, delude themselves about the nature and workings of romantic love when they speak of it as a sincere, self-less passion, through which the lovers merge into each other. Against this view, Nietzsche contends that in love "we [...] project our selves imaginatively upon a person whom we admire, and then relish the new image of our self, even though we call it by the name of the other person" (MOM 37). Nietzsche's contention in this aphorism clearly echoes Stendhal's concept of crystallization as an imaginative projection of the lover onto the beloved. (Even if Nietzsche does not actually have Stendhal in mind here, the concept of crystallization can help us to better understand and appreciate Nietzsche's observation about love.) Unlike Stendhal, however, Nietzsche is bitterly critical of this process. In Nietzsche's view, romantic love involves deceit, self-deceit, and egoism, and those who mistake it for a completely sincere and altruistic passion "commit a robbery from the treasury of knowledge: from which it follows what crime the saying, 'Know thyself!' warns us against" (MOM 37). I will focus on Nietzsche's attack on the common conception of love as an altruistic passion in Sections 3.3 and 4; for now let me say something more about his criticism of the deceit and self-deceit-involved love.

For Nietzsche, not only do people deceive themselves about the nature and workings of love, but the imaginative projection involved in love is itself nothing less than a crime against knowledge, especially against self-knowledge: In *Dawn*, Nietzsche argues that "[l]ove turns us into inveterate felons against truth," since, when we are under the spell of love, we "permit more to be true than seems true to us" (D 479). On the one hand, we lack honesty toward ourselves; and on the other, we fail to do justice—both epistemically and, as we will see, ethically—to the other person (cf. HH 69).

Still in *Dawn*, Nietzsche further develops his criticism of love as a crime against knowledge through a comparison with fear:

> *Fear and love.*—Fear has furthered the universal knowledge of humanity more than love, for fear wants to discern who the other person is, what he can do and what he wants: to deceive oneself here would mean danger and disadvantage [...]. Inversely, love has a secret impulse to see in the other as much of the beautiful as possible or to elevate the other as high as possible: for love to deceive itself here would mean pleasure and advantage—and so it does.
>
> (D 309)

In other words, whereas fear has an epistemic significance, love can be an obstacle to knowledge on account of its beautifying powers. Nietzsche's view of love in this aphorism (as "a secret impulse to see in the other as much of the beautiful as possible") is once again reminiscent of Stendhal's theory of crystallization. His view, though, has negative connotations, especially with respect to the significance of love for knowledge and to the practical implication of deceit and self-deceit for the lovers. Love is construed as a bias that tends to deceive by exaggerating the attractive characteristics of the beloved and to overlook or minimize their unattractive characteristics, distorting the lover's perception of the beloved to the point that the former's image of the latter diverging considerably from how the loved one really is. Moreover, Nietzsche affirms, "[L]ove is the secret impulse to elevate the other as high as possible"—above others as well as above oneself (D 379). This impulse leads the lover to debase themselves with respect to the beloved. If both lovers elevate the other and debase themselves, Nietzsche observes, they establish a relationship in which both individuals diminish themselves, deceptively idealizing the other (D 379).

### "Love Makes the Same"

In *Dawn*, Nietzsche scoffs at the common idea that the lover dissolves themselves in the beloved and that therefore "[*l*]*ove makes the same*" (D 532). For Nietzsche, not only does this idea involve deception and self-deception, but it also forms an undesirable fusion between the two lovers. Firstly, "[l]ove wants to spare the other to whom it consecrates itself every feeling of *being different*; consequently, it is full of dissembling and a show of similarity; it deceives continually and playacts a sameness that in truth does not exist" (D 532). In addition to deceiving themselves about the beloved, the lover more or less consciously deceives the beloved, playacting sameness rather than simply being themselves. This is because lovers who conceive of love as the feeling of being the same try to form an undifferentiated union that forbids the feeling of being different on both sides. As we will see in section 8, for Nietzsche, difference is vital for flourishing human relationships such as friendship—but also for more genuine forms of love.

Secondly, in the mutual playacting of sameness, each lover renounces—at least some parts of—themselves, sacrificing their individuality to imitate the other: "both relinquish themselves, feign sameness of the other and want to imitate that other and that other alone: and in the end neither knows any longer what one's imitating, why one's dissembling, who one's pretending to be" (D 532). The reciprocal mirroring between the two lovers creates a sort of void of identity instead of a *we* generated by the combination of two individual. As Nietzsche ironically puts it in *The Gay Science*, "for if both partners felt impelled to renounce themselves, we should then get—I do not know what: perhaps an empty space?" (GS 363). By clinging on to the ideal of love as the feeling of being the same—on to the romantic models of "forgetting oneself in love" and of "dissolving one's self in the other person"—the lovers relinquish their individualities and form a union in which both fail to actually participate in, and contribute to, the relationship as themselves. As we will see in Section 4, for Nietzsche self-relinquishment is a typical characteristic of the woman in love.

### *Love as a "Lust for Possession" in Disguise*

As we saw in Section 3.1, Nietzsche criticizes people who say that romantic love does *not* involve egoism (MOM 37). The criticism of the common conception of love as something entirely unegoistical is further developed in *The Gay Science*. Here, Nietzsche proposes the hypothesis that love and avarice, which people ordinarily take to be opposite, may in fact have a common origin in the same instinct—that is, a "lust for possession" (GS 14). His hypothesis is that "the concept of love as the opposite of egoism [...] may actually be the most ingenious expression of egoism" (GS 14; cf. D 145).

In this aphorism, Nietzsche suggests that different things that people generally call "love" (for example, love of our neighbor, love of knowledge and truth, pity, and sexual love) can be explained as a desire for possession and thus connected to avarice and egoism. In particular, for Nietzsche, "[s]exual love betrays itself most clearly as a lust for possession"—a desire to "change something new *into ourselves*": "the lover desires unconditional and sole possession of the person for whom he longs; he desires equally unconditional power over the soul and over the body of the beloved; he alone wants to be loved and desired to live and rule in the other soul as supreme and supremely desirable" (GS 14). If one considers this—among other things—Nietzsche observes, "then one comes to feel genuine amazement that this wild avarice and injustice of sexual love has been glorified and deified so much in all ages" (GS 14). In addition to attacking the misconception of love as something unegoistical, Nietzsche thus regards the lust for possession driving sexual and romantic relationships as an injustice toward the beloved—and, in a sense, toward the rest of the world.[4]

It is for this reason that in the conclusion of the aphorism, Nietzsche expresses his preference for friendship over romantic love. Friendship is "a kind of continuation of love in which this possessive craving of two people for each other gives way to a new desire and lust for possession—a *shared* higher thirst for an ideal above them" (GS 14). As such friendship, for Nietzsche, is a more just form of relationship between two individuals. Friends, unlike lovers, do not desire to *possess* one other; rather, they *share* a "higher thirst for an ideal above them"—that is, for a higher self. As Nietzsche sees it, friendship is a better opportunity for shared self-cultivation than love. In comparison to lovers, true friends are more truthful with one another, to the point that they can even be antagonistic; their honesty and frankness facilitates their pursuit of self-knowledge (Abbey 2000: 77; see also Ansell-Pearson and Bamford 2021: 183); they do not debase themselves to idealize the other but are in agonistic competition; they do not relinquish their individuality to playact sameness but confront their differences; they push each other to strive for ambitious goals (see, for example, Z On the Friend).[5]

Despite his criticism, it is important to note, Nietzsche does not simply believe that sexual love is to be unequivocally condemned and eradicated. On the contrary, he warns us against the demonization of eroticism and the deification of chastity that we can find, for example, in Christianity (D 76). Nietzsche thinks that friendship can remedy the shortcoming of some forms of romantic love: "Marriages made for love [...] have error as a father and penury as a mother" (HH 389); in contrast, "[a] good marriage rests upon the talent for friendship" (HH 378). This is because, for Nietzsche, "[s]ensuality often hurries the growth of love so that the root stays weak and is easy to tear up" (BGE 120); after all, one cannot promise a volatile emotion such as sexual love for ever (HH 58). Nietzsche goes as far as to say that "[o]ne ought not to be allowed to reach a decision [about marriage] affecting one's life while in the state of being in love, [...] on the basis of a heated whim: [...] and indeed precisely because one ought to take marriage unspeakably more seriously" (D 151). One way to take marriage more seriously, Nietzsche recommends, is to conceive of it as a "*a long conversation*" between friends,[6] for "everything else in marriage is transitory, but most of the time together is spent in conversation" (HH 406).[7]

In any case, Nietzsche believes free spirits, whom he characterizes as "men," "must prefer *to fly alone*" rather than living with women and getting married—for the sake of "truth-thinking and truth-speaking" (HH 426). Nevertheless, he hopes that in the future "noble, free-minded women" will consider "marriage [...] in its higher form, as a friendship of the soul between two human beings of different sex [...] for the purpose of engendering and educating a new generation" (HH 424). Such a marriage, for Nietzsche, will not be primary based on possessive erotic love but on a shared pedagogical project and will thus allow concubinage (HH 424).

## Nietzsche on the Different Roles of Men and Women in Love

In Sections 3.1-3, I discussed Nietzsche's criticisms of romantic love in general, without particular reference to gender roles. I now want to focus more specifically on the roles Nietzsche attributes to men and women in the romantic relationship. Let me begin by first saying something about friendship and gender. In line with GS 14, in *Dawn* Nietzsche states that the ancient Greek conception of friendship has an advantage over the modern obsession for "idealized sexual love" (D 503). In this context, though, Nietzsche adds: "All great abilities possessed by the people of antiquity took their purchase from the fact that *man stood beside man*, and that no woman was permitted to lay claim to being the nearest, highest, let alone exclusive object of his love—as sexual passion teaches us to feel" (D 503; cf. GS 61). Nietzsche's critique of erotic love here carries misogynistic implications. Although the primary target of his attack is the modern overvaluation of romantic love, he favors a patriarchal conception of friendship such as that of the ancient Greeks. As Nietzsche notes in *Human, All Too Human*, "Greek culture [...] is a culture of men [...]. [Social intercourses with women were important only in relation to procreation and sexual pleasure. No genuine love affairs]. Women themselves were excluded from [the social and cultural life]. Women had no further duties than producing beautiful, powerful bodies in which the character of the father could live on" (HH 259). On the basis of passages such as those, one may want to ask, is Greek-style friendship even possible between men and women for Nietzsche? And between women?[8] Bringing our focus back to romantic love, I want to ask now, does Nietzsche endorse the Greek view of the relationship between men and women? What is the role of women in love and in society for Nietzsche?

In Section 3.3, we saw that in GS 14 Nietzsche connects love to a desire for possession. As it turns out in the fifth book of *The Gay Science* (1887), that is for Nietzsche the conception men have of love (GS 363). Women, instead, have a different conception.

> For man and woman have different conceptions of love; and it is one of the conditions of love in both sexes that neither sex presupposes the same feeling and the same concept of "love" in the other. What woman means, by love is clear enough: total devotion (not mere surrender) with soul and body, without any consideration or reserve [...]. In this absence of conditions her love is a faith; woman has no other faith. Man when he loves a woman, wants precisely this love from her and is thus himself as far as can be from the presupposition of feminine love. [...] Woman wants to be taken and accepted as a possession, wants to be absorbed into the concept of possession, possessed. [Man's] love consists of wanting to *have* and not of renunciation and giving away.
>
> (GS 363)

The picture of the romantic relationship pictured in this aphorism is as simplistic as it is patriarchal—though as we will see in Section 5, not uninteresting. While men's love is a desire for possession, women's love is a desire to be possessed. Men play an active role, whereas women are essentially passive. I will return to this aphorism in the next section, suggesting that this can be used for a feminist critique of women's roles within a patriarchal society. To conclude this section, let me say something more about Nietzsche's view role of women in love and society in his middle period.

In contrast to GS 363, in his pre-Zarathustra writings Nietzsche acknowledges that in fact women do not play a purely passive role in the romantic relationship and that a subtle desire for possession is at work in their way of loving too. In *Human, All Too Human*, Nietzsche speculates that originally women consciously and cleverly made use of the idealizations of love (see Sections 1 and 3.1) to exercise their power over men (HH 415). At times, Nietzsche seems to praise women's—so to speak—Machiavellian "cleverness"; other times, he disapproves of their overreliance on the art of dissimulation for its contributing to exacerbating the deceit and self-deceit in love (HH 404).

As Nietzsche sees it, women end up falling pray of their own trap, identifying themselves with the role they originally playacted to have power over men (HH 415). Their identification with the role as objects of men's love has contributed to relegating women to a condition of passivity. Women are victims of their own "idolatrous attitude toward love" (HH 415): when they see their identity as uniquely defined by men's desire for possession, they remain unemancipated—both in the relationship and in society. "Perhaps," Nietzsche writes, "all this may change, but for now this is how it is" (HH 416). As things are in his time, he observes, there are not many "noble, free-minded women" who "oversee [their] own business and official duties separately from [their] husband" (HH 424). The vast majority of nineteenth-century women are largely dependent on their relationship with men. In such a situation of dependence, for Nietzsche, women's desire for possession cannot find full expression in romantic love and thus needs to be sublimated in maternal love: "The females find in their children satisfaction for their desire to dominate, a possession, an occupation" (GS 72).

Here, I agree with Willow Verkerk that, although Nietzsche does tend to see "the female as a lower type of human being" (Verkerk 2017: 132), "[he] provides a provocative and critical view of love that helps us to consider the extent to which love and friendship are shaped by gender constructs and inequalities" (Verkerk 2017: 151). However, as Verkerk argues, "Nietzsche is pointing to a problem that exists in love between men and women without making any suggestions for improvement" (Verkerk 2017: 138): "Nietzsche's woman is not given the opportunity to consider what she might be outside of a world that is defined by men" (Verkerk 2017: 152). While Verkerk aims to supplement Nietzsche's view on love and friendship with Luce Irigaray, in the following section I will show how Simone de Beauvoir uses Nietzsche's claim that "man and woman have different conceptions of love" (GS 363) for a feminist critique of the role of women in love in the context of a patriarchal society. In Section 6, I will then explore de Beauvoir's conception of an authentic kind of love. Finally, in Section 7 I will argue that Nietzsche too has a partly similar conception of authentic love.

## De Beauvoir on Inauthentic Love: A Feminist Use of Nietzsche

In *The Second Sex*, de Beauvoir explores the secondary condition of women in a world dominated by men. Here, we can find an important chapter on love, focusing on the subordinated role women play in the patriarchal romantic relationship. "The Woman in Love" opens with an extensive quotation of GS 363, wherein Nietzsche claim that men and women love differently. De Beauvoir subscribes to Nietzsche's distinction: "The word *love* has by no means the same sense for both sexes, and this is one cause of the serious misunderstandings that divide them" (Beauvoir 1953: 608). "For woman," de Beauvoir maintains, "to love is to relinquish everything for the benefit of a master" (Beauvoir 1953: 608). Women live love as an unconditional devotion and self-sacrifice akin to religious faith (Beauvoir 1953: 609); men "never abdicate completely; […] what they […] want is to take possession of [the beloved woman]; at the very heart of their lives they remain sovereign subjects; […] they wish to integrate her into their existence and nor to squander it entirely on her" (Beauvoir 1953: 608).[9]

Whereas Nietzsche construes the difference between women's and men's ways of loving as a "natural opposition" (GS 363), Beauvoir strongly asserts that "we have nothing to do here with laws of nature. It is the difference in their situations that is reflected in the difference men and women show in their conceptions of love" (Beauvoir 1953: 608). In other words, for de Beauvoir, the difference in their ways of loving is contingent upon the "different situations" women and men have in the Western, patriarchal society—that is, upon the lack of equality between them. Inequality in society thus creates inequality in the romantic relationship. As Tove Pettersen notes, the kind of love engendered by such injustice is "inauthentic," for both woman and man are fundamentally unable to realize their full human potential as free beings (Pettersen 2017: 160–4).

De Beauvoir focuses especially on disadvantaged condition of women in inauthentic love. In a patriarchal society, women's freedom to determine their own future possibilities is heavily limited by their situation of subordination and dependence. The only way to realize their dream of transcending their condition is through love. In the romantic relationship, women hope to indirectly participate in men's freedom and possibilities (Beauvoir 1953: 609). But this is a false or bad way to seek self-determination: "A woman who devotes herself completely to her partner does not take responsibility for herself and her life" (Pettersen 2017: 163). Ultimately, then, in inauthentic love women are unable to freely realize their full human potential.

**De Beauvoir on Authentic Love**

Pettersen points out that for de Beauvoir, however, "inauthentic love is not the only form of love possible between women and men. Authentic love between the sexes *is* achievable—but only when they acknowledge each other as equals and as unique. Hence, while inauthentic love can be described as patriarchal, authentic love can be labelled post-patriarchal since sexism must be eradicated for authentic relationships to flourish" (Pettersen 2017: 164). In contrast to inauthentic love, authentic or genuine love allows both the individuals in the relationship to realize their full human potential as free beings.[10]

De Beauvoir identifies two distinctive features of authentic love: (a) mutual recognition of each other's *differences* and (b) mutual recognition of each other's *equality* (Pettersen 2017: 165). (a) Authentic love is a human interaction between two individuals who recognize each other as different and unique beings: "An authentic love should accept the contingence of the other with all his idiosyncrasies, his limitations, and his basic gratuitousness. It would not pretend to be a mode of salvation, but a human inter-relation" (Beauvoir 1953: 619). As stressed by Pettersen, "[a]uthentic love requires both maintaining their individuality and self-respect, and acknowledging the differences between them" (Pettersen 2017: 165). On the contrary, as we have seen, the patriarchal conception of love is inauthentic and even destructive precisely because it demands women to renounce their individuality in the relationship. (b) "Genuine love ought to be founded on the mutual recognition of two liberties; the lovers would then experience themselves both as self and as other: neither would give up transcendence [i.e., the freedom to determine their own future possibilities], neither would be mutilated; together they would manifest values and aims in the world" (Beauvoir, 1953: 631). To recognize the other as an equal, Pettersen clarifies, means to recognize them as free being: "In authentic love relationship, each party must choose to respect their own freedom as well as that of the other" (Pettersen 2017: 166).

In summary, according to de Beauvoir, authentic love transcends the opposition of loving roles typical of patriarchal societies—the male desire for possession and the female submission. It is a "non-possessive and non-submissive" form of love, in which both lovers (a) accept each other's difference and uniqueness and (b) mutually recognize their freedom and equality (Pettersen 2017: 166). Is a similarly authentic form of love possible for Nietzsche? I address this question in the next section.

**Nietzsche on Learning How to Love Authentically**

We saw in Section 3 that Nietzsche is strongly critical of romantic love for its tendency to fuel self-deceit and world deceit (3.1). Moreover, like de Beauvoir, he disapproves of forms of love that involve sameness, self-relinquishment (3.2), and an untamed desire for exclusive possession (3.3). "Although Nietzsche acknowledges that women suffer from the adherence to male constructed gender roles," for Verkerk, "he does not think the solution is for women to attempt to be equal to, as in the same as, men" (Verkerk 2017: 144). Nietzsche is never willing to "admit the claim that man and women have *equal* right in love" (GS 363). Unlike de Beauvoir, then, Nietzsche does not seem to make any suggestion for redressing the gender inequalities of romantic relationships, nor does he seem to have a Beauvoirian-like conception of an authentic (non-possessive and non-submissive) form of love. Whereas for de Beauvoir authentic love involves the mutual recognition of each other's *differences* and *equality*, such a recognition for Nietzsche seems to be impossible in loving relationships. More likely, according to standard interpretations, a similar recognition can be found in Nietzschean friendship. "What seems certain from Nietzsche's writing on women and love," Verkerk concludes, "is that he does not think erotic love and friendship are compatible" (Verkerk 2017: 144). This, I want to argue in this section, is not as certain as it might seem—although, as we have seen, it is not completely mistaken either.

As Ansell-Pearson and Bamford duly note, despite his criticisms, in his middle writings "[Nietzsche] is not so skeptical about love as to not want to provide an alternative conception of our need and desire for love [...]. [H]e favors a mode of love where the two lovers do not become one but remain two; [...] a duality is respected and allowed to be cultivated and encouraged to flourish" (Ansell-Pearson and Bamford 2021: 182). This can be seen in an important, though often neglected, aphorism in *Mixed Opinions and Maxims*:

> *Love and duality.*—What then is love besides understanding and rejoicing in the fact that someone else lives, acts, and feels in a different and opposite way than we do? If love is to use joy to bridge over oppositions, it must not suspend or deny them.—Even love of self assumes an unalloyable duality (or multiplicity) within a *single* person as its precondition.
>
> (MOM 75)

In opposition to the idea that love makes the same, Nietzsche favors a mode of loving that not only understands or accepts duality but also rejoices in diversity and even oppositions.[11] Like de Beauvoir's authentic love (a), Nietzsche's love as duality preserves and encourages the diversity of the lovers. It forms a *we* in which the lovers maintain and cultivate their individuality, independence, and autonomy. Oppositions here are not suppressed in the name of the illusion of sameness but bridged in such a way that enables each lover to flourish—not only by letting the other be different but also, for example, by being partially transformed by them: interacting with a diverse, even opposed person, the lover explores alternative ways of living and opens themselves up to new possibilities for how to live. Nietzsche further states that rejoicing in difference and opposition is a precondition of self-love too. In other words, genuine self-love requires that one remains open to alterity and multiplicity—in oneself as well as in others. In *Dawn*, he claims that love for others is in fact vital to self-love: "*Most dangerous unlearning.*—One begins by unlearning how to love others and ends by finding nothing more worth loving in oneself" (D 401).

Importantly, for Nietzsche, love of difference and opposition is not just an emotion; rather, it is an art that can and ought to be learned. In *The Gay Science*, Nietzsche makes an intriguing comparison between developing an appreciation for music and learning how to love: just as coming to appreciate an unknown piece of music initially "requires some exertion and good will to *tolerate* it in spite of its strangeness, to be patient [...] and kindhearted about its oddity," so "we have *learned to love* all things that we now love"—including people (GS 334).

> In the end we are always rewarded for our good will, our patience, fairmindedness, and gentleness with what is strange; gradually, it sheds its veil and turns out to be a new and indescribable beauty. That is its *thanks* for our hospitality. Even those who love themselves will have learned it in this way; for there is no other way. Love, too, has to be learned.
>
> (GS 334)

One learns how to love—a piece of music or a person—by increasing their capacity for being open and hospitable to what is strange. Cultivating this capacity, one becomes gradually more able to appreciate the distinctive qualities of what one opens oneself to and thus comes to perceive its beauty.[12] This, it is important to note, is not yet another way to deceive oneself about the love object; it is rather a way to do full justice to it and to get to know it better (HH 621). Indeed, Nietzsche writes, "We need to be honest with ourselves and to know ourselves very well in order to be able to practice toward others that philanthropic dissimulation that goes by the name of love and kindness" (D 335). For Nietzsche, moreover, one *must* learn how to love—authentically—in order to be well and flourish: "We must learn to love, learn to be kind, from our youth on up; if education and chance provide us with no opportunity for practicing these feelings, then our soul will dry out" (HH 601). Only when one masters the art of loving, love becomes "a torch that can light [one] to higher ways" (Z I Marriage).

## Conclusion: De Beauvoir on Stendhal as a "Tender Friend of Women"

In *The Second Sex*, de Beauvoir explores the myth of woman in a number of authors, including Stendhal. Here, Stendhal is described as feminist, as "a man who lives among women of flesh and blood" (Beauvoir 1953: 246), and as a "tender friend of women [who] does not believe in the feminine mystery, precisely because he loves them as they really are; no essence defines woman once for all; to him the idea of 'the eternal feminine' seems pedantic and ridiculous" (Beauvoir 1953: 247). De Beauvoir's description will not surprise readers of Stendhal's novels, in which one can find flesh-and-blood representations of female characters and heroines that go way beyond the gender expectations of eighteenth-century French society.[13] For de Beauvoir, Stendhal clearly sees that "[t]he differences [...] between men and women reflect the difference in their situations"; and that "[t]he worst handicap they have is the besotting education imposed upon them; the oppressor always strives to dwarf the oppressed; man intentionally deprives women of their opportunities" (Beauvoir 1953: 247). In *On Love*, Stendhal openly champions the emancipation and education of women. He recognizes that men have been responsible for keeping women ignorant and away from responsibility: "Girls should have the same cultural opportunities as boys; they should not be allowed to grow up in ignorance of the facts of life and of society" (Stendhal 2004: Ch. 54).

By way of conclusion, I want to ask: can Nietzsche be similarly regarded as a tender friend of women? If Nietzsche is a friend of women, his friendship is certainly more problematic than Stendhal's—even according to a Nietzschean sense of friendship. We saw that although Nietzsche is aware of social inequalities with respect to gender roles, at times he tends to naturalize the differences between men and women and to merely see women as a passive type. If Nietzsche is a friend of women, this is more evident in his middle writings, wherein he expresses his hopes for "noble, free-minded women" of the future (HH 424). In contrast, in late writings such as *Beyond Good and Evil*, Nietzsche announces his uncomfortable truths about "woman in itself" (BGE 232–9), making a great number of misogynistic remarks that seems to be hardly compatible with a tender friendship with women. In *Ecce Homo*, Nietzsche is outspokenly contrary to the emancipation of women and sees it as "the instinctive hatred of *failed* women, which is to say infertile women, against those who have turned out well" (EH Books 5). In this context, he also sees "[l]ove [... as] the deadly hatred between sexes" and suggests that, to cure or redeem a women, one ought to "[g]ive her a baby" (EH Books 5).

Misogynist remarks about women such as those—be them literal, metaphorical, ironical, provocative, or strategic—are, in my view, inexcusable. However, as I see it the point is not much to find Nietzsche guilty or innocent with respect to the accusation of misogyny; it is rather to check whether, despite his misogynist remarks, he can provide us with helpful tools for thinking about the situation of women today. Nietzsche can become important for this task only if we recognize his limitations and try to overcome them, searching for solutions to the problems that he himself leaves unsolved.

Through the comparison with Stendhal and de Beauvoir, I have shown that Nietzsche can help us to distinguish between inauthentic (life-denying) and authentic (life-enhancing) forms of love and to identify some dangerous mechanisms of inauthentic love (e.g., self-deceit, other deceit, self-relinquishment, untamed desire for possession). Hopefully I have also shown that although Nietzsche does not offer a solution to the problem of gender equality in love and in society, his considerations of the loving roles of women and men bring to focus substantial inequalities and can be even used, as de Beauvoir does, for a feminist agenda. Finally, as we have seen, Nietzsche's conception of authentic love can provide us with an excellent model of a healthy, flourishing relationship, not only between men and women but also between individuals of whichever sex and gender—a relationship that respects and rejoices in otherness, differences, and oppositions.

## Notes

1. Nietzsche concentrates his attention on romantic relationships between women and men, but I believe much of what he says may be relevant also for loving relationships between individuals of the same sex and of nonbinary gender identities.
2. There are only few exceptions, including Cleary (2015: 71–98) and Ansell-Pearson and Bamford (2021: 182–3).
3. I am thankful to Keith Ansell-Pearson for inviting me to think about Stendhal, Nietzsche, and De Beauvoir on love, and for letting me present my argument as a guest lecture in the context of his 2019–2020 course on *Philosophy of the Emotions* at the University of Warwick.
4. Romantic love, for Nietzsche, as a lust for possession "means nothing less than *excluding* the whole world from a precious good, from happiness and enjoyment" (GS 14). Moreover, "to the lover himself the whole rest of the world appears indifferent, pale, and worthless, and he is prepared to make any sacrifice, to disturb any order, to subordinate all other interests" (GS 14).
5. On Nietzsche on friendship see, for example, Zavatta (2008), Miner (2010), and Verkerk (2019).
6. In a number of aphorisms in *Human, All Too Human*, Nietzsche identifies the capacity for conversation as an important aspect of friendship; see 197, 327, 406.
7. On Nietzsche on marriage see, for example, Nettleton (2009).

8   On these questions see Verkerk (2017, 2019).
9   A commentator clearly explains how this works in practice: "[i]n a traditional marriage, for example, women are expected to become part of the man's world by taking his name, joining his religion, following him where he wants to live" (Pettersen 2017: 161).
10  On de Beauvoir's conception of authentic love, see also Cleary (2017).
11  It seems that, nevertheless, there must be a limit to how much difference and opposition even this form of love can take. Love as duality, as other forms of love, is selective. That is to say, not all differences and oppositions will be bridgeable with joy. For example, it is unlikely that a feminist would love a sexist just because they are different and opposed. It seems that one of the constraints upon love of difference and opposition must be at least a form of mutual respect.
12  Of course, this presupposes that the love object has at least some valuable qualities.
13  On De Beauvoir's reading of Stendhal, see Scott (2008). On feminist readings of Stendhal, see Algazi (2005–2006).

12

# Nietzsche on Marriage and the Cultivation of Humanity

Marina García-Granero

## Introduction

Nietzsche's philosophy is oriented toward the future, especially humanity's future (Stegmaier 2016). His semantics of the future also reach the future of marriage (HH 434). His ideal of marriage aims to be future guaranteeing. Nietzsche calls to exhaustively research the conditions of our existence, including marriage (GS 7). Studying and comparing European culture with antique civilizations is fundamental to envisioning the optimal conditions for any elevation in love (Attali 2013: 143). The essential idea in Nietzsche's treatment of marriage is that it should not be motivated by passion or physical love, but rather by the superior love of humanity, or more concretely, the lineage or the offspring. Marriage becomes an aristocratic question, deeply connected to Nietzsche's thought of "breeding" or "cultivation" (*Züchtung*). With these terms, Nietzsche reflects on humanity's physiological and cultural formation and transformation.

I explore how Nietzsche's views on marriage connect with his anthropological philosophy—love, breeding/cultivation, heredity, vitalist/ascetic values, etc. Furthermore, I argue that Nietzsche's views on marriage can shed further light on his hereditary thinking. These ideas can be contextualized within his desire to promote human cultivation or breeding, a thought that obtains a programmatic character, especially in *Beyond Good and Evil*, in which Nietzsche aims to "teach humanity its future as its *will*, as dependent on a human will" and to "comprehend everything that *could be bred from humanity*" (BGE 203).

In the first instance, I analyze Nietzsche's assessment of marriage in the context of his critique of the morality of customs and the question of the free spirit in the earlier texts and the aphoristic books. Afterward, I concentrate on the more mature texts, where the task of "producing a better offspring" gains sense in the context of the will to power hypothesis. The last section addresses the possible "eugenical" dimension or implication of these ideas in light of Nietzsche's scientific and cultural context.

## The Free-Spirited Opposition to Marriage and the Tyranny of Customs

The first fragment in which Nietzsche uses the concept "*Züchtung*," in 1873, includes a mention of marriage:

> *Nationality* is, for the most part, only the *consequence* of rigid government measures, that is, a kind of breeding (*einer Art Züchtung*) through surrounding violence and taming (*Bändigung*), in addition to the compulsion to marry and to speak and live with one another.
>
> (PF 1873 29[48], my translation)[1]

This note encapsulates the core of the concept of "breeding" powerfully. This posthumous fragment, the first text in which *Züchtung* appears, is most likely a paraphrase from Walter Bagehot's book, *Physics and Politics, or Thoughts on the Application of the Principles of "Natural Selection" and "Inheritance" to Political Society* (1872).[2] Therefore, we cannot present this definition of nationality as if it were Nietzsche's own. Still, we can observe and assert that, as early as 1873, Nietzsche pictures "breeding" or "cultivation" as a social process favoring the appearance and maintenance of specific human types with specific instinctive behaviors. Marriage is an instrument to said breeding.

The example of nationality represents how the logic of breeding is, most of the time, unconscious or even undesired. "Breeding" in Nietzsche is a two-fold concept. It often has a descriptive sense: different cultures shape different types of human beings, consciously and unconsciously. In the middle works, the concept is mainly used to express how a habit or a value, for example, altruism, has been "bred," cultivated, inculcated, instilled, and taught, which are the more common verbs usually employed in the translations (GS 111). Nietzsche also argues, especially in *Beyond Good and Evil*, that morals and religion have been means to "discipline and breed" a particular type of person. Christianity, for example, is criticized for breeding a gregarious animal in *The Genealogy of Morals* (I 11 and II 1, 2, 3) and *The Anti-Christ* (A 62). But *Züchtung* also has a programmatic sense: from *Beyond Good and Evil* and on, Nietzsche queries what other types could represent the future of humanity and "should be *willed* as having greater value" (A 3).

National characteristics—considered representative of a particular people—are formed within customary groups. Not only are they formed, but they are also valued and recognized as belonging to that nation. Thus, there is a first selective process of specific ways of being and living. Compliance is encouraged to promote the correct coexistence of the group. Conformity is rewarded, and nonconformity is punished. In addition to unconscious imitation, this results in the group members becoming more and more similar, and thus the national character of the group is shaped.

Of course, Nietzsche recognizes that humans band together in groups for security and that there is a need for coexistence and self-preservation but warns of the dangers of adaptation and subordination to the community. Thus, the foundation of marriage is "shallow and silly," like any tradition (PF 1876 19[96]). There is no profound reason behind marriage as a tradition. In the following note, "cultivation" and marriage are again connected: Nietzsche claims marriage was promoted for utilitarian reasons of preservation and group survival: "The 'good' arises when one forgets the origin.—The parental instinct has only been bred (*grossgezüchtet*) in society, one needs offspring, so one protects marriage honors it" (PF 1876 19[115], my translation).

The ethicality of customs consists in the firm obedience to traditional habits, values, and acts instilled through education, suggestibility, and identification. The tyranny of custom played an essential role in evolutionism, and Nietzsche found it in several of his sources, for example, the anthropologist John Lubbock (Thatcher 1983). The example of marriage is used in Nietzsche's paradigmatic definition of the ethicality of custom in *Daybreak*.

> the chief proposition: morality is nothing other (therefore no more!) than obedience to customs, of whatever kind they may be; customs, however, are the traditional way of behaving and evaluating. [...] Originally all education and care of health, marriage, cure of sickness, agriculture, war, speech and silence, traffic with one another and with the gods belonged within the domain of morality: they demanded one observe prescriptions *without thinking of oneself* as an individual.
>
> (D 9)

Customary discipline is key to group survival but becomes a long-term obstacle to progress and development. Nietzsche critiques the oppression of customs (*Sittlichkeit*) and opposes them to freedom. Often, it is not the individual who chooses marriage, but society chooses for them (PF 1882 17[39]). Nietzsche instead presents a new figure of sovereignty: an individual freed from the ethicality of custom is autonomous in their actions and beliefs, strong, responsible, and in control of themselves and their circumstances (Bamford 2016). Also in *Daybreak*, Nietzsche claims that "one ought to take marriage enormously more seriously" (D 151); that is, it should represent something more than a mere tradition and have a higher end.

In the previous work, *Human, All Too Human*, the free spirit was portrayed as a critique of marriage. Marriage is a cage that trumps independence and intellectual development. The free spirit prefers to *"fly alone"* (HH 426). This is still Nietzsche's view in *On the Genealogy of Morality*: "the philosopher abhors *marriage*, together with that which might persuade to it—marriage being a hindrance and calamity on his path to the optimum" (GM III 7). Nonetheless, Nietzsche distinguishes between noble and unnoble types of marriage depending on their ends. He perceives these noble marriages to contribute to women's empowerment, as we will see in a moment.

Nietzsche was concerned about promoting the emergence of free spirits and ways for them to come into existence. This idea is further stressed in the preface of *Human, All Too Human*, added in 1886, where he suggests: "perhaps I shall do something to speed their coming if I describe in advance under what vicissitudes, upon what paths, I *see* them coming?" (HH P 2). As part of this dream, he contemplates breeding (*züchten*) a moral aristocracy through marriage. The "sense of marriage" is a child that will represent a higher type than their parents (PF 1882 4[232] and PF 1880 4[81]). Women seem to be subordinate to the purpose of an alleged higher development (Schank 2000: 398). Nietzsche writes that marriages should not be entered into so frivolously. One should only marry "for the purpose of higher development" and "to leave the fruits of such humanity"; otherwise, humanity suffers because of indiscriminate reproduction as people are primarily moved by the satisfaction of their instincts (PF 1880 5[38]). This is later reasserted in *Beyond Good and Evil* when he claims that "women are being made more hysterical by the day, and less capable of performing their first and last profession, the bearing of strong children" (BGE 239).[3] Surprisingly or not, the idea that motherhood could improve humanity and promote our path toward the overhuman was later re-appropriated and vindicated by Ellen Key, a Swedish-born conservative feminist (Diethe 2007: 151). In any case, Nietzsche considers women's ability to create life as a unique capacity, superior to the men of his epoch and their usual responsibilities. That is why he labels as "corrupters of women" those who "recommend that women defeminize themselves like this and copy all the stupidities that the 'man' in Europe, that European 'manliness' suffers from,—who would like to bring women down to the level of 'general education'" (BGE 239). Therefore, by imitating men, "*woman is regressing*" (BGE 334).

In Nietzsche's philosophy, institutions are worth as much as those who participate in them. Marriage, in itself, has no intrinsic value (PF 1887 10[76], PF 1887 10[109]). Nietzsche's critiques of marriage are mostly directed at the type of men and women that engage in it. In some notes, he claims, "Marriage is designed for ordinary people who are not capable of either extraordinary love or extraordinary friendship, in other words, for most people: but also (for) those scarce individuals who are capable of both love and friendship" (PF 1882 5[1] 46, trans. Loeb and Tinsley).[4] Friendship is a catalyzer or a force for a good marriage (HH 378).

Additionally, in said book, the goal of marriage, and even the purpose of women's emancipation, would be to produce (*erzeug*) a better generation ultimately.

> *From the future of marriage.*—Those noble, free-thinking women who set themselves the task of education and elevation of the female sex ought not to overlook one consideration: the higher conception of marriage as the soul-friendship of two people of differing sex—a conception it is hoped the future will realize—contracted for the purpose of begetting and educating a new generation.
> (HH 424)[5]

Such a marriage "employs the sensual as it were only as a rare, occasional means to a greater end," namely, the child. Thus, it probably requires, according to Nietzsche, "*concubinage*" outside the marriage. Again, according to Nietzsche, in this aphorism, the satisfaction of the husband's sexual needs would distract the wife from taking care of and educating their children. Although Nietzsche affirms that women can run their own business or job outside the household, they seem to acquire dignity in their task of educating and taking care of their offspring. And it seems to be out of the question that a woman might want to become a philosopher or a free spirit. Following the many ideas presented in the chapter "Woman and Child" of *Human All Too Human*, Nietzsche concludes that the free spirit should decide "whether he is created for a happy marriage" (HH 427). Even more so, in a letter to Reinhart von Seydlitz, Nietzsche alludes to the said chapter from *Human All Too Human* and states that "all women, reading such things, would wish not to have a free spirit for a husband: and by doing this I believe I have promoted marital happiness in general" (Letter no. 721 from 1879, my translation).[6]

## Marriage, Will to Power, and Sexed Genealogies

Nietzsche's anti-metaphysical understanding of truth and his evaluative stance toward it, with the will to power hypothesis, entail that his method of inquiry is also a method of transformation (Mitcheson, 2013). Humanity, as we know it, must be transformed and cultivated, and marriage, in Nietzsche's view, appears to be a technique to achieve said change, to direct their genealogies.

In my view, the most crucial text regarding the question of marriage is "Of Child and Marriage" from the first book of *Thus Spoke Zarathustra*. This chapter depicts the crucial discrepancies between Nietzsche and Schopenhauer regarding the conception of love and the (hetero)sexual union between a man and a woman. These divergences range from the most primary level—the physiological level of sexuality as the reproductive function of the species—and love, interpreted either as a product of the will to live (Schopenhauer) or will to power (Nietzsche).

"Of Child and Marriage" is an implicit discussion of Schopenhauer's thesis regarding the ultimate meaning of the sexual union between a man and a woman. For Schopenhauer, the procreative instinct of the species pushes people to bond sexually and affectively, but this is only a conditioned reflection of the will to live, an irrational and irrepressible desire to persevere in being, and nothing more than that. Nietzsche knew that the Schopenhauerian conception of love was the coherent conclusion of his pessimistic metaphysics and detachment from life. This was, according to Nietzsche, a reactive and ascetic notion of marriage and love.

Instead, Nietzsche's notion of marriage is a prolongation of the will to power: a principle of fertility, reproduction, and recreation in difference, in which people seek to prolong themselves in someone other than them with the added encouragement that their child will surpass or overcome them. It is not a matter of reproducing or propagating (*sich fort-pflanzen*) in the same plane of values but of pro-creating (*sich hinauf-pflanzen*) an elevation in the "garden of marriage." As Diethe noted—concerning feminist Helene Stöcker's reception of Nietzsche—Nietzsche's idea of reaching the heights means to produce offspring with the potential to improve humanity (Diethe 1996a: 163). Love catalyzes a yearning for the *Übermensch*, a love that aims to create above itself.[7] Moreover, this kind of love involves both self-dissatisfaction (contempt for oneself) and love for a higher self, a desire to create beyond oneself (McIntyre 1992).

In this discourse, Zarathustra asks whether one is allowed to long for a child and raise them, meaning whether we are noble enough for such an important task. That is why he enumerates a series of virtues, such as mastery of oneself. He then asks whether the source of our desire is mere solitude or our animal instincts. Finally, he proclaims the ethical imperative internal to noble marriage, which is to marry with the purpose of creating a higher kind of being:

> You should create a higher body, a first movement, a wheel rolling out of itself—a creator you should create.
> Marriage: that is what I call the will by two for creating the one who is more than those who created it. Respect for one another I call marriage, and respect for the one who wills such a willing.
>
> (Z I Marriage)

The earlier critique of marriage is then replaced by an exaltation of love and marriage when they serve as a spiritual guide to producing a higher type, a "creator," a person who will incorporate and practice affirmative values. Although the will to power is not explicitly mentioned, Nietzsche seems to reconsider marriage within its framework. The hypothesis of will to power is a conception or image of the organic world, presented in *Thus Spoke Zarathustra* and extended to the whole of reality in *Beyond Good and Evil*.

Heredity includes the transmission of values and psychological dispositions based on the correspondence between physiological and interpretive states. Interpretations are preferences that organize a particular way of life, and religions and philosophies are symptoms of bodily states. "Incorporation" (*Einverleibung*) is a synthetic faculty of assimilation at a physiological level. It is the process through which a value, a habit, or an interpretation is assimilated into the body, becomes instinctive, and thus obtains a secure and automatic functioning (GS 110). To incorporate means to internalize a value with such depth that it becomes unconscious, a regulation of the body, and ultimately, a condition of life. These interpretations determine our instincts and their rank within the hierarchical structure that is the body. As a result, in the long run, each morality contributes to raising or breeding some types of persons, to the detriment of others. Since the body is an instinctual configuration within the will to power hypothesis, values express phenomena typically considered physiological (BGE 36). Incorporation is the mechanism through which "breeding" operates and the mechanism of transformation, the process through which a second nature becomes first nature.

Nietzsche considers his exaltation of marriage to be a fidelity of spirit toward the ancient Greeks, who praised the active and vital forces of sexuality. He dedicates a specific section to sexuality and childbirth in *Twilight of the Idols* "What I Owe to the Ancients." The Greeks' ethics of time, and their social organization in general, are conveyed as follows: "the future promised by the past and the past consecrated to the future." In another paragraph from the *Twilight of the Idols*, Nietzsche presents "the right to procreate, for instance, the right to be born, the right to be alive" as depending on "the highest interest in lives, of ascending life," here again, in the context of a critique of Schopenhauer (TI Ancients 4, cf. TI Skirmishes 36, 39). This future-oriented project has a robust aristocratic character because it is centered around the transmission of noble forms of life and values throughout generations. Moreover, Nietzsche exalts the "intolerance" of marriage customs in aristocratic morality (BGE 262). Because of their usefulness in promoting aristocratic morality, the philosophers of the future should pay attention to marriage: "Preparation for becoming the legislators of the future, the masters of the earth, at least our children. Basic concern with marriages" (PF 1885 35[9], WP 132, see also PF 1884 26[90]).

The question of marriage contains elements that inform us of Nietzsche's thought on heritability: "He who sows in the spirit plants very slow-growing trees. What is inherited from father to son are the *most practiced* habits (*not* the most valued!) The son *betrays* the father" (PF 1881 11[168], my translation) because he reveals the father's true colors. Although I believe Nietzsche incorporated a Lamarckian framework,[8] widespread in his time, this specific note does not serve to support it. He refers to a cultural habit or virtue—industriousness, hardworking—and does not specify how it is transmitted: through imitation and education in life or through an instinctive heritage conveyed as a legacy from birth. In any case, this theory of the hereditary inscription of habits was widespread at the time and acted as one of the central premises of Francis Galton's theory (Haase 1989). Another aphorism in *Daybreak* highlights the role of imitation in education: children imitate as "born apes" and incorporate the inclinations and aversions that they perceive in their parents (D 34). This is an added motivation to self-cultivate and not let oneself go since children will imitate us.

One should not forget that "genealogy" traditionally possesses a naturalistic meaning, referring to natural history and evolutionism. Family trees are a biological classification of generations, ancestry, and descent. These (masculine) family trees are the subject of critical examination by feminist philosophers. Following Nietzsche, feminist philosophers, especially of sexual difference, highlight the noble connotations of genealogies. To be part of a genealogy means, above all, to be part of a line of power in such a way that these genealogical trees express the traditional transmission of men's knowledge and power. But Nietzsche adds a critical dimension when he develops his method instead of the mere natural history of morals from English evolutionists. Genealogy fulfills a specific function before transvaluation: as a method informed by evolutionism and the sciences of heredity, it provides the necessary knowledge to critique and heal European culture. Values are no longer perceived as immutable realities. Instead, they should be recognized as social instruments serving specific human groups. Nietzsche's original practice of truth contributes to this radical and experimental questioning of how human beings are raised.

> Having become free from the tyranny of "eternal" concepts, I am, on the other hand, far from plunging into the abyss of skeptical arbitrariness: rather, I ask to regard concepts as experiments with the help of which certain kinds of human beings are bred and tested for their durability and longevity.
>
> (PF 1885 35[36], my translation)

In his critical understanding of philosophy, Nietzsche insists that the traditional search for representational truth neglects the deeper conditioning of ideas and ways of thinking, which varies in each culture and operates through values. Concepts function in their task of expressing content because the same words are used for the same kind of internal experiences in a community. Thus, concepts require a common mutual experience. Members of the same people understand each other better and bond with greater strength and cohesion because of their shared experiences and affinity. *Züchtung* is a concept in the Nietzschean sense. It is a concept that responds to the need to problematize the phenomena to which it refers. It is not intended to search for the essence of "breeding" because the concept itself does not exist independently of the phenomenon. We coin the concept to grasp and understand the social process. But the concept in itself is not real; it is simply the instrument that allows us to articulate and interpret the variety and singularity of ways in which these cultivating processes are developed in societies.

As is well known, Nietzsche denounced the essential conception of truth and the will to truth as a supposedly disinterested search for objectivity. Weak wills long to discover value because they cannot create it (Oliver 1984: 186). Instead, Nietzsche does not renounce concepts but modifies their status and meaning, stresses their interpretive character and practical projection, and uses them to appraise value. As I have explained, analyzes in terms of "breeding" describe how different historical and cultural contexts form different types of human beings. Genealogy reinterprets historical transformations as breeding processes and problematizes the living conditions that sustain each cultural form. This broad use of culture designates human activities, politics, social organizations, and their products in morality, religion, art, philosophy, etc. A culture is defined by the values guiding people's lives.

In *Human, All Too Human*, Nietzsche presented an idyllic description of the physicians of the future, emancipated from ascetic ideals, and equipped with resources and knowledge of different disciplines. These physicians would oversee "the production of a spiritual-physical aristocracy (as promoter or preventer of marriages)" (HH 243). Later, in a note from 1888, he contends the necessity to divest priests of their power over marriages. Marriage is degraded when the priest, the "sworn anti-naturalist," is bestowed with the power of its blessing (PF 1887 10[156]). Thus, Nietzsche evaluated marriage depending on its mission and the specific values attached to it in different cultures, for example, the ascetic ideals of Christian matrimony or the more "vitalist" values of the Code of Manu, which, in any case, only win by default in comparison to Christian values (Brobjer 1998; Etter 1987). A vitalist model of marriage would act as a cultural therapy.

Some of Nietzsche's texts offer a nonessentialist, sympathetic reading of the female condition because "he establishes the limitations of men based on the latter's expectations of women, just as with their expectations of metaphysics, truth, history, science, religion, essences, and idols." Such expectations are symptomology of men's self-stunting development (Deutscher 2022: 66). Education was considered the privileged means to fight against the "eternal feminine." The eternal feminine consists of empty-headed, dependent women, as well as women who hate and compete with each other: "'woman' has historically been most despised by women themselves—and not by us [men] at all" (BGE 232). Willingly or not, the vast majority of women had to follow social norms; they had no other choice; they had to act hypocritically and artificially and saw each other as competition in the marriage mart (Diethe 1993: 45). Not getting married had negative social consequences. Nietzsche's feminist friends, particularly Meta von Salis, expanded this critique of women-hating women and reformulated it in a feminist manner. She criticized women whose ideal of happiness was to receive a man's kiss, that is, women whose lives revolve around men, in absolute heteronomy, and often being unsupportive and competitive with each other, instead of branching out on their own.[9]

In my view, this perspective anticipated some elements from the feminism of sexual difference, mainly present in France, Belgium, and Italy. Such a feminism of sexual difference criticizes, in a Nietzschean manner, the premise that equality implicitly presupposes the acceptance of the masculine symbolic order. Instead, these feminists argue that women should "start from themselves" (*partire da se*) in an open, future-oriented project. One of the significant legacies of Nietzsche for feminist philosophy is to avoid this mimetic repetition of masculine codes and to "break away from patterns of [phallogocentric] identification" (Braidotti 1993: 2).

Besides, or outside of this tradition of feminism of sexual difference, major contributions to Nietzsche studies have unveiled ideas like these in his texts. In her analysis of "Woman as Truth in Nietzsche's Writing," Kelly Oliver presents the "castrated woman" as a position of truth in which a woman de-sexes herself by imitating men and "assumes a position as the second type of man" (Oliver 1984: 187–8), thereby, renouncing to her authenticity as a woman. Likewise, Lawrence Hatab makes similar points:

> [I]f one were to admit a common assumption of "male chauvinism"—that our culture is a masculine product—then it seems to me that accusing Nietzsche of misogyny or male chauvinism entirely misses the point. There never has been a more severe critic of western culture than Nietzsche. Consequently, Nietzsche can be seen to be one of the most severe critics of the masculine principle.
> (Hatab 1981: 335)

We should also consider the even more poignant question: "In other words, how much of modern feminism is more accurately a 'masculinism'?" (Hatab 1981: 342). Masculinism is, in fact, a central critical concept in the feminism of sexual difference aiming to denounce the perspective of "equality" that often entails the ingenuous assumption of a masculine point of view, which does not allow for feminist social change. Luce Irigaray, a feminist of sexual difference attentive to Nietzsche's philosophy and Nietzsche studies, denounces that supposedly universal values result in the domination of one part of humanity over the other: men's world over women's world, and that patriarchal traditions have erased the traces of mother-daughter genealogies (Irigaray 1993b). The sexual difference should rather be understood as a contingent historical product: the sedimentation of a history that has shaped women's experiences as different human experiences. Feminine genealogies affirm the sexual difference with a positive meaning. This difference means that women would not need men to create the conditions of existence or self-understanding as women: the feminine is not reduced to its figuration. Authentically, women are not what men have made of them throughout history. The feminisim of sexual difference does not claim traditional femininity but an emancipatory ideal: it does not suppose a return to a so-called feminine essence but rather represents an opening, an invitation to self-discovery as a future-oriented project, much like Nietzsche's philosophy. Starting from oneself is a crucial revolution for women to affirm themselves outside the discourse of masculine truth and to build their individuality independent of the masculine symbolic order: the affirming woman creates "reality anew, not out of already existing materials" (Oliver 1984: 195).

## Nietzsche: A Eugenicist?

The section above revealed that Nietzsche scrutinizes marriage as a psychologist, moralist, cultural analyst, or even a "eugenicist," according to Éric Blondel's interpretation (Blondel 2017: 546). A passage that might support this view is the following posthumous note:

> In many cases, the first child of a marriage is reason enough not to bring more children into the world: and yet, the marriage is not dissolved but is *maintained*, despite the foreseeable inconvenience of having more children (to the detriment of the following)! How much blindness! But the State does not want and did not want quality, but rather *mass*! That is why it does not care about people's breeding [or cultivation (*Züchtung*)]!
>
> (PF 1881 11[179], my translation)

Undoubtedly, these are ideas in stark contrast with the formal character of modern liberalism and are sometimes associated with eugenics (Drochon 2010: 76). Nietzsche never used the term "eugenics"[10] but constantly spoke of *Züchtung*. Breeding includes a physiological dimension and ethical-political aspects, such as the transvaluation of values or Great Politics. Nietzsche's contribution posits that the complex formation called "morality" selects instincts considered apt for specific social ends. Nietzsche's uses of biological and racial words do not result in eugenics because they do not allude to an authoritarian or mechanical intervention in society. Breeding is not a eugenic program in Galton's sense (Haase 1989: 644).

Moreover, Nietzsche was not interested in contemporary Aryan theories such as Gobineau's.[11] When Nietzsche fantasizes about the conception of new types of human beings, he cares about cultural outcomes in terms of value. In Nietzsche's eyes, the unpredictable birth of exceptional persons does not preclude the possibility of working to foster the development of such persons. Nietzsche thought it imperative to overcome the *décadence* and degeneration of life. As part of his critique of social Darwinism, he argued that complex specimens of a species are more exposed to all kinds of decay because they coordinate a significantly larger sum of elements. Thus, their danger of disintegration is also greater. Decadence is an intermediate stage of fragility and complexity in the path toward a superior culture (Fornari 2006: 322; Moore 2002: Ch. 4).

This trial of "cultivation" or "breeding" provides a plausible solution in Nietzsche's social and scientific context. For example, in a fragment from 1886, Nietzsche writes: "In a marriage in the aristocratic, old-aristocratic sense of the word, it is a matter of the *breeding* of a race (does aristocracy still exist today? *Quaeritur*)" (PF 1886 4[6], trans. del Caro). In contexts like these, "race" means "a large human clade, i.e., a group of shared descent, which also shares a set of practices that enable *this* blood to live in this environment at this time" (Richardson 2008: 199–200). Nietzsche had no intention to develop any type of "race management" through the direct intervention of political authorities. Instead, he suggests a shift in values and taste and improving their members' "epistemic power." The contact or mixing between clades (or "races") favors freedom by taking distance from one's values and fosters a dialogue between multiple viewpoints to judge their limitations (García-Granero 2020).

Lamarckism enjoyed great popularity in enlightened circles during the expansion of evolutionary theories because it opened a space for improving humanity through education and culture. Indeed, later in the twentieth century, the Nazi regime adhered to Darwinism, rejected Lamarckism, and engaged with hard inheritance and racial inequality as key concepts (Weikar 2013). According to the idea of "hard inheritance," promulgated by the German biologist August Weismann, individuals do not transmit their acquired characteristics, only their parents' germ line. Therefore, environmental influences (education, culture) could not affect hereditary traits. Weismann rejected the Lamarckian idea that organisms develop by transmitting acquired characteristics to their progeny. Nazi ideology rejected the possibility of changing heredity through education and the environment and accused Lamarckism of being a Marxist doctrine (Weikar 2013: 537–56).

Within the philosophical project, whose aim is to elucidate "what we could do with humanity through its breeding," Nietzsche looked back at the prehistoric past and its moral legacy—namely, the ethicality of customs—but also looked toward the future. In *Beyond Good and Evil*, Nietzsche contended that culturally acquired qualities and preferences (what our ancestors did most willingly and consistently) are susceptible to be inherited by the following generations (BGE 264). This Lamarckian framework obtains the following form in Nietzsche's philosophy: given any community, successive generations slowly incorporate the absolute authority of norms and values reinforced by education and habits. Nietzsche conceives generations as a chain that never detaches, capitalizes on a force, and will bear fruit when the time comes (BGE 213).[12] Being an heir means to be part of a chain, share a heritage, and continue a lineage in humanity.

Inheritance and heritability were crucial both as a condition of possibility and a limiting framework. This soil sustains the conscious and methodical transformation that Nietzsche proposes. To "raise" or "breed" a person means to transform their hereditary qualities and preferences. Evolutionary and anthropological research provided information on traces that past cultures and civilizations have imprinted on us. Nietzsche adds a programmatic task to this dimension, progressively becoming more explicit over the years. Nietzsche argues that arbitrary criteria have governed customs and laws, but humanity can control its cultivation and inheritance.

A significant part of the argument of those who find a eugenic dimension in Nietzsche's philosophy stems from the assumption that Nietzsche would have adopted "the major ideas of the eugenics movement" and that "[h]e may even have been the only major modern philosopher to have done so" (Gayon 1999: 177). However, this unidirectional inspiration is unclear. The "eugenic movement" is not thinkable as a narrow circle of people isolated from nineteenth-century culture. These ideas were part, in varying degrees, of the cultural climate.

Nietzsche was concerned about alcohol abuse and sexually transmitted diseases and even raised the question of how good marriages could improve offspring. These are elements in common with the eugenic movement. But the history of medicine and eugenics needs to be addressed to determine Nietzsche's responsibility. According to Paul Weindling's detailed study of medicine in the nineteenth and twentieth centuries, eugenics did not emerge in the context of the Aryan ideology of anti-Semitism but in the fields of "public health, social policy, and biomedical sciences." The purpose of eugenics was supposed to be the improvement of living conditions. Therefore, there was an ambivalent character within eugenics. Only after the economic crisis of 1929 and the Nazi takeover did eugenics integrate an atrocious component of "racial hygiene" against Jewish people, Gypsies, and Slavs (Weindling 1989: 462).

Schank argues that "breeding" in Nietzsche, along with polemical concepts such as the "Party of Life" (EH Books BT 4), should be understood through the figure of the philosophical physician who cures diseases of the soul, since the premises for a biological breeding program (e.g., racist use of the concept of race and hierarchy among races) do not occur in Nietzsche's work. Schank's interpretation is that Nietzsche advocated elevating humanity and culture by educating different human types. He interprets Nietzsche's physiological program as a proposal for moral and cultural therapy, for the cure of diseases, under the aegis of the concept of the philosophical physician. Such a physician is, according to Schank, a healer (*Heiler*) and not a breeder (*Züchter*), even though Nietzsche plays on several occasions with the figure of the breeder (e.g., Z III Tablets 12, Z IV Sacrifice, BGE 207, 262). According to Schank, the healer and the breeder are based on entirely different premises. He even interprets Great Politics not from the figure of the philosopher legislator but the philosophical physician. Great Politics seeks the physiological healing of humanity by incorporating diet, clothing, food, health, and reproduction, as central problems (Schank 2000: 235, 359, based on the elements Nietzsche lists in PF 1888 25[1]).

Schank explains that Nietzsche's comments on alcohol, prostitution, sexual diseases, and marriage can be understood to consist with eugenical concerns with public health in which racism was not explicit (Schank 2000: 392–403; cf. Taylor 1990: 73). This first current promoted research on the human brain, hoping to find the cure for many mental illnesses. Popular campaigns against alcohol and tobacco argued that they interfered with biological inheritance and caused physical deformities in the offspring. Social utopians, like Edward Bellamy, admired Francis Galton, wished to cultivate "better" humanity in the colonies, and were convinced that this could be achieved by intervening in the environment and the workplace. They all shared an apparent concern for the welfare of humanity. The contamination of eugenics with explicitly racist and anti-Semitic ideas did not occur until decades after Nietzsche (Sommer 2012: 365). Regarding his responsibility for historical developments in the twentieth century, the most prudent or wisest position might be to avoid both absolute condemnation and total absolution (see Montinari 1982), and the same could be said concerning Nietzsche's misogyny or feminism.

## Conclusion

Nietzsche's orientation toward the future affects his perception and conception of marriage as a partnership for "breeding," cultivating, or upbringing future generations. Nietzsche's works cover almost every dimension of human life and culture, including marriage, love, and procreation. This aristocratic dimension of marriage, as care of the lineage, is the only one that most interests Nietzsche. This is shown in his call for parents to devote their body and soul to raising a noble—or "higher"—offspring. He is concerned with the cultural conditions to favor free spirits and good Europeans.

Nietzsche's philosophy treats the question of inheritance as a philosophical problem within the framework of his genealogical thought, whose aim is to think about human development on a large scale. His ideas are at the crossroads of a philosophical questioning of culture and an epistemological mutation of natural sciences. The transformation of humanity and cultural reform, Nietzsche thinks, will not be achieved through a simple discursive critique. Living conditions, i.e., ascetic values incorporated throughout centuries, do not change through mere awareness-raising. Instead, according to his scientific context, Nietzsche absorbs evolutionary ideas on inheritance and heritability. His ideal of marriage is just a necessary consequence of this.

Undoubtedly, a large part of Nietzsche's ideas or proposals are delicate and should be rigorously criticized and philosophically reformulated, following women's and LGBT+ rights, cultural and moral progress, and especially in the light of events in the twentieth century. At the same time, it might be intellectually dishonest to use Nietzsche as a scapegoat for a collective mindset that vastly exceeded him.

## Notes

1   I have only translated the texts myself where no English translation is available.
2   The German translation from 1874 is preserved in Nietzsche's library (Campioni et al. 2002: 129). On Nietzsche's reading of Bagehot, see Salaquarda (1979), Thatcher (1982), Brobjer (2008b), and Vivarelli (2008).
3   Nietzsche was attracted to motherly figures, in his friendships (for example, Malwida von Meysenbug) and potential spouses, resulting in unlikeness to further that end, as those women with children were already unavailable (Diethe 1996a: 26–30).
4   See also PF 1882 1[80] and PF 1883 25[343]: "A man who *has* nothing in his body but bestial appetites should not have the *right* to marriage" (my translation).
5   See also GS 71 for the paradoxical "knot" and "riddle" that is marriage for educated "upper-class women." According to Thorgeirsdottir, "Nietzsche explicitly criticizes the form of marriage where the woman forgets herself and closes her eyes to herself. Giving should not be confused with sacrificial care for the other and neglect for oneself" (Thorgeirsdottir 2017: 110).
6   For a detailed analysis on this question, see Marton (2021: Ch. 3) ("L'esprit libre, le mariage et le concubinage").
7   PF 1882 5[1] 53: "A child as the monument to the passion of two persons; a twosome's will to oneness." (trans. Loeb and Tinsley).
8   There is however intense discussion about this question in Nietzsche scholarship, the most important contributions on both sides being Clark (2013) and Schacht (2013).
9   See Diethe (1993: Ch. 3) for an extensive sketch of Nietzsche's feminist friends: Malwida von Meysenbug, Meta von Salis, and Resa von Schirnhofer.
10  Some scholars, like Jean Gayon (1999: 175–6), allude to a mention of the etymological root of "eugenics" in their efforts to portray Nietzsche as a eugenicist. In the first section of *On the Genealogy of Morals*, Nietzsche imagines the moment when the "nobles" coined the valuations "good" and "bad/evil" before the slave rebellion.

There, Nietzsche refers to "the well-born" who "felt they were 'the happy'; they did not need to construct their happiness artificially by looking at their enemies." Being naive means being honest and confident in their aristocratic character, as opposed to the reactive rationalizations of resentment: "While the noble man is confident and frank with himself (γενναίος, 'of noble birth,' underlines the nuance 'upright' and probably 'naïve' as well), the man of ressentiment is neither upright nor naïve, nor honest and straight with himself" (GM I 10). The paragraph in question is not about any eugenic project. It does not even mention *Züchtung*. It is about the provenance of value judgments and the antagonism between the master and slave morality. "Naivety" in Nietzsche is close to Schiller's: the spontaneity, passion, curiosity, and creativity characteristic of children. This connotation is present in his early writings on the Greeks (Martin 1996: 31–5).

11  Nietzsche's lack of interest in Gobineau is duly documented by Schank (2000: 425–33). See Martin (2004) for a comparison between Nietzsche and Gobineau.

12  See also PF 1884 26[409], a posthumous note that, in my view, has a robust Lamarckian character.

Part Five

# Feminist Strategies

# 13

# The Same Instinct Named Twice: The Drive to Possession and the Fettered Spirit in Nietzsche's Middle Period

Marisa E. Maccaro

## Introduction

At GS 14 Nietzsche offers a psychological analysis of "the things people call love" and concludes that friendship is love's highest form. There, he suggests that romantic/sexual love is not as selfless as it is commonly made out to be but a supremely egoistic expression of the drives to possess and be possessed. Crucially, these drives manifest in service of the drive to secure truth, incorporate it into oneself, and cease investigation into the nature of things and in opposition to the healthier drive to suspend judgment and accept uncertainty in the lifelong pursuit of truth, a drive exhibited by free spirits. In heteronormative romantic/sexual relationships, the details of these drives' expression are found in the traditional gender roles of dominance and submission—or, as Nietzsche calls them, "will and willingness." Although adhering to prescribed gender roles has significant social utility, the free spirit is marked by their rejection of this utility—of the comfort and security provided by the certainty of tradition—in favor of living autonomously and thereby "dangerously"[1] in pursuit of truth for its own sake.

Social utility aside, the ways in which the submissive role that women are socialized to play is harmful to their spirits are somewhat obvious, but the dominant role that men are socialized to play can be, according to Nietzsche, in spite of its utility, harmful to men's spirits as well insofar as it supports the unhealthy drive to possess an object that soothes, serves, and loves them unconditionally. Drawing on aphorisms from Nietzsche's middle period works, I will argue that the expression of the drives to possess and be possessed, specifically through gender roles, is detrimental to both men and women, both because the objects of these drives are mollifying and because they are illusory—they are the facades of subjects playing prescribed roles. I will then recommend curiosity as the higher ideal that ought to be cultivated between men and women and the key to the freedom of their respective spirits.

## The Free Spirit and the Fanatic

In the Preface of *Human, All Too Human*, Nietzsche identifies some preliminary characteristics of the free spirit, such as "strength and will to self-determination"[2] and "self-mastery and discipline of the heart."[3] As he develops this concept of "free-spiritedness" throughout the work, he describes the process of freeing the spirit as one that begins with questioning the external influences that act upon us, especially that of customary Christian morality. At HH 125 Nietzsche lists "[man's] origin, environment, his class and profession ... [and] the dominant views of the age" as sources of influence for which the free spirit "demands reasons."[4] By demanding such reasons, the free spirit is able to examine the values that these happenstances have imparted to them and decide whether they are worth adhering to—that is, whether they are grounded in some truth about themselves or the world that must be faced or grounded in untruth that must be overcome. This examination is a function of what Nietzsche calls the "intellectual conscience"—"the conscience behind your conscience."[5] Whereas conscience simpliciter is the herd instinct, the intellectual conscience is the drive to question the values of the herd. We develop our intellectual conscience when we recognize that our judgments have "a prehistory in [our] instincts, likes, dislikes, experiences, and lack of experiences" and ask "'*How* did [they] originate there?'" and "'*What* is it that impels me to listen to [them]?'"[6] On Alfano's account, the "intellectually courageous inquiry into oneself and one's community" facilitated by the intellectual conscience results in "*spernere se ipsum*."[7] Because unearthing the contemptible origins of one's drives or of the values of one's community can be painful, curiosity and courage are natural allies. It is this pain, however, that positions the spirit toward liberation by replacing trust in the herd—"trust in life"[8]—with existential problems that call for honest and courageous intellectual pursuit.

The "fettered spirit,"[9] on the other hand, is marked by the psychological state of fanaticism, a state in which one regards a belief that they wish were true as true because it is immediately advantageous to them, as is believing that they possess the truth.[10] The primary example of this fanaticism is "the man of faith," or the religious fanatic, who is comforted by the idea that there is a benevolent God watching over them, providing them with a moral code, and promising a superior life after death—and thus chooses to believe that this is the case. However, while it may be tempting to designate fanatical wishful belief to the realm of religious faith, Nietzsche believes that convictions of all kinds can be fanatical, such as the conviction of the scholar that understanding the world is superior to participating in it. On this kind of fanatic Nietzsche writes, "Most people take a thing that they *know* under their protection, as if knowledge of it sufficed to make it their property. The ego's desire for appropriation is boundless."[11] Fettered spirits such as these strive for knowledge because they have an "urgent need" for something certain to ground their existence, and the feeling of possessing this certainty results in "the experience of an increase in strength."[12] Thus, the pursuit of truth can manifest as an expression of the drive to dominate knowledge into truth, attain the satisfaction that comes from possessing certainty, and cease exploring alternate perspectives. Existence, however, is fundamentally uncertain, and to deny this fact is to deny life itself. The increase in strength experienced by the fettered spirit is therefore a deception produced by the fulfillment of the ascetic ideal, the essence of which is to weaken one's relationship with oneself and the world.

The free spirit and the spirit fettered by fanaticism are driven by differing manifestations of the will to truth. The free spirit, guided by the intellectual conscience, reasons in pursuit of truth, no matter how socially useless or personally unpleasant this pursuit or its object may be; whereas the fettered spirit "reasons" that "the personal *utility* of an opinion ... demonstrate[s] its truth."[13] The answer to Nietzsche's question at GS 110—"To what extent can truth stand to be incorporated?"—thus depends on the strength of an individual's instinct for self-preservation. When the truth cannot be incorporated into one's existing belief structures—into one's ego, that is—it turns destructive, demolishing one's faith that whatever beliefs one has inherited are in fact "conditions of life."[14] Unwilling to face such upheaval or unable to stomach the *spernere se ipsum* wrought from it, the fettered spirit contorts useful opinions into truths that conform to their worldview and often that justify disengaging from themselves and from the pursuit of truth altogether—truths about life after death, the value of selflessness, and the worthlessness of earthly pursuits. Conversely, the free spirit not only endures painful truths about the finitude and insignificance of human existence, they privilege truths that will inspire further engagement with the world anyway, on their terms, over the truths provided by religion, science, and metaphysics on which the fettered spirit rests and "deactivate[s] the will."[15]

**Gender Roles and Utility**

The utility of gender roles is that they prescribe distinct ideals to men and women that help guide their thoughts and actions. Contemporary proponents of gender roles often claim that it is easier to figure out how to be when the scope of what is acceptable and allowed is delimited. Moreover, traditional binary gender roles embrace both virtues and vices. For example, women are socialized to be sensitive to their emotions and the emotions of others, but they have also historically been encouraged to be physically weak and vain, i.e., spend an enormous amount of time and money on their appearances. Men are socialized to be strong and capable, but they are also encouraged to be aggressive and repress emotions other than anger. It is therefore easier to embody the ideals of femininity and masculinity than it is to achieve a gender-neutral ideal that excludes vices, like vanity and aggression, and even outright faults, like frailty and emotional incompetence. Furthermore, because these roles are so deeply entrenched in contemporary Western culture, there are often social consequences for departing from them and social rewards for successfully enacting them. Women who are "too masculine" and men who are "too feminine" are othered, ridiculed, and often have their sexual orientations called into question; whereas those who fulfill their roles well are lauded and garner social capital.

At GS 68 Nietzsche conceptualizes these roles as those of "will and willingness." In the language of contemporary feminist philosophy, these are the roles of dominance and submission or, in the language of existentialism, transcendence and immanence. Nietzsche writes:

> Someone took a youth to a wise man and said: "Look, he is being corrupted by women!" The wise man shook his head and smiled. "It is men who corrupt women," he exclaimed, "and the failings of women should be atoned for and set right in men—for man makes for himself the image (*Bild*) of woman, and woman shapes herself according to this image." "You are too gentle towards women," said one in the company; "you do not know them!" The wise man replied, "The way of men is will; the way of women is willingness—that is the law of the sexes; truly a hard law for women! All human beings are innocent of their existence; women, however, are *doubly innocent*. Who could have oil and mercy enough for them?" "Forget oil! Forget gentleness!" shouted someone else from the crowd; "one has to raise women better!" "One has to raise men better," said the wise man and beckoned to the youth to follow him.—But the youth did not follow him.
>
> (Emphasis mine)

Here Nietzsche exhibits sharply sympathetic insight into the social context that produces the ideal woman, a recurring theme in his considerations of women throughout his middle period. He recognizes, as many feminist philosophers have, that woman is defined in relation to man, rendering her subordinate to him. One of the primary roles that men play is that of creator: men have the economic and political power to produce and enforce the norms of femininity, norms that aim to shape women into passive servants to men's emotional, sexual, and domestic needs.

One of the key features of the fanatic's psychology is, according to Reginster, that they are "prepared to accept beliefs the particular content of which may be quite unpleasant or disturbing, provided he manages to convince himself that they represent the unconditional truth." Nietzsche is attentive to the fact that, like Christianity, womanhood exhibits no lack of "unpleasant and disturbing" content. At GS 71, "On female chastity," for example, Nietzsche considers how upper-class women are brought up to be ignorant about sex and instilled with "deep shame in the face of such things." All they know is that sex compromises their virtue by sullying their purity—that is, until their wedding night when they are forced "to experience all at once delight, surrender, duty, pity, terror at the unexpected proximity of god and beast, and who knows what else!" Nietzsche describes this custom as "amazing and monstrous" and marvels at how women are able to resolve such contradictory expectations:

> Even the compassionate curiosity of the wisest connoisseur of human psychology is insufficient for guessing how this or that woman manages to accommodate herself to this solution of the riddle and to this riddle of a solution, and what dreadful, far-reaching suspicions must stir in her poor, unhinged soul; indeed, how the ultimate philosophy and skepticism of woman casts anchor at this point! Afterwards, the same deep silence as before, and often a silence directed at herself; she closes her eyes to herself.

This passage contains two responses women might have to the "monstrous" social customs they find themselves subject to. The first response is that of the fanatic: to "clos[e] her eyes to herself," to the irresolvable contradictions she faces, and appeal to the values she has inherited, sacrificing personal comfort to some greater natural, social, or religious truth about womanhood. The second response is to cast the anchor of skepticism and follow it all the way down. At GS 64, Nietzsche states that old women harbor more skepticism in their hearts than any man and write that "they believe the superficiality of existence to be its essence, and all virtue and depth is to them merely a veil over this 'truth.'" That women are subject to and disadvantaged by a special set of restrictions puts them in a better position than men to see through the veil of value that is thrown over social constructs to obscure their contingency. By keeping their eyes open and demanding reasons for the norms and customs that harm them, women take the first step toward free spiritude. However, because rejecting their subordinate position can result in greater suffering than enduring it—in the form of various social consequences—it is more useful for women to believe that their subordination is ontologically grounded, though the realities of it are often unpleasant and disturbing.

That women suffer from their subordination but simultaneously reap benefits from it is a prominent theme in Nietzsche's analyses of women throughout *Human, All Too Human*. There, he pays special attention to the peace, comfort, and strength women are able to find in their socially conditioned subordination to men. As Nietzsche expresses at HH 412, "women have known through subordination to secure for themselves the preponderant advantage, even indeed the dominion." This advantage, he suggests, is that they do not have to work and earn money to take care of themselves; instead, they are taken care of. At D 66, Nietzsche writes that "[a]ll women are subtle in exaggerating their weaknesses" so that men not only do not hurt them but protect them and provide for them. Nietzsche characterizes these instances of subtle deception as victories of "female shrewdness"[16] but contemptible victories, nonetheless. Insofar as exploiting their role of willingness involves relying on others to satisfy their needs, the spirits of the women who do so remain unfree.[17]

Although there are obvious advantages to occupying the masculine role of will, Nietzsche nonetheless criticizes men for "corrupting" women by making them play the role of willingness and for desiring a willing being at their service in the first place[18]—"the free spirit does not want to be served,"[19] he states. At HH 435, Nietzsche suggests that millennia of occupying the role of willingness have conditioned women to "attach themselves ... to the wheels of a free-spirited, independent endeavor as brake on them." He further claims that the soothing qualities of femininity work to remove obstacles from men's paths.[20] While this "service" is performed in the name of "love," the free spirit rejects this kind of love; real love would place stones in his path to overcome. For this reason, when considering whether the free spirits of the future will live with women, Nietzsche determines that "like the truth-thinkers and truth-speakers of the present, they must prefer to fly alone."[21] Nietzsche offers Socrates, a truth-thinker and truth-speaker of the past, as an example of a man who flew alone; however, interestingly, he points out that Socrates did not do so out of spontaneous preference but to escape a bad wife. At HH 433, he describes Socrates as someone who sought a wife with the typical intention of securing a domestic servant; however, Xantippe "made his house and home" so "uncomfortable and unhomely to him" that he was driven into the streets where he would become one of the greatest philosophers that ever lived. Good women and, by extension, good wives, "always secretly intrigue against the higher being of their husbands; they desire to deprive them of their future for the sake of a quiet, comfortable present."[22] Thus, the social role of women actually works against the self-overcoming of men by seducing them into the comforts of a serene existence alongside a passive object that serves them and loves them unconditionally instead of challenging them. When men accept good wives as possessions they are entitled to, misconstrue their service as an act of love, and embrace this arrangement as evidence of their dominance, they too are kept from free spirithood. Moreover, because men's dominance is predicated on an unhealthy drive—the drive to possess—occupying the dominant position does not benefit men. Despite their social use-value, the roles of will and willingness are thus ultimately enacted to the detriment of both men and women.

## The Drive to Possession

At D 346, Nietzsche gives a brief character sketch of "misogynists" or men who see women as their enemy. He asserts that this view is born of "an immoderate drive which not only hates itself but its means of satisfaction as well."[23] The drive in question is none other than the drive to possess, and it is immoderate in that it can never truly be satisfied. On the one hand, acting on this drive can be understood as the misguided attempt to secure sexual gratification, as if the sex drive could be permanently satisfied, when it is in fact ever present, never ending, and bottomless. As Lucretius puts it in *De Rerum Natura*, "[n]othing else/inflames us, once we have it, with desire/of more and more and more."[24] On the other hand, the inclination to act on this immoderate drive extends beyond the desire for mere sexual gratification to the desire for the domestic and emotional comforts that women are meant to lend an irremediably uncomfortable existence. However, given that the drive for truth is similarly immoderate, it cannot be the immoderate nature of this drive that harms those in its grasp on Nietzsche's view. In actuality, the source of harm is the means of the drive's satisfaction: namely, women. Because women are constructed as obedient, passive objects to be cared for and possessed, but are actually subjects enacting the role prescribed to them, the means of the drive's satisfaction is illusory. Therefore, in addition to being insatiable, the drive to possess lacks a proper object. While it may be socially useful to believe that this drive can be satisfied and that the women who appear to be up to the task are what they seem, acting on this drive is ultimately a fool's errand. Misogyny is thus the product of the (unconscious or conscious) realization that this drive cannot be satisfied by its object.

That gender is a social construct rather than a natural kind does not make the roles of men and women any less real to Nietzsche—or to most people, for that matter. As he writes in GS 58,

> [the] reputation, name, and appearance, the usual measure and weight of a thing, what it counts for … all this grows from generation unto generation, merely because people believe in it, until it gradually grows to be part of the thing and turns into its very body. What was first appearance becomes in the end, almost invariably, the essence and is effective as such.

That is, what may have originated as a useful fiction of masculine and feminine essences has become reality with the force of generations of belief.[25] However, while this social transformation from appearance to essence may obtain when enacted upon inert "things," individuals are far less mutable. There is an important distinction between the reality of gender roles and the reality of the individuals enacting them. Gender roles, as they have been constructed, are not illusory—they are real to the members of the societies that uphold them. My point is rather that these roles are Procrustean disguises behind which individual males and females loom, striving to fulfill an impossible ideal. It is for this reason that women are illusory and both the drives to possess and to be possessed, as expressed through the roles of will and willingness, are doomed to dissatisfaction.

Crucially, the object of the drive to possess is not the only thing in disguise here—possessiveness itself notoriously masquerades as an expression of love.[26] At GS 14 Nietzsche calls love and greed "the same instinct, named twice," arguing that love, contrary to its popular characterization as the epitome of selflessness, is an essentially egoistic distraction from "higher"[27] and, perhaps, more perilous ideals. In explaining romantic/sexual love in terms of the drive to possess, he writes: "The pleasure we take in ourselves tries to preserve itself by time and time again changing something new *into ourselves*—that is simply what possession means."[28] However, by incorporating the beloved, and what the beloved stands for (i.e., beauty, "distinction,"[29] security, etc.), into one's own identity, one does not really come to possess the beloved but a fabricated idea of them as *same*,[30] or continuous with oneself. The object of the drive to possess is, once again, illusory—but this time the illusion is produced by the ego of the possessor and imposed on the object of possession rather than produced by the facade that the object of possession herself presents, although these two illusions certainly work together.

In light of Nietzsche's condemnatory view of romantic/sexual love, Verkerk offers Irigaray's account of wonder as a means of overcoming the drive for possession's damage to relationships between men and women. Irigaray describes wonder as "the appetite for knowledge of who or what awakens our appetite"[31] and belief in a "perpetual newness of the self, the other, the world"[32] that precludes fanatical convictions and invites curiosity. She writes: "Recognizing you means or implies respecting you as other, accepting that I stop before you as before something insurmountable, a mystery, a freedom that will never be mine, a subjectivity that will never be mine, a mine that will never be mine."[33] Irigaray, like Nietzsche, sees the pursuit of knowledge—of the world or of another person—as susceptible to corruption by the drive to possess certainty: to dominate information into submission by stamping it with the label "understanding" and filing it away to collect dust.[34] This drive constrains and defines the fanatic who has no use for that which is uncertain and therefore free. Although "the urge for certainty"[35] drives truth pursuit for the free spirit as well, the free spirit is able to keep this urge in check by recognizing that certainty is a destination that necessarily eludes us, an object beyond possession. With their wonder, or curiosity, about all there is to learn about "the self, the other, and the world" as a guide, they embrace the insurmountable, the mysterious, and the free. In this way, curiosity is antithetical to the greedy, domineering, ascetic valuation of utility that underlies adherence to custom.

## Conclusion

At GS 13 Nietzsche writes: "He who feels 'I am in possession of the truth'—how many possessions does he not renounce in order to save this feeling! What would he not throw overboard in order to stay 'on top'—that is, above the others who lack 'the truth!'" For both men and women, faith in the truth of gendered essences offers refuge from some of the most uncomfortable conditions of life: uncertainty, loneliness, contempt of self, and other. However, the comfort afforded by this refuge comes at the price of freedom, and insofar as the possession of truth is illusory, so are the feelings of strength and power that accompanies it. For this reason, Nietzsche advises "knowledge seekers" to "be robbers and conquerors as long as [they] cannot be rulers and possessors."[36] The project of the free spirit is to explore the innumerable perspectives of others and overcome the limitations therein. By embracing and sharing a "higher thirst for an ideal above them"[37]—namely, the *process* of truth-pursuit—men and women can replace the futile drives to possess and be possessed with a healthier drive to truth—about themselves, each other, and the world—and unfetter their spirits in tandem.

In response to gender roles, the free spirit thus casts the anchor of skepticism, opens their eyes to themselves, and proceeds courageously. Free spirithood requires an "openness to the world,"[38] a curiosity that runs counter to the blind valuation of the essences we are assigned at birth. Of course, doubting the reasons for one's gendered social position is not as useful as possessing certainty that the roles of will and willingness are grounded in some fundamental truth about the world. In fact, given the social consequences to which this skepticism can lead, it is an exercise of the "perilous curiosity" that Nietzsche describes at HH P3, that at GS 283 he calls "the secret to harvesting from existence the greatest fruitfulness and the greatest enjoyment." Uniting the virtues of curiosity and courage, the intellectual conscience makes possible the free spirit's confrontation of the "fearful and questionable that characterizes all existence,"[39] as well as its joyous outcome. The centrality of gender roles to human identities, with their ubiquitous demands and vicious limitations, makes them an obvious target of confrontation. Although this confrontation poses a threat to one's sense of self and well-being—survival even—within a society that not only values such roles but sees them as essential, the free spirit takes "delight in the danger of uncertainty"[40] and asks what modes of being and seeing one another can be found beyond gender.

## Notes

1. GS 283.
2. HH 7.
3. HH 8.
4. HH 125.
5. GS 335.
6. GS 335.
7. Alfano (2019: 262).
8. Alfano (2019: 262).

9  HH 225.
10  Reginster (2003: 53).
11  D 285.
12  Reginster (2003: 57).
13  HH 7.
14  GS 110.
15  Verkerk (2014: 283).
16  HH 416.
17  Abbey (2000: 115).
18  Oppel (2005: 29).
19  HH 432.
20  HH 431.
21  HH 426.
22  HH 434.
23  HH 259.
24  Lucretius (1968: 1088–90).
25  See GS 110.
26  Though at HH 10 Nietzsche only describes the possessive tendencies of women, stating that "women readily perceive in a man whether his soul has already been taken possession of" because "they wish to be loved without rivals," at GS 14 he indicates that this possessiveness is characteristic of both men and women in love, stating, "The lover wants unconditional and sole possession of the longed-for person; he wants power over her soul as unconditional as his power over her body; he wants to be the only beloved, to live and to rule in the other soul as that which is supreme and most desirable."
27  GS 40.
28  GS 40.
29  GS 40.
30  Verkerk (2017: 138).
31  Irigaray (1993a: 78).
32  Irigaray (1993a: 8).
33  Irigaray (2004: 8).
34  Verkerk (2017: 150).
35  GS 375.
36  GS 283.
37  GS 41.
38  Reginster (2013: 456).
39  HH AOM P6.
40  GS P3.

14

# An Affirming Feminism: Queering Nietzsche with Judith Butler

Marta Vero

## Overturning Nietzsche

It will undoubtedly strike some as odd to question Nietzsche's writings with the intention of contributing to a feminist strand of thought. In addition to the many places in his works where Nietzsche expresses misogynistic positions that go hand in hand with other racist and aristocratic positions, it would suffice to think of the frequently cited aphorism BGE 239 to conclude that Nietzsche's philosophy ought to be considered, at least in its intentions, as expressing an anti-feminist program. For according to Nietzsche, feminism as a political movement must be explicitly opposed by virtue of its "stupidity."[1] Anyone who reads this aphorism must deal with violent language and endure a succession of what, to put it mildly, are harsh judgments directed against those women who sought to emancipate themselves from the patriarchal societies of late nineteenth-century Europe, like those who seek to do so today.

Nevertheless, my aim here is not to refute Nietzsche's condemnations of feminism, nor to overturn the terms of his condemnation in order to dismiss him from accusations of misogyny. It is certainly possible to consider anti-feminism as one of Nietzsche's masks and therefore to read him "beyond" his misogynistic statements, as Ofelia Schutte has shown in her seminal book.[2] This would mean, as in the case of BGE 239, taking a closer look at the inconsistencies of Nietzsche's philosophy, namely considering his condemnation of feminism as deeply incompatible with his Dionysian program of a "new culture." Yet it must be admitted that in Nietzsche's works the *topos* of women is at least ambivalent. Scholars have noticed that he employed female mythological figures to represent the Dionysian instinct to life, showing himself capable of conceiving of women as a symbol of creative drives and, therefore, to go beyond his own masks (i.e., beyond his own misogynistic statements).[3]

In this chapter I dwell on Nietzsche's condemnation of feminism by considering feminism at its philosophical and methodological core. In BGE 239 Nietzsche opposes the feminists who believe they emancipate themselves by copying "all the stupidities that the 'men' in Europe, that European manliness suffers from."[4] It seems here that Nietzsche's "mansplaining" revolves around the paradoxical danger for feminists of "defeminizing" women, that is, negating the peculiarities of femininity in order to try to imitate masculinity. This might reveal a fatal error for feminism. Yet according to Nietzsche, European manliness is anything but a healthy ideal to emulate, for it is sick, supporting a culture that weakens individuals. Nietzsche's real target in this aphorism is the kind of feminist position that suffers from the same vice as does the dogmatic philosopher, insofar as it wants to "create a science of woman" to restore the same "tyrannical relation to truth" that motivated the metaphysical European philosophies of his age.[5]

There is a close connection in Nietzsche's thought between the problem of truth and the representation of women, as Kelly Oliver and other critics have observed. The "supposition" that "truth is a woman" in fact opens the preface to BGE.[6] For Nietzsche, dogmatic philosophy makes a fatal methodological mistake in that it claims to be able to identify truth with something like a specific object. Nietzsche deplores this "tyrannical" approach toward truth, as well as the "grotesque seriousness" and the awkward, grandiose tone that pertains to it.[7] The famous—and quite sexist—claim that, as in the case with truth, woman is elusive and fleeting, is employed by Nietzsche at the core of his preface to connect the tyrannical approach toward truth with a misconception of language:

> And perhaps the time is very near when we will realize again and again just *what* actually served as the cornerstone of those sublime and unconditional philosophical edifices that the dogmatists used to build—some piece of folk superstitions from time immemorial (like the soul-superstition that still causes trouble as the superstition of the subject or I), some word-plays perhaps, a seduction of grammar or an over-eager generalization from facts that are really very local, very personal, very human-all-too-human.[8]

By arguing that their philosophical edifices have been built upon superstitions and the fragile foundations of wordplay, Nietzsche means that dogmatists have interpreted the grammatical structures they used *as if* these structures revealed essential relations between things. The metaphysicians' mistake is therefore that of over-generalizing, which prevents them from grasping the multiplicity of things. This condemns their philosophical systems to remaining naively anchored to the grammatical structure of a language and to depicting mere linguistic relations between things as revealing their essential characteristics. For this reason, one can conclude that, for Nietzsche, a tyrannical approach toward truth, as that of the grandiose philosophical edifices built by dogmatists, corresponds to an essentialist, naive conception of language. This kind of tyrannical essentialism is the same "masculine" thought that Nietzsche claimed was weakening European culture, including the feminist movement.

At this point one can ask whether Nietzsche, albeit speaking from a position outside and probably opposed to feminist philosophy, is here making a criticism that is deserving of serious consideration. Should feminist philosophers embark on a critical investigation of grammatical and linguistic structures instead of taking them for granted? Should they recognize and deconstruct a *negative*, non-affirming conception of language in order to effectively pursue women's emancipation?

Moreover, the nexus between truth and woman also needs to be taken seriously. Nietzsche's argument might suggest that, in order to propose a non-tyrannical philosophical approach that might lead to women's emancipation, feminists should doubt their own choice of identifying "women" as feminism's object of inquiry. That the notion of "woman" may be as elusive as "truth" might mean that one cannot actually *define* what a woman is. The association of terms that Nietzsche proposes in BGE might help feminists to consider "woman" as too general a concept, the danger of which lies in underestimating its "local" existence, in favor of conceiving it in abstract, universal terms. In other words, raising a fixed concept of woman on the model of the old metaphysical edifices would completely erase humanity from that concept and reiterate an artificial idea of woman that would reinforce a tyrannical, negative view, precisely as has happened in the case of truth.

In order to emancipate women politically and philosophically, respecting their "womanhood" (whatever this means) and not assimilating them to men, feminism should, according to Nietzsche, desist from transforming women into mere objects of knowledge. Feminism should, in short, rely on an *affirming* philosophy, willing to doubt the linguistic structures that the term "woman" implies.

With regard to his position toward historical feminism, Nietzsche's claim is therefore still very much worth considering. Of course, many thinkers have examined Nietzsche's texts in order to answer the question of the "essence" of women. Notable among these is Carol Diethe, who has shown through an insightful inquiry that Nietzsche's philosophy had already generated such debate in the Wilhelmine era.[9] Like Diethe, I think feminism might dwell within Nietzsche's philosophy at a deeper level and that it can be used as a way to interrogate conventional feminism's *praxis*. For this reason, I question whether Nietzsche's philosophy might address feminism at a *methodological* level. If we accept Nietzsche's statement, according to which feminism should differentiate itself from masculine/Androcentric European thought, it follows that by critically interrogating feminism's language, we may disclose its future (authentically emancipatory) possibilities. Such a critical view of language would mark what I call an *affirming* feminism, that is, a philosophical interrogation of feminism that (1) engages in a critical-*genealogical* examination of language that subsumes Nietzsche's genealogical method in order to debunk the grandiose edifices of dogmatists, (2) admits the *elusiveness* of its findings, (3) takes an *ironic* approach to the language on which it relies, (4) considers its object *prospectively* and not *tyrannically* (i.e., rejects attempts to "make a science of woman," and corresponding generalizations), and (5) recognizes its *creative* capacity in juxtaposition to philological "sterility."[10]

In demonstrating the utility of Nietzsche's thought as a source of a truly emancipatory, affirmative feminism, I turn to Judith Butler's early works, for within them Butler conceives of feminism as an affirming view that combines all of the elements specified above.[11] Moreover, I argue that such an affirming interpretation of feminism differs from others in that it combines the debunking, philological, and "sterile" feature of genealogy—namely the genealogical investigation into the traces of what Nietzsche calls the "masculine stupidity" of the European use of language, with a creative impetus. This impetus allows us to imagine new practices and scenarios for the struggle against patriarchal oppression. For these reasons, I examine the ways in which

Butler's philosophy highlights a constitutive ambivalence in Nietzsche's program. This ambivalence originates in the twofold tension internal to the genealogical method: on the one hand the demystification of values and on the other the ironical subversion of the chain of interrelated meanings that genealogy uncovers. In what follows I assess the intersections between Nietzsche's and Butler's philosophies in order to deeply analyze this twofold tension and inquire into whether a "queer" interpretation of feminism might be considered an affirming one.

## A Feminist Genealogy: Skepticism and Grammar

References to Nietzsche's oeuvre are scattered throughout many of Butler's works. Some of them introduce the discussion of expressly methodological issues. Butler's appropriation of Nietzscheanism as a tool to doubt language embeds the fundamental features of an "affirming feminism." This is evident in the *genealogical* method that marks Butler's feminism. In *Gender Trouble* (GT), the book that is commonly taken to have inaugurated gender studies as a social and philosophical discipline, Butler endorses a Nietzschean (and Foucauldian) employment of genealogy. Butler's positioning with respect to the philosophical debate around the possibility of a feminist *praxis* in the twentieth century derives from this choice.

The first preface to the book reveals the strategic role of genealogy in Butler's early work. Genealogy is the most effectively philosophical strategy to bring into question the "epistemic/ontological regime" that sustains patriarchy, grounded in the "binary relation between 'men' and 'women.'"[12] Genealogy consists in an examination that takes place within language. Otherwise stated, to embark on a genealogical examination of such "foundational categories" as "sex, gender, and desire" means to identify language as the medium of our inquiry and, at the same time, to recognize it as the most important thing about which to be skeptical.[13] This echoes insights provided by Nietzsche. The appeal to deconstruct European philosophers' "belief in grammar," which is stated variously at different places in BGE, gives rise to a concerted linguistic exploration in *On the Genealogy of Morality* (GM).[14] In GM Nietzsche argues that the study of "linguistics" and "etymology" should have a prominent role in the investigation of the origins of morality.[15] In the first essay we find an etymological analysis in which the notions of good, bad, and evil are brought closer to etymologically related concepts.[16] This means that, for Nietzsche, a genealogy of morality is something that coincides with an investigation of the words we use, the worlds we inhabit, and the bodies we have.

It should be noted that, according to Nietzsche, the debunking action of grammatologists and philologists goes hand in hand with that of "physiologists and doctors." For Nietzsche it is necessary to examine bodies as well as language in order to uncover the a/effects of a normative value system. For in doing so we may reveal the physical symptoms and expressions of its moral structures, that is, the ways in which language imprints itself on the bodies and in the psyches of individuals. I will come back to this point later.

Butler decidedly inherits Nietzsche's "misologic" interpretation of genealogy in GT,[17] although she does not understand the inner tension of genealogy and language as the necessity of an etymological research.[18] Rather, she undertakes an investigation of the functioning of the linguistic predicates of sex, gender, and desire as *performative* predicates, namely as linguistic acts that bring a situation into being, affect a way of life, sanction a condition that can be experienced materially.[19] Genealogy prompts Butler to suspect that categories like manliness and womanhood, which are usually taken as "an internal essence," are in reality "manufactured through a sustained set of acts, posited through the gender stylization of the bodies."[20]

It is not a coincidence that, in the preface and throughout the book, Butler mentions Luce Irigaray's notion of "phallogocentrism" and Monique Wittig's opinions on the linguistic conflation between femininity and sexuality.[21] Along with Wittig and Irigaray, Butler believes that feminist philosophy should rely on a linguistic investigation.[22] Irigaray often referring in her philosophy to Nietzsche's representations of women and her contribution to feminism has shown that there is no place for women in a language shaped by men, namely "phallogocentrism."[23] This statement could be considered as agreeing with Nietzsche's controversial criticism of European feminism since it proceeds from the idea that manliness has produced a hegemonic language that completely ignores the essence of womanhood, and from this it draws, as Nietzsche would say, its "weakness." For her part, Wittig strongly criticizes a heteronormative, masculine-shaped society, as a result of which women are often sexualized, namely harnessed in the category of sex, which appears to be somehow prerational or even prelogical. These positions, one essentialist and the other materialist, have the merit of partially picking up on Nietzsche's plea to cast doubt on the dogmatist's language *vis-à-vis* the concept woman.[24] In particular, Wittig's criticism of the sexualization of woman helps to recognize a certain heteronormative tendency to identify women with something "other" than men, together with a "naturalization" of gender roles in language, insofar as they are generally traced back to sexual-biological motivations.

According to Butler, "if gender itself is naturalized through grammatical norms, as Wittig has argued, then the alteration of gender at the most fundamental epistemic level will be conducted, *in part*, through contesting the grammar in which gender is given."[25] This sentence allows one to understand the extent to which Butler employs Nietzsche's methodology in order to differentiate herself from "classical" European feminism—and thus to recognize the nexus between the first two features of affirming feminism I specified above. As a first step, Butler upholds the misologic aims of feminist philosophy, which was already recognized by those feminists who had read Nietzsche (like Irigaray), by openly attributing to it a *critical-genealogical* orientation (1). A linguistic genealogy prompts Butler to suspect that the entire sex-gender constellation is the result of performative, reiterated linguistic acts. In a genealogical view, the interconnected categories of "woman" and "female" must therefore be read as a kind of corollary of the thesis that gender is performative. According to Butler,

> to trace the political operations that produce and conceal what qualifies as the juridical subject of feminism is precisely the task of a *feminist genealogy* of the category of women. In the course of this effort to question "women" as a subject of feminism, the unproblematic invocation of that category may prove to *preclude* the possibility of feminism as a representational politics.[26]

This approach leads Butler to differentiate herself from other European feminists by being skeptical about "woman as such," which, distinct from essentialist notions, may be considered performative through genealogical and linguistic means.[27] This also applies to the entire sex-gender-desire constellation.

This kind of feminist genealogy is also affirming since it addresses itself to provisional, *elusive* findings (2), to the extent that it refuses to approach its "juridical" and philosophical subject in an "unproblematic" way. Her positioning with regard to the feminist landscape might also be confronted with Nietzsche's "problematic" approach toward morality and its origin.[28] In BGE he challenges European moralists who consider morality as something given. Using Butler, one might claim that even nature does not constitute something given. For not only is there no "natural woman"— meaning that our "feeling as natural women" must necessarily be questioned and criticized—but biological sex itself merely reflects existing power relations, since it is far from describing "essential" or "natural" relationships.[29]

Thus, unlike other feminists, and in force of her undertaking of a genealogical method, Butler engages her misological suspicion in order to question the same notion of "woman."[30] This term, just like its near equivalent "female," has become "unfixed," one far from conveying a "stable" notion.[31] Butler's employment of genealogy allows her to address language with the aim of recognizing the notion of womanhood as "elusive" and therefore connected with a wide "constellation"—to use Walter Benjamin's thought image—of strictly interconnected terms, such as femininity, sex, sexual orientation, and, of course, gender. Butler's distinctive feature in the landscape represented by this kind of feminist misology is that her approach is based precisely on the instability of the entire sex-gender constellation.

In this respect, Butler questions Nietzsche again, this time quoting Michel Haar's commentary on the German philosopher's criticism to the "metaphysics of substance."[32] According to Haar's interpretation, Nietzsche recognizes the dogmatists' edifices as "trapped" in illusions, such as "Being" and "Substance," which are "fostered by belief that the grammatical formulation of subject and predicate reflects the prior ontological reality of substance and attribute" (GT 27). Haar refers here to an aphorism, which has already been mentioned, in which Nietzsche claims that the existence of the antithesis between true and false might be revealed as "a fiction" grounded in grammar. As we saw, metaphysical language frequently entices its users to assume that grammatical laws equate with "true" philosophical principles.

At the end of the aphorism BGE 239, Nietzsche adds an important detail to his theory of non-correspondence between truth and language. Rising "above the belief in grammar," the philosopher should, according to Nietzsche, be "allowed to be a bit *ironic* with the subject," as she learns to be "with the predicate and the subject."[33] This aphorism, which Butler may have had in mind while composing GT, makes one reflect on at least two things. First, the toughest enterprise for the genealogist is to stand in front of the notion of subject, which necessarily has to be put into doubt, since the subject is one of the fundamental notions of the prevailing metaphysical use of grammar. Second, and consequently, the reason this task seems so difficult is that our thinking about human action, i.e., our functioning paradigm for human agency, is founded upon this grammatical notion of the subject. Nietzsche explains this at

GM I 13, in which he suggests that, just as it is incorrect to "separate the lightning from its flash," it is wrong for philosophers to distinguish between strength and its manifestations or a subject from their actions. It follows that the task of emancipating themselves from the notion of the subject is challenging for a philosopher, since it comprises the conceptual framework within which, as a human being, they may conceive the possibility of action.

To the question "how can a philosopher deconstruct the subject and conceive of her agency apart from it?," Nietzsche answers: by being ironic. Irony is about the ability to displace the subject, to consider it the result of its actions. Finally, for a philosopher being ironic toward the subject means being capable of destroying the same epistemic authority she contributed to building, to conceive her own philosophical activity as an ironic *performance*, that is, a parodic interpretation of the scientific narrative voice in order to replace it with something else.[34]

Butler uses Nietzsche's argument to reiterate her opposition to a normative use of the *topos* of identity in feminist politics. Above all, Nietzsche's plea for irony might turn out to be useful for her thesis of gender as a performance, as long as it allows feminists not only to get rid of a fixed identity (and in this way to be happy with the elusiveness (2) of their findings), but also to consider that our language, our minds, and, as we will see, our bodies are constructed through the reiteration of these linguistic acts. In other words, the grammatical fiction that we believe to be true erects the edifice of our self and constitutes the narrative in which we envision our agency and identity. The "doer is constructed in and through the deed," writes Butler, reformulating Nietzsche's aphorism.[35] Being ironic toward the subject means, finally, applying a genealogical method to our own experience and our own self. An affirming feminism is for this reason ironic (3), to the extent that it tries to "interrogate the *painful ironies* of being implicated in the forms of power that one explicitly opposes and trying to understand what kinds of agency might be derived from that situation."[36]

The emphasis that Nietzsche places on irony prompts reflection on the transformative outcomes of genealogy. Conceiving of his genealogical method ironically implies that Nietzsche's is a method that can be used on oneself. According to Thomas, *Ecce Homo* exhibits the extent to which Nietzsche applied this genealogical method to himself, in an intimate and singular way.[37] When we confer this intimate and ironical stance to a feminist genealogy, we can glimpse its transformative potential, insofar as feminism can function as a tool for women, together with all people oppressed by the androcentric, heteronormative political and discursive system, to investigate their repressive grammatical presumptions.

Emancipation, one could claim, comes in affirming feminism with a hammer. It is a long corridor of apparent "sterility" that drives the path of feminist emancipation.[38] I mean that the course of an affirming feminism must necessarily be composed of a *destructive* phase, in which genealogy (1) leads to deconstruct things that seemed essentially founded and unquestionable (such as the fixity (2) of notions like subject, womanhood, femininity, maleness, sex, gender) and to acquire an ironic (3) position toward one's grammar, experience, and self. By using a Nietzschean methodology Butler uncovers a creative, proactive capacity that marks the affirming aims of her interpretation of feminism. Moreover, Butler's focus on creativity and action depends on a particular interpretation of Nietzschean genealogy, which uncovers its "possibilising"[39] potential and its tight nexus with a dimension of futurbility.[40] In other words, a philological and etymological goal of her genealogy appears in affirming feminism through a transformative leap. In this way genealogy's "sterility" appears inextricably linked to its pro-active drive.

In order to focus on the *creative* (5) goal of this affirming feminism, one must nevertheless linger a little longer on the deconstruction of norms. In particular, one must ask what it means to move away from a tyrannical view of things, in the direction of a more perspectivistic (4) philosophical vision. I maintain that an affirming feminism must direct its gaze to bodies in order to discover how they are marked by tyrannical views of morality and gender and how such bodies can also be subversive by *performatively* and *creatively* (5) displaying their non-adherence to grammatical norms in an exploration of their multiple possibilities.

## Queer Bodies and Creativity

As noted above, Nietzsche denounces the "tyrannical" approach toward truth as a constitutive part of metaphysical systems. Moral edifices show an evident tendency to impress and to translate their own kind of truth onto living matter, to the extent that "every morality [...] is a piece of *tyranny* against both 'nature' and 'reason'" (BGE 188). A morality supported by a dogmatic philosophy treats truth *tyrannically*; namely it demands to find truth and possess it, enounce it, and enforce it as a value. Since such a morality claims to be conform to truth, nature, and reason, it strives to violently imprint its content on minds and especially on bodies, which will have to incorporate and perform these values in order to make them work. One can claim that, for Nietzsche, professing a tyrannical moral system affects the shared character and attitudes of a people, a mindset likely to be mocked by free spirits. In BGE Nietzsche makes fun of the way in which German people "perform" the moral values of profundity and honesty. The German "*drags* his soul around, he drags about everything he experiences. He digests his events badly [...]. And just as everyone who is chronically ill (all dyspeptics), tends towards comfortable things" (BGE 244).[41] In the case of Nietzsche's compatriots, profundity and honesty constitute their most successful "disguise," one that is bound up with sickness, depression, and a closely related sense of melancholy.[42]

Moreover, the same tendency that has been recognized as a part of the mystifying language of the metaphysicians, namely, to refer to certain fixed notions, is here transferred to a psychological and anthropological consideration, when the Germans' melancholic attitude is said to tend toward "comfortable things," namely toward (labile) securities. Nietzsche's ironic point of view confirms itself as a kind of antidote to the dominant attitude. He mocks Germans in order to distance himself from them and their sick attitude.

This is part of the reason Nietzsche argues that not only grammatologists and philosophers but also psychologists and physiologists need to cooperate in the pursuit of a genealogy of morality. The psychological, as well as the physical ways in which value systems are incorporated are worthy of being investigated together with an eye toward its narrative and linguistic peculiarities. That is to say, human psyches symptomize, just as human bodies bear the marks of sickness that decadent value systems promote.

Bodies, for Nietzsche, are constructed through a process of violent memorization, which has to be explained through genealogy (and indeed is partially discussed in the second essay of GM). Far from a spontaneous quality, the internalization and performance of memory is irreplaceable for any moral system. It does not instinctively pertain to the "animal, man," who has "a partly dull [...] inattentive mind" and who is the "personification of forgetfulness" (GM II 3). The "technique of mnemonics" might be defined as the process of violent inscription of values onto the bodies and minds of this "inattentive" animal, human:

> When man decided to make memory for himself, it never happened without blood, torments and sacrifice: the most horrific sacrifice and forfeit [...], the most disgusting mutilations (for example, castration), the cruelest rituals of all religious cults (and all religions are, at their most fundamental, systems of cruelty)—all this has its origin in that particular instinct which discovered that pain was the most powerful aid to mnemonics.
>
> (GM II 3)

The mutilated body of the ascetic, as well as the normative exaltation of the ascetic way of life, is for Nietzsche living proof of moral tyranny. Moral tyranny is therefore a powerful means of shaping and building bodies, the multitudinous possibilities of which are constrained through their formation by culture, which when decadent has maliferous effects. The psychology of human beings, as exhibited in their attitudes, is also conditioned by the violence employed of tyrannical systems of values. The resulting bodies, psychological dispositions, and the behaviors these impel are finally "metaphors" of morality that bear the scars of their violent conditioning.[43]

It should be noted that Butler also assigns a central role to the melancholic attitude that pertains to the heteronormative social standard. In GT, Butler turns, like Nietzsche, to psychology to interpret melancholy as the ground figure of gender performance.[44] Mainly by employing Freud's definition in *Mourning and Melancholia*—but also mentioning Klein, Kristeva, and Lacan—Butler suggests that gender identity is constitutively shaped through the heterosexual norm since it originates through prohibitions and taboos such as homoerotic desire or incest.[45] In other words, we identify with a gender, calling ourselves "women," through a constant *incorporation* of prohibitions and taboos. As women, we are for instance not allowed to desire to act, move, talk, desire like men do. Rather, we learn to take up less space, to walk and talk more quietly, to occupy our social role as though it were something given. Put differently, we learn to impersonate womanhood through the ritual repetition of gestures that prevent us from experiencing a loss, as should, according to Freud, occur in mourning.[46] As aforementioned, we take gender to be grammatically and naturally given, so do not normally identify the prohibition of homoerotic desire to constitute a loss or its elimination to be a source of real pain. This missed grief, so to speak, gives rise to the pathological nature of the continuous and repeated performance of gender. Using Nietzsche, one could claim that the melancholic configuration of gender is originated through a *tyrannical* prohibition, which prevents our desires to flourish, affects our psyche, condemns us to take refuge in "comfortable things," namely to confine ourselves within the "cage" of gender. This melancholic tendency to prefer comfortable things might be seen as the *dictamen* to "compulsory heterosexuality," which confirms the tight nexus between one's behavior and what she (thinks she) wants.[47] In a word, Butler's recourse to the psychological notion of melancholy allows her to dig deeper into the constellation sex-gender-desire, which allows her to identify the inadequacy of theories that fail to consider gender as a construct.

A perspectivist (4) approach to feminism must, for these reasons address bodies, and consider them as both melancholically and socially construed.[48] However, for Butler this does not mean that a feminist philosophy should imagine a body prior to "cultural inscriptions," or "signification and form,"[49] as Foucault and Nietzsche do.[50] Rather than imagining an *Ur*-body, still untouched by cultural and moral inscription and still in possession of its full potential, such a non-tyrannical approach turns its attention to those bodies that bear the marks of their non-conformity to the norms dictated by the patriarchal and heterosexual system. This means paying attention to the perspectives of bodies, memories, and psyches that are outside the dominant norm, who themselves have assumed, so to say, an *ironic* position toward the leading value system. Butler's refusal to consider a conjectural concept of original womanhood in order to distinguish it from today's feminine body, mutilated and marked by hetero-patriarchal norm, leads to the epochal broadening of feminist philosophy and its convergence with the aims of queer theory. An affirming feminism, via the force of its criticism of a fixed and non-elusive notion of womanhood, is able to go beyond itself and open its gaze to each body that ironically displaces itself from the norm. These are *real*, not conjectural, bodies that try to adopt a different gender performance from the ones to which they seem to be condemned. In considering an affirming feminism I now turn to the perspectives of *queer* bodies.

The shift of attention to "bodies that (normally do not matter)" has the merit of bringing attention to the possibly subversive and *creative* (5) outcome of an ironic (4) and, generally, of an affirming feminism. This is best captured by the word "queer." "Queer" initially denoted the aberration of the hetero-patriarchal norm. As Butler shows, referring to both 1980s ballroom culture and Nella Larssen's work *Passing*, the term "queer" has undergone a substantial redefinition, up to indicating a possible breakdown of the boundaries between genders, namely the ability to cross them. "To queer" means "to pass"—it refers to the opening of "a sudden gap in language."[51] The term, "queer," which was formerly used as an aspersion to repress putative abnormality, now means to subvert hetero-patriarchal normality and serves to denounce its artificiality and non-obviousness. Queer does not denote an alternative form of identity; rather it indicates the "discursive limits" of the notions of gender identity and sex. It explodes the internal contradictions of normalized identity.

Butler's accent on the resignification of the word "queer" allows reflection on the potentiality of linguistic shifts. The LGBT+ community's capacity to subvert the original derogatory meaning of the term produces a change of narrative which coincides with the experimentation of new forms of life. In chapter four of *Bodies that matter*, Butler comments on the 1990 documentary *Paris Is Burning* by Jenny Livingstone, which chronicled New York's ballroom and drag culture at the end of the 1980s. The chapter begins with by a quote taken from the second essay of GM, which, as I argue, is one of the main interlocutors of Butler's thesis on queer resignification.[52] According to the Nietzsche quote, a fatal flaw in genealogy would be to assume such things as a "purpose in law."[53] Nietzsche claims that there is no such thing as a clear purpose to the unique form of power that we, as genealogists, shall trace back. Things are more complex: "Everything in existence," writes Nietzsche, "having somehow come about, is continually interpreted anew, requisitioned anew, transformed, and redirected to a new purpose by a power superior to it; (…) dominating consists of re-interpretation, adjustment" (GM II 12).

To engage in an affirming feminism means to focus on the recurrent transformations of bodies, on the perennial revision of their meanings, and on unfixed, elusive findings. As genealogists we should try to grasp "the whole history of a 'thing', an organ, a tradition [that] can to this extent be a continuous chain of signs, continually revealing new interpretations and adaptions, the cause of which need not to be connected even amongst themselves, but rather sometimes just follow and replace one another at random."[54] Butler cites this passage once again in one of the concluding chapters of *BTM*, in claiming that "one might read a utopian investment in discourse"[55] in Nietzsche's genealogical program. Butler thereby glimpses the *creative* (5) potentiality of feminism in the assumption that the "chains of signs" (GM II 12), as Nietzsche refers to the interconnected meanings that constitute the history of a thing, might be interrupted, deflected, or directed toward new significances. The internal ambiguity of Nietzsche's project, which is its simultaneous drive toward the demystification of old values and the transvaluation or creation of new ones, is interpreted by Butler as a double tension within feminist philosophy: a skeptical, critical, debunking tension, and a resignifying, subversive, queering one.

At this point we must ask how this subversive and drifting potential of genealogy comes to light or how an affirming feminism might translate itself into a political and philosophical practice, or to use a Gramscian terminology (as Butler does), how a "re-articulation of hegemonies" works.[56] According to Butler, the LGBT+ community depicted in *Paris Is Burning* has to be credited with discovering the power of re-signification *vis-à-vis* their bodies and performances of gender. In their ballroom competitions participants performed different "categories" of hetero- and white normativity (e.g., femme queen, butch queen, female, or male figure, etc.). In these ballroom scenes, Butler glimpses a stimulus to reengage the sign-chains relating to sex, gender, desire, and the related notions of kinship, race, and class. Drag queens in ballroom culture demonstrate that the reiteration of "rituals," as Nietzsche would say, which erect gender identity as a performative fiction, might be interrupted and deviated.[57] According to Butler, the subversive potentiality of such a practice lies in the suggestion that "imitation is at the heart of the *heterosexual* project and its gender binarism: the drag is not a secondary imitation that presupposes a prior and original gender, but that hegemonic heterosexuality is itself a constant effort to imitate its own idealizations."[58] Furthermore, the ballroom competitions are judged by juries that evaluate the "realness" of the competitors to determine whether they appear authentic enough to be confused with (i.e., pass for) those benefitting from hetero—and white privilege. Put differently, to successfully imitate "realness" means to perform the hetero-patriarchal ideal of gender generated through the aforementioned chains of signification. This means, again, to lift gender categories out of naturalness, to consider them as discursive practices which can be discussed anew and subverted, to *create* new meanings that circulate and reinforce an affirming, perspectivist view. Drag queens show us that a feminist philosophy is fulfilled when it is brave enough to challenge received (anti-human) discourses, as Nietzsche commended. The ballroom context exposes the fictional character of gender as a "masquerade of styles" embodied in our melancholic behavior (BGE 223). Black and Latino gays, transgender individuals, prostitutes from New York's suburbs—all aberrations, violators of hegemonic norms, "bodies that do not matter"—affirm themselves in drag and voguing competitions that expose the artificiality of gender and de-naturalize sex by performatively challenging and subverting the decadent norms that exclude them.

As Michel Haar, an author whom Butler quoted several times, has pointed out, Nietzsche's project was grounded in reappropriation of "traditional" philosophical terms. This is the case with "will to power," "nihilism," "skepticism," "metaphysics," and "genealogy" itself.[59] According to Haar, Nietzsche insinuates himself in traditional philosophical language and tries to "subvert" it until he creates a "language of his own," where technical terms are resignified and turned against themselves. Nietzsche insinuates himself in the sign-chain of notions and tries to subvert them, opening up new possibilities, condensing the *creative* potentiality of genealogy. In this regard, Butler's project is similar to Nietzsche's: she thinks feminism should interrogate the meaning of the notion "woman" and redirect it to the related concept of gender performance, sex, desire, and body. They both formulate an affirming philosophy. Specifically, they comprise a *genealogy* without origins that accepts the (2) *elusive* nature of its results, in which the philosopher assumes (3) an *ironic* position toward norms and priorities of a (4) *perspectivist* point of view that is directed toward subversion and (5) the *creation* of new meanings. By focusing on certain uses of language, feminist philosophy can expose the history of oppression and violence behind conventional gender terms and make them subversive. After all, Butler did the same thing with aspects of Nietzsche's thought, proving that despite his misogynistic statements we can reappropriate his philosophical method for feminist purposes.

## Notes

1   BGE 238.
2   See Schutte (1984).
3   As in the case of the ancient goddess Baubo as an "affirming woman" (see Kofman 1998) or with Athena, Ariadne, and Persephone in Irigaray (1991). For feminist interpretations of Nietzsche, see also Oliver (1995), Oliver—Pearsall (1998), Call (1995), and Oppel (2005).
4   BGE 239. Of course I refute Nietzsche's accusations and tones, but they conceal an important point that deserves to be taken into account. According to Oliver (1984), Nietzsche's criticism is directed against the "castrated" feminists.

5   Oliver (1984: 187).
6   BGE P.
7   BGE P.
8   BGE P.
9   See Diethe (1996a, 1996b: 137–65).
10  See Blondel (1991: 97).
11  Actually Butler called out for "an affirmative view" of affirmative action in Butler (1996). This expression has indeed nothing to do with Nietzsche or philosophical Nietzscheanism. On the originality of Butler's reading of Nietzsche, see Call (1995).
12  Butler (1999); hereafter GT xxviii.
13  GT xxix.
14  BGE 34.
15  GM I, Note.
16  See the connection of "*schlecht*" and "*schlicht*"—bad and simple, in GM I 4, or of *malus* and *melas* in the following paragraph.
17  See Blondel (1991: 134 and ff.) (and *passim*).
18  Notwithstanding this, Butler envelopes an interesting analysis starting the etymological connection between the terms "*mater*," "matrix," and "matter" in Butler (1993) (hereafter BTM): 6–7. On the topic of the image of matrix and on geological metaphors in Rubin and Butler, see Pergadia (2018: 186 and ff.).
19  Butler endorses the theory of performative sentences or utterances, exposed first by Austin (1962), and applies it to the notion of gender. On this topic, see Butler (1988).
20  GT xv.
21  GT xxix.
22  See Butler (1992): "I am not at all interested in defending 'queer theory' or having it be something which is in opposition to feminism. I would actually like to see feminism rearticulated in light of some of those challenges, just as it has been forced to do in light of these challenges;" also cited in Pergadia (2018: 173).
23  See Irigaray (1991).
24  Nietzsche also conceives of his genealogy as something anti-essentialist but does not allow himself to be assimilated into materialist or utilitarian forms of genealogy. See Prinz (2016) for a comparison between Nietzsche's concept of genealogy, and the utilitarian and Marxist traditions.
25  GT xxix.
26  GT 9.
27  See GM III 11, in which Nietzsche claims that the most serious limitation of feminism consists in women's willingness to "justify 'woman as such.'"
28  Nietzsche's problematic approach toward the notion of origin was highlighted by Foucault (1977).
29  See GT 33-4.
30  For an extended criticism of Wittig, see GT 26.
31  GT xxix.
32  At GT 27, Butler refers precisely to Haar (1977).
33  BGE 34.
34  See Guay (2011: 38).
35  GT 181.
36  Butler (1992).
37  See Thomas (1993).
38  See Blondel (1991: 95).

39  See Lorenzini (2020).
40  See Thomas (1993).
41  Translation modified.
42  See Pippin (1999).
43  Blondel (1991: 135 and ff).
44  As she clarifies in the 1999 Preface, Butler has only anticipated the connection between melancholy and social performance in GT. This connection is further explored in Butler (1997), especially chapter 5.
45  See Butler (1999: 87–8).
46  See Freud (1964: 243–58).
47  Wittig's formula, which Butler uses repeatedly in Butler (1997, esp. 144 and ff.).
48  A connection between Butler and perspectivism has already been glimpsed by Piedra Alegria (2018).
49  GT 166.
50  Cf. Butler (1989).
51  BTM 130.
52  See Olson-Worsham (2000).
53  See Butler (1993: 81); Nietzsche engages in a strong criticism against traditional genealogists (like English moral philosophers, or Paul Ree), who are accused of mistaking the origin (*Ursprung*) as the sole purpose of genealogy.
54  Butler (1993: 81) Nietzsche engages in a strong criticism against traditional genealogists (like English moral philosophers or Paul Ree), who are accused of mistaking the origin (*Ursprung*) as the sole purpose of genealogy.
55  Butler (1993: 170).
56  Butler (1993: 91).
57  GM II 3.
58  Butler (1993: 85).
59  See Haar (1977).

15

# Hedwig Dohm's Feminist Revaluations of Nietzschean Nihilism

Katie Brennan

## Introduction

Hedwig Dohm (1831–1919) was a radical German feminist and author who wrote pamphlets, essays, novels, and short stories that address, among other things, the "*Frauenfrage*" (the woman question), women's education, the right to work, and the plight of elderly and single women. Dohm's work critically engages Nietzsche's writings, drawing on, adapting, and criticizing his theories on genealogy, religion, life affirmation, and science. In this article, I look to Dohm's critique of Nietzsche in order to reconstruct a feminist critique of Nietzschean nihilism. Famously, Nietzsche argues that nihilism is a form of life denial that makes it difficult to realize our highest and most actualized selves. Dohm's writings illuminate an oversight in Nietzsche's theory of nihilism. In Dohm's eyes, overcoming nihilism is going to require greater effort for a woman than it will for a man: one must first overcome the constraints of the societal expectations of women before one can begin to ask oneself who or what one is. Dohm emphasizes the challenges that women—and, by extension, perhaps other oppressed persons—face in overcoming nihilism. Women and other oppressed groups must first throw off the shackles of oppressive systems of social norms and institutions before they can discover a new or different way of interpreting themselves and their world.

In this chapter I develop and draw out the implications of a Dohmian critique of Nietzschean nihilism by looking closely at Dohm's novella *Become Who You Are!* [*Werde, die Du Bist!*] (1894). Dohm's writings on Nietzsche are not contained solely in this novella—she also discusses the topic in her essay "Nietzsche and Women" [*Nietzsche und die Frauen*] (1898) and employs Nietzschean concepts in many of her literary and political works. I focus on *Become Who You Are!* because it engages the concept of Nietzschean nihilism. In particular, I focus on Dohm's use of her protagonist

---

This chapter originally appeared in *The Journal of Nietzsche Studies*, vol. 52, 2021, 209–233; https://doi.org/10.5325/jnietstud.52.2.0209. It is used with permission from Penn State University Press.

I thank the members of the Extending New Narratives Works in Progress Seminar who provided feedback on an earlier version of this article, particularly Kaitlyn Creasy.

Agnes Schmidt to provide an extended case study of two distinct types of nihilism common to women living in Germany in the late nineteenth-century. Like many other women writers of this time period, Dohm's writings engage philosophical concepts through various genres of writing, including literature.

I use Dohm's writings to demonstrate two related points about Nietzschean nihilism. First, Nietzsche has a double standard. On Nietzsche's account, whether or not one subscribes to a nihilistic belief system depends, in part, on whether or not one is a man or a woman. Second, in spite of having a double standard for how nihilism is manifested in men and women, Nietzsche's writings nonetheless provide the conceptual resources to develop an account of nihilism in women and other oppressed peoples.

In the section that follows, I explain the relationship between the thought of Dohm and Nietzsche. Next, I outline the features of the sociocultural aspects of Nietzsche's account of nihilism, which is important for understanding Dohm's critique of Nietzschean nihilism. Finally, I look closely at the case of Dohm's protagonist Agnes Schmidt. In the novella *Become Who You Are!*, Dohm describes two distinct periods of Agnes's life. I demonstrate that in both of these periods Agnes is nihilistic.

## Why Dohm and Nietzsche?

On the first page of Dohm's novella *Become Who You Are!*, the reader is introduced to the protagonist Agnes Schmidt, a sixty-year-old woman interned in a mental hospital. In her description of Agnes, Dohm immediately invokes Nietzsche, describing her as someone whose "words breathed immeasurable melancholy or dithyrambic ecstasy" and as a woman who "uttered profound and sublime thoughts in a form that was reminiscent of Nietzsche's Zarathustra."[1] With this comparison to Nietzsche's character Zarathustra and Nietzschean concepts like dithyrambic ecstasy, Dohm begins her novella with an explicit nod to Nietzschean thought.[2]

Dohm's writings about Nietzsche are not restricted to *Become Who You Are!* She also praises and criticizes Nietzsche's thought in philosophical–political essays. For example, her essay "Nietzsche and Women" explores the contradictory nature of Nietzsche's comments on women. Dohm laments that a genius like Nietzsche is so thoroughly disappointing when it comes to his thoughts on women: "You [Nietzsche] can speak with God and gods, with the stars, with the ocean, with spirits and specters. Only you cannot speak with and about women."[3] Many of Dohm's other works, both literary and political, also employ Nietzschean concepts.[4] I focus particularly on the character of Agnes Schmidt as a case study of nihilism as experienced by women in late nineteenth-century Germany.

The novella *Become Who You Are!* maintains an ambivalence about Nietzschean thought. Dohm is clearly influenced by Nietzsche, employing his concepts of the Übermensch, the Dionysian, nihilism, and life affirmation.[5] Yet, as in her essay on Nietzsche and women, Dohm employs these notions in a critical way, aimed at demonstrating how difficult it is to overcome nihilism as a woman. On her first page, Dohm states that Agnes has "the eyes of a seer."[6] Yet she follows that with the statement, "One would have believed that this old woman had been a great poetess and that an excess of intellectual provocation caused the mental disturbance. The opposite was the case."⁷ Dohm goes on to explain the contours of Agnes's life and how she came to be who she is. We soon learn that Agnes lived the majority of her life in the service of others: first her parents, then her husband, and finally her children. As a widow with grown children, Agnes is left with no one to serve but herself, and her process of "becoming who she is" can finally begin. In her search for her own identity, Agnes becomes unconventional, adopts a Dionysian perspective (a concept borrowed from Nietzsche), and is labeled insane and institutionalized. Dohm's narrative emphasizes the challenges that women face in affirming their own lives, overcoming nihilism, and becoming who they truly are. In doing so, Dohm confronts Nietzsche's conception of nihilism from a feminist standpoint.[8]

Dohm is part of a larger feminist movement in Germany, of which Nietzsche was critical.[9] In the late nineteenth and early twentieth centuries, conceptions of gender were largely based on an assumption about the inherent differences between men and women. Scientific, medical, philosophical, legal, and psychological texts supported the notion that men and women are naturally different. This natural difference was used to justify the division of labor and power between men and women. Women were expected to be wife and mother with limited access to the public sphere. This so-called natural division between men and women was not only advocated by male authors but was prevalent in the conservative and moderate wings of the feminist movement, which argued for separate roles for men and women.[10] While there was a radical wing of the feminist movement in Germany that pushed back against this so-called natural division between the genders, the majority of mainstream feminists accepted the division, arguing instead for women's education and access to professions (like teaching) that did not fundamentally challenge the gender divide.[11] Dohm's work marks an exception to this trend. Instead of arguing that women and men are naturally different, she argues that perceived differences are the result of social norms, not nature.[12] Dohm was influenced by the liberal tradition of thinkers like John Stuart Mill and advocated for women's rights as a form of basic human rights.[13]

One aspect common among many members of the women's movement in Germany—conservative, moderate, and radical—is the desire to develop one's personality.[14] This imperative can be seen in the novellas of German women like Dohm, Lou Andreas-Salomé, and Gabriele Reuter, who all participated in the salons hosted at Dohm's home in Berlin.[15] In spite of having different takes on feminism (Dohm considered Lou Andreas-Salomé an anti-feminist), these authors share an interest in grappling with their subjective identities. Importantly, they develop their inquiry into women's subjectivity through similar literary genres, including fragmentary diary entries, letters, and recollections. Texts written in this way bring into question the coherence of the individual's subjective identity and challenge the reliability of the narrator as self.[16] This trend is more than evident in *Become Who You Are!*, where Dohm uses diary entries as a literary device for describing her awakening from the social burdens of womanhood. In this novella, she grapples with who she is as a person and implies that the formation of the self is something that must be developed by struggling to free oneself from social constraints.

Dohm's concern with developing her personality and subjectivity are closely linked to Nietzsche's own worries about the possibility of overcoming nihilism. Indeed, even the title of Dohm's novella echoes Nietzsche's advice in *GS*: "What does your conscience say?—'You should become who you are' [Was sagt dein Gewissen?—'Du sollst der werden, der du bist.']" (GS 270). This phrasing is also used in the subtitle of Nietzsche's *EH* (1880): *How One Becomes What One Is* [Wie man wird, was man ist]. For Nietzsche, this saying has deep implications for self-discovery, self-actualization and, in some cases, overcoming nihilism. Becoming what you are is necessary for overcoming nihilism and for living a fully actualized life. Dohm picks up on this theme in Nietzsche's work and explores it in her novella, exposing both her affinity for and problems with Nietzsche's ideas.

**Nietzsche and Nihilism**

It is outside the scope of this chapter to provide a complete account of Nietzschean nihilism. Instead, I follow Kaitlyn Creasy, who attempts to offer an overarching account. Creasy argues that we should understand nihilism as what Nietzsche calls life denial or the negation of life.[17] Nihilism understood as life denial is not a negation of the phenomenon of life (understood as an abstract principle) but rather my experiencing *my life* as negated. On Creasy's account, nihilism as life denial is a "phenomenon that either (1) involves an explicitly or implicitly negative evaluation of life or (2) results in the degradation of the will (BGE 208) or the mere preservation of weak forms of life (BGE 61; GM III 25)."[18] For Creasy, the common thread that unites the many different manifestations of nihilism Nietzsche discusses is that they all deny life: "all of the beliefs, norms, institutions, practices, and psychophysiological phenomena Nietzsche frames as either nihilistic or as characteristic of the nihilist deny life in some way."[19] For the remainder of this chapter, I follow Creasy's definition of nihilism as a form of life denial. In other words, I assume life denial is the key element that not only unifies the complex cast of nihilistic Nietzschean characters but can also account for the cognitive, affective, and sociocultural aspects of nihilism.

Nietzschean nihilism is a complex phenomenon with *cognitive, affective*, and *sociocultural* dimensions.[20] The dimension of Nietzschean nihilism that we will focus on in the rest of this article is its *sociocultural* manifestation. On my view, the sociocultural dimensions of nihilism appear in two different ways. First, certain types of belief systems, which operate at a sociocultural level, are taken by Nietzsche to be nihilistic because of the life-denying ideals they espouse. Nihilistic sociocultural belief systems include religions like Christianity and Buddhism (A 20), philosophical schools of thought like that of Schopenhauer (A 7, TI Skirmishes 21), and modes of thought like scientific positivism, or what Nietzsche sometimes calls the "will to truth" (BGE 10, GM III 24). Nietzsche takes these belief systems to be particularly dominant within Europe and sees them as a part of the downfall of modern society.

Second, the sociocultural manifestation of nihilism can be understood as a mismatch between the dominant values of society and the types of values that would most benefit the individual. In other words, sometimes the values that would allow an individual to flourish conflict with the values espoused by society. I use this conception of sociocultural nihilism to understand the way certain historical and political situations lead to nihilism in different ways for different individuals.[21] This conception of sociocultural nihilism situates the nihilistic trouble at the nexus between the individual and society. The way that nihilism is inherent in particular sociocultural systems of belief is commonly observed, but commentators do not look specifically at the socially mediated ways in which these systems of belief impact different individuals in different ways. On my reading, then, sociocultural nihilism manifests in two separate ways: either when the dominant ideology in society itself is fundamentally nihilistic or when the individual is at odds with the dominant ideology.

The latter aspect of sociocultural nihilism, which emphasizes how the sociocultural impacts the individual, gains support from Nietzsche's praise of solitude and critique of the herd: "That's why I go into solitude—so as not to drink out of everyone's cistern. When I am among the many I live as the many do, and I do not think as I really think; after a time it always seems as though they want to banish me from myself and rob me of my soul" (*D* 491; see also *D* 323). Nietzsche's praise of solitude demonstrates the tension between the highest aims of the individual and the aims of society. In another passage from the notebooks, Nietzsche describes how being solitary has helped him both to experience and to escape nihilism:

> He that speaks here, conversely, has done nothing so far but reflect: a philosopher and solitary by instinct, who has found his advantage in standing aside and outside, in patience, in procrastination, in staying behind; as a spirit of daring and experiment that has already lost its way once in every labyrinth of the future [...] as the first perfect nihilist of Europe who, however, has even now lived through the whole of nihilism, to the end, leaving it behind, outside himself.
>
> (*KSA* 13:11[411])[22]

In this passage, Nietzsche discusses the importance of solitude for both discovering and, eventually, overcoming nihilism. Like his character Zarathustra, Nietzsche cites the importance of taking time away from society in order to clear one's mind of the nihilistic belief systems inherent in modern, European culture.

## Agnes Schmidt's Nihilism

In what follows, I use Dohm's *Become Who You Are!* to understand the two different manifestations of sociocultural Nietzschean nihilism outlined above. It turns out, on a Nietzschean reading, Dohm's protagonist Agnes Schmidt exists in a nihilistic state for her entire life. At first, Agnes is nihilistic because she lives completely for others and according to the customs of Christian morality. This is the version of sociocultural nihilism in which someone is nihilistic because the belief system they adhere to is itself nihilistic. Later, Agnes is nihilistic because she realizes that the value system of society does not allow her to fully become who she is. This is the version of sociocultural nihilism in which the individual is at odds with the dominant social ideology. These two states of being are nihilistic in different ways. In what follows, I examine the way nihilism operates in each phase of Agnes's life. In doing so, I provide a feminist critique of Nietzsche's view of nihilism, arguing that Nietzsche has a double standard when it comes to women and nihilism.

## The Nihilism of Selflessness

Throughout her childhood and in the majority of her adult life, Agnes lives for others just as her mother, who "rigorously paid attention to order and decorum," lived for others: "What others did, that was the right thing for her."[23] From early childhood, Agnes is raised to be obedient to social conventions: "Barely twelve years old, I helped with the household, in the kitchen, with the laundry, in the free time that I had from school. I did it all gladly; it didn't even occur to me that things could have been different."[24] Agnes admits that during her childhood she was "cheerful, content, and very healthy."[25] Yet her attempts to express herself meet with resistance: "Once I had to recite a Schiller poem. I did it with glowing cheeks and so solemnly that the whole class laughed. I was ashamed of myself, never did it again, and from then on monotonously recited the poems just like the others did."[26]

Once grown and married, Agnes transfers the source of authority from her parents to her husband: "That he was convinced of his superiority over me, was somewhat willful and strict in his demands on me, did not disturb the peace of our marriage. I never opposed him, rather arranged everything quite as he wished it."[27] Agnes describes their relationship as a "cloudless marriage that lasted 33 years."[28] During this time, Agnes has two daughters, Grete and Magdalene, who are "hearty and lively children whom I loved with my whole heart, but who saw to it that I had to work vigorously."[29] Agnes's married life goes quickly and smoothly: "And one day was like the next. As if on wheels, my life glided forward, quickly, quickly."[30] Once her children are grown and successfully married off, Agnes hopes to finally have time to travel. However, her plans are soon thwarted when her husband becomes ill, not to be well again: "For eight years I cared for him. With the loving stubbornness of a sick person, he would take nothing, not even the smallest assistance, from anyone except me."[31] This period of Agnes's life, like all the previous ones, is dominated by care for others: "Never had every hour of my life been filled up as during this long illness."[32]

During this stage of her life, Agnes believes herself to be happy. She accomplishes all of the things befitting a woman of her time—marriage, children, homemaking—and lives a full life. Yet, even during this period of purported happiness, Agnes's life would be considered nihilistic on Nietzsche's account. We can come more clearly to understand Agnes's nihilism by looking closely at Nietzsche's critique of selflessness, with GS 21 as an emblematic passage.[33] Agnes's early life resembles what Nietzsche describes as the socially supported phenomenon (particularly in Nietzsche's Germany) of "blindly raging industriousness." Here Nietzsche criticizes "the teachers of selflessness" and argues that "the virtues (such as diligence, obedience, chastity, piety, justice) are mostly harmful to their possessors." The harm of this type of selflessness (and the reason why we should consider it nihilistic) lies in the fact that it is based on a life-denying disregard for the well-being of the individual for the sake of the greater good. Like Agnes, whose life is completely devoted to others, those who are selflessly and blindly industrious are incapable of fully realizing their own needs and desires. Nietzsche is critical of a society that "praises the diligent even if he should harm his vision or the originality and freshness of his spirit," where the selfless are nothing more than a "devoted tool, ruthless towards itself." For Nietzsche, blindly raging industriousness is the "typical virtue of an instrument." This is an example of the first type of sociocultural nihilism, in which an individual subscribes to a social ideology that is itself nihilistic.

For Nietzsche, the virtues of selflessness and industriousness (which, Dohm points out, are also the types of virtues demanded of women in society) involve an implicitly negative evaluation of life because it is misleadingly represented as "the road to riches and honor," while in reality these virtues are filled with "extreme dangerousness." These dangerously deceptive virtues are promulgated through education, which "tries to condition the individual through various attractions and advantages to adopt a way of thinking and behaving that, when it has become habit, drive, and passion, will rule in him and over him *against his ultimate advantage* but 'for the common good.'"[34] Nietzsche rejects the virtue of selfless industry because it works only for the preservation of weak forms of life. Strong individuals, alternatively, refuse to trade their own well-being for the good of society. They have the strength to go against society for the sake of their *own* highest values. Indeed, Nietzsche argues that selflessness for the sake of the common good is actually harmful to society as a whole: "Perhaps one also asks whether it would not have been more useful to society if he had worked in a way that was less negligent towards himself and had preserved himself longer."[35] The virtue of selflessness is harmful to society as a whole because it promotes values that deny life in its fullest existential realization.

Nietzsche argues in GS 21 that the logic of "blindly raging industriousness" is not based on the value of selflessness but on the fact that selflessness brings advantages to those who associate with the selfless:

> The praise of the selfless, the self-sacrificing, the virtuous—that is, of the person who does not apply his entire strength and reason to his *own* preservation, development, elevation, promotion, and expansion of power, but rather lives, as regards himself, modestly and thoughtlessly, maybe even with indifference and irony—this praise is certainly not born out of the spirit of selflessness! The "neighbor" praises selflessness because *it brings him advantages*! If the neighbor himself thought "selflessly," he would reject this decrease in strength, this harm for his benefit; he would work against the development of such inclinations, and above all he would affirm his selflessness by *not* calling it *good*!

Those who praise selflessness fool themselves into thinking they are acting morally. However, on Nietzsche's account, this morality lacks a genuine source. This praise of *selflessness* is actually based in *selfishness*. The selfless acts of "good" and "moral" people serve only to further the ends of others. Therefore, the virtue of selflessness is harmful to both the individual and their highest ends and also to the society that supports and encourages it.

What is relevant here is that Nietzsche himself might not have considered Agnes's early life nihilistic. This is because, unlike for a man, who should strive toward "his ultimate advantage," the most important and appropriate role for women is to procreate and be submissive to men.³⁶ For example, Nietzsche claims that the "first and last profession" of women is "the bearing of strong children" (BGE 239).³⁷ Nietzsche again emphasizes the importance and value of breeding when the character of Zarathustra speaks: "Everything about a woman is a riddle, and everything about a woman has one solution: pregnancy ... A man should be raised for war and woman for the recreation of the warrior" (Z I Women).

Nietzsche is critical of modern social movements like women's suffrage and the "democratic tendencies" of Europe, which have caused woman to "forget her fear of man: but the woman who 'forgets fear' abandons her most feminine instincts" (BGE 239). Nietzsche's critique of women's emancipation and their orientation in society extends beyond his thinking on women and can also be applied to society writ large. Nietzsche views fear as a helpful part of what he deems a "healthy" society:

> Broadly speaking, it is by no means the fear of man one might wish lessened: for this fear compels the strong to be strong, in some cases to be terrible—it keeps the well-formed type of human *upright*. What is to be feared, what has a doomful effect such as no other doom, would not be the great fear but rather the great *disgust* at man; likewise the great *compassion* for man.
>
> (GM III 14)

Later in this passage, Nietzsche argues that compassion and disgust for man would lead to a "will to nothingness, nihilism" (GM II 14). Nietzsche's critique of women is a subset of his critique of modern society. Like society in general, women's desire for equal rights is a sign of decline: "While women are seizing new rights in this manner, trying to become 'master [*Herr*]' and writing 'progress' for women on their flags and pennants, the opposite is taking place with terrifying clarity: '*women are regressing*'" (BGE 239).³⁸

On Nietzsche's account, democratic ideals of equality are a problem for everyone in society, not just for women.³⁹ Yet his critique of the regression of women is noteworthy for the simple fact that it does not apply to men. Nietzsche's discussion of nihilism and critique of democracy are intended as a corrective to what he deems an unhealthy society. In this way, he leaves open the possibility that certain individuals may overcome nihilism. But women, given their "natural" profession of procreation and their inherently subservient position, are not given even the smallest hope of overcoming the type of industrious and selfless nihilism experienced by Agnes Schmidt. Instead, this type of nihilism is seen by Nietzsche as appropriate and natural to women. Nietzsche has a double standard when it comes to overcoming nihilism. If we are to believe Nietzsche, a woman should live her life in a way that would be considered nihilistic if she had been born a man.

Dohm's criticism of Nietzsche in her essay "Nietzsche and Women"—that "You [Nietzsche] can speak with God and gods, with the stars, with the ocean, with spirits and specters. Only you cannot speak with and about women"⁴⁰—comes into focus when we examine the nihilism of young Agnes. While Nietzsche is keen to point out how harmful the virtue of selflessness would be for a man, he does not view these same cultural norms as harmful for women. Nietzsche, as we saw above, believes that the virtue of selflessness is ultimately harmful not only to the individual but also to society as a whole. Yet this same virtue is supposedly beneficial to women. Dohm's critique of Nietzsche is centered on this double standard and Nietzsche's unwillingness to see women as individuals similar to himself. As she states: "Friedrich Nietzsche is no Socrates; he does not know what he does not know."[41] Through the story of Agnes's early life, Dohm provides a critique of the gender roles imposed upon women and Nietzsche's double standard that women should exist in a state of nihilism, while men should strive to overcome it.

## The Nihilism of the Criminal

After the death of her husband, Agnes is left with a lot of free time. A few weeks after her husband's funeral, she notes: "I was tired from the hard, daily work of the past years. I was allowed to take a rest. Why did rest not come? It didn't come. And now it started, quite gradually—the strangeness, the gnawing, the ruminating, the frightfulness."[42] With her daughters married and living far away, Agnes finds herself with nothing to keep her occupied. She takes up reading, but it is not enough to fill the void. She asks herself: "Now what? I water the plants, which have enough water; I wipe dust from the furniture on which no more dust lies."[43] Eventually, Agnes gives up on her old way of life and becomes introspective. She visits her daughters' families but realizes that she is just in the way. Her sons-in-law have no respect for her and call her "*Mämmchen*": "'Mother', a nice word, '*Mämmchen*' is as if they didn't take their mother seriously, only as a comical, old woman, as if it didn't oblige them to anything."[44] After several failed attempts at making herself useful to her daughters and grandchildren, Agnes gives up and returns home, lamenting: "I am no personage, I am no one. That's also why no one can like me, even my children—barely—barely."[45]

It is at this point that Agnes begins to realize there is more to life than selfless industriousness. Looking back on her earlier life, she says, "They had chained up my nature. Now I've been unleashed [*losgelassen*], and I wander about in a new, strange world."[46] As Agnes begins to distance herself from her former life of dutiful obedience, she laments its futility:

> Living for others ought to be the right, the true thing. If that were so, and everyone lived for others, then indeed others also would have had to live for me, and then it just would be the same and much simpler if everyone lived for himself from the beginning. A mother ought to be there only for the children! So I should only live and work for my daughter, and the daughter in turn should only be there for her children. What a senseless, fruitless, circular course.[47]

Here, Dohm, speaking through her character Agnes, differs from Nietzsche in her rejection of the idea that women are useful only for the creation and care of children. Yet she also employs Nietzschean ideas in her rejection of this social norm. Like Nietzsche, who argues that the virtue of selflessness is dangerous to the individual because it distracts from achieving one's highest ends and allows one to be exploited by others, Agnes conjectures that life would be "much simpler if everyone lived for himself from the beginning."[48] As Nietzsche says, selflessness in fact helps the neighbor who "praises selflessness because *it brings him advantages!*" (GS 21).

As Agnes puts more and more distance between her current self and her past life, the questions she asks herself become more urgent. For example, "Did Eduard have the right to say: live for me! Did my parents have it? My children?"[49] Agnes questions the social conventions that held her in place, becoming increasingly disenchanted with her past self: "But yet I was always satisfied? I? But I wasn't even an 'I.' Agnes Schmidt! A name! A hand! A foot, a body! No soul, no brain. I have lived a life in which I wasn't even present."[50] Dohm emphasizes the social conventions that held Agnes in place: "Or do we perhaps only have pangs of conscience when we do something that stands in contradiction with that which is held by general opinion to be good[?]"[51]

At this point in Agnes's life, she decides to do what *she* wants. She inherits a sum of money and decides to do something she had always wanted to do—travel. She starts dressing in a strange way, always wearing "a black, wool dress from the era of Marie Antoinette" with her "full gray hair, a little curly on the ends" that "fell almost to her shoulders."[52] She even develops a romantic interest in a young doctor named Johannes, for which she is accused of "erotic insanity."[53]

Agnes's rejection of the social order lands her in a mental institution for the remainder of her life. Her reflections on "madness" demonstrate the different expectations of men and women. For example, while older men date younger women all the time, if an older woman becomes enamored of a younger man, she is deemed insane. Agnes reflects on this double standard, noting that she does not see any problem with it when she is alone, "but as soon as I am among people, I see through the eyes of others, think the thoughts of others, then I feel I am guilty of a ridiculous anachronism, and I feel ashamed."[54]

The final stages of Agnes's life are very different from her youth. Yet, in spite of these differences, Agnes's late life would still be considered nihilistic on a Nietzschean account. In this stage of her life, Agnes's nihilism is a result of a mismatch between her highest aims and the dominant values of society. This disjunction maps onto the second iteration of sociocultural nihilism outlined earlier. Agnes's late life resembles what Nietzsche calls the nihilism of the criminal.[55] In a helpful passage in TI, Nietzsche describes the criminal type as "a strong type of person under favorable conditions, a strong person made ill" (TI Skirmishes 45).[56] The criminal's illness is not his own doing. Indeed, this person is strong. What causes him to be nihilistic is the mismatch between his individual desires and the expectations of society:

> His *virtues* are ostracized by society; his liveliest drives quickly fuse with depressive affects, with suspicion, fear, dishonor. But this is almost the *recipe* for physiological degeneration. When somebody is forced into secrecy and suspense, forced to be cautious and sly for a long time just to do what he does best and likes to do most, he will become anemic; and because he only ever experiences danger, persecution, and disaster from his instincts, even his feeling turns against these instincts—he feels them fatalistically.

Nietzsche describes what happens when one's own virtues are ostracized by society. The conflict between the virtues of an individual and the virtues of society eventually leads to negative effects on the individual, including depressive affects like fear, suspicion, and dishonor. When one is consistently forced to hide oneself from society, to keep one's innermost desires secret on pain of punishment, they internalize the danger and persecution they experience. Nietzsche blames this form of nihilism on "our tame, mediocre, emasculated society" in which "a natural person from out of the mountains or the adventures of the sea necessarily degenerates into a criminal."[57] This criticism is part of Nietzsche's larger critique of modern, European culture and the slave morality it subscribes to.

While Nietzsche does not himself relate this category of nihilism to the plight of women, he does explicitly say that we can generalize the case of the criminal to the "Chandala": "If we generalize from the case of the criminal: we can imagine beings who, for some reason, lack public approval, who know that they are not seen as beneficial or useful,—that Chandala [Untouchable] feeling that you are not seen as equal but as excluded, unworthy, polluted." While Nietzsche is not thinking about women here, he *is* thinking about another oppressed group: "Chandala" refers to the lowest caste in India. In his discussion of the criminal, Nietzsche mentions the Chandala several times, arguing that even the greatest of men, who eventually overcome nihilism, have experienced the feeling of being ostracized from society:

> All innovators of the spirit have at some point had that pale and fatalistic sign of the Chandala on their foreheads: *not* because they were seen this way, but rather because they themselves felt a terrible gap separating them from everything conventional and honorable. Almost every genius has experienced the "Catilinarian existence" as one aspect of his development: a hateful, vengeful, rebellious feeling against everything that already *is*, that has stopped *becoming* … Catiline—the pre-existing form of *every* Caesar

In this passage, Nietzsche uses Julius Caesar as an example of an exemplary human who has rejected social conventions and uses his own power to shape the world. Caesar is an example of someone who "proves stronger than society" and who has overcome nihilism. In spite of Caesar's eventual success, he nonetheless had to endure a phase where his vision was not shared by the rest of society. In this phase, even the strongest person is bound to experience nihilism because he feels "a terrible gap separating them from everything conventional and honorable." This is something that every genius operating under Christian morality must face: it is "one aspect of his development." Like Catiline, a Roman senator who was accused of trying to overthrow the senate, the genius must go through a phase of "hateful, vengeful, rebellious feeling against everything that already *is*" before he can overcome nihilism.

It is important to note here that the problem is not simply that society is against the nihilistic criminal. The problem is much more insidious. The mismatch between society and the individual eventually becomes internalized, leaving criminals with a "subterranean hue to their thoughts and actions" that forces them to live in a "half-funeral atmosphere." When someone is "forced into secrecy and suspense, forced to be cautious and sly for a long time just to do what he does best and likes to do most, he will become anemic." This is because following his "liveliest instincts" ultimately leads to danger, persecution, and disaster. These experiences teach him to doubt his own instincts and ultimately lead to a form of nihilism.

The nihilism of Agnes's late life follows the same form as the criminal and the "Chandala." No longer useful for procreation, housekeeping, or childcare, Agnes becomes a social pariah whose choices of clothing and behavior land her in a mental institution. She becomes someone who can no longer be understood by society. Agnes, like other would-be geniuses, is on the path to overcoming the nihilism imposed on her by society. Yet, as a woman, she has little hope of being taken seriously even on that front. While Nietzsche praises figures like Caesar or Cataline for managing to overcome the nihilism of the criminal, he would likely condemn a woman who tried to overcome the social conventions oppressing her because, as discussed above, he seems to believe that many of the social roles ascribed to women—mother, caregiver, and so on—are appropriate to their "nature."

Nietzsche's discussion of the nihilism of the "Chandala" makes his estimation of women even more problematic. It demonstrates that Nietzsche understands the way that social conventions can have a deleterious effect on members of oppressed groups, potentially leading to nihilism. Yet Nietzsche fails to extend this understanding to the plight of women. In other words, while Nietzsche clearly does have the conceptual tools to understand a nihilism like Agnes's, he does not apply it to the case of women. In spite of this, Nietzsche's acknowledgment that the nihilism of the criminal is similar to the experience of the "Chandala" indicates the potential for extracting a theory of oppression as a form of sociocultural nihilism from a Nietzschean framework.

## Conclusion

Dohm's novella lays the groundwork for a feminist critique of the sociocultural aspects of Nietzschean nihilism. In both phases of her life, Agnes is nihilistic but for different reasons. In the first phase of her life, Agnes subscribes to the socially accepted virtues of compassion and living for others, which Nietzsche deems nihilistic (for men at least). This maps onto the first type of sociocultural nihilism in which an individual is nihilistic because they subscribe to a belief system that is itself nihilistic. In the second phase of her life, Agnes abandons her previous social role yet still finds herself in a nihilistic predicament. In this state, her nihilism resembles that of the criminal, whose values conflict with that of society. This maps onto the second type of sociocultural nihilism, which can be understood as a mismatch between an individual's highest ends and the ends of society.

Dohm's novella is particularly helpful at demonstrating that Nietzsche has a double standard when it comes to nihilism. While he thinks that men should try to overcome nihilism, he does not apply that same thinking to women. Instead, Nietzsche argues that women are naturally suited to take on the social role of submission, compassion, and motherhood. Fulfilling these social roles as women would not be, on a Nietzschean reading, a cause for nihilism. Yet, if a man were to take on these same roles, he would be considered nihilistic. In this way, Nietzsche has two sets of rules for men and women. Dohm's novella highlights the double standard in Nietzsche's theory of nihilism and opens the door for a theory of Nietzschean nihilism that can account for the nihilism of women and other oppressed people.

## Notes

1   Dohm (2006: 1).
2   "Dithyrambic ecstasy" is a term associated with Nietzsche's concept of the Dionysian, which he views as the ultimate life-affirming symbol for overcoming the problem of nihilism: "the highest state a philosopher can attain: to stand in a Dionysian relationship to existence" (KSA 12:10[3], 13:16[32]).
3   Dohm 2021: 137.
4   As well, for example, of criticizing Nietzsche. See Dohm (2021).
5   Dohm (2006: 56).
6   Dohm (2006: 1).
7   Dohm (2006: 1).
8   In using the term "standpoint" here I allude to Feminist Standpoint Epistemology. See, for example, Hartsock (1983), Harding (1991), Hill Collins (2004), Haraway (1988).
9   Nietzsche argues against the emancipation of women, claiming that "women are regressing" as a result of their newly acquired rights (BGE 239). See BGE 232: "Women want to become independent, so they are beginning to enlighten men about the 'woman *an sich*'—*this* is one of the worst developments in Europe's general trend towards increasing ugliness"; see also GM III 25. In GS 363, Nietzsche argues that, in love relationships, women are naturally disposed to want to be treated as a possession: "A man who loves like a woman becomes a slave, but a woman who loves like a woman becomes a more perfect woman […] Woman wants to be taken, adopted as a possession […] consequently she wants someone who takes." Nietzsche calls this a "natural opposition," arguing that women are naturally made to be possessed. Feminism is also something that Nietzsche rejects: "I regard every type of 'feminism' espoused by people, men as well as women, as the closing of a door: you will never enter this labyrinth of daring knowledge" (EH Books 3).
10  See Weedon (1994: 183).
11  Helene Lange is an example of such a feminist. Lange was a German feminist who attended a salon regularly hosted by Dohm and frequented by other German female intellectuals, including Adele Schreiber, Lou Andreas-Salomé, Else Lasker, and Gabriele Reuter. Lange, like Dohm, advocated for girls' education but, unlike Dohm, opposed women entering the workforce (except as teachers), arguing that it would cause women to live their lives as "manly women" (quoted in Diethe 1996b: 74). Echoes of Lange's sentiments can be found in BGE 144: "When a woman has scholarly inclinations, there is usually something wrong with her sexually. Even sterility makes her prone to a certain masculinity of taste; man is, if you will, 'the sterile animal.'"
12  See, for example, Dohm's *Der Frauen Natur und Recht* (2015), which argues for the idea that women's roles are socially constructed.

13 Weedon (1994: 183).
14 Diethe (1996b: 72–3); see also Woodford (2016: 336–49).
15 Weedon (1994: 184).
16 Diethe (1996b: 70) and Woodford (2016: 337).
17 Creasy (2020: 27).
18 Creasy (2020: 27–8).
19 Creasy (2020: 60).
20 In this delineation of the different dimensions of Nietzschean nihilism, I follow Creasy (2020). For an account that focuses on the cognitive aspects of nihilism, see Reginster (2006). For an account that focuses on the affective aspects of nihilism, see Creasy (2020).
21 My reading of sociocultural nihilism does not rule out the idea that oppression should be understood as operating on social groups rather than at the level of the individual. Compare Marilyn Frye, for example, who defines oppression as a type of social pressure applied to groups of people: "One is marked for application of oppressive pressures by one's membership in some group or category" (2000: 16). According to Frye, much of one's suffering and frustration befalls one because one is a member of a particular group or category. See also Young's (2004) description of oppression as something that happens to a member of a group.
22 KSA 12:10[192].
23 Dohm (2006: 11).
24 Dohm (2006: 10).
25 Dohm (2006: 10).
26 Dohm (2006: 10).
27 Dohm (2006: 12).
28 Dohm (2006: 12).
29 Dohm (2006: 12).
30 Dohm (2006: 13).
31 Dohm (2006: 14).
32 Dohm (2006: 14).
33 Until otherwise noted, all quotations in this and the following paragraphs are from GS 21.
34 This section of GS also contains an important criticism of utilitarianism. See Anomaly (2005: 1–15).
35 Agnes Schmidt echoes this sentiment when she says, "Our duties! Shouldn't they be such that they make us better, nobler and not the other way around? Are they allowed to push us downwards onto a lower niveau?" (Dohm 2006: 32).
36 Nietzsche's estimation of women as inherently different from men was common in his time. As Chris Weedon notes, "ideas about gender in Germany were profoundly influenced by dualistic theories which stressed differences between men and women" (1994: 182). Marianne Dekoven argues that in the modernist period (1880–1920) there was a new preoccupation with gender that came about as a reaction against the feminist movements of the time: "Much of this preoccupation expressed a male modernist fear of women's new power, and resulted in the combination of misogyny and triumphal masculinism that many critics see as central, defining features of modernist work by men" (1999: 174).
37 Some argue that Nietzsche's discussion of women and procreation, particularly the one found in BGE 234–39, must either be understood metaphorically or contextualized within his body of work (or both). For example, Hatab argues that

Nietzsche does not believe in masculine superiority because "he speaks of 'woman as such' (*Weib an sich*), not 'women.'" Hatab takes this as evidence that "Nietzsche is pursuing something deeper than sexual differences … a principle which is neither biological nor sociological but archetypal" (1981: 333–35, 333). Clark argues that "the misogyny exhibited there [in BGE VII] is on the level of sentiment, not belief, and that it is used by Nietzsche to illustrate points he is trying to make about philosophy and the will to truth" (1994: 3–12, 4). It is outside the scope of this chapter to take up these arguments. I note however that Dohm thought Nietzsche was a misogynist.

38  Diethe notes that "Nietzsche's pun on the word *Herr* (master/man) descends to the level of a sexist slur, but Nietzsche was by no means alone in assuming the 'manishness' of the feminist; it serves to remind us of how inimical to his philosophy he thought the feminist demands were" (Diethe 1996b: 70).
39  Nietzsche's critique of democracy can be seen throughout his writings. For paradigmatic passages, see BGE 22, 202; GS 356, and TI Skirmishes 39.
40  Dohm (2021).
41  Dohm's observation about Nietzsche's lack of knowledge about women is worth quoting for its cunning and wit (often deployed in the form of *ad hominem* attacks throughout her essay): "It almost forces a laugh from us when Friedrich Nietzsche speaks so confidently of the tiger claws, of the dangerous, beautiful cat woman, of her untamable wildness—this celibate man, stranger to women, who certainly never felt the smallest female tiger claw on his own body, never experienced how these predatory creatures, like tragedy, 'beguile, while they tear apart.' Perhaps he dreamt of them precisely because of this, like Saint Antonious dreamt of the seductive she-devils: hallucinations from too great abstinence" (Dohm 2021: 134).
42  Dohm (2006: 15).
43  Dohm (2006: 16).
44  Dohm (2006: 18).
45  Dohm (2006: 20).
46  Dohm (2006: 32).
47  Dohm (2006: 32).
48  Dohm (2006: 32).
49  Dohm (2006: 32).
50  Dohm (2006: 33).
51  Dohm (2006: 36).
52  Dohm (2006: 2).
53  Dohm (2006: 5, 61).
54  Dohm (2006: 60).
55  I borrow this insight from Creasy (forthcoming), who uses the example of the criminal type to understand the plight of women in society.
56  Nietzsche quotations in the remainder of this section are from TI Skirmishes 45.
57  Here we again see resonances with Nietzsche's Zarathustra. In this book, Zarathustra is a creature who has overcome nihilism and has been hiding from society in the mountains. Agnes Schmidt also turns to nature in her later years, taking solace in the ocean and travel.

# Bibliography

Abbey, Ruth (2000), *Nietzsche's Middle Period*, Oxford: Oxford University Press.
Abbey, Ruth (1996), "Beyond Misogyny and Metaphor: Women in Nietzsche's Middle Period", in *The Journal of the History of Philosophy*, 34(2), 233–56.
Acampora, Christa Davis and Keith Ansell Pearson (2011), *Beyond Good and Evil: A Reader's Guide*, London: Continuum.
Ahern, Daniel R (1995), *Nietzsche as Cultural Physician*, Philadelphia: The Pennsylvania University Press.
Alfano, Mark (2019a), *Nietzsche's Moral Psychology*, Cambridge: Cambridge University Press.
Alfano, Mark (2019b), "Nietzsche's Affective Perspectivism as a Philosophical Methodology," in *Nietzsche's Metaphilosophy: The Nature, Method, and Aims of Philosophy*, ed. Paul S. Loeb and Matthew Meyer, 127–45, Cambridge: Cambridge University Press.
Algazi, Lisa G. (2005–2006), "Feminists Read Stendhal (or Do They?)," in Nineteenth-Century French Studies, 34(1), 11–20.
Anomaly, Jonny (2005), "Nietzsche's Critique of Utilitarianism," in *The Journal of Nietzsche Studies*, 29(1), 1–15.
Ansell-Pearson, Keith (1993), "Nietzsche, Woman and Political Theory," in *Nietzsche, Feminism and Political Theory*, ed. Paul Patton, 27–48, London: Routledge.
Ansell-Pearson, Keith, and Rebecca Bamford (2021), Nietzsche's Dawn: Philosophy, Ethics and the Passion of Knowledge, Hoboken, NJ: Wiley Blackwell.
Ansell-Pearson, Keith (2006), "A 'Dionysian Drama on 'The Fate of the Soul'": An Introduction to Reading *on the Genealogy of Morality*," in *Nietzsche's On the Genealogy of Morals: Critical Essays*, ed. Christa Davis Acampora, 19–38, Lanham, MD: Rowman & Littlefield Publishers.
Attali, Patrick (2013), "Par-delà tout ce qu'on a vu dans l'"amour"," in *Nietzsche-Studien*, 42, 116–50.
Austin, J. L. (1962), *How to Do Things with Words*, Oxford: Clarendon Press.
Autiero, Serena (2014), "Terracotta Figurines from Egypt as Agents of Cultural Globalisation," in *Current Research in Egyptology 2014: Proceedings of the Fifteenth Annual Symposium*, ed. Pinarello, M. S., et.al., 90–9, Oxford: Oxbow Books.
Aydin, Ciano (2007), "Nietzsche on Reality as Will to Power: Toward an 'Organization-Struggle' Model," in *The Journal of Nietzsche Studies,* (33), Spring 2007, 25–48, Penn State University Press.
Bachofen, Johann Jakob (1954), *Das Mutterrecht Und Urreligion*, Stuttgart: Alfred Kroner Verlag.
Bagchi, Jasodhara (2017), *Interrogating Motherhood*, London: Sage Publications.
Bagchi, Jasodhara (2010), "Representing Nationalism: Ideology of Motherhood in Colonial Bengal," in *Motherhood in India. Glorification without Empowerment*, ed. Maithreyi Krishnaraj, 158–85, New York: Routledge.

Bagehot, Walter (1874), *Der Ursprung der Nationen. Betrachtungen über den Einfluss der natürlichen Zuchtwahl und der Vererbung auf die Bildung politischer Gemeinwesen*, Leipzig, F.A.: Brockhaus, (BN).
Bamford, Rebecca (2016), "The Ethos of Inquiry: Nietzsche on Experience, Naturalism, and Experimentalism," in *The Journal of Nietzsche Studies*, 47(1), 9–29.
Beauvoir, Simone de (1972), *The Second Sex*, Harmondsworth: Penguin.
Beauvoir, Simone de (1953), *The Second Sex*, trans. H. M. Parshley, London: Jonathan Cape.
Behler, Diana (2010), "Nietzsche's View of Woman in Classical Greece," in *Nietzsche-Studien*, 18(1), 359–76.
Bergoffen, Debra B. (1996), "Nietzsche's Women," in *The Journal of Nietzsche Studies*, 12, 19–26.
Binion, Rudolph (1968), *Frau Lou: Nietzsche's Wayward Disciple*, Princeton, NJ: Princeton University Press.
Bishop, Paul (2022), *Nietzsche's The Anti-Christ*, Edinburgh: Edinburgh University Press.
Blondel, Eric (2009), "Nietzsche: a vida e a metáfora," in *Nietzsche, um "francês" entre os franceses*, Scarlett Marton, ed., Fernando de Moraes Barros, trans., São Paulo: Discurso; 53–92, Barcarolla.
Blondel, Eric (1991), *Nietzsche: The Body and Culture, Philosophy as a Philological Genealogy*, trans. Séan Hand, Palo Alto, CA: Stanford University Press.
Blondel, Éric (2017), "Mariage (*Ehe*)," in *Dictionnaire Nietzsche*, ed. Dorian Astor, 546–7, Paris: Robert Laffont.
Bollas, C. (2018), *The Shadow of the Object: Psychoanalysis of the Unthought Known*, New York: Routledge.
Braidotti, Rosi (1993), "Embodiment, Sexual Difference, and the Nomadic Subject," in *Hypatia*, 8(1), 1–13.
Brandchaft, Bernard (2010), *Towards an Emancipatory Psychoanalysis: Brandchaft's Intersubjective Vision*, New York: Routledge.
Brennan, Katie (2021), "The Nihilism of the Oppressed: Hedwig Dohm's Feminist Critique of Nietzschean Nihilism," in *The Journal of Nietzsche Studies*, 52, 209–23.
Brobjer, Thomas (2008a), *Nietzsche's Philosophical Context: An Intellectual Biography*, Urbana: University of Illinois Press.
Brobjer, Thomas (2008b), *Nietzsche and the English, The Influence of British and American Thinking on His Philosophy*, Amherst, NY: Humanity Books.
Brobjer, Thomas (1998), "The Absence of Political Ideas in Nietzsche's Writings. The Case of the Laws of Manu and the Associated Caste-Society," in *Nietzsche-Studien*, 27, 300–18.
Butler, Judith (1999), *Gender Trouble: Feminism and the Subversion of Identity*, (2nd edition), London: Routledge.
Butler, Judith (1997), *The Psychic Life of Power*, Palo Alto, CA: Stanford University Press.
Butler, Judith (1996), "An Affirmative View," in *Representation*, 55, 74–83.
Butler, Judith (1993), *Bodies That Matter: On the Discursive Limits of "Sex"*, New York: Routledge.
Butler, Judith (1992), "The Body You Want: An Interview with Judith Butler, by L. Kotz," in *Artforum*, https://www.artforum.com/print/199209/the-body-you-want-an-inteview-with-judith-butler-33505 (accessed March 15, 2022).
Butler, Judith (1990), *Gender Trouble: Feminism and the Subversion of Identity*, London: Routledge.

Butler, Judith (1989), "Foucault and the Paradox of Bodily Inscriptions," in *The Journal of Philosophy*, 86(11), 601–7.
Butler, Judith (1988), "Performative Acts and Gender Constitution: An Essay in Phenomenology and Feminist Theory," in *Theatre Journal*, 40(4), 519–33.
Call, Lewis (1995), "Woman as Will and Representation: Nietzsche's Contribution to Postmodern Feminism," in *Women in German Yearbook*, 11, Lincoln: University of Nebraska Press, 113–29.
Campbell, Joseph (1964), *The Masks of God*, vol. 3, New York: Viking.
Campioni, Giuliano (2016), *Nietzsche e o espírito latino*. Tradução de Vinícius de Andrade, São Paulo: Edições Loyola.
Campioni, Giuliano (2009), *Der französische Nietzsche*, trans., Renate Müller-Buck e Leonie Schröder, Berlin: De Gruyter.
Campioni, Giuliano et. al., (2002), *Nietzsches persönliche Bibliothek* (BN), Berlin: De Gruyter.
Catani, Stephanie (2005), *Das fiktive Geschlecht. Weiblichkeit in anthropologischen Entwürfen und literarischen Texten zwischen 1885 und 1925*, Würzburg: Königshausen & Neumann.
Cavalcanti, A. H. (2005), *Símbolo e Alegoria: a gênese da concepção de linguagem em Nietzsche*, São Paulo: Annablume.
Cavell, Stanley (1990), *Conditions Handsome and Unhandsome: The Constitution of Emersonian Perfectionism*, Chicago: University of Chicago Press.
Clark, Maudemarie (2015), *Nietzsche on Ethics and Politics*, Oxford: Oxford University Press.
Clark, Maudemarie (2013), "Nietzsche Was No Lamarckian," in *The Journal of Nietzsche Studies*, 44(2), 282–96.
Clark, Maudemarie (1998), "Nietzsche's Misogyny," in *Feminist Interpretations of Friedrich Nietzsche*, ed. Kelly Oliver and Marilyn Pearsall, University Park, PA: Pennsylvania State University Press, 187–98.
Clark, Maudemarie (1994), "Nietzsche's Misogyny," in *International Studies in Philosophy*, 26(3), 3–12.
Cleary, Skye C. (2017) (online edition), "Simone de Beauvoir on Love," in *The Oxford Handbook of Philosophy of Love*, ed. Christopher Grau and Aaron Smuts, Oxford: Oxford University Press, https://doi.org/10.1093/oxfordhb/9780199395729.013.25 (accessed July 26, 2022).
Cleary, Skye C. (2015), *Existentialism and Romantic Love*, New York: Palgrave Macmillan.
Clement of Alexandria (1960), *The Exhortation to the Greeks*, trans. G. W. Butterworth, Cambridge: Harvard University Press.
Conant, James (2001), "Nietzsche's Perfectionism," in *Nietzsche's Postmoralism: Essays on Nietzsche's Prelude to Philosophy's Future*, ed. Richard Schacht, Cambridge: Cambridge University Press, 181–257.
Creasy, Kaitlin (forthcoming), "Sexism is Exhausting: Nietzsche and the Affective Dynamics of Sexist Oppression," in *Nietzsche and Politicized Identities*, ed. Rebecca Bamford and Allison Merrick, Albany: State University of New York Press.
Creasy, Kaitlin (2020), *The Problem of Affective Nihilism in Nietzsche: Thinking Differently, Feeling Differently*, New York: Palgrave Macmillan.
Cross, Stephen (2013), *Schopenhauer's Encounter with Indian Thought: Representation and Will and Their Indian Parallels*. Honolulu: University of Hawaii Press.
Cruz, M. A. (2015), "Nietzsche and the Nineteenth-Century Debate on Teleology," in *Nietzsche and the Becoming of Life*, ed. Vanessa Lemm, New York: Fordham University Press, 67–82.
Dekoven, Marianne (1999), "Modernism and Gender," in *The Cambridge Companion to Modernism*, ed. Michael Levenson, 174–93, Cambridge: Cambridge University Press.

Derrida, Jacques (1998), "The Question of style," in *Feminist Interpretations of Friedrich Nietzsche*, ed. Kelly Oliver and Marilyn Pearsall, 50–65, Philadelphia: Pennsylvania State University Press.
Derrida, Jacques (1997), *Of Grammatology*, trans., Gayatri Chakravorty Spivak, Baltimore: Johns Hopkins University Press.
Derrida, Jacques (1979), *Spurs: Nietzsche's Styles*, trans., Barbara Harlow, Chicago: University of Chicago Press.
Deleuze, Gilles (1983), *Nietzsche and Philosophy*, trans., Hugh Tomlinson, New York: Columbia University Press.
Deutscher, Penelope (1993), "'Is It Not Remarkable that Nietzsche Should Have Hated Rousseau?' Woman, Femininity: Distancing Nietzsche from Rousseau," in *Nietzsche, Feminism and Political Theory*, ed. Paul Patton, 162–88, London: Routledge.
Deutscher, Penelope (2022), "Sexual Difference and the Conduct of Critique (Nietzsche and Irigaray)," in *Enrahonar: An International Journal of Theoretical and Practical Reason*, 68, 63–74.
Devereux, Georges (1983), Baubo: la Vulve Mythique, Paris: Jean-Cyrille Godefroy.
Diethe, Carol (2007), *Historical Dictionary of Nietzscheanism*, Second Edition, Lanham, MD: Scarecrow Press.
Diethe, Carol (1996a), *Nietzsche's Women: Beyond the Whip*, Berlin: De Gruyter.
Diethe, Carol (1996b), "Nietzsche and the Early German Feminists," in *The Journal of Nietzsche Studies*, 12, 69–81.
Diethe, Carol (1993), "Nietzsche and the Pathos of Distance," in *Nietzsche, Feminism and Political Theory*, ed. Paul Patton, 1–26, New York: Routledge.
Diethe, Carol (1989), "Nietzsche and the Woman Question," in *History of European Ideas*, 11, 865–76.
Diethe, Carol (1989), "Nietzsche, Ethics and Sexual Difference," in *Radical Philosophy*, 52, 27–33.
Diprose, Rosalyn (2002), *Corporeal Generosity. On Giving with Nietzsche, Merleau-Ponty, and Levinas*, Albany: State University of New York Press.
Diprose, Rosalyn (1993), "Nietzsche and the Pathos of Distance," in *Nietzsche, Feminism and Political Theory*, ed. Paul Patton, 1–26, New York: Routledge.
Diprose, Rosalyn (1989), "Nietzsche, Ethics and Sexual Difference," in *Radical Philosophy* 52, 27–33.
Dohm, Hedwig (2006), *Become Who You Are*, trans. Elizabeth G. Ametsbichler, Albany: State University of New York Press.
Dohm, Hedwig (2015), *Der Frauen Natur und Recht*, Berlin: Holzinger.
Dohm, Hedwig (2021), "Nietzsche and Women," trans. Anna Ezekiel, in *Women Philosophers in the Long Nineteenth Century*, ed. Kristin Gjesdal and Dalia Nassar, 122–53, Oxford: Oxford University Press.
Draz, Marie (2018), "Burning It In? Nietzsche, Gender, and Externalized Memory," in *Feminist Philosophy Quarterly*, 4(2) Art. 1.
Dries, Manuel (2008a), "Nietzsche's Critique of Staticism," in *Nietzsche on Time and History*, ed. Manuel Dries, Berlin: De Gruyter, 1–19.
Dries, Manuel (2008b), "Towards Adualism: Becoming and Nihilism in Nietzsche's Philosophy," in *Nietzsche on Time and History*, ed. Manuel Dries, 113–45.
Drochon, Hugo (2010), "The Time Is Coming When We Will Relearn Politics," in *The Journal of Nietzsche Studies*, 39(1), 66–85.
Erndl, K. M. (2000), "Is Shakti Empowering for Women? Reflections on Feminism and the Hindu Goddess," in *Is the Goddess a Feminist? The Politics of South Asian*

*Goddesses*, ed. Alf Hiltebeitel and Kathleen M. Erndl, 91–101, New York: New York University Press.

Etter, Annemarie (1987), "Nietzsche und das Gesetzbuch des Manu," in *Nietzsche-Studien*, 16, 340–52.

Faustino, M. (2017), "Nietzsche's Therapy of Therapy," in *Nietzsche-Studien*, 46(1), 82–104.

Faustino, M. (2016), "Grande saúde e filosofia do futuro [Great Health and the Philosophy of the Future]," in *Estudos Nietzsche*, 7(1), Espírito Santo, 8–30.

Figl, Johann (2007), *Nietzsche und die Religionen: Transkulturelle Perspektiven seines Bildungs- und Denkweges*, Berlin: Walter de Gruyter.

Firestone, Shulamith (2015), *The Dialectic of Sex: The Case for Feminist Revolution*, London: Verso.

Fornari, Maria Cristina (2006), *La morale evolutiva del gregge*, ETS.

Foucault, Michel (1977), "Nietzsche, Genealogy, History," in *Language, Counter-Memory, Practice: Selected Essays and Interviews by Michel Foucault*, ed. Donald F. Bouchard, trans. Donald F. Bouchard and Sherry Simon, Ithaca: Cornell University Press, 139–64.

Freud, Sigmund (2001), "New Introductory Lectures on Psychoanalysis," in *The Standard Edition of the Complete Psychological Works of Sigmund Freud*, vol. XXII (1932–6), trans. James Strachey, London: Vintage.

Freud, Sigmund (1964), "Mourning and Melancholia," in *The Standard Edition of the Complete Psychological Works of Sigmund Freud*, ed. James Strachey, London: Hogarth, 243–58.

Freud, Sigmund (1961), "Fetishism," in *The Standard Edition of the Complete Psychological Works of Sigmund Freud*, vol. XXI (1927–31), trans. James Strachey, 147–58, London: The Hogarth Press and the Institute of Psychoanalysis.

Frye, Marilyn (2000), "Oppression," in *Gender Basics: Feminist Perspectives on Women and Men*, ed. Anne Minas, Belmont, CA: Wadsworth.

Frye, Marilyn (1983), *The Politics of Reality: Essays in Feminist Theory*, New York: Crossing Press.

Ganapathy, T. N. (2003), "The Way of the Siddhas," in *Hindu Spirituality: Postclassical and Modern*, ed. K. R. Sundararajan and Bithika Mukerji, Delhi: Motilal Banarsidas Publishers.

García-Granero, Marina (2020), "La raza como problema filosófico en los escritos de Nietzsche," in *Anales del Seminario de Historia de la Filosofía*, 37(1), 73–84.

Gayon, Jean (1999), "Nietzsche and Darwin," in *Biology and the Foundations of Ethics*, ed. Jane Maienschein and Michael Ruse, Cambridge: Cambridge University Press.

Geuss, Raymond (2002), "Genealogy as Critique," in *European Journal of Philosophy*, 10(2), 209–15.

Geuss, Raymond (1994), "Nietzsche and Genealogy," in *European Journal of Philosophy*, 2(3), 274–92.

Gemes, Ken (2006), "'We Remain of Necessity Strangers to Ourselves': The Key Message of Nietzsche's *Genealogy*," in *Nietzsche's On the Genealogy of Morals: Critical Essays*, ed. Christa Davis Acampora. Lanham, MD: Rowman & Littlefield, 191–208.

Gemes, Ken and C. Sykes (2015), "The Culture of Myth and the Myth of Culture," in *Individual and Community in Nietzsche's Philosophy*, ed. Julian Young, New York: Cambridge University Press.

Giacoia Jr., Oswaldo (2002), *Nietzsche e o Feminine*, São Paulo: Natureza humana, vol. 4, n. 1, 9–31.

Goethe, Johann Wolfgang von (2014), *Faust I & II*, ed. and trans. Stuart Atkins, with a new introduction by David E. Wellbery, Princeton: Princeton University Press.

Goethe, Johann Wolfgang von (2011), Fausto: uma tragédia, Segunda parte, trans. Jenny Klabin Segall, ed., Marcus Vinicius Mazzari. São Paulo.
Goethe, Johann Wolfgang von (1984), *Faust I & II*, trans., Stuart Atkins, Princeton: Princeton University Press.
Goethe, Johann Wolfgang von (1962), *Faust*, trans. Walter Kaufmann, New York: Anchor Books.
Goswami, Jayadeva (2017), Sri Gita-Govinda, revised 2nd edition, trans. Bhaktivedanta Narayana Gosvami Maharaja, New Delhi: Spectrum Printing Press.
Guay, Robert (2011), "Genealogy and Irony," in *The Journal of Nietzsche Studies*, 41(1), 26–49.
Guay, Robert (2022), *Nietzsche's On the Genealogy of Morality*, Edinburgh: Edinburgh University Press.
Haar, M. (1977), "Nietzsche and Metaphysical Language," in *The New Nietzsche: Contemporary Styles of Interpretation*, ed. Allison, D. B., Cambridge: MIT Press, 5–36.
Haase, Marie-Luise (1989), "Friedrich Nietzsche liest Francis Galton," in *Nietzsche-Studien*, 18, 633–58.
Haraway, Donna (1988), "Situated Knowledges: The Science Question in Feminism and the Privilege of Partial Perspective," in *Feminist Studies*, 14(3), 579–99.
Harding, Sandra (1991), "Feminist Epistemology," in *Whose Science, Whose Knowledge?*, ed. Sandra Harding, Ithaca, NY: Cornell University Press.
Hartsock, Nancy (1983), "The Feminist Standpoint: Developing the Ground for a Specifically Feminist Historical Materialism," in *Discovering Reality*, ed. Merrill Hintikka and Sandra Harding, Norwell, MA: Kluwer.
Hatab, Lawrence J. (2015), "Nietzsche, Nature, and Life Affirmation," in *Nietzsche and the Becoming of Life*, ed. Vanessa Lemm, New York: Fordham University Press.
Hatab, Lawrence J. (1981), "Nietzsche on Woman," in *the Southern Journal of Philosophy*, 19(3), 333–45.
Hayman, Ronald (1984), *Nietzsche, A Critical Life*, New York: Penguin Press.
Heidegger, Martin (1996a), *Gesamtausgabe*, 6.1, Frankfurt am Main: Vittorio Klostermann.
Heidegger, Martin (1996b), *Gesamtausgabe*, 6.2, Frankfurt am Main: Vittorio Klostermann.
Heidegger, Martin (1991), *Nietzsche*, vol. 1, David F. Krell, trans., New York: Harper Collins.
Heidegger, Martin (1976), Zur Seinsfrage. *Gesamtausgabe*. 1. Abteilung, Veröffentlichte Schriften (1914–1970), Bd 9, Frankfurt am Main: Vittorio Klostermann.
Heidegger, Martin (2009), *Interprétation de la deuxième considération intempestive de Nietzsche*, trans. Alain Boutot, Paris: Gallimard.
Held, Virginia (2006), *The Ethics of Care*, Oxford: Oxford University Press.
Hemelsoet, D., K. Hemelsoet, and D. Devreese (2008), "The neurological illness of Friedrich Nietzsche," in *Acta Neurol Belg*, 108(1), March, 9–16. PMID: 18575181.
Higgins, Kathleen Marie (1996), "*The Whip Recalled*," in *The Journal of Nietzsche Studies*, (12), 1–18.
Hill Collins, Patricia (2004), "Learning from the Outsider within: The Sociological Significance of Black Feminist Thought," in *The Feminist Standpoint Reader: Intellectual and Political Controversies*, ed. Sandra Harding, New York: Routledge.
Huddleston, Andrew (2019), *Nietzsche on the Decadence and Flourishing of Culture*, Oxford: Oxford University Press.
Hurka, Thomas (2007), "Nietzsche: Perfectionist," in *Nietzsche and Morality*, ed. Brian Leiter and Neil Sinhababu, Oxford: Oxford University Press, 9–31.

Ingram, David (2003), "Foucault and Habermas," in *The Cambridge Companion to Foucault*, ed. Gary Gutting, Cambridge: Cambridge University Press, 240–83.
Irigaray, Luce (1993a), *An Ethics of Sexual Difference*, trans., Carolyn Burke and Gillian C. Gill, London: Athlone Press.
Irigaray, Luce (1993b), *Sexes and Genealogies*, New York: Columbia University Press.
Irigaray, Luce (2004), *Key Writings*, London: Continuum/Bloomsbury.
Irigaray, Luce (1991), *Marine Lover of Friedrich Nietzsche*, trans. Gillian C. Gill, New York: Columbia University Press.
Jaggar, Alison M. (1983), *Feminist Politics and Human Nature*, Oxford: Rowman & Littlefield Publishers, Ltd.
Jantz, Harold (1953), "*The Place of the "Eternal-Womanly" in Goethe's Faust Drama*," in PMLA, 68(4), 791–805.
Jayadeva and Lee Siegel (2008), *Gita Govinda*, trans., C. J. Holcombe, Santiago: Ocaso Press.
Jeong, J. (2021), "Nietzsche's Early Concept of Culture," in *Revista Trans/Form/Ação*, Marília, 44(4) October and December, 229–44.
Jeong, J. (2019), *Nietzsche on the Social Whole and Unity* (unpublished doctoral thesis), Coventry: University of Warwick.
Judith, Anodea (2004), *Eastern Body Western Mind. Psychology and the Chakra System as a Path to the Self*, New York: Crown Publishing Group.
Kapferer, Norbert (1984), "Nietzsches philosophischer Antifeminismus," in *Mythos Frau. Projektionen und Inszenierungen im Patriarchat*, ed. Barbara Schaeffer-Hegel and Brigitte Wartmann, 79–90, Berlin: Publica.
Kaufmann, Walter (1974), *Nietzsche: Philosopher, Psychologist, Antichrist*, New York: Vintage.
Keller, M. A. (2014), "Goddess Spirituality," in *Encyclopaedia of Psychology and Religion*, 2nd edition, ed. D. A. Leeming 729–33, New York: Springer.
Kempton, Sally (2013), *Awakening Shakti: The Transformative Power of the Goddesses of Yoga*, Louisville, CO: Sounds True Publishing.
Kerenyi, Carl (1976), *Dionysos*, Princeton: Princeton University Press.
Kittay, Eva Feder (2019), *Learning from My Daughter: The Value and Care of Disabled Minds*. Oxford: Oxford University Press.
Kittay, Eva Feder (1999), *Love's Labor*, New York: Routledge Press.
Klossowski, Pierre (1990), *Diana at Her Bath: The Women of Rome*, Boston: Eridanos Press.
Kofman, Sarah and Madeleine Dobie (1995), "The Psychologist of the Eternal Feminine (Why I Write Such Good Books, 5)," in *Yale French Studies*, 87, 173–89.
Kofman, Sarah (1998), "Baubô: Theological Perversion and Fetishism," in *Feminist interpretations of Friedrich Nietzsche*, ed. Kelly Oliver and Marilyn Pearsall, 21–49, University Park, PA: Pennsylvania State University Press.
Kofman, Sarah (1985), "O/Os "conceitos" de cultura nas Extemporâneas," in, *Nietzsche hoje? Colóquio de Cerisy*, Scarlett Marton, ed., Milton Nascimento e Sônia Salzstein Goldberg, Trad., São Paulo: Brasiliense.
Kohler, Joachim (2002), *Zarathustra's Secret: The Interior Life of Friedrich Nietzsche*, trans., Ronald Taylor, New Haven: Yale University Press.
Kopp, B. (1974), *Beiträge zur Kulturphilosophie der deutschen Klassik*. Eine Untersuchung im Zusammenhang mit dem Bedeutungswandel des Wortes Kultur, Meisenheim am Glan: Hain.
Kramrisch, Stella (1956), "An Image of Aditi-Uttānapad," in *Artibus Asiae*, 19(3/4), 259–70.

Krell, David F. (1986), *Postponements: Woman, Sensuality, and Death in Nietzsche*, Bloomington: Indiana University Press.
Lacoue-Labarthe, P. (1986), "Histoire et mimesis," in *Typographies 2 – L'Imitation des modernes*, 100–103, Paris: Galilée.
Leelamma, K. P. (1998), *Devi Mahatmyam*, Cochin: Sri Ramkrishna Math.
Lemm, Vanessa (2020), *Homo Natura: Nietzsche, Philosophical Anthropology and Biopolitics*, Edinburgh: Edinburgh University Press.
Lemm, Vanessa (2009), *Nietzsche's Animal Philosophy: Culture, Politics, and the Animality of the Human Being*, New York: Fordham University Press.
Lidke, J. S. (2017), *The Goddess within and beyond the Three Cities: Sakta Tantra and the Paradox of Power in Nepala-Mandala*, Delhi: DK Printworld, Pvt., Ltd.
Lorenzini, Daniele (2020), "On Possibilising Genealogy," in *Inquiry*, DOI: 10.1080/0020174X.2020.1712227.
Lorraine, Tamsin E. (1998), "Nietzsche and Feminism: Transvaluing Women in Thus Spoke Zarathustra," in *Feminist Interpretations of Friedrich Nietzsche*, ed. Kelly Oliver and Marilyn Pearsall, 119–29, University Park, PA: Pennsylvania State University Press.
Lubell, Winifred (1994), *The Metamorphosis of Baubo*, Nashville: Vanderbilt University Press.
Lucretius, Titus (1968), *The Way Things Are: The De Rerum Natura of Titus Lucretius Carus*, Rolfe Humphries, trans., Bloomington: Indiana University Press.
Machado, R. (1984), *Nietzsche e a Verdade*, Rio de Janeiro: Rocco.
Malan, Gert J. (2016), "Ricoeur on myth and demythologising," in HTS Teologiese Studies/Theological Studies, 72(4), a2998.
de Man, Paul (1979), *Allegories of Reading: Figural Language in Rousseau, Nietzsche, Rilke, and Proust*, New Haven: Yale University Press.
Marion, Jean Luc (2001), *The Idol and Distance: Five Studies*, trans. Thomas A. Carlson, New York: Fordham University Press.
Marques, A. (2003), *A filosofia perspectivista de Nietzsche* [Nietzsche's perspectivist philosophy], São Paulo: Discurso Editorial.
Martin, Nicholas (2004), "Breeding Greeks: Nietzsche, Gobineau, and Classical Theories of Race," in *Nietzsche and Antiquity: His Reaction and Response to the Classical Tradition*, ed. Paul Bishop, 40–53, Rochester, NY: Camden House.
Martin, Nicholas (1996), *Nietzsche and Schiller: Untimely Aesthetics*, Oxford: Clarendon Press.
Marton, Scarlett (2022), *Nietzsche e as Mulheres*, Belo Horizonte: Autêntica.
Marton, Scarlett (2021), *Les ambivalences de Nietzsche: Types, images et figures féminines*, Paris: Editions de la Sorbonne.
Marton, Scarlett (2009), "*Do dilaceramento do sujeito à plenitude dionisíaca*," in Cad. Nietzsche, (25), 53–82.
May, Regine and Stephen J. Harrison, eds. (2020), *Cupid and Psyche. The Reception of Apuleius' Love Story since 1600*, Berlin: Walter de Gruyter.
May, Simon (2011), *Love: A History*, New Haven: Yale University Press.
McDaniel, J. (2004), *Offering Flowers, Feeding Skulls: Popular Goddess Worship in West Bengal*, Oxford: Oxford University Press.
McIntyre, Alex (1992), "'Virtuosos of Contempt': An Investigation of Nietzsche's Political Philosophy through Certain Platonic Political Ideas," in *Nietzsche-Studien*, 21, 184–210.
McNeal, Michael J. (2022), "The Free Spirit's Dionysian Mirth: A Laughing Storm to Herald Philosophers of the Future," in *Joy and Laughter in Nietzsche's*

*Philosophy: Alternative Liberatory Politics*, eds., Paul Kirkland and Michael J. McNeal, 191–213, London: Bloomsbury Academic.

McNeill, William (2006), "A Wave in the Stream of Chaos: Life beyond the Body in Heidegger's *Nietzsche*," in *Philosophy Today*, 50, Supplement, 156–61.

Messerschmidt, Mat (forthcoming), "The Body and the Completion of Metaphysics: A Critical Analysis of Heidegger's Nietzsche," in *Nietzsche-Studien*.

Meyers, Diana (1989), *Self, Society, and Personal Choice*, New York: Columbia University Press.

Miner, Robert C. (2010), "Nietzsche on Friendship," in *The Journal of Nietzsche Studies*, 40, 47–69.

Mitcheson, Katrina (2013), *Nietzsche, Truth and Transformation*, London: Palgrave Macmillan.

Moore, Gregory (2002), *Nietzsche, Biology and Metaphor*, Cambridge: Cambridge University Press.

Metropolitan Opera, The (2014), *Carmen*, Milwaukee: Amadeus Press.

Montinari, Mazzino (1979), "Nietzsche zwischen Alfred Baeumler und Georg Lukács," in *Basis*, 9, 188–223.

Montinari, Mazzino (1982), *Nietzsche lesen*. Berlin: De Gruyter.

Morrison, I. (2021), "Patterns of Sickness: Nietzsche's Physio-Historical Account of Asceticism," in *British Journal for the History of Philosophy*, 30, 109–29.

Mukhopadhyay, Anway (2019), "Everyday Aesthetics and the Indic Goddess Traditions: An Aurobindonian Approach," in *Journal of Comparative Literature and Aesthetics*, 42(2), Autumn.

Müller-Lauter, Wolfgang (1999), *Über Werden und Wille zur Macht. Nietzsche Interpretationen I*. Berlin: De Gruyter.

Nehamas, Alexander (1996). "Nietzsche, Modernity, Aestheticism," in *The Cambridge Companion to Nietzsche*, ed. Bernard Magnus and Kathleen Higgins, 223–51, Cambridge: Cambridge University Press.

Nehamas, Alexander (1985), *Nietzsche: Life as Literature*. Cambridge: Harvard University Press.

Nettleton, Skye (2009), "Ten Tips for a Great Marriage According to Friedrich Nietzsche," in *Indo-Pacific Journal of Phenomenology*, 9(2), 1–9.

Neumann, Erich (1969), *The Origins and History of Consciousness*, Princeton, NJ: Princeton University Press.

Noddings, Nell (2003), *Caring: A Feminist Approach to Ethics and Moral Education*, 2nd ed. Berkeley: University of California Press.

Norlock, Kathryn (2019), "Feminist Ethics," in *The Stanford Encyclopedia of Philosophy*, ed. Edward N. Zalta, URL: https://plato.stanford.edu/archives/sum2019/entries/feminism-ethics/.

O'Brien, E. P. (2012), "The Meaning of the Eternal Feminine in Goethe's Drama Faust," Retrieved from http://purl.flvc.org/fsu/fd/FSU_migr_etd-5076.

Oliver, Kelly and Marilyn Pearsall (1998), "Why Feminists Read Nietzsche," in *Feminist Interpretations of Friedrich Nietzsche*, ed. Oliver, Kelly and Marilyn Pearsall, University Park, PA: Pennsylvania State University Press.

Oliver, Kelly (1995), *Womanizing Nietzsche: Philosophy's Relation to the "Feminine,"* New York: Routledge.

Oliver, Kelly (1984), "Woman as Truth in Nietzsche's Writing," in *Social Theory and Practice*, 10(2), 185–99.

Olson, G. and L. Worsham (2000), "Changing the Subject: Judith Butler's Politics of Radical Resignification," in *JAC*, 20(4), 727–65.
Oppel, Francis N. (2005), *Nietzsche on Gender: Beyond Man and Woman*, Charlottesville: University of Virginia Press.
Opsopaus, John (1994), "The Parts of the Soul—A Greek System of Chakras," http://opsopaus.com/OM/BA/JO-TEP.html.
Osho (1997), *Kundalini Yoga: In Search of the Miraculous*, vol. 1, New Delhi: Sterling Paperback.
Osho (1976), *The Discipline of Transcendence*, vol. 2, Discourses on the 42 Sutras of Buddha, http://www.alaalsayid.com/ebooks/OSHO%20pdf/The%20Discipline%20 of%20Transcendence,%20Vol%202.pdf.
Osterkamp, Ernst (2012), "Amor e Violência: a Natureza do Fausto," in *Fausto de Goethe no século XXI: questões fáusticas na contemporaneidade*, ed. Izabela Kestler and Moura, Magali dos Santos, Rio de Janeiro: Rio de Letras.
Owen, David (1998), "Nietzsche's Squandered Seductions: Feminism, the Body, and the Politics of Genealogy," in *Feminist Interpretations of Friedrich Nietzsche*, ed. Kelly Oliver and Marilyn Pearsall, 306–26, University Park: Pennsylvania State University Press.
Pande, Mrinal (2003), *Stepping Out: Life and Sexuality in Rural India*, Penguin Books: New Delhi.
Patton, Paul (1993), "Child of English Genealogists: Nietzsche's Affiliation with the Critical Historical Mode of the Enlightenment," in *Nietzsche, Feminism and Political Theory*, ed. Paul Patton, 204–24, New York: Routledge.
Pergadia, Samantha (2018), "Geologies of Sex and Gender: Excavating the Materialism of Gayle Rubin and Judith Butler," in *Feminist Studies*, 44(1), 171–96.
Petterson, Tove (2017), "Love According to Simone de Beauvoir," in *A Companion to Simone de Beauvoir*, ed. Laura Hengehold and Nancy Bauer, Hoboken: Wiley & Sons, 160–73.
Picart, Caroline J. S. (1999), *Resentment and the Feminine in Nietzsche's Politico-Aesthetics*, University Park, PA: Penn State University Press.
Picart, Caroline J. S. (1996), "Classic and Romantic Mythology in the (Re)Birthing of Nietzsche's Zarathustra," in *The Journal of Nietzsche Studies*, 12, 40–68.
Piedra Alegria, J. (2018), "A Queer Nietzsche: Intersections between Nietzschean Thought and Queer Theory," in *Praxis. Revista de Filosofia*, 77, 1–19.
Pippin, Robert B. (2014). "Self-Interpreting Selves: Comments on Alexander Nehamas's Nietzsche: Life as Literature," in *The Journal of Nietzsche Studies*, 45(2), 118–33.
Pippin, Robert B. (2010), *Nietzsche, Psychology, and First Philosophy*, Chicago: The University of Chicago Press.
Pippin, Robert B. (2001), "Morality as Psychology, Psychology as Morality: Nietzsche, Eros, and Clumsy Lovers," in *Nietzsche's Postmoralism: Essays on Nietzsche's Prelude to Philosophy's Future*, ed. Richard Schacht, Cambridge: Cambridge University Press, 79–99.
Pippin, Robert B. (1999), "Nietzsche and the Melancholy of Modernity," in *Social Research*, 66(2), 495–520.
Pletsch, Carl (1991), *Young Nietzsche: Becoming a Genius*, New York: Free Press/Macmillan.
Pratt, James Bissett (2005), *India and Its Faiths*, New York: Cosimo Classics.
Prideaux, Sue (2018), *I Am Dynamite: The Life of Friedrich Nietzsche*, London: Faber & Faber.

Prinz, J. (2016), "Genealogies of Morals: Nietzsche's Method Compared," in *The Journal of Nietzsche Studies*, 47(2), 180–201.
Rashinkar, Vinita (2019), *Sri Chakra Yantra (Manifest Anything with the Symbol of Everything)*, Chennai: Notion Press.
Reginster, Bernard (2013), "Honesty and Curiosity in Nietzsche's Free Spirits," in *Journal of the History of Philosophy*, 51(3), 441–63.
Reginster, Bernard (2006), *The Affirmation of Life: Nietzsche on Overcoming Nihilism*, Cambridge, MA: Harvard University Press.
Reginster, Bernard (2003), "What Is a Free Spirit? Nietzsche on Fanaticism," in *Archiv Fuer Geschichte Der Philosophie*, 85(1), 51–85.
Reichard, Joy (2011), *Celebrating the Divine Feminine: Reclaiming Your Power with Ancient Goddess Wisdom*, San Francisco: Bush Street Press.
Reschke, R. (Hg.) (2012), *Frauen-Ein Nietzschethema? – Nietzsche: Ein Frauenthema? Nietzscheforschung*, Bd., 19, Berlin: Akademie Verl.
Richardson, John (2020), *Nietzsche's New Values*, Oxford: Oxford University Press.
Richardson, John (2008), *Nietzsche's New Darwinism*, Oxford: Oxford University Press.
Ricoeur, Paul (1967), *The Symbolism of Evil*, trans., E. Buchanan, Boston: Beacon Press.
Roberts, Tyler (1998), *Contesting Spirit: Nietzsche, Affirmation, Religion*, Princeton: Princeton University Press.
Rutherford, Donald (2018), "Nietzsche as Perfectionist," in *Inquiry*, 61(1), 42–61.
Safranski, Rüdiger (2002), *Nietzsche, A Philosophical Biography*, trans., Shelley Frisch, New York: W. W. Norton & Company.
Salaquarda, Jörg (1979), "Der unmögliche Shelley," in *Nietzsche-Studien*, 8, 396–7.
Schacht, Richard (2013), "Nietzsche and Lamarckism," in *The Journal of Nietzsche Studies*, 44(2), 264–81.
Schank, Gerd (2000), *Rasse und Züchtung bei Nietzsche*, Berlin: De Gruyter.
Schutte, Ofelia (1984), *Beyond Nihilism: Nietzsche without Masks*, Chicago: University of Chicago Press.
Scott, Maria (2008), "Simone de Beauvoir on Stendhal: In Good Faith or in Bad?," in *Irish Journal of French Studies*, 8, 55–71.
Seung, T. K. (2005), *Nietzsche's Epic of the Soul: Thus Spoke Zarathustra*, Lanham, MD: Lexington Books.
Sevenhuijsen, Sibyl (1998), *Citizenship and the Ethics of Care*, London: Routledge Press.
Shankaranarayanan, S. (2002), *The Ten Great Cosmic Powers*, Chennai: Samata Books.
Shastri, P. D. (1911), *The Doctrine of Maya in the Philosophy of Vedanta*, London: Luzac & Co.
Silk, M. S. and J. P. Stern (1983), *Nietzsche on Tragedy*, Cambridge: Cambridge University Press.
Singh, S. K. (2020), *51 Shaktipithas*, New Delhi: Diamond Pocket Books.
Sloterdijk, Peter (2013), *You Must Change Your Life: On Anthropotechnics*, trans., W. Hoban, Cambridge: Polity Press.
Solomon, Robert (2003), *Living with Nietzsche: What the Great "Immoralist" Has to Teach Us*, Oxford: Oxford University Press.
Sommer, Andreas Urs (2012), *Nietzsche-Kommentar. Der Fall Wagner. Götzen-Dämmerung*, Berlin: De Gruyter.
Sommer, Andreas Urs (2016), *Kommentar zu Nietzsches Jenseits von Gut und Böse*, Berlin: De Gruyter.
Sri Aurobindo (1920), *The Superman*, Pondicherry: Sri Aurobindo Ashram Trust.
Staten, Henry (1993), *Nietzsche's Voice*, New York: Cornell University Press.

Stegmaier, Werner (2016), "Nietzsche's Orientation toward the Future," in *the Journal of Nietzsche Studies*, 47(3), 384–401.
Stellino, Paolo (2015), *Nietzsche and Dostoevsky: On the Verge of Nihilism*. Bern: Peter Lang.
Stendhal (Beyle, Marie-Henri) (2004), *On Love*, Gilbert and Suzanne Sale, translators, London: Penguin Books.
Stern, D. (2009), *Partners in Thought: Working with Unformulated Experience, Dissociation, and Enactment*, New York: Routledge.
Stiegler, Barbara (2005), *Nietzsche et la critique de la chair*, Paris: Presses Universitaires de France, 179–202.
Stolorow, R. D., B. Brandchaft, and G. E. Atwood (1987), *Psychoanalytic Treatment*, Hillsdale, NJ: The Analytic Press.
Syea, Emma (2016), "Nietzsche on Greek and Indian Philosophy," in *Universe and Inner Self in Early Indian and Early Greek Thought*, ed. Richard Seaford, Edinburgh: Edinburgh University Press.
Taylor, Seth (1990), *Left-Wing Nietzscheans. The Politics of German Expressionism 1910-1920*, Berlin: De Gruyter.
Temp, D. (2019), *As Anotações de Nietzsche Sobre Teleologia* [Nietzsche's Notes on Teleology], Pelotas: Dissertatio [50], 203–22.
Thatcher, David (1983), "Nietzsche's Debt to Lubbock," in *Journal of the History of Ideas*, 44(2), 293–309.
Thatcher, David (1982), "Nietzsche, Bagehot and the Morality of Custom," in *Victorian Newsletter*, 62, 7–13.
Thomas, D. (1993), "Utilising Foucault's Nietzsche: Nietzsche, Genealogy, Autobiography," in *The Journal of Nietzsche Studies*, 6, 103–29.
Thorgeirsdottir, Sigridur (2017), "Love of the Sexes in Nietzsche's Philosophy: From Opposition to Transformative Interaction," in *Nietzsche-Studien*, 46, 105–13.
Thorgeirsdottir, Sigridur (2012), "Baubo, Laughter, Eroticism, and Science to Come," in *Nietzscheforschung*, 19(1), Berlin: De Gruyter, 65–73.
Thorgeirsdottir, Sigridur (2010a), "Nietzsche's Philosophy of Birth," in *Birth, Death, and Femininity: Philosophies of Embodiment*, ed. Robin May Schott, 157–85, Bloomington: Indiana University Press.
Thorgeirsdottir, Sigridur (2010b), "The Natal Self," in Robin May Schott, ed., *Birth, Death, and Femininity: Philosophies of Embodiment*, 186–208, Bloomington: Indiana University Press.
Thorgeirsdottir, Sigridur (2004), "Nietzsche's Feminization of Metaphysics and Its Significance for Theories of Gender Difference," in *Feminist Reflections on the History of Philosophy*, ed. L. Alanen and C. Witt, Dordrecht/New York: Kluwer Academic Publishers, 51–68.
Tirrell, Lynne (1995), "Sexual Dualism and Women's Self-Creation: On the Advantages and Disadvantages of Reading Nietzsche for Feminists," in *Nietzsche and the Feminine*, ed. Peter J. Burgard, 158–82, Charlottesville: University of Virginia Press.
Toscano, Alberto (2001), "The Method of Nature, the Crises of Critique. The Problem of Individuation in Nietzsche's 1867/1868 Notebooks," in *Pli, The Warwick Journal of Philosophy*, 11, 36–61.
Tronto, Joan (1993), *Moral Boundaries: A Political Argument for an Ethic of Care*, New York: Routledge.
Ure, Michael (2008), *Nietzsche's Therapy: Self-Cultivation in the Middle Works*. New York: Lexington Books.

Van der Laan, J. M. (2007), *Seeking Meaning for Goethe's Faust*, New York: Continuum.
Vasu, Srisa Chandra (1914), *The Siva Samhita*, Bahadurganj: Bhuvaneswari Asrama.
Verkerk, Willow (2019), *Nietzsche and Friendship*, London: Bloomsbury.
Verkerk, Willow (2017), "On Love, Women, and Friendship: Reading Nietzsche with Irigaray," in *Nietzsche-Studien*, 46, 135–52.
Verkerk, Willow (2014), "Nietzsche's Goal of Friendship," in *The Journal of Nietzsche Studies*, 45(3), 279–91.
Vivarelli, Vivetta (2008), "Der freie Geist, die amerikanische Rastlosigkeit und die Verschmelzung der Kulturen," in *Nietzsche—Philosoph der Kultur(en)?*, ed. Andreas Urs Sommer, 185–208, Berlin: Walter de Gruyter.
Weber, Courtney (2021), *Hekate: Goddess of Witches*, Newburyport, MA: Red Wheel/Weiser Books.
Weedon, Chris (1994), "The Struggle for Women's Emancipation in the Work of Hedwig Dohm," in *German Life and Letters*, 47.
Weikar, Richard (2013), "The Role of Darwinism in Nazi Racial Thought," in *German Studies Review*, 36(3), 537–56.
Weindling, Paul (1989), *Health, Race and German Politics between National Unification and Nazism 1870–1945*, Cambridge: Cambridge University Press.
White, Alan (1990), *Within Nietzsche's Labyrinth*, London: Routledge.
Williams, Bernard (1993), "Nietzsche's Minimalist Moral Psychology," in *The European Journal of Philosophy*, 1(1), 4–14.
Wolfenstein, Eugene Victor (2000), *Inside/Outside Nietzsche: Psychoanalytic Explorations*, Ithaca: Cornell University Press.
Wollstonecraft, Mary (1998), *A Vindication of the Rights of Woman*, New York: Norton.
Woodford, Charlotte (2016), "Female Desire and the Mind-Body Binary in *Fin De Siècle* Fiction by Hedwig Dohm, Lou Andreas-Salomé and Gabriele Reuter," in *German Life and Letters*, 69.
Woodroffe, John (2009), *Sakti and Sakta*, Leeds: Celephaïs Press.
Young, Iris Marion (2004), "Five Faces of Oppression," in *Oppression, Privilege, and Resistance*, ed. Lisa Heldke and Peg O'Connor, Boston: McGraw-Hill.
Young, Julian (2013), "Nietzsche and Women," in *The Oxford Handbook of Nietzsche*, ed. Ken Gemes and John Richardson, 46–62, Oxford: Oxford University Press.
Zavatta, Benedetta (2008), "Nietzsche and Emerson on Friendship and Its Ethical-Political Implications," in *Nietzsche, Power and Politics: Rethinking Nietzsche's Legacy for Political Thought*, ed. Herman Siemens and Vasti Roodt, Berlin: De Gruyter, 511–40.
Zuckert, Catherine (1976), "Nature, History and the Self: Friedrich Nietzsche's Untimely Considerations," in *Nietzsche Studien*, 5, Berlin: De Gruyter, 55–82.
Zurn, Perry (2021), *Curiosity and Power: The Politics of Inquiry*, Minneapolis: University of Minnesota Press.

# Name Index

Abbey, Ruth 9, 166, 199
Acampora, Christa Davis 99, 100
Ahern, Daniel R. 149
Alfano, Mark 107, 192, 198
Algazi, Lisa G. 174
Anomaly, Jonny 228
Andreas-Salomé, Lou 7, 8, 26, 29, 54, 161, 217, 227
Ansell-Pearson, Keith 72, 99, 100, 163, 166, 170-1, 173
Aristotle 93, 113
Autiero, Serena 109
Attali, Patrick 175
Austin, J. L. 213
Aydin, Ciano 114

Blondel, Éric 94, 101, 138, 184, 213-14
Bagchi, Jasodhara 103
Bagehot, Walter 187
Bamford, Rebecca 1, 163, 166, 170-1, 173, 177
Beauvoir, Simone de 12, 71, 115, 161-2, 168-74
Behler, Diana 72
Benjamin, Walter 206
Bergoffen, Debra B. 72
Binion, Rudolph 29
Bishop, Paul 14
Bizet, Georges 82, 150
Blondel, Eric 94, 101, 138, 184, 213-14
Bollas, C. 52
Braidotti, Rosi 183
Brandchaft, B. 52-3
Brobjer, Thomas 116, 163, 182, 187
Butler, Judith 13, 74, 75-6, 79, 83, 87-8, 99, 203, 204-7, 209-14

Campbell, Joseph 28
Campioni, Giuliano 65, 163, 187
Cavalcanti, A. H. 149
Cavell, Stanley 155

Caesar, Gaius Julius 225-6
Clark, Maudemarie 46, 54, 91, 99, 187, 229
Cleary, Skye C. 173-4
Clement, of Alexandria 79-80
Conant, James 155
Creasy, Kaitlin 215, 218, 228-9

Dekoven, Marianne 228
Deleuze, Gilles 99
Derrida, Jacques 31, 35-6, 40-1, 72, 74, 83, 91, 99, 108-09, 117
Deutscher, Penelope 46, 54, 63, 182
Devereux, Georges 79
Diethe, Carol 14, 178-9, 182, 187, 203, 213, 227-9
Diprose, Rosalyn 54
Dohm, Hedwig 13, 215-19, 221-29
Dries, Manuel 100
Drochon, Hugo 184

Erndl, K.M. 105
Etter, Annemarie 182

Faustino, M. 133, 149
Figl, Johann 116
Fornari, Maria Cristina 184
Foucault, Michel 88, 99, 210, 213
Freud, Sigmund 52, 78, 83, 209, 214
Frye, Marilyn 228

Ganapathy, T.N. 113
Gayon, Jean 185, 187
Gemes, Ken 150
Giacoia, Oswaldo 61-2
Gobineau, Arthur 188
Goethe, Johann Wolfgang von 5, 10, 46, 58-67, 70-2, 106, 123
Goswami, Jayadeva 117
Guay, Robert 14, 213
Geuss, Raymond 99

Haar, Michael 206, 212–14
Haase, Marie-Luise 181, 184
Haraway, Donna 227
Harding, Sandra 227
Hartsock, Nancy 227
Hatab, Lawrence J. 9, 10, 13, 113, 183, 228–29
Heidegger, Martin 74, 93, 98, 101–2, 113–15, 117, 149
Held, Virginia 154
Higgins, Kathleen Marie 72
Hill Collins, Patricia 227
Huddleston, Andrew 149
Hurka, Thomas 155

Irigaray, Luce 72, 115, 168, 183, 197, 199, 205, 212–13

Jantz, Harold 59, 60, 72
Jeong, J. 146, 149, 150
Judith, Anodea 117

Kant, Immanuel 33, 81, 99, 120, 124, 137, 149
Kaufmann, Walter 1, 2, 13, 17, 28, 74
Keller, M. A. 103
Kerenyi, Carl 21, 28
Kittay, Eva Feder 154
Klossowski, Pierre 131
Kofman, Sarah 72, 77, 90, 99, 142–3, 145–6, 212
Kopp, B. 149
Kramrisch, Stella 109
Krell, David F. 9, 108

Lacoue-Labarthe P. 141–2, 146
Leelamma, K. P. 113
Lemm, Vanessa 90, 99, 100
Lidke, J. S. 108, 111
Livingstone, Jenny 210
Lorraine, Tamsin 73, 74
Lorenzini, Daniele 214
Lubell, Winifred 78
Lucretius, Titus 196, 199

Machado, R. 149
Malan, Gert J. 104
de Man, Paul 100
Marion, Jean Luc 101

Marques, A. 137, 140
Martin, Nicholas 188
Marton, Scarlett 70, 149–50, 187
May, Regine 114
May, Simon 161
McDaniel, J. 115
McIntyre, Alex 179
McNeal, Michael 14
McNeill, William 101
Mill, John Stuart 217
Miner, Robert C. 173
Moore, Gregory 14, 184
Metropolitan Opera, The 82
Mitcheson, Katrina 179
Montaigne, Michel de 126–7, 134
Montinari, Mazzino 79, 83, 186
Morrison, Iain. 52, 55
Mukhopadhyay, Anway 104, 107
Müller-Lauter, Wolfgang 72

Nehamas, Alexander 120–7, 131–3
Nettleton, Skye 174
Neumann, Erich 17, 24
Noddings, Nell 154
Norlock, Kathryn 154

O'Brien, E. P. 71
Oliver, Kelly 8–10, 14, 72, 76, 78, 82–3, 115, 138, 140, 182–3, 202, 212–13
Olson, G. and Worsham, L. 214
Oppel, Francis N. 9, 109, 199, 212
Opsopaus, John 111
Osho 109
Osterkamp, Ernst 60

Pande, Mrinal 115
Patton, Paul 8, 50
Pearsall, Marilyn 8, 83, 212
Petterson, Tove 169, 170, 174
Pergadia, Samantha 213
Picart, Caroline J. S. 9, 72
Piedra Alegria, J. 214
Pippin, Robert B. 13, 100, 120, 122–9, 131, 133–4, 214
Plato 33, 62, 71, 77, 93, 100, 111, 127
Pletsch, Carl 14
Pratt, James Bissett 103
Prideaux, Sue 14, 109
Prinz, J. 213

Rashinkar, Vinita 111
Reginster, Bernard 114, 194, 199, 228
Reichard, Joy 108
Richardson, John 84, 184
Ricoeur, Paul 104
Roberts, Tyler 133
Rutherford, Donald 155

Salaquarda, Jörg 187
Salis, Meta von 182, 187
Schacht, Richard 187
Schank, Gerd 177, 186, 188
Schutte, Ofelia 201, 212
Scott, Maria 174
Schopenhauer, Arthur 12, 19, 133, 135, 139, 142, 149, 155, 179, 180, 218
Seung, T. K. 101
Sevenhuijsen, Sibyl 154
Shankaranarayanan, S. 107, 112
Shastri, P. D. 108
Silk, M. S. 102
Singh, S. K. 105
Sloterdijk, Peter 107
Solomon, Robert 161
Sommer, Andreas Urs 81, 186
Staten, Henry 101
Stegmaier, Werner 175
Stellino, Paolo 52
Stendhal, Marie-Henri Beyle 12, 161–3, 165, 172–4
Stern, D. 52
Stern, J. P. 102
Stiegler, Barbara 94, 101–2
Stolorow, R. D., Brandchaft, B., and Atwood, G. E. 52
Syea, Emma 116

Taylor, Seth 186
Temp, D. 149
Thatcher, David 177, 187
Thomas, D. 207, 213–14
Thorgeirsdottir, Sigridur 9, 46, 69, 72, 80–1, 83–4, 97, 99, 102, 187
Tirrell, Lynne 46, 48
Toscano, Alberto 149
Tronto, Joan 154

Ure, Michael 133

Van der Laan, J. M. 72
Verkerk, Willow 168, 170, 173–4, 197, 199
Vivarelli, Vivetta 187

Wagner, Cosima 7
Wagner, Richard 8, 47, 65–6, 149
Weber, Courtney 108
Weedon, Chris 227–8
Weikar, Richard 185
Weindling, Paul 186
White, Alan 111
Williams, Bernard 91
Wittig, Monique 205, 213
Wolfenstein, Eugene Victor 14
Woodford, Charlotte 228
Woodroffe, John 108

Young, Iris Marion 228
Young, Julian 46

Zavatta, Benedetta 173
Zuckert, Catherine 149
Zurn, Perry 54

# Subject Index

Active 13, 70, 88, 92, 95, 98–9, 142, 167, 180, 208
Aesthetics 21, 23–4, 37, 58, 60, 65, 69, 80, 119, 120–22, 124, 129–30, 133
Affirmation 23, 57, 66, 69, 73, 110, 116, 128, 130, 132–33, 146, 215–16
Aim 1–2, 6, 9–10, 12, 25, 34, 38, 40, 48, 75, 79, 81, 110–11, 113, 120–22, 127, 137, 148, 155, 157, 168, 170, 175, 179, 183, 185, 187, 194, 201, 205–07, 210, 216, 219, 224
Androcentric 203, 207
Androgyny 22, 25–7
Aphrodite 60, 114
Apolline 119, 124, 129, 131
Apollo 20–24, 88,
Apollonian 25–26, 28, 36–7, 136, 140, 145, 149
Allegory 149
Amor Fati 96
Anti-essentialism 105, 213
Ariadne 11, 88–9, 92–8, 101–2, 110, 117, 119–20, 130–33, 212
Art 10, 18, 20, 48, 58–62, 65–8, 70, 72, 107–9, 113–15, 119, 122, 124, 126, 141–2, 145–6, 148–9, 168, 171–2
Artist 2, 4, 11, 24, 32, 35–41, 128–29, 132
Asceticism 12, 47, 68, 179, 197, 209
Ascetic ideal 14, 182, 193
Ascetic values 6, 65, 175, 187
Authentic 38, 104, 135, 141, 144, 148, 161, 168–74, 183, 203, 211

Bad 187, 204, 213
Barbarism 144–5, 147
Baubo 11, 67, 72, 78–81, 108, 212
Beauty 18, 20, 22, 67, 114, 124, 142, 171, 197
Beautiful 21, 36, 71, 95, 120, 128, 130, 149, 164, 167, 229

Becoming 5–7, 10–11, 18–20, 26, 28, 35, 37–9, 46, 58, 69, 71, 76, 93–8, 100–1, 107–8, 115, 121, 125, 127–32, 136, 139, 140–2, 146–8, 158, 176, 180, 185, 217–18, 224–5
Binary 7, 13, 75, 78, 81, 173, 193, 204, 211
Birth 11, 22, 29, 60, 68–9, 79–81, 109, 114, 116, 180–1, 184, 188, 198
Blindness 114–15, 148, 184, 198, 220–21
Body 26, 36, 38, 41, 52, 62, 64–6, 68, 70, 80–1, 94, 97–8, 101–2, 105, 108, 110–11, 113, 116, 165, 167, 180, 187, 193, 196, 199, 209–10, 212, 224, 228–9
Breed (and 'breeding') 12, 175–7, 180, 182, 184–6, 222

Care (and 'caring') 2, 7, 9, 12, 17, 19, 24, 48, 62, 73, 133, 143, 153–59, 177–8, 184, 186–7, 195–6, 220, 223, 226
Carmen (Bizet's opera) 82, 150
Causality 136
Cause 5, 48, 77, 120, 136, 169, 211, 227
Certainty 191–2, 197–8
Chaos 20, 71, 101, 105, 114, 129, 132–3
Coherence 75, 89, 91, 142, 144, 148, 217
Compassion 12, 153–9, 222, 226
Conformity 144, 147, 176, 210
Courage 5, 45, 78–9, 192, 198
Criticism 8, 14, 57, 61, 73, 75, 90, 112, 122, 148, 157–8, 163–7, 170, 202, 205–6, 210, 212–14, 222, 225, 228
Culture 3, 10, 12, 17, 19, 20–5, 28, 35, 58–9, 61–3, 65–6, 69, 100, 104, 110, 125, 135–6, 141–9, 167, 175–7, 181–7, 193, 201–2, 209–11, 219, 225
Curiosity 13, 45, 128, 188, 191–2, 194, 197–8
Criminal 223–6, 229
Cruelty 23, 28–9, 143, 209

Death 6, 22, 60, 71, 80, 111, 115, 128, 131–2, 145, 147, 192–3, 223
Death of God 3, 6, 24, 107, 113
Decadent 3, 4, 10, 11, 61–3, 209, 212
Decadence 1–7, 9, 10, 19, 68, 75, 77, 80, 184
Deify 11, 22, 28, 111, 120, 124, 127, 128–33, 166
Demeter 72, 78–80, 109, 114
Democracy 4–5, 25–7, 48, 222, 229
Demythologization 104
Devalue 19, 46–7, 122
Devi 103–4, 107–8, 111, 113, 117
Dionysiac 107–9, 124, 129
Dionysian 10, 11, 13, 20–6, 28–9, 37–41, 57, 58, 65–72, 90, 92–3, 95–8, 102, 105, 119, 124, 129, 132, 140, 145, 201, 216–17, 227
Dionysus 11, 20, 22, 24, 28, 38, 67, 68, 80–1, 88, 92–3, 95–7, 110, 120, 129–33
Discipline 47, 155, 176, 177, 192
Disintegration 47, 70, 120, 148, 184
Disgust 38, 63, 143, 209, 222
Dithyrambic 216, 227
Drag 13, 211–12
Drive 2, 13, 25, 65, 92, 94, 107, 112, 125, 128, 147, 157, 191–3, 196–8, 201, 207–8, 211, 221, 224
Dynamic 2, 70, 88, 95, 98, 101, 113–14, 146–9

Egoism 21, 50, 74, 112–13, 164–5, 192–3, 197
Egoistic 13, 50–1, 53, 191, 197
Eleusinian mysteries 105, 108
End 25, 33–5, 37, 137, 177–8, 187
Epistemology 2, 9, 80, 104, 107, 132, 135–6, 139, 141, 187, 227
Eugenic 175, 184–8
Europe 1–5, 7, 18–19, 33, 48, 83, 89, 103–4, 106, 178, 187, 201, 218–219, 222, 227
European 3, 5, 19, 33, 46, 61, 63, 106, 175, 178, 181, 187, 201–6, 219, 225
Essentialism 2, 5, 7, 11, 17, 21, 57, 65, 69, 70, 81, 87, 90, 105–6, 146–8, 167, 175, 177, 182, 197–8, 202, 205–7
Eternal-masculine 64

Eternal return 11, 68, 69, 94, 128
Existence 4, 34, 40, 45, 50, 60, 67, 71, 77–8, 83, 96, 105–8, 114, 119, 124, 136, 139–40, 142–3, 145, 147–9, 169, 175, 177, 183, 192–6, 198, 203, 206, 211, 225, 227
Existential 21, 112, 115, 119, 192–3, 221
Expediency 137, 139, 140–2, 144
Experiments 4, 5, 6, 7, 11, 27, 103, 120, 125, 157, 181, 219
Experimental 125, 181
Experimentation 7, 105, 210

Faith 3, 103, 167, 169, 192–3, 198
False 32, 39, 49, 64, 87, 108, 141, 143, 144, 145, 147–8, 169, 206
Fate 20, 23, 28, 65, 71, 82, 96, 120, 125, 127, 129, 132
Faust 46, 58–61, 64, 66–7, 71, 106
Fear 21, 26, 28, 47–9, 52, 69–70, 89, 90, 92, 96, 108, 115, 164, 198, 222, 224–5, 228
Feminism 3–5, 7, 9–10, 13, 17, 23–7, 34–5, 45–6, 61, 63, 76, 81, 183, 186, 201–5, 207–8, 210–13, 217, 227
Feminist 1–5, 7–10, 13–14, 23, 26–7, 32–6, 40, 51–2, 57, 71, 73–6, 79, 81, 83, 88, 105–6, 162, 168, 172–4, 178–9, 181–3, 187, 193–4, 201–7, 210–12, 215, 217, 220, 226–9
Fertility 147, 179
Fertilization 57–8
Fictional 93, 95–6, 138, 140, 142–4, 146, 212
Finitude 94, 97, 101, 193
Force 19, 20, 22–5, 28, 37–9, 40, 47–9, 51, 58, 60, 65, 69–70, 88, 95, 98–9, 107–8, 112–13, 119, 120, 124–5, 128–9, 132, 134, 140, 145, 180, 185
French 14, 18, 90, 98, 126, 172
Free spirit 1, 4, 6–7, 14, 166, 175, 177–9, 187, 191–3, 195–8, 208
Friendship 13, 18, 104, 158, 161, 165–8, 170, 172–3, 178, 187, 191
Future 3, 6, 11–13, 38, 51, 60, 80, 87, 94, 97, 116, 120, 132, 137, 156, 166, 169, 170, 172, 175–6, 178, 180, 182–3, 185–6, 195–6, 203, 219

Gender 1–7, 9, 11, 13, 25–7, 69, 74–6, 81, 83, 87–90, 94, 100–1, 105–6, 162, 167–8, 170, 172–3, 191, 193, 196–8, 204–13, 217, 223, 228
Genealogy 13, 75, 76, 87, 88, 99, 181–2, 203–9, 211–15
Genealogical 13, 69, 88, 179, 181, 183, 187, 203–7, 211, 214
Genealogist 206, 211, 214
Germany 8, 145, 216–17, 220, 228
Greece 21, 69, 70, 96
Greek (and 'Greeks') 11, 20, 22, 28–9, 68–72, 75, 78–9, 93, 102, 104, 105, 107, 110, 115–16, 119, 124, 129, 143, 146–7, 167, 180, 188
Guilt 27, 47, 173, 224

Health 4, 8, 34, 48, 65, 79, 80, 90, 104, 114, 126–8, 135, 142–9, 163, 173, 177, 186, 191, 198, 202, 220, 222
Hecate 11, 108
Herd 4, 24, 29, 192, 219
Hereditary (and 'heredity') 12, 139, 175, 180–1, 185
Hermeneutic 12, 74
Hermaphrodite 64
Heteronormative 191, 205, 207, 209
Heterosexism (and 'heterosexist') 6, 7,
Heterosexual (and 'heterosexuality') 100, 209–11
Homoerotic 209
Homophobia 7
Homosexual (and 'homosexuality') 8, 26
Human rights 217

Ideal 3, 6, 10, 13, 20, 27, 45, 50–4, 61–2, 64–7, 69, 88, 95, 96, 98, 103, 106, 120, 121, 124–28, 133–34, 141, 144–6, 149, 162, 165–8, 175, 182–83, 187, 191, 193–94, 197–98, 202, 211–12, 218, 222
Idealism 4, 10, 46–9, 51–2, 54–5, 57, 59, 61–3, 65, 69, 106
Idealist (and 'idealistic') 51, 59, 62, 70, 139
Idealization 57, 61, 66, 71, 162, 168, 211,
Impulse 4, 69–71, 93, 125, 128–9, 140, 142, 144, 146, 148, 162, 164
Inauthentic 90, 168–70, 173
India 11, 22, 28, 103–5, 116, 225

Indian 103–5, 111–12, 115–16
Instinct 4–5, 9, 13, 18–20, 23–4, 26, 28, 32–4, 37–9, 47–9, 51, 57, 64–6, 68–9, 80, 89–90, 106, 113, 125, 129, 142–3, 165, 172, 176–81, 184, 192–3, 197, 201, 209, 219, 222, 224, 226
Instinctual 90, 180
Intellect 23, 45, 47, 88, 116, 136–9
Intellectual 9, 22, 45, 47, 88, 116, 138, 139, 177, 187, 192–93, 198, 217, 227
Intellectual conscience 192–3, 198
Ironic 59, 61, 64, 81, 109, 165, 173, 203–4, 206–8, 210, 212
Irony (and 'ironies') 62, 82, 90, 109, 207, 221

Jewish 186
Judgment 2, 49, 82, 122, 188, 201
Justification 37, 40, 53, 93, 119–22, 124–8, 130–2

Kali 103
Knowledge 3, 19, 22–4, 33, 47, 64, 79, 107, 110–11, 116, 135–8, 140–1, 144, 147–8, 163–6, 181–2, 192, 197–8, 203, 227, 229

Lack 33, 48, 52, 59, 61, 64, 70, 1, 74, 77–8, 83, 92, 116, 127, 135, 144–45, 164, 169, 188, 192, 196, 198, 221, 229
Lamarckian 181, 185, 188
Language 13, 39, 59, 60, 66, 76–8, 83, 104, 116, 125, 128–29, 133, 149, 193, 201–8, 210, 212
Laughter 7, 11, 27, 67, 72, 76, 79–80
LGBT+ 27, 187, 210–11
Life-affirmation (and 'life-affirming') 6–7, 10, 20, 67, 215–16, 227
Life-denial (and 'life-denying') 3, 12, 49, 52–3, 65, 173, 218, 220
Literary 96, 103, 121–4, 126, 128, 131–2, 162, 215–17
Literature 60, 72–3, 120–4, 127, 130, 132, 161, 216
Love 2, 11–13, 18, 21, 24, 31, 34–5, 38, 59–60, 66–7, 82–3, 92–3, 95–8, 130–1, 148–9, 161–75, 178–80, 186, 191, 195–7, 199, 220, 227
Lovers 71, 88, 100, 110, 162–66, 170–1
Lust 47, 80, 109, 165–6, 173

Male 3, 6, 12, 18-19, 21, 23-4, 27, 32-4, 38-9, 48, 57-8, 62, 64-6, 69, 71, 74, 76-7, 81-4, 87-92, 106, 108, 110, 122-3, 126, 144-5, 148, 162, 167-70, 172, 178-9, 183, 187-8, 192, 194-5, 199, 209, 215-16, 218, 221-2, 224, 227, 229
Manliness 19, 33, 106, 178, 201-2, 205
Manu 182
Marriage 6, 8, 9, 12, 14, 109, 166, 174, 175-82, 184-7, 220
Masculine 1, 2, 3, 5, 8-11, 17-29, 32, 46, 64, 75, 81, 96-8, 109, 150, 181, 183, 193, 195, 197, 202-3, 205, 229,
Masculinism (and 'masculinist') 1, 7, 25, 88, 93, 98, 100, 183, 228
Metaphor (and 'metaphorical') 2, 10-12, 31, 37-9, 64, 69, 73-4, 78, 80-81, 103, 135-8, 140-2, 144-5, 147-48, 162, 173, 209, 213, 228
Metaphysics 9, 19, 35-8, 40, 46, 48, 66-7, 75, 77, 82, 97-99, 101, 179, 182, 193, 206, 212
Metaphysical 2, 26, 46, 50, 52-3, 57-8, 61-2, 64, 66-7, 69-70, 74-5, 78, 80-2, 98, 106-7, 113, 116, 119, 134-5, 139, 141, 145, 179, 202-3, 206, 208
Metaphysician 14, 33, 35-6, 38
Misogyny (and 'misogynist') 1, 13, 17, 20, 28, 54, 73, 83, 87-92, 96, 98-100, 108, 161, 167, 172-3, 183, 186, 196, 201, 212, 228-9
Misologic (and 'misology') 204-6
Modern 2-4, 10, 18, 25-6, 48, 58-9, 61-6, 68-9, 89-90, 103-4, 112, 117, 120, 124, 129, 141, 144-5, 148, 153, 167, 183-5, 218-19, 222, 225, 228
Modernity (and 'late-modernity') 1-6, 9-10, 63, 66, 71, 90
Modesty 127, 138, 147-8, 221
Immodesty 73
Mother 11-12, 14, 19, 22, 28, 38, 40, 46, 60, 81, 103-5, 108-9, 115, 135-8, 140-5, 148-9, 166, 183, 187, 217, 220, 223, 226
Motherhood 11, 178, 226
Morality 4, 40, 52, 54, 60, 76, 106, 110, 112, 116, 175, 177, 180, 182, 184, 188, 192, 204, 206, 208-9, 219, 221 225

Morals 4-6, 14, 34, 51, 53, 61-2, 70, 106, 110, 121, 130, 148, 155, 176-7, 181, 185-7, 192, 204, 208-10, 214, 221
Multiplicity 12, 32-4, 36-7, 54, 81, 129, 136-9, 142, 146, 147, 171, 202
Music 41, 58, 62, 66, 171
Myth 39, 41, 71, 79, 104-6, 109, 114-16, 143, 172
Mythology 22, 93, 102, 104, 105, 107, 115, 116, 201

Naked (and 'nude') 36, 109, 131, 138, 140, 147, 148
Nature 12, 19-24, 26-8, 33, 35, 37, 41, 47, 49, 52-3, 60, 63, 65, 69-71, 77-80, 82, 92, 100, 105-6, 114, 135-8, 140-50, 155, 163-4, 169, 180, 191, 196, 206, 208-9, 212, 216-17, 223, 226, 229
National ('nationalism' and 'nationality') 9, 60-1, 70, 103, 176
Naxos 110, 130
Negation 145-7, 218
Nihilism 1-2, 7, 13, 69, 75, 77, 107, 111-12, 215-29
Noble 61, 65, 69, 92, 95, 98, 149, 166, 168, 172, 177-81, 187-8, 228
Nourishment 45, 107, 112, 115

Oedipus (and 'Oedipean') 138, 148
Ontological 2, 9, 204, 206
Organic (and 'organicity') 80, 98, 135-6, 141-2, 147, 180
Organism 137, 139-42, 185
Overcome (and 'self-overcoming') 4, 6, 10, 13, 23, 28, 37, 39, 47, 62-3, 74, 76, 80-1, 98, 107, 109-10, 112, 115, 125-6, 131, 173, 179, 184, 192, 195-8, 215-19, 222-3, 225-7, 229
Overfull ('overfullness') 38, 51, 54

Pathos of distance 110
*Paris is Burning* (the film) 210-11
Passion 12-13, 19, 33, 47, 49, 51, 65, 97-8, 115, 125, 131, 156-7, 161-4, 167, 175, 187-8, 221
Passive 92, 95, 156, 167-8, 172, 194, 196
Passivity 13, 96, 168
Past 94, 130, 138, 180, 185, 195

Perfectionism 12, 34, 59–60, 71, 153, 155–6, 158–9, 162–3
Performative 13, 75, 130, 205–6, 211, 213
Perspective 4, 6, 9–11, 13, 35, 37, 39, 47, 52, 54–5, 58, 60, 62–3, 65, 68–9, 71, 73–6, 79–83, 92, 98, 107, 110, 120–2, 124, 126, 128, 130, 136, 138–41, 155, 161, 183, 192, 198, 210, 217
Perspectivism 106–7, 110, 137, 214
Phallogocentrism 205
Philosopher (and 'philosophers') 2, 6, 11, 13, 17, 33, 36, 38–40, 45–7, 57, 68, 71, 73–8, 82–3, 88, 91, 93–4, 98, 100, 103, 120, 122–3, 129, 131–32, 134, 142, 144, 177–8, 180–1, 185–6, 194–5, 202, 204, 206–8, 212, 214, 219, 227
Philistine 141, 144–9
Physiology 51–2, 65, 69, 91–4, 97–8, 111, 175, 179–80, 184, 186, 218, 224
Physiologist (and 'physiologists') 52, 91, 204, 208
Pity (and 'pitying') 21, 71, 165, 194
Poetry 60, 65, 70
Possession 18, 93, 147, 165–70, 173, 196–9, 210, 227
Possibility 26, 49, 54, 58, 75, 80–1, 97, 111, 114–15, 128, 130, 139, 145, 154, 157–8, 184–5, 204–5, 207–8, 218, 222
Postmodern 13
Praxis 203–4
Pregnancy (and 'pregnant') 11, 29, 38, 40, 51, 57, 60, 68–9, 79, 81, 108, 132, 140, 222
Priest (and 'priests') 65, 182
Procreation 38–9, 57, 68–9, 167, 186, 222, 226, 228
Psychologist 5, 10, 21, 45–6, 49–50, 52–4, 57–8, 68, 70, 99, 105–6, 163, 184, 208
Psychological 2, 5, 13, 45, 47–53, 108, 113, 116, 125–6, 162–3, 180, 191–2, 208–10, 217
Psychology 2, 6, 51, 68–70, 113, 117, 194, 209

Queer ('queered' and 'queering') 9, 13, 204, 210–11, 213

Reactive (and 'reactivity') 12, 38–9, 54, 63, 88–90, 92, 98–100, 106, 179, 188
Reason (and 'reasoning') 19–20, 23, 34, 75–8, 81, 83, 90, 93–6, 98, 100, 110, 137, 144, 193, 208, 221
Redemption 60, 81, 106, 120, 126–7, 133
Renaissance 10, 60, 63, 65, 72
Reproduction 38, 146, 178–9, 186
Ressentiment 3, 132, 188
Revaluation 2, 6, 14, 68, 74–6, 81, 83, 106, 127
Romanticism 10, 12–13, 19, 58–63, 65–8, 130, 161–70, 173, 191, 197, 224

Sahasrara 111, 113
Science 2, 33–7, 40, 49, 63, 104, 112, 116, 181–2, 186–7, 193, 202–3, 215
Scientific ('scientificity' and 'scientism') 5, 18, 20, 24, 48–9, 175, 184, 187, 207, 217–18
Self-creation 4, 54, 127, 133
Self-determination 126, 169, 192
Self-mastery 126, 192
Self-overcoming 13, 63, 109–10, 125–6, 131, 196
Selflessness 51, 53, 191, 193, 197, 220–24
Sex 2, 4–5, 13–14, 18, 19, 27, 33, 71, 75, 79, 81–3, 89–90, 92, 166, 168, 173, 178, 194, 196, 204–7, 210–12,
Sexual (and 'sexuality') 2, 4–8, 11–14, 18–19, 24, 27–8, 33, 64–5, 68–9, 74–5, 81–3, 89–90, 93, 105, 109, 131, 165–7, 178–81, 183, 186, 191, 193–4, 196–7, 204–7, 210–12, 227, 229
Sexism (and 'sexist') 1–3, 9, 17, 91, 92, 153, 169, 174, 202, 229
Sexual difference 11, 17, 74, 181, 183, 229
Sexualization (and 'sexualized') 88, 205
Shaktipitha 105
Shaktism 11, 103–8, 110–11, 113, 116
Sick (and 'sickness') 3–4, 19, 23, 39, 52, 65, 80, 93, 112–13, 126, 143–4, 146–7, 177, 202, 208–9, 220
Sign chains 211
Skeptical 13, 82, 154, 170, 181, 204, 206, 211
Skepticism 48, 91, 194–5, 198, 212
Solitude 112–13, 179, 219

Spiritual 3, 5, 11, 22–3, 103–6, 108, 110, 112, 114–15, 156, 180, 182
Spirituality 11, 22, 103, 110, 112
Style 7, 12, 24, 53, 81, 108–9, 121–3, 133, 142–8, 167, 212
Suffering 1, 8, 10, 21, 33, 68, 71–2, 79–81, 92, 95, 105–6, 109, 112, 119–20, 125, 127–8, 130–2, 157–8, 170, 178, 195, 201–2, 228
Suffrage 48, 222
Suffragette 5–6

Theodicy 120, 124
Tragedy 20–1, 24, 28, 60, 66, 70–1, 119–20, 124–5, 129, 131, 229
Tragic 20–2, 25, 36, 38, 66, 68–72, 82, 94, 120, 124–5, 129, 142–3, 145
Transfigure 2, 6, 7, 11, 32, 109, 120–33, 163
True 28, 33–5, 66–8, 74–5, 77, 82, 83, 91, 93, 106, 108, 113, 119, 131, 135, 140–9, 161, 164, 166, 181, 193, 206, 207, 223
Truth 2–3, 7, 17, 34–5, 61–2, 73, 75, 82, 91–2, 99, 135, 141, 166, 172, 193

Übermensch (and 'Übermenschlich') 6, 12, 29, 179, 216
Uncertainty 10, 51, 191, 198

Unegotistical 50–1, 53, 165–6
Unity 12, 60, 88, 98, 120–2, 125, 133, 135, 137–49
Utility 7, 191, 193, 197, 203

Values (and 'valuing') 2–6, 9–11, 14, 19–20, 23–5, 32, 34–5, 37, 39, 45, 47, 52–4, 57–63, 65, 67–71, 74–77, 79–84, 88, 105–7, 110, 114, 120, 122, 132, 137, 145, 148, 155–7, 159, 163, 170, 175–85, 187–8, 192–3, 195–6, 198, 204, 208–11, 218–19, 221–2, 224, 226
Veil 12, 14, 33, 71, 104, 106, 108–9, 135–9, 140–5, 147–8, 171, 195
Vital (and 'vitality') 4, 47, 65, 108, 115, 142–3, 149, 165, 171, 180,
Vitalist 175, 182

Wagnerian 58, 63
Wilhelmine 14, 203
Will to Power 10, 12, 31–3, 37–40, 70, 72, 88, 94, 98, 113–14, 175, 179–80, 212
Womb 11, 38–40, 78, 104, 140

Zarathustra 11, 28–9, 67, 73, 82, 93–6, 98, 101, 108–9, 111, 114–15, 128, 158, 179, 216, 219, 222, 229

www.ingramcontent.com/pod-product-compliance
Lightning Source LLC
Chambersburg PA
CBHW071817300426
44116CB00009B/1347